Refiguring the Body

I0644879

Refiguring the Body

Embodiment in South Asian Religions

Edited by

Barbara A. Holdrege and Karen Pechilis

SUNY
PRESS

Cover art by Asha Tyska McLaughlin

Published by State University of New York Press, Albany

© 2016 State University of New York

All rights reserved

Printed in the United States of America

No part of this book may be used or reproduced in any manner whatsoever without written permission. No part of this book may be stored in a retrieval system or transmitted in any form or by any means including electronic, electrostatic, magnetic tape, mechanical, photocopying, recording, or otherwise without the prior permission in writing of the publisher.

For information, contact State University of New York Press, Albany, NY
www.sunypress.edu

Production, Ryan Morris
Marketing, Fran Keneston

Library of Congress Cataloging-in-Publication Data

Names: Holdrege, Barbara A., editor. | Pechilis, Karen, editor.
Title: Refiguring the body : embodiment in South Asian religions / edited by Barbara A. Holdrege and Karen Pechilis.
Description: Albany : State University of New York Press, 2016. | Includes bibliographical references and index.
Identifiers: LCCN 2016007753 (print) | LCCN 2016037354 (ebook) | ISBN 9781438463155 (hardcover : alk. paper) | ISBN 9781438463148 (pbk. : alk. paper) | ISBN 9781438463162 (e-book)
Subjects: LCSH: Human body—Religious aspects. | South Asia—Religion. | Buddhism—South Asia. | Hinduism—South Asia.
Classification: LCC BL65.B63 R44 2016 (print) | LCC BL65.B63 (ebook) | DDC 294—dc23
LC record available at https://lccn.loc.gov/2016007753

10 9 8 7 6 5 4 3 2 1

For Selva,
who inspired us all

Contents

Introduction

Body Matters in South Asia

Barbara A. Holdrege

In the past decades, theories of the body have proliferated in the social sciences and humanities, representing a range of disciplinary perspectives and generating a host of contending categories of the body, such as the lived body, the mindful body, the social body, the body politic, the medical body, the alimentary body, the sexual body, and the gendered body. Among the plethora of theories, as I have discussed at length elsewhere, three areas of scholarship in particular have had a significant influence on studies of the body in religion: the body in philosophy, the body in social theory, and the body in feminist and gender studies.[1]

For the purpose of the present analysis I would like to briefly highlight the contributions of several theorists whose work is particularly germane to the essays in this volume. (1) *The body in philosophy*: With respect to the contributions of philosophy, one of the most important trends of analysis stems from the philosophical phenomenology of Maurice Merleau-Ponty, who proposes a theory of embodiment founded on the notion of the "lived body," which posits a continuum of consciousness-body-world that seeks to overcome the dualities of subject/object and mind/body.[2] (2) *The body in social theory*: Among the various theories of the body developed by anthropologists, sociologists, and historians, the seminal contributions of Pierre Bourdieu and Michel Foucault are of particular significance. Bourdieu posits the notion of the "socially informed body" that is inscribed with sociocultural taxonomies through the logic of practice and that functions as the principle that generates and unites all practices. Foucault emphasizes the "biopolitics of power" in which the body is regulated and disciplined as a site of sociopolitical control on which are inscribed relations of power.[3] (3) *The body in feminist and gender studies*: Among the wide-ranging theories of the body in feminist and gender studies, one of the most important trends of analysis is inspired by the French scholars Julia Kristeva, Luce Irigaray, and Hélène Cixous, who maintain that the body is a text inscribed by the structures of language and signification, and hence there is no experience of the body apart from discourse. Irigaray and Cixous, as exponents of *écriture féminine* (feminine writing), propose "writing the body" and generating new inscriptions of the female body that are liberated from "phallocentric" discursive practices and that celebrate the alterity of woman's sexual difference.[4] The notion of sexual difference has been developed in a variety of distinctive ways by Anglo-American feminists such as Judith Butler. Butler is a critical interlocutor in ongoing debates about the relationship of the sexed body to the gendered body, with the validity of the distinction between sex (male or female) and gender (masculine or feminine) itself a topic of contention.[5]

This collection of essays advances the field of body studies in significant ways by bringing together in a single volume eleven scholars to engage in a sustained interrogation of categories and models of the body that are grounded in the distinctive idioms of South Asian religious traditions, with particular focus on Hindu and Buddhist traditions. The contributors engage in various ways the prevailing theories of the body in the Western academy—in particular, the theories of Merleau-Ponty (Skora), Bourdieu (Holdrege), Foucault (Radich, Pintchman), the exponents of *écriture féminine* (Radich), and Butler (Anderson, Pintchman). At the same time, however, as part of the postcolonial turn, we recognize the limitations of applying Western theoretical models as the default epistemological framework for understanding notions of embodiment that derive from the "Rest of the World," and more specifically from premodern non-Western cultures. One of the principal purposes of this collection of essays is to establish "theory parity"[6] in our investigations and to re-figure body theories by taking seriously the contributions of South Asian discourses to theorizing the body. While a number of the essays bring these indigenous South Asian discourses of embodiment into conversation with Western theoretical models, not all of the essays explicitly address contemporary Western body theories.

The contributors employ a range of methodologies to explore discursive representations and practices pertaining to the body in diverse South Asian religious communities across various registers, including different historical periods, geographic regions, languages, and social locations. The contributors' explorations of formulations of embodiment in distinct religiocultural, historical, geographic, and linguistic environments not only contribute toward re-figuring theories of the body but also serve to illuminate the intimate connections between categories of embodiment, notions of the person and the self, and representations of religious experience.

The Essays

The eleven essays are organized thematically in three parts that explore the interrelations between embodiment and selfhood (part 1), divine bodies and devotional bodies (part 2), and gendered and engendering bodies (part 3).

Part 1: Material Bodies, Embodied Selves, and Perfected Embodiments

The four essays in part 1 interrogate the interrelations between embodiment and selfhood in a variety of South Asian traditions, ranging from notions of the material body and the embodied self in the classical medical texts of Āyurveda to theories of perfected embodiment in Mahāyāna Buddhist and Kashmir Śaiva traditions to constructions of performative selfhood in contemporary South Indian performance contexts.

In "Perfected Embodiment: A Buddhist-Inspired Challenge to Contemporary Theories of the Body," Michael Radich argues that contemporary theories of the body in the social sciences and humanities are bound by "materialist" and "descriptivist" assumptions in which the material human body—and more specifically the biophysical body composed of flesh and blood with an anthropomorphic shape—is the default template for what constitutes the body. He suggests that these contemporary academic theories can be fruitfully re-visioned by bringing them into genuine conversation with the radically different models of embodiment found in many premodern religious traditions. While most religious traditions may take as their starting point ordinary modes of human embodiment, at the same time they posit a range of extraordinary modes of embodiment, which are primarily ascribed to two classes of beings: divine beings or other beings who are invested with the status of ultimate reality; and human beings who have undergone some form of bodily transformation, which may entail realization of an ideal or perfected form of embodiment. Radich grounds his general reflections in a close analysis of Mahāyāna Buddhist constructions of two pivotal categories of embodiment: *sat-kāya-dṛṣṭi,* mistaken identification with the ordinary mode of human embodiment comprising the material psychophysical complex; and *dharma-kāya,* realization of an alternative perfected embodiment in gnostic identity with the ultimate truth of all things. He concludes with a consideration of the challenges posed by Buddhist theories of embodiment to contemporary scholarly theories that are predicated on the ordinary flesh-and-blood body.

Anthony Cerulli, in "Body, Self, and Embodiment in the Sanskrit Classics of Āyurveda," provides an analysis of the terminology and taxonomies used in the Sanskrit medical literature of classical Āyurveda to articulate the nature of human embodiment, focusing on two distinct Āyurvedic typologies: those that emphasize the material body, and those that emphasize the embodied self, which includes the material body together with the *ātman*. His analysis includes an examination of the multivalent significations ascribed to the term *ātman* and the matrix of socioreligious practices with which the term is associated in the *Caraka Saṃhitā* (ca. second century BCE to first century CE) and other classical medical texts and commentaries. While the term *ātman* is at times used to designate the physical body or the empirical self, it is most frequently used to designate the transcendent Self, which in its essential nature is nonmaterial and is represented in relation to the material psychophysical organism as the "knower of the field" in relation to the "field." In contrast to Western allopathic medicine, which is almost exclusively concerned with healing the diseased material body, Cerulli emphasizes that Āyurveda is concerned with establishing and maintaining the health, longevity, well-being, and happiness of the embodied self by providing a comprehensive system of "body *dharma*" and "self-cultivation" that is designed to enliven the connections between the microcosmos and the macrocosmos, align the individual physiology with the cosmic physiology, and ensure that all aspects of an individual's life—physical body, mind, social relations, environment, and the transcendent Self—are properly coordinated and function together in balance and harmony.

In "Bodily Gestures and Embodied Awareness: *Mudrā* as the Bodily Seal of Being in the Trika Śaivism of Kashmir," Kerry Skora explores tantric formulations of embodiment as expounded by Abhinavagupta (ca. 975–1025 CE), the eminent exponent of the nondual Trika Śaivism of Kashmir, and his disciple Kṣemarāja (ca. 1000–1050 CE). He focuses in particular on the role of *mudrās*, or bodily gestures, in the tantric system of ritual and meditative practices (*sādhana*), which serve as the means through which the finite body of the practitioner is "sealed" with the absolute consciousness of Śiva, the ultimate reality. Skora concludes with a description of the perfected body of the realized tantric practitioner (*sādhaka*) as exemplified by Abhinavagupta, who in the poetic evocation of his disciple Madhurāja (ca. 1000–1050 CE) is celebrated as Śiva himself embodied in human form, his every posture and gesture a spontaneous manifestation of absolute consciousness.

Harshita Mruthinti Kamath, in "Bodied, Embodied, and Reflective Selves: Theorizing Performative Selfhood in South Indian Performance," interrogates the interrelations between embodiment and selfhood in contemporary South Asian performance through proposing a theory of "performative selfhood" that distinguishes between three categories: the bodied self, or physical body of the performer; the embodied self, which comprises the psychoemotional faculties within the performer's corporeal form; and the reflective self, or self-conscious faculty beyond the body through which the performer reflects upon and controls both the bodied self and the embodied self. She distinguishes her theory of performative selfhood from classical Indian aesthetic theories of *rasa* and utilizes her threefold theoretical framework to examine two case studies of South Indian performance: ritual possession and the classical dance forms of Kathakali and Kuchipudi.

Part 2: Divine Bodies and Devotional Bodies

The four essays in part 2 explore the ways in which various types of divine and human bodies are represented, cultivated, and transformed in the epic narratives, devotional poetry, theological discourses, and embodied practices of a range of Hindu traditions in the period between the second century BCE and the sixteenth century CE, including the epic formulations of the Mahābhārata, the Tamil Śaiva and Tamil Vaiṣṇava *bhakti* (devotional) traditions of South India, and the Gauḍīya Vaiṣṇava *bhakti* tradition of North India.

Kendall Busse, in "Observations on the Bodies of the Gods in the Mahābhārata," provides a close analysis of the semantics of divine embodiment in the Mahābhārata (ca. second century BCE to second century CE), including a consideration not only of representations of the bodies of *devatā*s, gods, but also of the bodies of subtle beings such as *yakṣa*s (chthonic spirits) and *rākṣasa*s (demons). She focuses in particular on the terms *vigraha* and *mūrti* and the broader semantic fields in which they are embedded in the epic. Her analysis suggests that the term *vigraha* refers to the human-like bodies that the gods assume on the gross material plane in order to interact with human beings, while the term *mūrti* refers to the multiple bodies that the gods manifest, particularly through the agency of *yoga*. She also provides a brief consideration of the relationship of epic terminology for divine bodies to earlier Vedic constructions of divine embodiment and to post-epic formulations concerning sculpted images.

In "*Bhakti* and Embodiment: Bodies of Devotion and Bodies of Bliss in Kṛṣṇa *Bhakti*," I interrogate the role of embodiment in *bhakti* traditions. I argue that an exploration of the connections between *bhakti* and embodiment is not only critical to understanding the transformations that characterize the historical shift from Vedic traditions to post-Vedic *bhakti* traditions in the period between 200 BCE and the early centuries of the Common Era, but, more importantly, it is critical to understanding the myriad forms that *bhakti* has historically assumed up to the present time. I focus in particular on the Gauḍīya Vaiṣṇava tradition, an important *bhakti* tradition that originated in the sixteenth century in the northeastern region of India now known as Bengal, which provides a robust example of the multileveled models of embodiment and systems of embodied practices that are integral to many *bhakti* traditions. My analysis centers on Gauḍīya constructions of three categories of embodiment: *ananta-rūpa*, the limitless divine bodies of Kṛṣṇa, the supreme Godhead, that interweave the various planes of existence; *sādhaka-rūpa*, the sexually marked material body of the practitioner that is transformed through devotional practices; and *siddha-rūpa*, the perfected devotional body of the practitioner that is an eternally gendered nonmaterial body of bliss.

Karen Pechilis, in "To Body or Not to Body: Repulsion, Wonder, and the Tamil Saint Kāraikkāl Ammaiyār," analyzes the poetic vision of Kāraikkāl Ammaiyār, a renowned sixth-century Tamil Śaiva *bhakti* saint, who is the only woman among the sixty-three Tamil Śaiva Nāyaṉārs to leave a legacy of devotional poetry. She contrasts Kāraikkāl Ammaiyār's poetic vision, as expressed in her own voice through her poetry, with the portrayals of the poet-saint by Cēkkiḻār, her twelfth-century male biographer, in his narrative the *Periya Purāṇam*. Pechilis argues that in her poetry Kāraikkāl Ammaiyār constructs a devotional subjectivity in which she deploys an "aesthetics of repulsion" in celebration of the fearsome appearance of the divine body of Śiva, Lord of the cremation ground, thereby subverting the distinctions between beauty and repulsion, purity and pollution, life and death. Cēkkiḻār, in contrast, in his biographic portrayal deploys an "aesthetics of wonder" in celebration of the bodily transformation of the female poet in which, as a visible sign of her all-consuming devotion to her majestic Lord Śiva, she sheds her female beauty and assumes the form of an emaciated ghoul among the host of the Lord's attendants.

In "Bodies of Desire, Bodies of Lament: Marking Emotion in a South Indian Vaiṣṇava Messenger Poem," Steven Hopkins explores the charged emotional landscapes of divine, human, and animal bodies in the *Haṃsasandeśa* (The Goose Messenger), a fourteenth-century Sanskrit messenger poem (*sandeśa-kāvya*) by Veṅkaṭeśa (ca. 1268–1369 CE), the acclaimed South Indian *bhakti* poet-saint and theologian of the Śrīvaiṣṇava community in Tamil Nadu. He examines the ways in which Veṅkaṭeśa refashions the story of Lord Rāma and his consort Sītā and marks emotional landscapes—the agonies of love-in-separation, the torment of loss, and the madness of longing—onto the divine bodies of the lover and his beloved and also onto the animal body of the messenger, a royal goose.

Part 3: Gendered and Engendering Bodies

The three essays in part 3 examine the gendered logics through which female and male bodies are represented, defined, and regulated in the monastic rules and narratives of the Pāli Buddhist canon and in the literature and practices associated with contemporary Hindu women's votive rituals (*vrat*s).

In "Defining Women's Bodies in Indian Buddhist Monastic Literature," Carol Anderson provides an analysis of the ways in which female bodies are classified and regulated in Indian Buddhist traditions. She is concerned in particular with the taxonomic schemas deployed in Indian Buddhist monastic literature to classify anomalous women's bodies that deviate from the normative heterosexual two-sex system. She focuses more specifically on a list of eleven anomalous physical conditions that afflict biologically sexed women, which is found in the Vinaya-Piṭaka, the section of the Pāli Buddhist canon of the Theravāda school that delineates monastic regulations for monks and nuns. Women who are afflicted by these conditions, which include various types of abnormal genitalia and menstrual disorders, are disqualified from becoming nuns, just as men with nonnormative bodies are disqualified from becoming monks. Anderson concludes with a series of reflections on the implications of such body taxonomies for illuminating Indian Buddhist understandings of the relationship between sex and gender.

Liz Wilson, in "Murderer, Saint, and Midwife: The Gendered Logic of Engendering in Buddhist Narratives of Aṅgulimāla's Conversion," explores the gendered logic through which male and female bodies are invested with different forms of generativity in the literary imagination of redactors and commentators of the Pāli Buddhist canon. She focuses in particular on narratives of the Buddha's conversion of the serial murderer Aṅgulimāla (Garland of Fingers), who wears the severed fingers of his victims as a garland around his neck. In the first phase of her analysis, she argues that the Buddha's intervention, which stops Aṅgulimāla from killing his own mother by converting him, may be viewed as a male form of generativity in which the Buddha gives birth to a new being, a transformed Aṅgulimāla, who through his ordination as a monk is born anew in the noble lineage of the Buddhas. Thus engendered by the Buddha, Aṅgulimāla himself assumes the role of a male midwife, in which he helps a woman deliver a healthy child after an extended period of difficult labor and continues to be invoked to the present day as the patron saint of childbirth by expectant mothers in Theravāda Buddhist communities. In the second phase of her analysis, Wilson argues that the commentarial sources ultimately emphasize the interdependence of female and male forms of generativity by showcasing the critical role of women—in particular, Aṅgulimāla's mother and the woman whose childbirth he facilitated—in fostering Aṅgulimāla's transformation from a heartless killer into an *arhat*, awakened being, whose male fecundity is expressed as a fertile "field of merit" for his lay supporters.

In "Fruitful Austerity: Paradigms of Embodiment in Hindu Women's *Vrat* Performances," Tracy Pintchman examines the role of Hindu women's *vrat*s, or votive rituals, in the religious management and regulation of householder women's bodies, focusing on one particular votive ritual, the Chaṭh *vrat*. Her analysis draws on Hindi narratives associated with the Chaṭh *vrat* and her own field research on contemporary Hindu women's observance of this votive ritual in the city of Vārāṇasī in North India. She argues that the Chaṭh *vrat*, as represented in the narratives and actualized in contemporary practices, functions as a performative field in which three models of embodiment—the ascetic body, the purity body, and the devotional body—are interwoven in support of the dominant paradigm of the religiously regulated body at work in this votive ritual: the auspicious female body.

Contributions to Re-figuring Body Theories

As a heuristic device to highlight the contributions of the essays in this volume to re-figuring theories of the body in the human sciences, I will employ Radich's distinction between ordinary modes of human embodiment, which are predicated on the material psychophysical complex, and extraordinary modes of embodiment, which include divine bodies, absolute bodies, and transformed human bodies. I would argue that, in contrast to the prevailing academic theories for which the biophysical human body is the default template, all of the South Asian traditions addressed in this volume frame their notions of ordinary human embodiment in relation to some form of extraordinary embodiment.

Beyond Human Embodiment

A number of essays highlight the pivotal role that South Asian traditions ascribe to various types of extraordinary bodies beyond the human realm.

These extraordinary modes of embodiment include the bodies of gods, *devatās*, who are represented in the epic formulations of the Mahābhārata as having the capacity to maintain their subtle material forms in their luminous celestial abodes while at the same time manifesting a variety of gross material forms on the earthly plane. The epic also posits various classes of subtle beings, such as *yakṣa*s and *rākṣasas*, who inhabit subtle worlds between the divine and human realms and who each have their own distinctive forms of embodiment (Busse).

In *bhakti* traditions the devotional gaze centers on the divine body of the supreme Godhead, who is celebrated as the ultimate reality and the object of devotion. In the devotional poetry of the Tamil Śaiva *bhakti* poet-saint Kāraikkāl Ammaiyār, the female poet constructs her devotional subjectivity in dynamic engagement with her beloved Lord Śiva, celebrating the fearsome appearance of his divine body (Pechilis). In his messenger poem the *Haṃsasandeśa*, the Śrīvaiṣṇava *bhakti* poet-saint and theologian Veṅkaṭeśa deploys his literary imagination to mark emotional landscapes, ranging from the agonies of love-in-separation to the hoped-for consummation of erotic union, onto the divine bodies of Lord Rāma and his consort Sītā (Hopkins). With the Gauḍīya Vaiṣṇava tradition we shift from South India to North India and from devotional poetry to *bhakti-śāstra*, a formal discourse of *bhakti*, that constructs a multileveled theology centering on the absolute body of Kṛṣṇa, which consists of *sat-cit-ānanda*—being, consciousness, and bliss—and which manifests on the transcosmic, macrocosmic, microcosmic, and mesocosmic planes in innumerable divine forms that are its partial manifestations (Holdrege).

Transforming Human Bodily Identities

In addition to positing a variety of models of divine embodiment, the South Asian traditions addressed in this volume present a range of models of human embodiment that involve some form of bodily transformation. In order to illuminate the interrelations among these various models, I will distinguish three phases in the transformation of bodily identities: from (1) the *ascribed identity* associated with the karmically constructed material body to (2) the *inscribed identity* in which the material body is reconstituted through a designated regimen of practices to (3) the *realized identity* in which a perfected form of embodiment is attained.

(1) Ascribed identity. Most of the traditions addressed in the essays take as their starting point the notion of an *ascribed identity* that is determined at birth and circumscribed by the karmically constructed material body, which is sexually marked as either male or female and, in the case of certain Hindu traditions, may be further classified as part of a social class (*varṇa*) and caste (*jāti*). Mistaken identification with the material body, which is represented as a psychophysical continuum that includes the physical body, senses, and mental faculties, is considered the root cause of bondage and suffering. In certain Buddhist formulations this mistaken identification with the material psychophysical complex is termed *sat-kāya-dṛṣṭi* and needs to be rooted out in order for liberation to be attained (Radich). In Gauḍīya Vaiṣṇava formulations the material psychophysical complex is termed the *sādhaka-rūpa,* which is glossed as the "body as it is" (*yathāvastitha-deha*) and is deemed the body of bondage prior to its transformation through the Gauḍīya regimen of *sādhana-bhakti* (Holdrege).

(2) Inscribed identity. Although not every tradition addressed in the essays is explicitly concerned with the mechanisms of bondage and liberation, they share a common concern: to transform the material body that is delimited by the markers of *ascribed identity* through a designated regimen of practices that—invoking Bourdieu's notion of the logic of practice—serves as a means of *inscribing* the body with the socioreligious taxonomies of the particular religious community. In my own work on Hindu discourses of the body, I have distinguished a number of modalities of the human body, which I term "processual bodies,"[7] that mediate transactions with other bodies in distinctive ways and that are each constituted by a specific regimen of practices: the ritual body, the ascetic body, the purity body, the tantric body, and the devotional body.[8] Several traditions addressed in this volume adopt a system of practices that is designed to constitute a particular modality of human embodiment: for

example, the tantric body constructed by the Kashmir Śaiva system of tantric *sādhana* (Skora) or the devotional body fashioned by the Gauḍīya Vaiṣṇava regimen of *sādhana-bhakti* (Holdrege). Other modalities of the human body brought to light by the essays include the medical body cultivated by the medical regimes of Āyurveda (Cerulli) and the performative body constructed by possession rituals or the disciplines of classical Indian dance (Kamath). Several of the essays suggest that the means for transforming the material body and constituting alternative modes of embodiment assume distinctive forms depending on whether the biological body is sexually marked as male or female. For example, in the case of the Chaṭh *vrat* performed by Hindu women in Vārāṇasī, the ascetic body, the purity body, and the devotional body are refashioned as integral components of a single performative field aimed at constituting an auspicious female body (Pintchman). Indian Buddhist monastic literature constructs elaborate taxonomies that distinguish men and women whose bodies conform to the normative two-sex system—male or female—from those with anomalous bodies that diverge from the norm and hence are barred from undertaking the monastic disciplines necessary for constructing a monastic body (Anderson).

(3) Realized identity. In several traditions addressed in this volume the process of transformation culminates in a state of liberation or realization in which the empirical self casts off its mistaken identification with the material psychophysical complex and realizes a perfected form of embodiment. In Theravāda Buddhist traditions the process of transformation finds fruition in attainment of the status of an *arhat*, an awakened being who is liberated from the fetters of material embodiment (Wilson). In certain Mahāyāna Buddhist formulations awakening is envisioned as realization of the *dharma-kāya*, perfected embodiment in gnostic identity with the ultimate truth of all things (Radich). In Kashmir Śaiva formulations the process of transformation culminates in realization of a perfected tantric body that is the manifest expression of the absolute consciousness of Śiva (Skora). In the case of the Gauḍīya Vaiṣṇava tradition, the ultimate goal is realization of a *siddha-rūpa*, a perfected devotional body that is ontologically distinct from the transformed *sādhaka-rūpa* and is eternal, nonmaterial, and, like the absolute body of Kṛṣṇa himself, constituted of *cit* and *ānanda*, consciousness and bliss.

Notes

1. For a discussion of recent trends of scholarship on the body in philosophy, social theory, and feminist and gender studies and more specifically

in religious studies, along with relevant references, see Holdrege 2015: 7–11; Holdrege forthcoming.

2. See Merleau-Ponty 1962.

3. See Bourdieu 1977, 1984, 1990; Foucault 1973, 1979, 1980, 1988–1990.

4. See Kristeva 1980, 1982, 1986; Irigaray 1985a, 1985b, 1993; Cixous 1976, 1994; Cixous and Clément 1986.

5. See Butler 1993, 1999, 2004.

6. This expression derives from Cabezón 2006: 31.

7. The term "processual body" reflects the Hindu notion that the human body is not "individual" but is rather "dividual"—to use McKim Marriott's (1976) term—that is, a constellation of substances and processes that is connected to other bodies through a complex network of transactions.

8. For an extended study of the discursive representations and practices associated with these five processual bodies in distinct Hindu discourses of the body, see Holdrege forthcoming. For brief analyses of a range of Hindu discourses of the body, see Holdrege 1998, 2008.

References

Bourdieu, Pierre. 1977 [1972]. *Outline of a Theory of Practice*. Translated by Richard Nice. Cambridge: Cambridge University Press.

Bourdieu, Pierre. 1984 [1979]. *Distinction: A Social Critique of the Judgement of Taste*. Translated by Richard Nice. Cambridge: Harvard University Press.

Bourdieu, Pierre. 1990 [1980]. *The Logic of Practice*. Translated by Richard Nice. Stanford: Stanford University Press.

Butler, Judith. 1993. *Bodies That Matter: On the Discursive Limits of "Sex."* New York: Routledge.

Butler, Judith. 1999 [1990]. *Gender Trouble: Feminism and the Subversion of Identity*. 2nd ed. New York: Routledge.

Butler, Judith. 2004. *Undoing Gender*. New York: Routledge.

Cabezón, José Ignacio. 2006. "The Discipline and Its Other: The Dialectic of Alterity in the Study of Religion." *Journal of the American Academy of Religion* 74, no. 1: 21–38.

Cixous, Hélène. 1976. "The Laugh of the Medusa." Translated by Keith Cohen and Paula Cohen. *Signs* 1, no. 4: 875–893.

Cixous, Hélène. 1994. *The Hélène Cixous Reader*. Edited by Susan Sellers. New York: Routledge.

Cixous, Hélène, and Catherine Clément. 1986 [1975]. *The Newly Born Woman*. Translated by Betsy Wing. Minneapolis: University of Minnesota Press.

Foucault, Michel. 1973 [1963]. *The Birth of the Clinic: An Archaeology of Medical Perception*. Translated by A. M. Sheridan Smith. New York: Random House, Pantheon Books.

Foucault, Michel. 1979 [1975]. *Discipline and Punish: The Birth of the Prison*. Translated by Alan Sheridan. New York: Random House, Vintage Books.

Foucault, Michel. 1980. "Body/Power." In *Power/Knowledge: Selected Interviews and Other Writings 1972–1977*, ed. Colin Gordon, 55–62. Translated by Colin Gordon et al. New York: Random House, Pantheon Books.

Foucault, Michel. 1988–1990 [1976, 1984]. *The History of Sexuality*. 3 vols. Translated by Robert Hurley. New York: Random House, Vintage Books.

Holdrege, Barbara A. 1998. "Body Connections: Hindu Discourses of the Body and the Study of Religion." In *The Study of Hinduism and the Study of Religion*, special issue, *International Journal of Hindu Studies* 2, no. 3: 341–386.

Holdrege, Barbara A. 2008. "Body." In *Studying Hinduism: Key Concepts and Methods*, ed. Sushil Mittal and Gene Thursby, 19–40. New York: Routledge.

Holdrege, Barbara A. 2015. *Bhakti and Embodiment: Fashioning Divine Bodies and Devotional Bodies in Kṛṣṇa Bhakti*. New York: Routledge.

Holdrege, Barbara A. Forthcoming. *The Body and the Self: Hindu Contributions to Theories of Embodiment*.

Irigaray, Luce. 1985a [1974]. *Speculum of the Other Woman*. Translated by Gillian C. Gill. Ithaca: Cornell University Press.

Irigaray, Luce. 1985b [1977]. *This Sex Which Is Not One*. Translated by Catherine Porter with Carolyn Burke. Ithaca: Cornell University Press.

Irigaray, Luce. 1993 [1984]. *An Ethics of Sexual Difference*. Translated by Carolyn Burke and Gillian C. Gill. Ithaca: Cornell University Press.

Kristeva, Julia. 1980 [1969, 1977]. *Desire in Language: A Semiotic Approach to Literature and Art*. Translated by Thomas Gora, Alice Jardine, and Leon S. Roudiez. Edited by Leon S. Roudiez. New York: Columbia University Press.

Kristeva, Julia. 1982 [1980]. *Powers of Horror: An Essay on Abjection*. Translated by Leon S. Roudiez. New York: Columbia University Press.

Kristeva, Julia. 1986. *The Kristeva Reader*. Edited by Toril Moi. New York: Columbia University Press.

Marriott, McKim. 1976. "Hindu Transactions: Diversity without Dualism." In *Transaction and Meaning: Directions in the Anthropology of Exchange and Symbolic Behavior*, ed. Bruce Kapferer, 109–142. Philadelphia: Institute for the Study of Human Issues.

Merleau-Ponty, Maurice. 1962 [1945]. *Phenomenology of Perception*. Translated by Colin Smith. London: Routledge and Kegan Paul.

Part 1

Material Bodies, Embodied Selves, and Perfected Embodiments

Chapter 1

Perfected Embodiment

A Buddhist-Inspired Challenge to Contemporary Theories of the Body

MICHAEL RADICH

Theories about the body and embodiment in the contemporary academy are consistently bounded by "materialist" and "descriptivist" assumptions. Acceptance of these assumptions amounts to an impasse for all theorization interested—as any such theory should be—in exploring the full range of human embodiment and how it can be understood. These assumptions are especially counterproductive and restrictive for politically radical currents in contemporary theory, such as Foucauldian and feminist discourses, that are not satisfied merely with supposedly objective "descriptions" of a given and immutable status quo but seek rather to deploy theory as an "intervention," a strategy to bring liberatory change to bodies and the existential status and experience of the subjects embodied in them.

Many religious traditions, by contrast, are not at all bound by this almost hardwired modern materialism. They propose a vast range of possible and ideal modes of embodiment, quite apart from anything that looks like the biophysical, anthropomorphic body of an ordinary worldly human being. At first blush such models of embodiment look outlandish to the modern gaze. On close and creative examination, however, they may have the potential to suggest new directions for theoretical work in our own time.[1] I will try to demonstrate the promise of such ideas by taking one rather surprising and abstruse set of ideas about perfected embodiment from Buddhist traditions and "translating" them from their technical Buddhist idiom into more familiar terms to yield a set of claims for contemporary scholarship to consider.

This essay attempts to squarely face the wide gulf between our modern standpoint and other worldviews and to contribute to constructing serviceable bridges across that gulf. In one sense I hope that this essay will demonstrate the benefits of taking the ideas of other traditions such as Buddhist traditions seriously—of treating them not simply as objects of study but as worthy interlocutors who might have something to teach us. I also hope that my analysis will help scholars, including Buddhologists, pay more serious attention to Buddhist ideas about perfected Buddha bodies as an integral part of the Buddhist vision of the salvific project. Moreover, my analysis will suggest some of the implications of the fact that Buddhist liberation is conceived of in terms of *embodying* and *being embodied in* what is true and real.

The Materialist, Descriptivist Limitations of Contemporary Body Theories

For purposes of analysis, contemporary body theories[2] might be divided into six main currents:[3] (1) theories of the body as *constructed by social forces* and inscribed by social meanings,[4] in which broad category I include Foucauldian theories of the body as a site of subjection to power;[5] (2) *phenomenological analysis* of the body as the means, locus, or agent of experience and certain kinds of knowledge;[6] (3) philosophical or comparative attempts to counter or *challenge mind/body dualism;*[7] (4) theories of the body as the means, locus, or agent of significant, embedded, and *epistemologically consequential practice;*[8] (5) quasi-ethological analysis of the body as *animal organism*, biological mechanism, and vessel of genetic heredity;[9] and (6) theories of the body as a key component in the *construction of gender* and the perpetuation of patriarchal gender inequities.[10]

Despite their profusion and apparent variety, such contemporary theories of the body are almost universally confined within a set of assumptions that I call "materialist" and "descriptivist."[11] By "materialist" I do not necessarily mean what we might call "hard" materialism—that is, the metaphysical position that all that exists is exclusively composed of physical matter. I mean rather a looser, more inclusive materialism, defined for our present purposes specifically with reference to the question of what constitutes the human body. The hallmark of this materialism is the assumption that human embodiment ultimately always prototypically includes, has reference to, or is grounded upon biological matter, and more specifically a living physical organism with an anthropomorphic shape. This assumption is a common thread that arguably binds together all members of the large family of modern body theories, however much they may otherwise vary in their claims about the extent to which such bodies are also elastic in the ways they are socially encoded, phenomenologically experienced, and so on.

This materialist assumption is often coupled with a "descriptivist" stance that is common to many other modern intellectual endeavors. By this I mean the widespread assumption that the proper role of conceptual inquiry is to describe as accurately as possible an object or state of affairs. The target of description is understood to exist independently of the description and ideally to remain pristinely untouched by it, whether the description succeeds or fails. In theories about the body, this translates into the more specific assumption that the task of theorization is to accurately and adequately capture a type (or types) of given, already existing embodiment. Theorization will make a difference only to the state of our knowledge about that embodiment, not to embodiment itself. Such theories do not take as part of their task to normatively stipulate better or ideal modes of embodiment, or to help to bring them into being.

These two assumptions are intertwined, perhaps not by dint of any a priori link between the project of description and the material-biological anthropomorphic body as its object, but by the purportedly empirical fact that descriptive endeavor only discovers such bodies wherever it looks. However, we must ask whether the tail is wagging the dog so that we only discover such bodies because our attention is directed by materialist assumptions.

Thus, returning to the six broad currents in contemporary body theories outlined earlier, we see that these various theories all assume what I am calling the materialist understanding of body. The bodies they imagine, in the final analysis, are ordinary human bodies: subject to birth and death; gendered; composed of flesh and blood; with two arms and two legs and a head and a heart and a stomach; able to move, walk, talk, breathe, ingest food, and excrete waste, but not able to fly, or evanesce, or walk through solid objects.[12] This is true regardless of claims that the body is also inscribed with social meanings or otherwise socially constructed, regardless of claims that it is not merely an object of knowledge but an intimate component in the construction of that knowledge, regardless of claims that it is not merely a prior requisite for our being and identity but the very medium and axis of that identity, and regardless of claims that it is not in fact as clearly separable from "mind" as "Cartesian dualism" leads us to believe. It is even true of the most radical claims for the relativity of embodiment to the nonuniversal parameters of culture, gender, class, sexuality, social role, and so on. It is also even true of theories that propose that current modes of embodiment dominant in our societies are repressive, unjust, and the means of our subjugation to alienating powers and therefore agitate for some sort of change in embodiment. Through all these theories one particular body—the ordinary living human body—runs like a relentless *idée fixe*, and, we might say, the outlines of the ordinary human body demarcate the limits beyond which all such theories will not or cannot think.

In this dogged adherence to a single, shared, broad underlying model of human embodiment, most of these contemporary theoretical discourses are descriptive in the sense that they adopt a rhetorical stance of abjuring normative questions. They are also descriptive in the deeper sense that this rhetorical stance of objectivity, in conjunction with the unanimity of all theories on the question, lends the air of an empirical truth to the assumption that the material body is the only kind of body possible or conceivable.

A partial exception to both the materialist and descriptivist stances is presented by politically radical theories. I am thinking primarily of Foucault (and those inspired by him) and currents in radical feminist theory usually inspired at some remove by psychoanalysis. Both lines of thought reject descriptivism insofar as they refuse to believe that "what you see is what you get"; their critiques imply that we do not have to like or lump the status quo, but rather we can and should resist current exploitative modes of embodiment and work for better.

I find no indication, however, that even Foucauldian theory rejects the materialist premise. For instance, for such theory bodies are particularly effective sites for the construction and maintenance of power precisely insofar as they are ordinary human bodies, subject to ordinary human pleasure and pain.[13] To my knowledge, Foucault never considers, as part of his theorization of the body, any claim about alternative types of bodies to material human bodies, nor does he ever propose bodies radically unrelated to the ordinary human body in any emancipatory project.[14]

More radical currents in continental feminism, represented by the so-called *écriture féminine* of Irigaray, Cixous, and Kristeva, perhaps come closest of all the modern theories surveyed to challenging the materialist assumption.[15] It is instructive therefore to observe the limits beyond which even these writers will not go in abandoning the archetype of the flesh-and-blood human body. They are famous for proposing that the body—particularly, for their purposes, the body of woman—is only text. The project is therefore to reinscribe this text, to generate new texts free of the phallocentric, phallocratic norms hidden in patriarchal discourse, which will furnish women with new, liberatory modes of embodiment. On the surface of it, this is a radical departure from the idea of the body as physical matter, as biological organism, as living animal, and so on. However, even these new "textual bodies" teem with anatomical details—genitalia, bodily fluids, body cavities, breasts[16]—that reveal the persistence of the biophysical body as a template. The body may well be text, but it turns out that it is always written as palimpsest on the parchment of our given physicality. For all it might be supposed that we can overwrite it, perhaps in a language utterly new, it does not seem to be imagined that we can transform the physical body into, or substitute for it, a different medium altogether. Thus even those theories that appear to present the most radical departure from the materialist premise end up not departing from it very far at all.

Insofar as even these most "radical" theories do not divest themselves thoroughly of the materialist assumption, it is arguable that, despite their willingness to risk a normative rhetoric and the abstract possibility of radical change, they also do not get past the descriptivist orthodoxy. For modern theories, it seems, it is simply an incontrovertible fact that "body" *means* the given human body, and that is exactly where all exploration of the question stops.

Beyond Modern Assumptions: Alternative Models from Religious Traditions

The materialist and descriptivist limits I have pointed to in modern body theories are not shared by a wide range of religious traditions, especially premodern traditions, which have elaborated a host of ideas about special bodies beyond the wildest dreams of modern theorists.[17] Such special bodies are in the main ascribed to two classes of beings: (1) divine beings or other beings ascribed the status of ultimate reality;[18] and (2) human beings who are rendered temporarily or permanently "holy" by some means.

Divine beings or other beings who are ascribed the status of ultimate reality can have as their bodies (be embodied in) such things as: special knowledge (gnosis); light; the word of the dispensation, holy texts, divine names, or other kinds of special language; the entire world in various senses; man-made objects like temples and images; religious communities; sacrificial food; relics; partially or entirely zoomorphic bodies; titanic bodies of immeasurable strength or invulnerable bodies of adamant; bodies distinguished by special physiognomic marks; flesh-and-blood bodies of apparently anatomically normal humans (for example, Christ or the Hindu *guru*); stones; and geographic features of the natural landscape.

Originally ordinary human beings who undergo temporary or permanent sanctification—ritualized transformation, salvific transformation, apotheosis, or other forms of transformation—can thereby enter into various kinds of extraordinary embodiment. For example, they can become immortal or immensely long-lived; they can be bodily resurrected after death; they can take a new form of nonmaterial body in some postmortem state; they can be mummified; they can be purified or otherwise sanctified by means ranging from ritual action to excruciating torture and death; they can be miraculously healed; or they can be transformed into other bodies such as those of birds and animals. In some cases, they can even remain physically untransformed while sanctification is bestowed upon them by external grace or revealed in them by sudden insight.

These understandings of extraordinary or perfected bodies are often not merely peripheral curiosities at the fringes of the worldviews that produce them, however "fringe" they might look from our modern vantage point. The understanding of ordinary human embodiment in religious systems that propound such ideas is intimately connected with these models of extraordinary embodiment. Ideas about extraordinary embodiment are not merely proposed, they are *celebrated*; they present not merely "an" alternative, but a much better alternative. In fact, the models proposed are often intended as visions of embodiment *perfected*, and the clear implication is that ordinary embodiment is inadequate and unsatisfactory at every point where it departs from that perfected ideal. Such perfected bodies, then, are often at the very center of what a given tradition has to say about embodiment, particularly about its existential or salvific significance.

The clear implication is that unless we understand perfected bodies and take them seriously, we miss a very large dimension of even how these traditions understand ordinary bodies. Even for the less radical and ambitious purpose of accurately *describing* the full range of human experience of and ideas about embodiment, then, it is necessary for us to move beyond the boundaries of the materialist and descriptivist assumptions. Unfortunately, however, most studies of the body in religious studies to date have been restricted in one way or another by precisely these assumptions.[19]

The question of the implications of this descriptive problem for religious studies and body theories is too complex to be adequately addressed in this essay. In the present analysis I will attempt rather to go one step further and ask what might be the challenges to contemporary body theories if we take seriously, as possible *contributions* to our theoretical discourses about the body, such claims from beyond the pale of our common contemporary assumptions. Before I can do so, however, I must address an important conceptual obstacle that lies in our path.

Against an Exclusively Metaphorical Hermeneutic

Too easily, and too commonly, modern observers tend to automatically interpret ideas about extraordinary bodies as "just a metaphor."[20] In using the word "metaphor" here, I mean to include all interpretations that do not read the notion of "body" as literal but rather understand it as a figure of speech, or as an allegory, or as somehow symbolic. Such metaphorical uses of any term have in common precisely the fact that they are not meant literally.[21] We might say that in such cases the term is used to refer to something that falls outside the usual class of its referents, with respect to some definitionally salient feature or features. Thus if I say metaphorically that "Mary is a jackass," no one will understand me as asserting that she has four hooved feet and a tufted tail, is male, can only bray, and cannot speak.

The problem of course is that correct identification of metaphor can hinge in large part on definitions of what literally is or can be the case. When we are dealing with statements made from within a worldview other than our own, we must therefore be careful not to assume that all statements that strike *us* as literally implausible are therefore necessarily intended to be understood metaphorically. The pertinent standard is rather, in the first instance, what would be literally plausible to subscribers of the worldview from which the statement originates. We know of many cases in which at least some adherents of other worldviews ascribe literal truth to propositions most moderns find implausible: for example, that the world is arranged around a massive central mountain; that certain ghosts hunger for human afterbirth; that worms are generated from fallen horsehairs after rain; that many diseases in women are caused by the uterus roaming from its rightful place inside their body. Such cases should give us pause. Just because we think we know that the only real bodies that exist in the world are animal bodies (including those of the human animal), this does not mean we can assume that this "truth" has also been self-evident to all peoples in all times and places and therefore that no one ever spoke literally when they spoke of other bodies.

How then should we proceed? If it is true that our metaphysical and ontological preconceptions might lead us into incorrect metaphorical interpretations of literal statements from other worldviews, we should at least attempt to develop some criteria for judging the issue independent of our preconceptions. We cannot go fully into this complex question here, but some possibilities suggest themselves immediately. (1) Does the text or other source say in some way that the idea is intended metaphorically? For instance, parables and allegories, in which the elements of the narrative are not meant literally, are often followed by a handy auto-gloss or key ("Here the gold is [means, represents] Buddha-nature . . ."). In such cases we are obviously justified in interpreting the idea metaphorically. (2) Is metaphor an obvious general feature of the language in the particular context? In poetic language, for instance, we commonly see metaphors follow one another in quick and rich succession ("*take arms* against a *sea of troubles* . . . to die, *to sleep* . . . bear *the whips* and scorns of time . . .") in a manner that makes it obvious that they cannot all can be meant literally, because no real context can be imagined in which they would all co-occur. Similarly, figurative speech often applies multiple metaphors to the same topic so that the combination might illuminate it better, by a kind of triangulation, than any one alone ("You are our life, Your Majesty, our sun, the wind in our sails . . ."). Here too grounds for reading each separate notion metaphorically are strong. (3) Do people behave toward the thing named as they behave toward its literal referents? For example, Bette Midler might well say, "You are the wind beneath my wings," but the fact that she means it metaphorically is shown when she is (presumably) unwilling to cast herself from a clifftop and try to fly, even with her lover's "support." (4) Does the language used have a more literal counterpart or translation? If so, what is it? If we are to treat an idea in the form in which it is given to us as a metaphor, then we must logically have some idea of what we take to be the literal denotation it implies. For example, if someone claims, "He is an ox," we must know, in order to interpret this metaphor correctly, that it is intended to mean, "He is very strong." If pressed, we can then translate it into more concrete terms like, "He is thickly muscled," "He can move unusually heavy weights." (5) Finally, before assuming that a statement from another worldview is intended to be understood metaphorically, we should consider whether a direct, literal interpretation of the statement is conceivable. Remembering the hermeneutical principle of charity, we must be as vigorous, generous, and well informed as possible in attempting to elaborate a conceivable interpretation before we give up.

This list of criteria could certainly be expanded. For our purposes, the main point is not so much the exact nature of the criteria by which we test for literality or metaphoricity but the more basic need to apply some test in the first place, as some kind of control against our assumptions.

When we turn to religious ideas about extraordinary bodies, I believe we frequently find a number of indications, along the lines of these types of criteria, that strongly indicate that the usages in question are not exclusively metaphorical. Take the relics of the Buddha, for example.[22] We know these are bodies because they are named as such: the most common designation for relics is *śarīrāṇi*, literally, "bodies." One important way in which this designation is not metaphorical is that there is no other term that is commonly used for relics as there is, for example, for a king who is at times called a "lion"—"bodies" *is* the word.[23] Buddhist texts also never turn around after using this "body" language and say to us, "Now what we *really* mean here is . . ." We are also directed away from a metaphorical reading by the fact that relics are substituted interchangeably with other bodies of the Buddha in certain key doctrinal formulae. Furthermore, relics are treated in many respects as if they are bodies. For example, Gregory Schopen has documented the notion that destruction of relics is considered equivalent to a murder,[24] and he and other scholars have also argued persuasively that the Buddha is understood as present in his relics.[25] Devotees also behave toward relics as they would behave in the presence of a Buddha, and relics are thus the functional equivalent of other Buddha bodies. Relics are worshiped and are held to be identical to the Buddha himself as a field of merit.[26] Moreover, relics are functionally equivalent to the Buddha not only for his devotees but also for his own purposes (*svārtha*) in the sense that they can undertake acts he might actively undertake, in some cases for his own benefit rather than the benefit of others. Thus relics can perform miracles,[27] and in some miracles relics transform themselves precisely into other kinds of Buddha bodies.[28] Relics are also ascribed the status of a "legal person" who can legally hold property.[29]

In all these respects, then, we seem to be dealing with a use of the notion of body that goes beyond metaphor. As applied to relics, the "body trope," if we want to call it that, does not necessarily appear in poetic contexts where metaphor is otherwise at play. It is not a passing fancy conjured up to give momentary vividness to another, separately identifiable idea, and it is also not presented as one of a number of different ways we might think about relics "in a manner of speaking." It is rather the main way of speaking and thinking about the phenomenon in question, and as such it is remarkably sustained in historical time and cultural space.[30] That this "trope" is ascribed a reality that goes beyond the figurative is also powerfully underscored by the many important ways in which people behave toward the relics as if they were authentic bodies.

Turning to the fourth criterion listed earlier, it also does not seem clear, in the case of the Buddha's relics, that an interpreter who claims that the idea of relic as body is a metaphor would be able to identify what supposedly literal idea lies behind it. If we want to assert that the relic is not literally the Buddha's body, what relation do we think the tradition does claim holds between the Buddha and his relics? How will we translate this claim into an allegedly nonfigurative counterpart? If we cannot so translate, are we sure it is meaningful to speak of a metaphor in this case?

Part of the problem here is that we are dealing with claims about extraordinary states of being—what might be justly described as the "supernatural." Such states are presumably beyond ordinary experience. Religious traditions often claim that they can only with difficulty be approximated in ordinary language at all, and they celebrate this fact. It is possible, then, that the ordinary language we call "literal" pertains only to the ordinary world of "natural" experience and that in application to ideas or phenomena ostensibly beyond its sphere, the very notion of literality versus metaphoricity breaks down.

Another part of the problem, however, may be connected to the very nature of the body. It is important in this context to introduce a terminological distinction between "body" and "embodiment." I hold that our intuitive concept of "body" (being careful to define in terms general enough to admit the nonhuman, nonanthropomorphic extraordinary bodies whose status as body is precisely my topic of investigation here) means something like "a perceptible, tangible form in which a subjective (experiencing, knowing, acting) being is present in the world, both for itself (in order to experience, know, act, and so on) and for others." For analytical purposes, then, we might stipulate that "body" refers to the form (organism, vessel, vehicle) in which the being is so presenced in the world. "Embodiment," by contrast, we can stipulate to mean something like "being-in-the-body," meaning that the being in question is presenced in and through the body, which is the mode in which it is so present, including the relations that inhere between being and body.[31] Such a distinction, I believe, clarifies an ambiguity and confusion that characterize contemporary body theories, in which what is actually at issue is often, according to my definition, not just "body" but "*em*bodi*ment*" (for example, the symbolic inscription of the body with social meanings).

With these definitions in hand, I think we can see more clearly—as is indeed so often pointed out in various ways by contemporary body theories—that what I am calling "*em*bodi*ment*" is a phenomenological, subjective matter. It is defined by modes of experience and structures of meaning, as well as by the physical or otherwise tangible form in which the embodied is embodied, which we might conventionally call "body." The key point for our discussion here is that there may be no language for any experiential or subjective states that is not purportedly metaphorical. It is very often observed, for instance, that our language about our ordinary moods, emotions, and dispositions—"up," "down," "dark," "bright," "heartsick," "beside oneself," "cold," "hot," "calm," "agitated," and so on—is overwhelmingly metaphorical and indeed, if we pursue etymology far enough, perhaps universally so.[32] However, it should be obvious that this is because of a materialist, objectivist bias in what we recognize as the literal senses of words—that they refer first and foremost to things of the external world and that in the final analysis this is what we mean by "literal." If it is true that subjective, experiential states are necessarily spoken of in metaphorical terms, this means that there is no more literal language to translate them into, and I return to my basic contention: in the absence of a more literal alternative against which to define it, to claim that embodiment talk of any kind is a metaphor may be, beyond a certain point, misleading and even meaningless.

This brings us to the fifth criterion in my list: Is a nonliteral interpretation of the body trope in question conceivable? It is here that I believe modern analysis has generally not tried hard enough, or imagination has failed us. Thus we have too often said, "There is no way that can be meant (or understood) literally," and that has been the end of our interpretive process. This problem of literal conceivability, applied to the specific case of ideas about remarkable, ideal bodies, will be the main focus of the remainder of this essay.

In the case of relics, especially in light of the evidence just reviewed, this question of conceivability seems trivial. We can certainly imagine a worldview in which the Buddha or a Christian saint is believed to literally act and be present in his or her relics. After all, we have no trouble conceding that there are worldviews in which it is literally believed that

Christ ascended bodily into heaven, or rain is brought by the activity of dragons. Precisely because the range of things we can imagine might genuinely be held by other worldviews is so large, the problem may lie elsewhere, in the question of whether or not we can think of an understanding of the idea in question that is plausible *to us*—that is, reconcilable with our own worldview. As I suggested earlier, this may be the reason literalist readings of ideas about extraordinary bodies are so readily ruled out of court. However, once we bracket our own materialist biases and recognize that such literalist readings might not historically have been unheard of or impossible, we should surely ask whether there might be stronger senses in which ideas about extraordinary bodies are workable or true for us. If such ideas were plausible and compelling to such a wide range of cultures and peoples, why not for us too?

Current directions in body theories open up a space for such considerations. A range of contemporary theories urge that the body or embodiment is not reducible to the physical organism; instead, it is conditioned and constituted to a considerable degree by processes like identification, meaning-making, ritual, and experience. If this is true, just how elastic is the category "body"? If the body is a phenomenological matter, how can we be so sure that only the biophysical flesh-and-blood organism that *we* take as the literal referent of the term body is indeed the limit of possible embodiment as experience? How will we find out unless by trying out other alternatives?

I propose, then, that the question of whether a nonfigurative reading of a given model of embodiment can be made plausible to us is not only critical to accurate interpretation of ideas from other traditions and cultural worlds. It is also a vital question for our genuine intercourse with these ideas. Unless we can ourselves intuitively "see" how the ideas might be more than flights of imagination, how can they ever amount to more than conceptual curiosities for us? Where will we find the points of contact where we can engage in dialogue with our own ideas? To the same end, the creative, open attempt to find a way such ideas are plausible on a level beyond metaphor might itself be taken as an independent test of their ontological and metaphysical status—a kind of thought experiment. To be sure, such an exercise could claim no adjudication over historical questions of how literally the ideas were intended or understood by their authors and recipients at their source. But I intend to proffer such a thought experiment to a different end: the creative extension and rejuvenation of our own theoretical discourses about the body.

To this end, we should adopt a different hermeneutic. The exclusively metaphorical hermeneutic is the interpretive corollary of the materialist-descriptivist assumption, which furnishes the criterion for deciding what qualifies as literal, against which all else is relegated to the category of metaphor. In order to explore the possibility that some surprising ideas may nonetheless be more than figurative, I suggest that we instead begin with the assumption that the ideas under consideration are meant literally until they are proven metaphorical. We can then see how far we can follow the thinking behind them from that point of view. The exclusively metaphorical hermeneutic is a closed hermeneutic, and, as such, it automatically admits no possibilities other than those that are already part of our received worldview. By contrast, this alternative hermeneutic is open. Only by means of such an open approach will we have the opportunity to discover something new.

The Rejection of *Sat-kāya-dṛṣṭi* and the Realization of *Dharma-kāya*

In the remainder of this essay I propose to conduct one such thought experiment, using as my base a particular set of ideas about extraordinary, perfected embodiment from Buddhist traditions. These ideas are explicitly normative and claim that (1) human well-being and truth can only be realized if we completely reject and overcome identification with our ordinary, given embodiment (*sat-kāya-dṛṣṭi*); and (2) perfection, or Buddhahood, consists in the realization of an alternative embodiment in perfect gnostic identity with the highest metaphysical truth that inheres in all things (*dharma-kāya*).[33]

I should stress that the ideas that follow are best understood as inspired by Buddhist ideas, although I will do my best to accurately present what the Buddhist texts say. In the end, these ideas have obviously been modulated by their passage through the filter of my own understanding and sensibilities. Since I do not identify as a Buddhist or speak from a position of faith (for want of a better term), I therefore make no claim to speak for Buddhist traditions.

I turn first to the notion of *sat-kāya-dṛṣṭi*.[34] At first sight, this term would literally appear to mean "the view (*dṛṣṭi*) that [one] is (*sat*, from Sanskrit root *as*, 'to be') the body (*kāya*)" or "the view that the body exists (*sat*)."[35] More technically, we might paraphrase the concept in question as "the mistaken view that a self exists in some sense in, of, or as one or more of the five *skandhas*." The five *skandhas* (aggregates or faggots[36]) are five classes of phenomena into which Buddhist traditions analyze the putative person and its world of experience: (1) visible, tangible material forms (*rūpa*); (2) sensation (*vedanā*); (3) conception (*saṃjñā*); (4) reaction/volition (*saṃskāra*); and (5) consciousness (*vijñāna*). Strictly speaking, then, the term refers to identification not just with the body defined as the biophysical flesh-and-blood organism (which would be covered by the first *skandha* only, *rūpa*) but with any aspect of embodiment—that is, the overall psychophysical complex we normally think of under the heads of both body and mind, including sense perception, ideas, affect, and awareness.

Canonical texts repeatedly emphasize that clinging to (*upādāna*, which we might more loosely translate "identification with" or "attachment to" in modern parlance) any part of this personal psychophysical complex constitutes the existential stance termed *sat-kāya*, and this attitude is existentially inadequate and dissatisfactory—in Buddhist terms, it is attended by suffering, *duḥkha*. *Sat-kāya-dṛṣṭi* so defined is treated as a subspecies of a broader mistaken and harmful view known as *ātma-dṛṣṭi*, "mistaken belief in a self."[37] Doctrine concerning *sat-kāya-dṛṣṭi* is presented not just as a set of abstract propositions but as a meditative curriculum of practice to systematically undo this identification (clinging). Success is equated with full liberation in the fundamental salvific terms of the Four Noble Truths.[38]

Although the false identification termed *sat-kāya* is thus larger in its scope than our ordinary understanding of the word "body," the word *kāya* in the term *sat-kāya-dṛṣṭi* nonetheless literally refers to "body" in the ordinary sense.[39] This apparent tension might be reconciled in more than one way. For instance, it is possible that *kāya*, body, refers to *rūpa*, material form—which is, with reference to the makeup of the psychophysical complex of the putative person, understood primarily with reference to the physical body—and thus labels the overall complex of the five *skandhas* by synecdoche. Another possibility is that the notion of *kāya* here refers to all five *skandhas*, not by synecdoche but equally and directly. In this interpretation, *kāya* refers to the entire state of being-in-the-body, conceived in terms broader than only its physical dimension to include what we might call its "psychological" aspects and concomitants. Such a broader interpretation of what body means for ordinary personhood seems better captured by the term "*em*bodi*ment*" (as previously defined), which conveys the sense that not only is there a body, but there is a being of some sort "in" or by means of the body. It also seems closer to the sorts of nondualist, post-Cartesian understandings of body toward which many contemporary body theories have been working.[40]

Setting aside philological problems of exactly how the element *kāya* might have been intended in canonical Buddhist texts, I will take it as a warrant to consider an interpretation in which the object of the problematic identification that produces suffering is intimately bound up with our ordinary embodiment. I hope to show in what follows that such an interpretation fits very neatly with other Buddhist claims that liberation, or the attainment of Buddhahood, entails an absolute transformation of embodiment involving the substitution of ordinary embodiment by a radically different alternative. I will thus translate *sat-kāya-dṛṣṭi,* perhaps with some latitude, as "mistaken identification with ordinary embodiment as self."

The salient points for my thought experiment are these—and here I begin translating from strictly Buddhist terminology into broader terms. It is proposed that our ordinary state of human embodiment, as we intuitively tend to understand it, is radically inadequate to our true existential makeup. It therefore leads to unhappiness, lack of fulfillment, and misery. The core of this problematic state of embodiment is a mistaken identification with an embodiment predicated on the ordinary flesh-and-blood body.[41] This identification goes beyond the biophysical organism alone and includes identification with the whole gamut of mental contents conditioned by the operation of the body and reactions to them, including sense perception, a particular ideational map of the world, affect, and consciousness (at least its ordinary contents). We "identify" with all of this inasmuch as we take it all as intrinsic and central to our very identity, our being as persons. In this we are wrong. Not only is this identification—and the identity so constructed—dispensable, it is harmful, and overcoming it is an urgent task for our well-being.

It should be immediately obvious what a radical challenge this Buddhist perspective presents to modern theories of the body, which, as we have seen, do not usually contemplate any alternative to embodiment predicated on the ordinary body (even on those rare occasions when these theories are not entirely comfortable with our given state of embodiment, as in radical critiques). The obvious question is: What do Buddhist traditions propose instead? A fuller answer, I believe, is that they propose not just one but several quite radical alternatives.[42] In the present analysis, however, I will focus on one model in particular: the idea of *dharma-kāya* in Mahāyāna Buddhist discourse. The concept of *dharma-kāya* proposes that the Buddha is embodied in (*-kāya,* takes as his body) the ultimate truth of all things, as he realizes it in the gnosis that constitutes his complete liberation.[43] In order to understand this notion, we need to understand a few constituent concepts first, more specifically the term *dharma*.

Dharma is a notoriously complex and polysemous term in Indian religions in general and even within the more restricted context of Buddhist traditions alone.[44] For our purposes we need to have before us three different but interrelated senses. (1) *Dharma* (conventionally often capitalized in this sense in English) refers to the teachings of the Buddha about the salvific truth, the path to its realization, and obstacles in that path. (2) Especially in schools of Abhidharma and their heritors,[45] *dharma* refers to a "real," or irreducible, building block among a limited number (several dozens, or a hundred, say) into which an apparently much more multifarious reality can be analyzed by correct doctrinal and meditative effort. In this sense, Abhidharma is a pluralist-realist philosophy, and *dharma*s are the root categories it recognizes. This sense of *dharma* is related to the first in that Abhidharmic *dharma*s are the constituents of the reality described by Dharma as a discourse. (3) By extension and loose application, *dharma* comes in post- (or anti-) Abhidharmic Mahāyāna discourse to mean just "thing." Even Abhidharmic *dharma*s are deconstructed and denied ultimate reality. With that privileged status stripped from it, the term *dharma* is freed up for a much more general use in which it means something like "any apparent or putative thing," "any phenomenon"—that is, anything that presents itself as an object to cognition or for philosophical-doctrinal consideration. However, to discuss a putative thing under the head of *dharma* rather than by other names still implies that one is considering it from a kind of ultimate point of view, in terms of such true reality as can be imputed to it (if any), rather than under the aspect it presents to the ordinary (*saṃsāric*) world.

This third sense most concerns us here because of a widely shared Mahāyāna philosophical position about *dharma*s that informs the notion of *dharma-kāya*. Early Mahāyāna texts elaborated, and later Mahāyāna texts universally followed,[46] a doctrine that "all *dharma*s are empty" (*sarva-dharma-śūnyatā*). "Empty" here means specifically "devoid of independent self-identity and essence (*sva-bhāva*),"[47] inasmuch as all things (*dharma*s) are held to be radically mutually dependent in a relational web of causes and conditions (*pratītya-samutpāda*) that accounts exhaustively for all aspects of their (apparent) "being."[48] In crude terms, "nothing is real"—understanding "real" in the extremely strong and robust sense of "existing autonomously and eternally."[49] However, it would be erroneous to understand this as an assertion that "there is absolutely nothing."[50]

Thus the reality of all things (*sarva-dharma*), or the nearest they ever come to reality, consists precisely and paradoxically in their *un*reality. To keep this difficult proposition in the forefront of our minds, I will call it "reality-cum-unreality." The status of this reality-cum-unreality can be partly clarified by understanding it as a second-order proposition. At the first order of what we presume to be "things in themselves," nothing answers to our craving for the real in that nothing holds eternally and universally; all is unstable and in flux and subject to coming into and going out of being. However, at the second order of what can be known about things, this very instability, recognized as a universal truth, promises to salvage from the storm a single thread of security: the very proposition that nothing is eternal and universal is itself, at least on one level, eternal and universal.[51] Such a second-order, abstract reality-cum-unreality might appear to be a thin-blooded substitute for the reality we initially craved, but in the Mahāyāna Buddhist perspective it is not only enough, it is the fountainhead of all the bliss and power of the Buddhas themselves.

The Mahāyāna tradition has some specific terms for this reality-cum-unreality of all *dharma*s, understood specifically as it relates to (for example, is instantiated in) individual *dharma*s. Sometimes it is called *dharmatā*, "*dharma*-ness"—which we might translate "the thingness of things"—referring to the fact that in this Buddhist view the only candidate for a common characteristic in all things, by which they can be known to be "things," is precisely this emptiness. Given that we can understand emptiness precisely as a failure to be a thing in the manner we usually imagine things, we might equally call this "the unthingness of things," or their "thingness-cum-unthingness."

Sometimes the reality-cum-unreality of all *dharma*s is also called the *dharma-dhātu*. *Dhātu* here is itself a multivalent word, meaning most basically such things as "primary element," "raw material," or "primitive matter." In this sense we might understand *dharma-dhātu* to suggest a kind of matrix or inchoate potential state from which apparently individuated *dharma*s arise, a kind of quasi-ground constituting the uniform reality underlying their apparent phenomenal multiplicity.[52] In Buddhist parlance *dhātu* is also often taken to mean something like "domain," "range," or "realm," and awakening is sometimes spoken of as "entry into the *dharma-dhātu*."[53] Here we might perhaps imagine each apparently individuated phenomenal thing as a door or gate (cf. Chinese *famen*, literally, "*dharma* gate") such that if we can disentangle its misleading apparent autonomy and particularity from its underlying participation in emptiness *qua dharmatā*, we can proceed via the thing into the universal realm of truth in which it partakes.

This same reality-cum-unreality of things is also called *tathatā*, "Thusness," meaning roughly the fact of things in truth being the way they are.[54] *Tathā* is an ordinary Sanskrit adverb meaning "so, thus, in such a manner, like this," and *-tā* is a nominalizing suffix (like English -ness, -ity, -itude; also found in the term *śūnyatā*, "emptiness," discussed earlier). *Tathatā* thus refers to the aspect of all things whereby they are as they are (in truth)—that is, whereby they are empty of autonomous self-essence, as discussed earlier.

The terms *dharmatā*, *dharma-dhātu*, and *tathatā* are germane here because Mahāyāna texts sometimes speak of *dharma-kāya* in terms related to them. *Dharma-kāya*, in the specific sense in which we are considering it here, is sometimes called **dharmatā-kāya* (embodiment in *dharmatā*).[55] On other occasions we notice in the history of a text that the term *dharma-kāya* gradually comes to replace the term *dharma-dhạtu*, or that the Buddha is identified with the *dharma-dhātu* in a manner that closely parallels the statement that he is "embodied in *dharma*."[56] The implication is clear that *dharma-kāya* can be interpreted as meaning "embodied in the *dharma-dhātu*." Finally, *tathatā* is also one of the most important of a network of parallel terms into which *dharma-kāya* was gradually woven as the tradition developed. In other words, *dharma-kāya* is *tathatā* ("Thusness" of all things) and vice versa.

In understanding the force of the notion of embodiment here, I think it helps further to consider the Buddhist understanding of the nondual nature of the Buddha's perfected, liberatory gnosis (*buddha-jñāna, prajñā*). Especially in the Mahāyāna school known as Yogācāra (practice of meditation) or Vijñaptimātra (mental representations only), Buddhist theorists explicitly emphasize that the deluded ignorance that leads to our suffering is characterized by its organization around a foundational false dualism (a kind of alienation, we might say) between subject (*grāhaka*, "apprehender") and object (*grāhya*, "[that which is] apprehended"). Against this, they claim that the Buddha's gnosis is nondual (*advaya*) such that knower and known are identical, and self-knowing knowledge is thereby perfectly adequate to itself *qua* its own (non)object. The Buddha thus "*real*izes" the truth in the double sense that he fully *knows* it and in the process *makes it real* in his own very being. This nondualism translates directly into the full and perfect identity of the Buddha and the *dharma* he knows. Here the three senses of *dharma* outlined earlier collapse into one another, since the Buddha's teaching (Dharma) is about the real (*dharma*) he has realized, which is the single universal true aspect of all things (*sarva-dharma-dharmatā, dharma-dhātu*) and is therefore no longer plural, as in Abhidharma philosophy, but itself transcendentally one.

In the notion of the Buddha as *embodied* in *dharma,* the nondualism of (former) subject and object in perfected gnosis maps onto another key and mysterious nondualism: that of body and mind. Just as (in the selfsame moment when) the Buddha, in perfecting his special gnosis of the truth, becomes perfectly self-identical with that truth, so too his "mind" (if the term still holds in this strange new nondualistic world) becomes entirely one with his "body," such that there is no difference between what he knows and what he *is*—that is, what he is in knowing.[57]

Here I think we may find another unexpected congruence with inklings in modern theories, although Buddhist traditions have characteristically taken the insights concerned much further. In contemporary body theories, especially in currents stemming from or addressing phenomenology, epistemology, and neuroscience,[58] there is an emphasis on the idea that knowledge is often located in the body and that knowledge that is more embodied, as it were, is more intimate, closer to our very identity, and so on. From the point of view of such theories, we can easily understand the idea that the truth is only *really* known—only fully *real*ized—when it is taken into or even becomes the body and person of the knower. We should not let this parallel lead us to overlook a key distinction, however. In these Buddhist ideas, rather than nondualism meaning that we (descriptively) locate modes of worldly (often practical) knowledge as actually in the body defined in materialist terms,[59] we see a much more radical alternative nondualism: the complete "upload," in a manner of speaking, of embodiment into otherworldly, transcendent knowledge.

The notion of *dharma-kāya,* which we might now translate as "being embodied in the liberatory truth of all things," conveys this understanding powerfully and vividly, in a manner that arguably mirrors exactly the structure of the kind of embodied knowing it describes. Far more is at stake than just knowing something in a propositional sense. It is a matter of knowing in a full, existential manner, to the very core of one's being—not just knowing but *being* the truth, which then becomes inalienable because one knows it merely by reflexive self-awareness. The initially counterintuitive language that states that one takes this knowledge *as one's body* is effective in conveying this notion precisely because it is structured to transcend (or stymie) the very dualistic assumptions about what knows and is known, along with the respective functions and nature of body and mind, that are at issue in *saṃsāric* ignorance as distinct from the cognition of the Buddha. In this sense too the idea of *dharma-kāya* is no metaphor, in that there is no other more literal language into which it can be translated.

Much more could be said of course about this notion of *dharma-kāya,* but the little I have already presented will hopefully be enough to proceed with the thought experiment that is my main purpose here. I will now try to extricate these Buddhist ideas from the thickets of technical terms they usually inhabit and translate them into a form hopefully more generally accessible to our own discourses.

We already saw earlier that Buddhist traditions propose that *sat-kāya-dṛṣṭi*, our identification with our ordinary given embodiment in all its dimensions corporeal and cognitive/psychological, is a harmful mistake and that liberation comes by undoing that identification completely. In the notion of *dharma-kāya* we see a sophisticated articulation of an ideal state of embodiment that replaces that mistake when a being is fully perfected and becomes *buddha*, "awakened." This liberated state is defined primarily by full experiential knowledge of the true fundamental nature of all that "exists," which counterposes, against deep-rooted and even unconscious hypostatizing intuitions about the seeming autonomy, self-identity, and aseity of things, a clear awareness of their utterly conditioned and processual (temporal) character. This insight into the true nature of things brings about, and is predicated upon, profound transformations in the affective structure of the person so that he or she no longer forms ultimately painful attachments and aversions to ephemeral phenomenal objects.

Paramount and paradigmatic among the things so understood and the objects of these transformed relations is the embodiment of the person. Mistaken hypostatization and attachment take the ordinary, given, flesh-and-blood body to be an integral component of the self. *Dharma-kāya* doctrine claims that in place of this erroneous and insalubrious identification, the liberated person instead forms a truthful, salvific identification, even more existentially intimate and foundational because utterly nondual, with the liberatory truth he or she knows. Gnosis of this truth is so supremely valuable and transformative that it becomes the primary criterion for the very being of the one it liberates. The same gnosis is so complete, direct, and intimate that the usual apparent alienation of subject from object that characterizes the ordinary benighted mindset collapses or disappears, and the liberated "person" becomes identical with the gnosis that defines him or her. With the disappearance of this dualism, the ordinary dualism between mind and body also disappears, and the most meaningful sense in which the language of embodiment can be used in application to the new, liberated state is to say that the liberated being is *embodied in* the self-identity of perfect gnosis with what it knows. The "body" of the liberated being—its being-in-the-world and vehicle of being for the world—*is* its perfect, self-aware "mind," which in turn *is* all reality, as knower and not just known.

Challenges for Contemporary Body Theories

I remind the reader that I am not pleading for the accuracy or truth-value of these Buddhist ideas in the translation I give them here. My aim rather is to describe them in such a way that we can use them to engage in a thought experiment, in which we see how plausible such an alternative notion of ideal embodiment can be rendered to contemporary thought. My aim in engaging in this thought experiment is also to find ways in which radically different models of embodiment, like those found in premodern religious traditions, can be brought into dialogue with modern body theories. At this very preliminary stage of such work, I only hope to carry this dialogue far enough to sharpen our sense of what sorts of challenges and alternative models might be derived from ideas like these, in contrast to the usual modern materialist-descriptivist assumptions and stereotypes. At the very least, I hope by this example to begin to show how very many possibilities remain to be explored by modern body theories in religious studies, far beyond the close boundary line traced by the outline of the materialist-descriptivist body.

I suggest that we can identify four main levels at which these Buddhist ideas challenge modern body theories. These four levels can be arranged in a nested hierarchy, proceeding from the most specific and concrete version of the Buddhist ideas in question to the most basic and general.

(1) Appropriation of the Buddhist model of embodiment. This is the level already described in my translation of *dharma-kāya* doctrine into more general terms at the end of the preceding section. At this level we would consider, against the materialist-descriptivist modern paradigm, all four of the following propositions that are integral to the Mahāyāna Buddhist model of embodiment that I have described: (a) ordinary embodiment is not in fact the only mode of embodiment possible for human beings; (b) ordinary embodiment is constitutionally dissatisfying and harmful to the proper *telos* of human beings and is existentially inadequate; (c) the solution to this existential problem is not only disentangling ourselves from ordinary embodiment but *re*embodiment in a perfected alternative, comprising complete knowledge of and identification with (embodiment in) an existentially salvific, liberatory truth of the world; (d) the liberatory truth in question is best captured by the Mahāyāna understanding that our main cognitive problem is our inveterate hypostatization of putative "things," whereas in truth all things are empty. At this level the basic project for modern theory and practice, especially where it aims at genuine human *liberation,* would be to translate much further

the doctrines concerned into terms comprehensible and functional for contemporary use and to recover, adopt, or elaborate regimes of practice to facilitate realization of the model it articulates.

(2) Acceptance of the possibility of liberatory reembodiment in existential truth, with the content of that truth open to question. At a second level we might consider the challenge posed to modern body theories by all but the last of the four propositions just listed. In other words, modern theorists could consider the possibility that ordinary given embodiment is inadequate and that liberation from it is desirable and to be achieved by realization of (reembodiment in) a salvific existential truth, but the Buddhists may have been wrong about the concrete nature of the liberatory truth in question. In this version the challenge to modern theoretical presuppositions would still be powerful, since the model would not be based solely on the ordinary body and we would have to consider the proposition that salvific gnosis could constitute an alternative embodiment. The project would be expanded to include the discovery of the salvific truth that constitutes ideal embodiment, in addition to the elaboration of practices for the realization of that truth.

(3) Rejection of ordinary embodiment without promotion of a gnostic alternative. At a third level we might also strip away the claim that an alternative perfected embodiment consists in the attainment of identity with a liberatory gnosis. The claim would still be that ordinary embodiment is neither sufficient nor existentially salubrious for us as human beings. We might call this the rejection of *sat-kāya-dṛṣṭi* without *dharma-kāya*. At this level of specificity, our Buddhist-inspired challenge could be considered in two forms: (a) The first form would be open to the possibility that an alternative embodiment might replace ordinary embodiment, but it would be prepared to entertain models of such ideal embodiment other than the model of embodiment in gnostic truth. This is effectively the level at which the many other models of ideal embodiment in Buddhist traditions and other religious traditions would come into play. In this case the project for modern theorists would be to explore other models of alternative perfected embodiment and to consider possibilities of translation and adaptation like those we have pointed to here for *dharma-kāya*. (b) A second form of Buddhist-inspired challenge would reject embodiment completely as an entirely negative influence on human being. Such a form would presumably propose as a normative goal something like "disembodiment," disidentification with embodiment, to extricate it from our identity and core being.[60] The project for modern theorists might then be the elaboration of practices—including systems of critical ideas considered as praxis or

as intervention—to effect such disembodiment, alongside explorations of reasons that embodiment per se is deleterious to human well-being, implications for our philosophical anthropology, and so forth.

(4) Rejection of the constitutive nature of ordinary embodiment without any normative imperative to reject it. At a fourth level we might again strip away the next proposition in our list: the normative claim that ordinary embodiment is somehow harmful or inadequate to our being. We would then retain only the first proposition: that ordinary embodiment is not a constitutive aspect of our being and other possibilities are also open to us. Even at this most general and basic level, the Buddhist-inspired challenge we are exploring here is potentially extremely powerful. Whereas modern discourses only seriously consider embodiments anchored in or somehow defined by a relation to the biophysical flesh-and-blood human body, this opens up the possibility that there may be whole worlds we have been missing. Without the normative value-judgments Buddhist traditions attach to their rejection of ordinary embodiment, the exploration of other possibilities might proceed in a mode of fun and play, as the generation of creative and even recreational possibilities.

When we strip away the specificities of Buddhist *dharma-kāya* doctrine and consider the more open-ended possibilities of my third and fourth levels, the relevance to contemporary politically radical discourses about the body—like those proposed by the exponents of continental feminism and Foucauldian theory mentioned earlier—becomes especially apparent. Like Buddhists, such contemporary theorists are interested in human liberation, but they are arguably caught somewhere between partial versions of each of these levels. Like proponents of the *sat-kāya-dṛṣṭi* model of what is wrong with human beings, they are convinced that something about ordinary embodiment (the given status quo) is harmful (alienating, emasculating, disempowering, and so on). They are also sometimes even willing to entertain a half-blooded version of the idea that the biophysical body is not constitutive of or pivotal to all possible forms of human being, as is seen most vividly in the initially startling proposal of proponents of *écriture féminine* that body is text.

From the perspective of the Buddhist ideas we have considered, however, even our radical theorists might not be radical enough. Their theories do not have the full courage of their intuitions and stop only halfway. They do not make their ideas truly *radical*—that is, they do not interrogate the supposed body right to its fleshly *root*. As I argued earlier, all contemporary theories that I know of stop short of dispensing entirely with the biophysical, given human organism as the definitive point of reference and entertaining truly thoroughgoing alternatives. This means that they only overlap in part with even the stripped-back third- and fourth-level versions of the Buddhist challenge.

The Buddhists I have been ventriloquizing might rejoin that it is little wonder if true liberation has not ensued from such theories, or if it has not even been perceived by many as a plausible goal. Buddhists, along with the exponents of many other religious systems, would propose that there is something utterly out of joint not just about the social inscriptions of the body with power or meaning but about our umbilical tie of identity to the mortal, decaying flesh itself.[61] If this is so, then perhaps no amount of tweaking the relatively superficial level of reinscribing or reconfiguring social symbols and power will ever address the whole problem at the level where it actually inheres.

In this essay I have worked through this challenge with reference to the specific example of the Buddhist doctrines of *sat-kāya-dṛṣṭi* and *dharma-kāya*. However, as I tried briefly to suggest earlier, the religious traditions of the world actually propose a very wide range of alternative, ideal, perfected embodiments for divine beings and sanctified humans. The larger point of the exercise is that we moderns almost universally assume a particular, limited model of human embodiment, while many serious, sophisticated systems of human existential meaning and practice do not. Even if the particular exercise I have undertaken here is unconvincing in its details, I would nevertheless urge modern theorists of the body to hunt through these various traditional religious models of embodiment for inspiration that might point ways out of their general materialist impasse. This holds especially true for theorists of a radical stripe who are looking for radical alternatives to the world as they find it. To my mind, political questions aside, this radical group should on some level include all scholars and theorists, whose job it is to be curious about ways in which reality might prove completely different from our presuppositions.

Buddhists, I think, would not propose that realizing such a radical, liberatory reembodiment or achieving such a radically different understanding of embodiment will be easy. On the contrary, there is every indication—for example, in Buddhist models of countless eons of *bodhisattva* practice aimed at realizing the goal, or ideas about the inadequacy of all theoretical formulations and the difficulty of really grasping truth—that Buddhists would consider such work arduous and perilous. But I think the Buddhists whose ideas I have borrowed here would also say that we stand to win everything—complete freedom from all existential misery, fear, and dissatisfaction—and stand to lose only the chains of our "selves."

Notes

I thank Barbara Holdrege for her support and encouragement in the writing of this essay, for long and illuminating discussions that helped lead to the ideas it contains, and for her meticulous and generous editing. I also thank organizers of the Conference on the Study of Religions of India at Albion College, Michigan, September 13–16, 2007, and especially the late Selva J. Raj, for their support for related work. I am also grateful to fellow participants in the conference for their valuable discussion and feedback. In addition, I am grateful to colleagues at Victoria University of Wellington in New Zealand, especially Chris Marshall, for feedback on related work presented at a seminar in May 2008 (Radich 2008) that also stimulated some of the thinking set out here.

1. These resources are of course in many cases very old, but they may nonetheless be regarded as new for the purposes of the contemporary discourses that have hitherto ignored them or at best have interpreted them through hermeneutical schema that rob them of all their power to challenge us.

2. Obviously the pertinent literature is vast, and my treatment here is necessarily as abbreviated as I can make it. I survey the main currents I identify here in more detail in my paper "The Neglected General Problem of Holy Bodies and Some of Its Implications" (Radich 2008), which I hope to publish in the near future. Other useful general reviews or anthologies of various parts of this large literature, sometimes in the context of programmatic calls for greater attention to the body in particular disciplines, can be found in Asad 1997; Bynum 1995: esp. 3–5; Coakley 1997; Culianu 1991; Feher, Naddaff, and Tazi 1989; Frank 1990; Freund 1988; Hancock et al. 2000; Holdrege 1998: esp. 341–346; Johnson 2002: esp. 170–182; Maissonneuve 1976; McGuire 1990; Midgley 1997; Scheper-Hughes and Lock 1987; Shilling 1993; Sullivan 1990; Synnott 1993; Turner 1991, 1997; Williams and Bendelow 1998.

3. This schema is of course only a heuristic. Boundaries between its categories are permeable, and this is not the only way approaches to the body could be divided for purposes of summary. For alternatives, see, for example, Johnson's seven bodies (2002: 173–181); McGuire's division into "the body and self experience," "the body and social meanings," and "the body and power relations" (1990: 285–294); and Holdrege's analysis in terms of "the body in philosophy, the body in social theory [including 'social body' and 'body politic'], and the body in gender studies" (1998: 342–345).

4. See, for example, Burton 2001; Douglas 1996; McGuire 1990; Ruth 1974; Turner 1984.

5. Key works here are Foucault 1975, 1977, 1980, 1988–1990. Foucault's approach has of course been extremely influential. Of particular relevance for us is his impact on medical sociology and anthropology, as exemplified by Turner 1992, and on studies of sexuality and gender, as exemplified by Gallagher and Laqueur 1987.

6. Foundational thinkers are Merleau-Ponty (1962) and Binswanger (1975). The core phenomenological idea of the body as the site and organ of knowledge, and knowledge as therefore an embodied state, has been influential in anthropology thanks to Csordas 1990, 1993. See also Jackson 1983. We also see attempts to work out the implications of this approach in gender studies, as in Jaggar and Bordo 1989. Related moves have been made in more recent Anglo-American philosophy to recuperate the body for epistemology and explore phenomenological lines of inquiry. See, for example, Johnson 1987; Levin 1985; Zaner 1971.

7. See, for example, Spicker 1970; Warner and Szubka 1994. Comparative work sometimes makes the claim that mind/body dualism is a parochial Western problem and perceives alternatives in the positions promulgated by Asian and other traditions. See, for example, Kasulis, Ames, and Dissanayake 1993; Yuasa 1987.

8. I am thinking here particularly of Mauss and Bourdieu. See, for example, Mauss 1973; Bourdieu 1977. This work also forms an important basis for the hybrid Merleau-Pontean-cum-Bourdieuan theory of Csordas, set forth in his prize-winning article "Embodiment as a Paradigm for Anthropology" (1990).

9. See, for example, Guthrie 1976; Morris 1967; Blacking 1977. Into the same broad category, we might also place the huge wave of recent work in neuroscience (brain anatomy) and genetics, which in various ways attempts to trace determinants of (or at least contributing factors to) human behavior and psychophysical characteristics to microscopic features of our physical bodies.

10. See, for example, Brook 1999; Gallop 1988; Grosz 1994; Jacobus, Keller, and Shuttleworth 1990; Laqueur 1990; Wyke 1998. For works regarding *écriture féminine* as espoused (broadly) by Kristeva, Irigaray, and Cixous, see, for example, Kristeva 1986; Irigaray 1991; Cixous 1994; Dallery 1989. Among works in religious studies, see Cooey 1994; Miles 1989; Wilson 1996; and the essays by Sharrock, Cartledge, King, and Clark in Wyke 1998.

11. In attempting to identify limitations of this large body of theoretical discourses and areas in which it might be supplemented or extended, I do not mean to imply it is without value. On the contrary, my clear debt in what follows to many of the insights of the founding theorists who have participated in these discourses will be a clear sign of my appreciation for them.

12. Obviously sickness, deformity, mutilation, or accident can interfere with this archetypal form; it remains nonetheless the default norm.

13. This is brought out especially clearly by Lingis (1999).

14. From my limited knowledge of Foucault's project, it seems difficult to tell how much Foucault formulated a clear vision of alternative embodiment beyond his critiques of the way "biopower" is exercised on and through modern bodies. One possibility is that his later studies of classical techniques for the "care of the self" somehow imply, at least in part, a liberatory alternative to the bleak modern scenario whose several dimensions he surveys in his earlier work. It seems that his later studies of classical material depict practices and processes

that leave more room for subjective agency and empowerment than his earlier work on modern practices. However, drawing such a bald contrast between antiquity and the modern on this score would seem to imply a naive romanticization of antiquity, which I hesitate to impute to him. It also remains equally possible that the alienation-disempowerment thematic in Foucault's early work and the exercise of self-constructive agency that seems part of the "care of the self" in his later work are complementary aspects of a single, coherent theoretical picture, intended to be generally applicable, but the two parts just happen to have been worked out in relation to epochs and contexts remote from one another in history. Still a third possibility is that Foucault's interests and convictions changed over his career and that the less dystopian note of the later work signals that change. In this case these differences would not be special properties of the historical cultures he studies in each respective phase, but we would also equally be chasing mirages if we attempted to discern some unified underlying theoretical plan. The problem in part is that, at least to my knowledge, Foucault does not seem to have clearly stated the programmatic relation between these components of his larger project as they do or do not contribute to a larger view that balances critique with a concrete, contentful emancipatory vision. For our present purposes, however, it should suffice to observe that even though Foucault formulates no positive vision of a better alternative, his consistent critique of the modern implies at least a belief in the bare possibility of attaching value-judgments to facts and also the possibility of an alternative. In this respect it is clearly normative.

15. I call these currents "radical" in the precise, limited sense that, in the respects I am about to describe, they challenge certain fundamental, "root" assumptions about human ontology. I do not mean to make any judgment about whether they are more or less politically subversive or effective in bringing about profound political change.

16. To give only a couple of examples: Irigaray's "speculum" in the title of her *Speculum of the Other Woman* (1985a) clearly figures her writing as an instrument or glass through which to examine woman's "sex" in a manner that puns on the double sense of "sex" as genital organs and biological femaleness. Similarly, her *This Sex Which Is Not One* (1985b) takes as its eponymous starting point a supposed plurality of female genitalia, viewed as counterpoint to the unary phallus and a raft of attendant forms of thought understood to derive from it. Kristeva's *chora* is based upon the (imagined) interior body cavity of the mother. The congruence of these ways of thinking with psychoanalytic methods and preoccupations scarcely needs pointing out, from Freud's foundational dictum that "the ego is first and foremost a body-ego" (1927: 26) through the imaginary infant-maternal landscape of Melanie Klein. Irigaray and Kristeva were of course powerfully influenced by psychoanalysis via Jacques Lacan. See Irigaray 1985a, 1985b; Fisher 1992.

17. I can here only gesture very briefly at the extraordinary range of these ideas, which I gather and generalize from a wide range of religious traditions.

For details and references I refer readers to my unpublished paper, Radich 2008, mentioned in n. 2.

18. I mean these terms to be as inclusive as possible and to capture tricky cases like the one God of Christianity and also the Buddhist "absolute" by any of its many names.

19. Generally speaking, studies of the body in religious studies, although often extremely instructive, are prey to the following limitations. (1) They generally assume and take as their object the ordinary, biological body (as dictated by materialist-descriptivist assumptions). (2) When they do study this or that extraordinary religious body, or multiple such ideas in a given religious system, they stop at a kind of "thick description" by the methods of ethnography, textual scholarship, and so on. The materialist premise still intervenes insofar as it prevents scholars from treating the ideas in question as genuinely describing bodies in a strong sense commensurable with the paradigmatic ordinary human body. Rather, they treat such extraordinary bodies as bodies only in some allegorical or metaphorical sense—not least by implication, as when they simply fail to notice or address the very question of what on earth might be meant if the bodies in question are seriously intended *as* bodies. (3) Perhaps because each individual set of ideas about extraordinary bodies is thus treated as a mere imaginative flourish, the extent to which traditions propose such ideas seems not to have struck scholars as an interesting larger problem. There is virtually no systematic general study of extraordinary bodies. I have attempted to strike out in this direction in Radich 2008.

20. The question of what metaphor is, and what counts as such, is complicated, and I confine myself here to one dimension of the question.

21. For example, the *Oxford English Dictionary* defines metaphor thus: "A figure of speech in which a name or descriptive word or phrase is transferred to an object or action *different from*, but analogous to, *that to which it is literally applicable*" (my emphases).

22. This is a highly condensed summary of contentions documented in detail in my dissertation, Radich 2007: Chapter 4.1 (447–592), esp. §4.1.1 (458–487).

23. There are of course other terms for relics—notably *dhātu*, for instance, which we will meet again later—but it is not the case that these are the literal designations for relics while *śarīrāṇi* is in some contrastive sense figurative.

24. Schopen 1997a: 128–130; 1998: 260, citing *Cūlavaṃsa* from Geiger 1980: vol. 1, 133; 1996.

25. See, for example, Sharf 2004: 179; Schopen 1997b: 148, 158–159; 2005: 364; Kinnard 2004: 117–118; Collins 1992: 238.

26. See, for example, *The Mahāvastu*, trans. Jones 1973–1978: vol. 2, 328–354, analyzed in Radich 2007: 474–477. For other examples from the *Saddharmapuṇḍarīka*, *Adbhutaparyāya*, *Bodhisattvabhūmi*, and *Mūlasarvāstivāda Vinaya*, see Radich 2007: 477–478.

27. See the example from the *Mahāvaṃsa* cited in Falk 1977: 284.

28. For examples, see Radich 2007: 279–280.

29. Schopen 1997a: 129–130.

30. In the relevant portions of my dissertation (Radich 2007), I cite examples from South, Southeast, and East Asia, covering at least a millennium. This range could easily be extended with further research.

31. The terms of this definition of embodiment are unavoidably dualist, predicated as they are upon the provisional opposition between being and body. However, there is still ample room for use of the term to discuss claims about nondualism. It is simply a matter of stipulating that the mode of being-in-the-body in question is sufficiently intimate that the relation labeled by the notion of embodiment is indeed nondual. In fact, "being-in-the-body" could be stipulated to mean precisely that we are speaking of a being that *is* only by virtue of "being *in the body*."

32. This is one of the main domains in which the insights of Lakoff and Johnson about the pervasion of thought by metaphor are most relevant and persuasive. See, for example, Lakoff and Johnson 2003, 1999; Johnson 1987. However, Lakoff and Johnson tend in their work to ally their observations about metaphor with strong claims about cultural relativism that I believe are overstated and flawed. They seem almost to assume that metaphor is necessarily arbitrary (perhaps following a somewhat dogmatic ghost of Saussure) and thus that metaphor and universality are two mutually exclusive options that between them exhaust the field of possibility. I see no reason why there might not be universal metaphors, or metaphors that, if not universal, are very widespread and repeatedly rediscovered by independent polygenesis. Indeed, I think a glance at the stock of imagery in mutually unrelated languages empirically supports the hypothesis that there are. This is important for our present purposes, because it seems likely that very many metaphors derived from the body might fall precisely in this group.

33. Some Buddhological caveats: (1) I will treat these Buddhist concepts at a level of generality where my characterizations apply broadly to most traditions. I also aim, where possible, to treat these ideas in a manner that is not too controversial, especially in the definitions of these terms, characterizations of how they are discussed in primary sources, and equations drawn between them and other concepts. In other words, while acknowledging that some of the material I treat entails difficult philological problems, I hope to sidestep these problems for the present to concentrate on the task at hand. (2) At the same time, I must acknowledge that my interpretations are indeed likely to be controversial. My reading of *kāya* in *sat-kāya-dṛṣṭi* as referring to the ordinary body runs against a tendency in Buddhological scholarship to interpret the term as referring to something more abstract like "personality" or a "collectivity," as I discuss in the relevant portion of Radich 2007 (cited in n. 34). I refer interested readers to that discussion for details. Similarly, my reading of *kāya* in *dharma-kāya* as reflecting a strong claim about a nonfigurative embodiment is at odds with the instincts of many Buddhologists who prefer, for example, to read it as referring to an abstract

collection (for example, of qualities unique to a Buddha, *āveṇika-dharmāḥ*), or as making a figurative claim about the equal authority of the Buddha's teachings (Dharma) and the Buddha himself. I suspect that to some extent we can detect in these readings the workings of the same materialist-descriptivist assumptions I discussed earlier. In any case, the question of the extent to which a stronger, nonfigurative reading is possible or warranted is precisely the nub of the issue, and on this score I cannot avoid a controversial stance, although I must largely relegate discussion of complex textual evidence supporting my interpretations to other arenas. (3) To some degree, I will knowingly commit anachronisms. *Sat-kāya-dṛṣṭi* was apparently most salient as a concept or rubric for practice earlier in the tradition than *dharma-kāya,* although later (and Mahāyāna) texts continue to invoke *sat-kāya-dṛṣṭi* and attempt to relate it to other concepts. However, I believe that the concepts as I characterize them are compatible and cast light upon one another. Indeed, this fact itself may bespeak a continuity in Buddhist traditions on aspects of the question of embodiment, which undergirds the surface history of changes in terminologies, texts, and schools. (4) Apart from such Buddhological concerns, my primary aim here is to provide a set of ideas that might shift the terms of our usual body theories in the contemporary context. Any inadvertent Buddhological errors of fact that I might commit need not be fatal to the present project, so long as the ideas that result achieve the desired goal. Indeed, in the attempt to achieve that goal, I will be so bold as to translate these Buddhist ideas into terms I hope will be more relevant and comprehensible to participants in contemporary theoretical discourses. This is not standard Buddhological method, for the usually excellent reason that every interpretive step away from the terms of the texts themselves risks introducing further layers of subjective judgment and additional misinterpretation. This has seemed to me an appropriate and worthwhile risk. I can only beg Buddhological colleagues, to whose ears such translation might sound reckless and dissonant, to tolerate the experiment and judge it in terms of its intended goals.

34. *Sat-kāya-dṛṣṭi* is Sanskrit; the Pāli equivalent is *sakkāyadiṭṭhi.* I use the Sanskrit for consistency with other terms used later in this essay in the discussion of *dharma-kāya,* despite the fact that most of the sources on which I base my discussion of *sat-kāya-dṛṣṭi* here are earlier, Pāli sources. For more detail on *sat-kāya-dṛṣṭi* and references to primary sources upon which my generalizations here are based, see Radich 2007: §2.1.1.3 (100–117). See also Schmithausen 1979; Collins 1982: 93–94, 117–118, 133; Wayman 1979: 375–380; Edgerton 1998: s.v. *satkāya;* La Vallée Poussin 1980: vol. 4, 15–17 (La Vallée Poussin's footnote to *Bhāṣya* to verse 5.7).

35. The two alternative meanings depend upon whether one ascribes a copulative or existential meaning to the verb root *as,* "to be." Both are possible in Sanskrit (and Pāli). My interpretation here hinges on reading it as a copula of identity, which I believe is warranted by the primary texts, but I believe this interpretation puts me in a minority of Buddhological interpreters of the term.

36. I use the word "faggot" here in its most basic sense of "a bundle of firewood." There is most likely a pun here that conveys the notion that these

"collections" (*skandha*) of phenomena are in fact fuel (*skandha*) to the flames of suffering, which need to be put out (root *vā* + *nir*), thus attaining "extinction" of the flames, or *nirvāṇa*. See Gombrich 1996: 67–68.

37. "Nonself," "not-self," or "no-self" (*anātman*) is of course one of the foundational Buddhist doctrines. Briefly it can be taken as the claim that the self as ordinarily conceived does not exist, or that anything identified as self by ordinary, benighted consciousness is not in fact a self. Exactly how this doctrine is to be interpreted, and what alternative state ensues upon liberation from this delusion, is one of the most difficult problems in the interpretation of Buddhist traditions. Two key studies in this area are Collins 1982 and Harvey 1995.

38. See, for example, the relatively extended presentation placed in the mouth of the *bhikkhunī* (nun) Dhammadinnā in Majjhima Nikāya 44, Cūḷavedalla Sutta, trans. Ñāṇamoli and Bodhi 1995: 396–403.

39. It can also be used in Sanskrit to refer to a collectivity, much as in English we say "a body of work" or "a body of water." However, I believe contemporary Buddhological studies of Buddhist body discourses may have made too much of this semantic latitude.

40. I believe it should in fact be possible to argue that there is such an implicit understanding in Buddhist traditions of the problem of embodiment and that the entire fivefold *skandha* schema is a model of (sufferingful, religiously problematic) embodiment. However, I have yet to attempt such an analysis in print. It obviously leads immediately to the difficult problems of "what" is so embodied, if all five *skandha*s are in some sense body or embodiment (we normally think in terms of "embodiment of X in Y"), and "what" might be liberated from such an embodiment, if it is not an inevitable and inescapable dimension of all possible modes of our being. These problems are in turn cognate with core problems in the interpretation of no-self doctrine: What transmigrates? What is liberated? What is the subject or ground for a free will that might choose actions tending toward liberation, rather than actions tending toward entrapment in *saṃsāra*? There obviously can be no question of broaching such large questions here. Relevant, however, are considerations explored in Albahari 2002; Thanissaro 1993a, 1993b. I am grateful to Benno Blaschke for bringing these works to my attention.

41. Whether *kāya* in *sat-kāya-dṛṣṭi* means only the physical body or all the *skandha*s, it certainly refers to a collectivity that at least includes the physical body.

42. The attempt to map a substantial number of these models is the project of my entire dissertation (Radich 2007).

43. Those familiar with this complex concept will know that there are at least two other important interpretations besides the one I take up here. (1) The Buddha is understood as embodied in his teaching (also called Dharma). This concept is of partial relevance but is not central to present considerations. (2) The Buddha is understood to be embodied in special qualities (also *dharma*, plural *dharmāḥ*) unique to a Buddha, the realization or possession of which defines him as a Buddha. Lists of these qualities vary, but the most central is almost

certainly the eighteen *āveṇika-dharmas*, "unique (unshared) qualities" comprising ten special powers, four kinds of confidence, great compassion, and three bases of mindfulness. In Radich 2007 I argue at length that the actual historical sequence and relative predominance of these other models to the "absolute" *dharma-kāya* I treat here are empirically different from the way they have usually been understood by modern scholarship. However, such historical questions need not detain us here. For our present purposes all that matters is that some Buddhist texts do indeed propose the absolute model I discuss here, which I do not think is controversial. These other models can be safely set aside as not relevant to the present exercise.

44. Still worth consulting is Stcherbatsky 1970.

45. Abhidharma is the earliest scholastic systematization of Buddhist teachings and, in large part as a natural outgrowth of the scholastic commentarial impulse, the broad current of systematic Buddhist philosophy. It came to include multiple competing schools, and some of these flourished well into the first millennium in parallel with other (Mahāyāna) schools of later origin. The prefix *abhi-* has more than one meaning, and while the term *abhidharma* probably originally labeled discourse "about (*abhi*) the teaching," it came (presumably partly through self-aggrandizement) to mean "higher (*abhi*) teaching," "the acme of the Dharma."

46. I agree with interpretations, best articulated by Ruegg, that hold that even doctrines of *tathāgata-garbha*, "Buddha nature," that proclaim a certain kind of *aśūnya* (nonempty) aspect to the ultimate are properly to be interpreted in dialectical terms as a further negation (or sublation) of emptiness itself, which does not necessarily bring us back full circle to a substantialist starting point. Thus even these doctrines, appearances notwithstanding, do not necessarily constitute an exception to the universal validity of *śūnyatā* for the Mahāyāna. See Ruegg 1969, 1989.

47. Emptiness is understood as a final and complete generalization of the original doctrine of "not-self" or "no-self" from "persons" (*pudgala*) to include all things (*dharma*). This is termed the "absence of self in [both] persons and things" (*pudgala-dharma-nairātmya*).

48. We have to pick our terms carefully here. We might leap to the conclusion that this doctrine allows us to characterize the failure of autonomy in things by saying they are radically heteronomous, but at least in Nāgārjuna's seminal *Mūlamadhyamakakārikā* (Root Verses on the Happy Medium), heteronomy (*para-bhāva*) too is deconstructed in the same breath as autonomy (*sva-bhāva*).

49. This claim might appear to construct a straw man. We might object that no one means "perfectly autonomous and eternal" when they impute reality or existence to a thing. However, as I understand it, the Buddhist claim is this: We might *think* that we know what we think, but these opinions about our own ideas obtain, at best, when we are reflective and level-headed. What counts much more is what we "think" at an affective and existential level. At

this level—perhaps unwittingly—we *do* in fact ascribe such a strong reality to objects. Our ignorance consists precisely in this ascription, which, according to the Second Noble Truth, is a (even *the*) root cause of our suffering.

50. The "middle way" (*madhyamā pratipad*), a root conceit in the tradition for depicting the overall Buddhist stance, is interpreted as a "happy medium" between two metaphysical extremes: hypostatization (reification, eternalism, the imputation of excessive being) and nihilism (the imputation of excessive nonbeing), both being seen as equally wrongheaded. This position is so central that it is the source of the eponymous designation for the main school propounding this position: Madhyamaka ([School of the] Happy Medium), which strikes a happy medium between the two extremes.

51. If we say the only universally true statement is that nothing is universally true, this immediately casts us on the horns of a dilemma structured exactly like the "Cretan Liar" paradox, in which a Cretan declares, "All Cretans always lie." This means it is equally untenable to claim both that (1) a supposed law of emptiness holds for emptiness itself and (2) the law is its own only exception. Each of the horns of this dilemma points down the line of an important current in the subsequent interpretation of emptiness doctrine, epitomized by positions known in Tibet as *rang stong* (void of itself) and *gzhan stong* (void [only] of [what is] other), which part company over the question, "Is emptiness itself empty?" This is what I mean by saying "unreality-cum-reality" itself appears real "on one level"—that is, with respect to one horn of this dilemma only. There is thus a double sense in which whatever "reality" is ascribed to "reality-cum-unreality" is in fact *un*real: not only in the sense that its ground is the *un*reality of all things apart from it but also in the sense that, considered from one point of view, it too must be regarded as just as unreal as real. These complications powerfully suggest that whatever un/reality we might be talking about is strictly ineffable, but at the same time, if we are to proceed with the discussion at all, we must adopt *some* terms. This is indeed what Buddhist traditions themselves would point to by saying that whatever language we use is only "provisional," "conventional" (*vyavahāra, prajñapti*).

52. Such talk is bound to appear controversial, because it is considered standard for Buddhist traditions to deny such a metaphysical ground. I believe empirical exceptions can be pointed to, as, for example, in some discussions about *prajñā-pāramitā* "producing" or "consummating/bringing to completion" all *dharmas*, as in Lokakṣema's *Aṣṭasāhasrikā* (for example, T224:8.466c20–21; T224:8.467a06–07; T224:8.467a01). Another exception can be seen in the treatment of Buddha, *dharma-dhātu*, or Buddha nature (**buddha-dhātu*) as congruent with the neo-Daoist *li* (理, principle) in Chinese texts (where it has often been interpreted as a sign of supposed "sinification"). However, such historical considerations need not detain us here, so long as we remember that insofar as it is the *emptiness* of all *dharma*s that constitutes the *dharma-dhātu*, it can only constitute at best a kind of paradoxical "groundless ground" or

"ungroundedness-cum-ground," if some sort of "ground" is indeed connoted by the use of this term.

53. We might note two other echoes of the term *dhātu*. (1) Although scholarship has not been able to agree on a Sanskrit antecedent for the notion of "Buddha nature" (*foxing*) so important in East Asian Buddhist traditions, one strong candidate is **buddha-dhātu*. This term, which is roughly coterminous with *tathāgata-garbha* (embryo/womb of the Buddha), refers to a germ of potential or latent Buddhahood within all beings. As such it is often depicted in corporeal terms, through corporeal images, which are quite salient to the theme of embodiment that concerns us here. For instance, it is represented as a miniature Buddha (or his image, in either case anthropomorphic) contained within the body of the aspirant, or it is held to be within the person as a fetus is within the pregnant mother. The notion of such a **buddha-dhātu* as the "raw material" (*dhātu*) for Buddhahood also suggests that *dharma-dhātu* might be read in parallel as the raw material for the (realization of the) Dharma, or *dharmatā*. (2) *Dhātu*, as noted earlier (see n. 23), is one of the standard terms for a Buddha relic (apparently because cremation was imagined as a kind of reduction of the body to its constituent elements, *dhātūni*). Scholars have suggested, in connection with the concept of Buddha nature, or **buddha-dhātu*, that the term might have arisen in part out of an attempt to promote *tathāgata-garbha* texts and their ideas as a direct alternative for popular relic worship. See, for example, Shimoda 1997: 39[L]. Given the arguments I rehearsed earlier about the genuinely bodily status of relics, this may suggest that the idea of *dharma-dhātu* itself was already involved in the widely ramified dialectic of the corporeal trope, even before it entered into such terms as *dharma(dhātu)kāya*. Exploration of this possibility, however, demands further research.

54. "Thusness" or "Suchness" is the usual Buddhist Hybrid English translation for this concept. Although it perhaps conveys little to an ordinary English reader, it does come close to the literal semantic structure of the Sanskrit.

55. See, for example, Radich 2007: 460–461, n. 952, citing the **Mahāprajñāpāramitopadeśa*, *faxing shen*, *faxing foshen*, T1509:25.121c26–122c10; trans. Lamotte 1966–1980: 513.

56. See the ideas from Lokakṣema's *Lokānuvartanā* discussed in Radich 2007: §4.2.9 (659–669)—for example, T807:17.753a28–29, 753b01–03. These passages were first pointed out in Harrison 1992. Lokakṣema's *Druma-kinnara-rāja-paripṛcchā* has *fashen* (usually **dharma-kāya*) where the extant Tibetan has *dharma-dhātu* (*chos kyi dbyings*) and where Kumārajīva has the equivalent *fajie* (Harrison 1992: 61–63). So too in passages from his *Ajātaśatru-kaukṛtya-vinodanā* (Harrison 1992: 64). Xuanzang's massive **Mahāprajñāpāramitā* declares, "All the Tathāgatas, in accordance with *saṃyak-saṃbodhi*, penetrate completely to Thusness, the *dharma-dhātu*, *dharmatā*, the *bhūta-koṭi*, and so on, by means of *prajñāpāramitā* and thereby realize the *dharma-kāya*" (T220:7.781c03–08). For discussion and further examples, following Harrison, see Radich 2007: §4.3.9 (766–772).

57. From either vantage point, the nondualism is presented as an extraordinary state and a goal to be attained by almost superhuman practice,

not as a given starting point. Where a nondualism is so hard won and cause for such celebration, there was surely a very troublesome and ornery dualism in its way that had to be overcome. This, I think, poses a significant challenge to crude comparativist claims that nondualism is somehow a simple given of ordinary human ontology for Buddhist traditions, as in other "Asian" systems of thought, and thus can serve as a stark point of contrast to supposedly parochial "Western" "Cartesian" mind/body dualism. Detailed consideration of this complex problem, however, must await future work.

58. For a glimpse of the tip of an entire iceberg of such work, see Barsalou et al. 2005. I am grateful to Joe Bulbulia for referring me to this article.

59. Particularly seminal here of course is Mauss 1973.

60. Such indeed may historically have been the main model for ideal embodiment—no embodiment at all—entailed by *sat-kāya-dṛṣṭi* doctrine in the context of its first elaboration in older strata of Buddhist traditions.

61. A striking feature of modern body theories, in contrast to ideas about the body in traditional religious systems, is how seldom the topic of mortality is even mentioned in passing.

References

Note: References to canonical Chinese Buddhist texts are to Chinese Buddhist Electronic Text Association 2008. References are formatted to follow the order: text number, volume number, page number, register, and line number. Thus, for example, T225:8.483b17 is text number 225, volume 8, page 483, second register, line 17. References to entire texts give the text number only—for example, T224.

Ajātaśatru-kaukṛtya-vinodanā-sūtra [*Asheshi wang jing*]. T626.

Albahari, Miri. 2002. "Against No-*Ātman* Theories of *Anattā*." *Asian Philosophy* 12, no. 1: 5–20.

Asad, Talal. 1997. "Remarks on the Anthropology of the Body." In *Religion and the Body*, ed. Sarah Coakley, 42–52. Cambridge: Cambridge University Press.

Aṣṭasāhasrikā-prajñāpāramitā-sūtra [*Dao xing bore jing*]. T224.

Barsalou, Lawrence W., Aron K. Barbey, W. Kyle Simmons, and Ava Santos. 2005. "Embodiment in Religious Knowledge." *Journal of Cognition and Culture* 5, no. 1–2: 14–57.

Binswanger, Ludwig. 1975. *Being-in-the-World: Selected Papers of Ludwig Binswanger*. Translated by Jacob Needleman. London: Souvenir Press.

Blacking, John, ed. 1977. *The Anthropology of the Body*. London: Academic Press.

Bourdieu, Pierre. 1977 [1972]. *Outline of a Theory of Practice*. Translated by Richard Nice. Cambridge: Cambridge University Press.

Brook, Barbara. 1999. *Feminist Perspectives on the Body*. London: Longman.

Burton, John W. 2001. *Culture and the Human Body: An Anthropological Perspective*. Prospect Heights: Waveland Press.

Bynum, Caroline Walker. 1995. "Why All the Fuss about the Body? A Medievalist's Perspective." *Critical Inquiry* 22: 1–35.
Chinese Buddhist Electronic Text Association. 2008. *Taishō shinshū daizōkyō*. Edited by Takakusu Junjirō and Watanabe Kaigyoku. Tokyo: Taishō shinshū daizōkyō kankōkai/Daizō shuppan, 1924–1932. CBReader v. 3.7.
Cixous, Hélène. 1994. *The Hélène Cixous Reader*. Edited by Susan Sellers. New York: Routledge.
Coakley, Sarah. 1997. "Introduction: Religion and the Body." In *Religion and the Body*, ed. Sarah Coakley, 1–12. Cambridge: Cambridge University Press.
Collins, Steven. 1982. *Selfless Persons: Imagery and Thought in Theravāda Buddhism*. Cambridge: Cambridge University Press.
Collins, Steven. 1992. "Nirvāṇa, Time, and Narrative." *History of Religions* 31, no. 3: 215–246.
Cooey, Paula M. 1994. *Religious Imagination and the Body: A Feminist Analysis*. New York: Oxford University Press.
Csordas, Thomas J. 1990. "Embodiment as a Paradigm for Anthropology." *Ethos* 18, no. 1: 5–47.
Csordas, Thomas J. 1993. "Somatic Modes of Attention." *Cultural Anthropology* 8, no. 2: 135–156.
Culianu, Ioan P. 1991. "A Corpus for the Body." *Journal of Modern History* 63, no. 1: 61–80.
Dallery, Arleen B. 1989. "The Politics of Writing (the) Body: Écriture Féminine." In *Gender/Body/Knowledge: Feminist Reconstructions of Being and Knowing*, ed. Alison M. Jaggar and Susan R. Bordo, 52–67. New Brunswick: Rutgers University Press.
Douglas, Mary. 1996 [1970]. "The Two Bodies." Chapter 5 of *Natural Symbols: Explorations in Cosmology*, 72–91. 2nd ed. New York: Routledge.
Druma-kinnara-rāja-paripṛcchā-sūtra [*Dunzhentuoluo suowen rulai sanmei jing*]. T624.
Edgerton, Franklin. 1998 [1953]. *Buddhist Hybrid Sanskrit Grammar and Dictionary*. 2 vols. Delhi: Motilal Banarsidass.
Falk, Nancy. 1977. "To Gaze on the Sacred Traces." *History of Religions* 16, no. 4: 281–293.
Feher, Michel, with Ramona Naddaff and Nadia Tazi, eds. 1989. *Fragments for a History of the Human Body*. 3 vols. New York: Zone Books.
Fisher, David. 1992. "Kristeva's *Chora* and the Subject of Postmodern Ethics." In *Body/Text in Julia Kristeva: Religion, Women and Psychoanalysis*, ed. David R. Crownfield, 91–106. Albany: State University of New York Press.
Foucault, Michel. 1975 [1963]. *The Birth of the Clinic: An Archaeology of Medical Perception*. Translated by A. M. Sheridan Smith. New York: Vintage Books.
Foucault, Michel. 1977 [1975]. *Discipline and Punish: The Birth of the Prison*. Translated by Alan Sheridan. New York: Pantheon Books.
Foucault, Michel. 1980. *Power/Knowledge: Selected Interviews and Other Writings, 1972–1977*. Edited by Colin Gordon. Translated by Colin Gordon et al. Brighton: Harvester Press.

Foucault, Michel. 1988–1990 [1976, 1984]. *The History of Sexuality*. 3 vols. Translated by Robert Hurley. New York: Vintage Books.

Frank, Arthur W. 1990. "Bringing Bodies Back in: A Decade Review." *Theory, Culture and Society* 7, no. 1: 131–162.

Freud, Sigmund. 1927. *The Ego and the Id*. Translated by Joan Riviere. London: Hogarth Press and the Institute of Psychoanalysis.

Freund, Peter E. S. 1988. "Bringing Society into the Body: Understanding Socialized Human Nature." *Theory and Society* 17, no. 6: 839–864.

Gallagher, Catherine, and Thomas Laqueur, eds. 1987. *The Making of the Modern Body: Sexuality and Society in the Nineteenth Century*. Berkeley: University of California Press.

Gallop, Jane. 1988. *Thinking through the Body*. New York: Columbia University Press.

Geiger, Wilhelm, with the assistance of Mabel Haynes Bode, trans. 1980 [1912]. *The Mahāvaṃsa, or The Great Chronicle of Ceylon*. London: Pali Text Society.

Gombrich, Richard F. 1996. *How Buddhism Began: The Conditioned Genesis of the Early Teachings*. London: School of Oriental and African Studies.

Grosz, Elizabeth. 1994. *Volatile Bodies: Toward a Corporeal Feminism*. St. Leonards: Allen and Unwin.

Guthrie, R. Dale. 1976. *Body Hot Spots: The Anatomy of Human Social Organs and Behavior*. New York: Van Nostrand Reinhold.

Hancock, Philip, Bill Hughes, Elizabeth Jagger, Kevin Paterson, Rachel Russell, Emanuelle Tulle-Wilson, and Melissa Tyler. 2000. *The Body, Culture and Society: An Introduction*. Buckingham: Open University Press.

Harrison, Paul. 1992. "Is the *Dharma-Kāya* the Real 'Phantom Body' of the Buddha?" *Journal of the International Association of Buddhist Studies* 15, no. 1: 44–94.

Harvey, Peter. 1995. *The Selfless Mind: Personality, Consciousness and Nirvāṇa in Early Buddhism*. Richmond, Surrey: Curzon Press.

Holdrege, Barbara A. 1998. "Body Connections: Hindu Discourses of the Body and the Study of Religion." *International Journal of Hindu Studies* 2, no. 3: 341–386.

Irigaray, Luce. 1985a [1974]. *Speculum of the Other Woman*. Translated by Gillian C. Gill. Ithaca: Cornell University Press.

Irigaray, Luce. 1985b [1977]. *This Sex Which Is Not One*. Translated by Catherine Porter with Carolyn Burke. Ithaca: Cornell University Press.

Irigaray, Luce. 1991. *The Irigaray Reader*. Edited by Margaret Whitford. Cambridge: Basil Blackwell.

Jackson, Michael. 1983. "Knowledge of the Body." *Man*, n.s., 18, no. 2: 327–345.

Jacobus, Mary, Evelyn Fox Keller, and Sally Shuttleworth, eds. 1990. *Body/Politics: Women and the Discourses of Science*. New York: Routledge.

Jaggar, Alison M., and Susan R. Bordo, eds. 1989. *Gender/Body/Knowledge: Feminist Reconstructions of Being and Knowing*. New Brunswick: Rutgers University Press.

Johnson, Mark. 1987. *The Body in the Mind: The Bodily Basis of Meaning, Imagination, and Reason*. Chicago: University of Chicago Press.

Johnson, Paul Christopher. 2002. "Models of the 'Body' in the Ethnographic Field: Garifuna and Candomble Case Studies." *Method and Theory in the Study of Religion* 14, no. 2: 170–195.

Jones, J. J., trans. 1973–1978 [1949–1956]. *The Mahāvastu*. 3 vols. London: Pali Text Society and Routledge and Kegan Paul.

Kasulis, Thomas P., with Roger T. Ames and Wimal Dissanayake, eds. 1993. *Self as Body in Asian Theory and Practice*. Albany: State University of New York Press.

Kinnard, Jacob N. 2004. "The Field of the Buddha's Presence." In *Embodying the Dharma: Buddhist Relic Veneration in Asia*, ed. David Germano and Kevin Trainor, 117–143. Albany: State University of New York Press.

Kristeva, Julia. 1986. *The Kristeva Reader*. Edited by Toril Moi. Oxford: Basil Blackwell.

Lakoff, George, and Mark Johnson. 1999. *Philosophy in the Flesh: The Embodied Mind and Its Challenge to Western Thought*. New York: Basic Books.

Lakoff, George, and Mark Johnson. 2003 [1980]. *Metaphors We Live By*. Chicago: University of Chicago Press.

Lamotte, Étienne, trans. 1944–1980. *Le traité de la grande vertu de sagesse de Nāgārjuna (Mahāprajñāpāramitāśāstra)*. 5 vols. Louvain: Institut Orientaliste de Louvain.

Laqueur, Thomas. 1990. *Making Sex: Body and Gender from the Greeks to Freud*. Cambridge: Harvard University Press.

La Vallée Poussin, Louis de, trans. 1980 [1923–1931]. *L'Abhidharmakośa de Vasubandhu*. 6 vols. Brussels: Institut Belge des Hautes Études Chinoises.

Levin, David Michael. 1985. *The Body's Recollection of Being: Phenomenological Psychology and the Deconstruction of Nihilism*. London: Routledge and Kegan Paul.

Lingis, Alphonso. 1999 [1994]. "The Subjectification of the Body." In *The Body*, ed. Donn Welton, 286–306. Malden: Blackwell.

Lokānuvartanā-sūtra [*Nei zang bai bao jing*]. T807.

**Mahāprajñāpāramitā-sūtra* [*Da bore boluomi jing*]. T220.

**Mahāprajñāpāramitopadeśa* [*Da zhi du lun*]. T1509.

Maissonneuve, Jean. 1976. "Le corps et le corporéisme aujourd'hui." *Revue Française de Sociologie* 17, no. 4: 551–571.

Mauss, Marcel. 1973 [1935]. "Techniques of the Body." Translated by Ben Brewster. *Economy and Society* 2: 70–88.

McGuire, Meredith B. 1990. "Religion and the Body: Rematerializing the Human Body in the Social Sciences of Religion." *Journal for the Scientific Study of Religion* 29, no. 3: 283–296.

Merleau-Ponty, Maurice. 1962 [1945]. *Phenomenology of Perception*. Translated by Colin Smith. London: Routledge and Kegan Paul.

Midgley, Mary. 1997. "The Soul's Successors: Philosophy and the 'Body.'" In *Religion and the Body*, ed. Sarah Coakley, 53–68. Cambridge: Cambridge University Press.

Miles, Margaret R. 1989. *Carnal Knowing: Female Nakedness and Religious Meaning in the Christian West*. Boston: Beacon Press.

Morris, Desmond. 1967. *The Naked Ape: A Zoologist's Study of the Human Animal*. London: Cape.

Ñāṇamoli, Bhikkhu, and Bhikkhu Bodhi, trans. 1995. *The Middle Length Discourses of the Buddha: A New Translation of the Majjhima Nikāya*. Boston: Wisdom Publications.

Radich, Michael. 2007. "The Somatics of Liberation: Ideas about Embodiment in Buddhism from Its Origins to the Fifth Century C.E." PhD diss., Harvard University.

Radich, Michael. 2008. "The Neglected General Problem of Holy Bodies and Some of Its Implications." Unpublished paper presented in The Body in the Study of Asian Religions Seminar Series, co-sponsored by the Asian Studies Institute and the Religious Studies Programme, Victoria University of Wellington, New Zealand, May 30.

Ruegg, David Seyfort. 1969. *La théorie du tathāgatagarbha et du gotra: Études sur la sotériologie et la gnoséologie du bouddhisme*. Paris: École Française d'Extrême-Orient.

Ruegg, David Seyfort. 1989. *Buddha-Nature, Mind and the Problem of Gradualism in a Comparative Perspective: On the Transmission and Reception of Buddhism in India and Tibet*. London: School of Oriental and African Studies, University of London.

Ruth, David N. 1974. "The Social Reference of Body Symbols in Religion." In *Changing Perspectives in the Scientific Study of Religion*, ed. Allan W. Eister, 227–247. New York: John Wiley and Sons.

Scheper-Hughes, Nancy, and Margaret M. Lock. 1987. "The Mindful Body: A Prolegomenon to Future Work in Medical Anthropology." *Medical Anthropology Quarterly*, n.s., 1, no. 1: 6–41.

Schmithausen, Lambert. 1979. "Gaken ni kansuru jakkan no kōsatsu: sakayaken, gaman, osen'i." *Bukkyōgaku* 7: 1–18.

Schopen, Gregory. 1996. "The Suppression of Nuns and the Ritual Murder of Their Special Dead in Two Buddhist Monastic Texts." *Journal of Indian Philosophy* 24: 563–592.

Schopen, Gregory. 1997a [1987]. "Burial *Ad Sanctos* and the Physical Presence of the Buddha in Early Indian Buddhism: A Study in the Archaeology of Religions." Chapter 7 of *Bones, Stones, and Buddhist Monks: Collected Papers on the Archaeology, Epigraphy, and Texts of Monastic Buddhism in India*, 114–147. Honolulu: University of Hawaii Press.

Schopen, Gregory. 1997b [1988]. "On the Buddha and His Bones: The Conception of a Relic in the Inscriptions of Nāgārjunikoṇḍa." Chapter 8 of *Bones,*

Stones, and Buddhist Monks: Collected Papers on the Archaeology, Epigraphy, and Texts of Monastic Buddhism in India, 148–164. Honolulu: University of Hawaii Press.

Schopen, Gregory. 1998. "Relic." In *Critical Terms for Religious Studies*, ed. Mark C. Taylor, 256–268. Chicago: University of Chicago Press.

Schopen, Gregory. 2005 [1994]. "*Stūpa* and *Tīrtha*: Tibetan Mortuary Practices and an Unrecognized Form of Burial *Ad Sanctos* at Buddhist Sites in India." Chapter 14 of *Figments and Fragments of Mahāyāna Buddhism in India: More Collected Papers*, 350–369. Honolulu: University of Hawaii Press.

Sharf, Robert. 2004. "On the Allure of Buddhist Relics." In *Embodying the Dharma: Buddhist Relic Veneration in Asia*, ed. David Germano and Kevin Trainor, 163–191. Albany: State University of New York Press.

Shilling, Chris. 1993. *The Body and Social Theory*. London: Sage Publications.

Shimoda, Masahiro. 1997. *Nehangyō no kenkyū: Daijōkyōten no kenkyū hōhō shiron*. Tokyo: Shunjusha.

Spicker, Stuart F., ed. 1970. *The Philosophy of the Body: Rejections of Cartesian Dualism*. Chicago: Quadrangle Books.

Stcherbatsky, Th. 1970 [1923]. *The Central Conception of Buddhism and the Meaning of the Word "Dharma."* Delhi: Motilal Banarsidass.

Sullivan, Lawrence E. 1990. "Body Works: Knowledge of the Body in the Study of Religion." *History of Religions* 30, no. 1: 86–99.

Synnott, Anthony. 1993. *The Body Social: Symbolism, Self and Society*. New York: Routledge.

Thanissaro, Bhikkhu. 1993a. *The Mind Like Fire Unbound*. Barre: Dhamma Dana Publications, Barre Centre for Buddhist Studies.

Thanissaro, Bhikkhu. 1993b. "The Not-Self Strategy." *Access to Insight*. http://www.accesstoinsight.org/lib/authors/thanissaro/notself.html.

Turner, Bryan S. 1984. *The Body and Society: Explorations in Social Theory*. Oxford: Basil Blackwell.

Turner, Bryan S. 1991. "Recent Developments in the Theory of the Body." In *The Body: Social Process and Cultural Theory*, ed. Mike Featherstone, Mike Hepworth, and Bryan S. Turner, 1–35. London: Sage Publications.

Turner, Bryan S. 1992. *Regulating Bodies: Essays in Medical Sociology*. New York: Routledge.

Turner, Bryan S. 1997. "The Body in Western Society: Social Theory and Its Perspectives." In *Religion and the Body*, ed. Sarah Coakley, 15–41. Cambridge: Cambridge University Press.

Warner, Richard, and Tadeusz Szubka, eds. 1994. *The Mind-Body Problem: A Guide to the Current Debate*. Cambridge: Blackwell.

Wayman, Alex. 1979. "The Twenty Reifying Views (*sakkāyadiṭṭhi*)." In *Studies in Pali and Buddhism: A Memorial Volume in Honor of Bhikkhu Jagdish Kashyap*, ed. A. K. Narain, 375–380. Delhi: B. R. Publishing.

Williams, Simon J., and Gillian Bendelow. 1998. *The Lived Body: Sociological Themes, Embodied Issues*. New York: Routledge.

Wilson, Liz. 1996. *Charming Cadavers: Horrific Figurations of the Feminine in Indian Buddhist Hagiographic Literature*. Chicago: University of Chicago Press.

Wyke, Maria, ed. 1998. *Gender and Body in the Ancient Mediterranean*. Malden: Blackwell.

Yuasa, Yasuo. 1987 [1977]. *The Body: Toward an Eastern Mind-Body Theory*. Translated by Shigenori Nagatomo and Thomas P. Kasulis. Edited by Thomas P. Kasulis. Albany: State University of New York Press.

Zaner, Richard M. 1971 [1964]. *The Problem of Embodiment: Some Contributions to a Phenomenology of the Body*. 2nd ed. The Hague: Martinus Nijhoff.

Chapter 2

Body, Self, and Embodiment in the Sanskrit Classics of Āyurveda

ANTHONY CERULLI

The body is the lodestar for deliberations on health and illness in the Sanskrit sources of Āyurveda, one of India's classical medical systems, whose literary tradition crystallized around the turn of the Common Era. Over the course of about seven centuries the "big three" (*bṛhat-trayī*) Sanskrit medical classics were redacted in the form of the *Caraka Saṃhitā*, *Suśruta Saṃhitā*, and *Aṣṭāṅgahṛdaya Saṃhitā* that are extant today. A number of terms in these sources designate the material human body, among which *śarīra*, *deha*, *tanu*, *kāya*, and *vapus* are the most common. Occasionally the terms *gātra* and *aṅga*, meaning "component" or "part" (frequently translated as "limb" by nineteenth-century Sanskrit lexicographers), synecdochically signify the entire physical body as well. The term *ātman*, usually understood as the nonmaterial self in popular and scholarly writings on Hindu traditions and Indian philosophy, also at times denotes the physical body in Āyurvedic sources.

In this essay I will examine representations of the body in the Sanskrit classics of Āyurveda and will focus in particular on the body's role as an instrument that is crucial not only for achieving long life (*āyus*), the grand goal of classical Āyurveda, but also for gaining knowledge of the self and fulfilling one's *dharma*, "duty" in a broad social and ethical sense. It is important to note in this context that expositions of the body and the self in the Āyurvedic classics are not always consistent; the body is not conceived in a standardized way in the Sanskrit sources. Anatomical minutiae, such as the number of bones, tendons, ligaments, and layers of skin, often differ from source to source.[1] There are many possible reasons for these differences. One reason stems from the expansive period of time over which the Sanskrit medical sources were compiled and composed, sometimes spanning centuries. People from different generations with different knowledge of, and access to, the human body redacted, emended, and added to these works. This diversity of authorship, even within an individual "school" (such as the Ātreya school or the Dhanvantari school), may account for many of the anatomical inconsistencies we find in the sources. Another reason may have to do with the fact that—apart from physicians trained according to the *Suśruta Saṃhitā* (ca. second century CE), which specializes in surgery and contains the most elaborate anatomical accounts among the Āyurvedic classics—from the classical era onward, most physicians appear to have had little experience in the practice of dissection, which is central to anatomical explanation.[2] Prevalent concerns about ritual purity and pollution in Hindu societies in classical India suggest a third possible reason, for anxiety over ritual purity could have deterred physicians from engaging in dissection since the practice naturally involves contact with polluting substances.

Moreover, the very genre adopted by the compilers of the Sanskrit medical sources—the *saṃhitā*, which is a Sanskrit word meaning "union" or "connection" and, by extension, any systematically arranged collection of treatises or verses—misleadingly advertises a coherency that is not always present in the Sanskrit medical classics. As Francis Zimmermann has noted, the medical *saṃhitā* routinely "enfolds a multiplicity of alternative doctrines that are added or withdrawn at different periods, and it refers to various levels of medical practice."[3] To parse the shifting layers of somatic detail in these works, pictographic representations of the medical body would be useful. Āyurveda's classics contain no illustrations, however. It is not until well after the classical era, around the late eighteenth century, that we find medical manuscripts in South Asia with anatomical illustrations.[4] Illustrations are not utterly indispensable for us, as contemporary scholars, to ascertain the classical Āyurvedic understanding of human anatomy. Yet without these visual aids we are forced to imagine the body according to the descriptive skills of the sources' authors. We must try to be, like the classical compilers of Āyurveda, morphologically articulate about the human body.

Excavating material across the Āyurvedic classics that addresses the general parameters of the body brings to light a dynamic notion of embodiment in the tradition. Embodiment in this context is an articulation of the principle of well-being actualized in lived experience. The notion of embodiment highlights a distinctive body typology in Āyurveda that emphasizes an "embodied self": a nonmaterial self, *ātman*, in relation to a physical somatic structure. The embodied self stands apart from the tradition's other body typology, the "material body," which is the cadaver-like body most often portrayed in the literature. This material body may be treated in isolation, as an independent object to be studied and manipulated as such. The embodied self typology, in contrast, presents a modal case of being-in-the-world; it presents a portrait of an active patient whose experience of health or illness cannot be fully knowable apart from her or his relationships with other people and the natural world.

To make sense of these two body typologies in the literature, I will consider uses of the Sanskrit term *ātman* and the matrix of practices with which *ātman* is associated in the earliest and most voluminous of the big three classics, the *Caraka Saṃhitā* (ca. first century BCE to first century CE), while occasionally commenting on other sources and their commentaries. Regular associations in the *Caraka Saṃhitā* between the material body and the *ātman* point to a uniquely medical directive concerning the notion of self-cultivation, which I take to be a loose translation of *ātma-hita* (literally, "self-good"). I will reflect on the Āyurvedic notion of self-cultivation as a therapeutic process that situates the human body within the broad expanse of nature—what I call the "cosmic physiology"—and is vital to ensure the successful achievement of an individual's *dharma*, or social, legal, and ethical responsibilities as defined in classical Dharmaśāstra literature. The ability to cultivate oneself, I suggest, is entwined in a process of learning how to know oneself. For one commentator on the Sanskrit medical classics, Cakrapāṇidatta, self-knowledge is the single most important requirement for identifying and cultivating the things that are good for the self. I will examine in particular an idea that motivates the entire classical "Āyurvedic enterprise" and that sets Āyurveda's knowledge and treatment of the body apart from (as uniquely therapeutic) and simultaneously makes it vital to (as indispensable) other classical Indian knowledge systems: the Sanskrit medical classics promote the idea that the body is the foundational dharmic instrument for human flourishing. Self-cultivation produces health in the body, and bodily health is the unequivocal precondition needed to uphold one's dharmic duties throughout one's life. A person's obligation to his or her body—what I call the "body *dharma*" of Āyurveda—is the foundational *dharma* to which all people must attend before everything else in their lives to ensure optimal performance of the complex array of all other *dharma*s in the social and religious arenas.

Self and Somatic Well-being

Information about the nature of the *ātman*, self, is interspersed throughout Āyurveda's classical literature. The compilers and redactors of this literature rarely addressed the topic with direct and sustained comments. It is nevertheless possible to distinguish a coherent, if multipart, vision of the self in the Āyurvedic corpus. Four articulations of the *ātman* are especially significant to the classical accounts of the body and the embodiment of well-being in Āyurveda:

(1) *ātman* is the material body

(2) *ātman* is the transcendent self

(3) *ātman* and the material body together constitute the "person" (*puruṣa*)

(4) *ātman* and the material body are vital complements in the production of somatic fitness (*sātmya*) and happiness (*sukha*)

These four formulations are linked to classical Āyurvedic nosology, the system's arrangement and classification of diseases. For example, the *Caraka Saṃhitā* lists three types of disease that may afflict human bodies: endogenous diseases, which are produced internally; exogenous diseases, which are produced externally; and mental diseases, which are produced in the mind. Endogenous diseases are generally attributable to the morbidity of the body's humors (*doṣa*s) and inadequate diet. Exogenous diseases are attributable to influences external to the body, such as demons, gods, poisons, and combat. The *Caraka Saṃhitā* explains that a person's actions (*karman*s) also may create diseases of the exogenous type. Mental diseases arise from a combination of desires and acquisitions, especially the incongruity between a person's desires and acquisitions. Of these three types of disease, the mental type in particular is a useful starting point from which to begin exploring the nature of the self in classical Āyurveda. It is useful because it signals the ways in which Āyurvedic views of the self as both a nonmaterial principle and a physical, flesh-and-bones entity influence the tradition's thoughts about the body and the lived experience of well-being or embodiment.

The *Caraka Saṃhitā* succinctly states that mental diseases arise when a person "does not get what is wanted and gets what is not wanted."[5] There are variants of this verse that say "from getting what one wants, and not getting what one doesn't want," which, as Dominik Wujastyk has noted, "scarcely seems a reason for derangement."[6] Brahmadathan U.M.T. and I have argued elsewhere that Cakrapāṇidatta, in the *Āyurvedadīpikā* (eleventh century CE), his commentary on the *Caraka Saṃhitā,* suggests in his comments on this passage (in the standard edition as well as in the variant readings to which Wujastyk refers) that the basis of mental affliction is neither getting nor not getting, but simply desire, thirst, or craving.[7] About this Cakrapāṇidatta has the following to say:

> When a person gets what is desired, this generates satisfaction, happiness, and so on. When a person gets what is not desired and is separated from pleasurable things, then grief and so on arise. However, it was just read [in the *Caraka Saṃhitā* that mental illness arises] "from not getting what is wanted and from getting what is not wanted." But on this reading, because of the particle "and" (*ca*), even getting what is wanted should be known as the cause [of mental illness].[8]

According to Cakrapāṇidatta, both the attainment of things that are wanted and the attainment of things that are not wanted result in mental afflictions. Even though the wanted and the unwanted both cause mental disease, the paths they take to produce disease are different. Feelings such as grief introduce mental afflictions when one acquires things that are unwanted. Feelings of satisfaction, ecstasy, and so on are generated from the procurement of things that are wanted, and this, too, Cakrapāṇidatta asserts, results in mental afflictions. Why would getting something that is wanted cause mental illness? Cakrapāṇidatta's interpretation that mental illness may arise in people for simply having wanted something and then getting that thing "suggests that people want things without knowing whether or not they are suited for the objects of their desire."[9] Mental illness, according to the *Caraka Saṃhitā,* is a matter of self-understanding. Thus the central question in mental illness cases is not about getting and not getting things that are wanted and not wanted. Rather, the task that the compilers of the *Caraka Saṃhitā* set for their students when attempting to discern the causes of mental distress—a task that Cakrapāṇidatta emphasizes in his commentary—involves a mode of questioning and knowledge acquisition that amounts to the discovery of the self of the patient.

After declaring that mental diseases arise because a person does not get what is wanted and gets what is not wanted, the *Caraka Saṃhitā*'s next verse states several things that a person burdened with mental illness ought to do for treatment. These things include commonsense discriminations between actions and social associations that are good and bad and the pursuit of the three aims of human existence (*trivarga*) that are often advocated in Āyurveda and in classical Hindu traditions: *kāma*, sexual pleasure; *artha*, prosperity; and *dharma*.[10] Moving beyond the external actions and objects that the mentally ill should bring into or separate from their lives, the *Caraka Saṃhitā* quickly gets to the crux of the issue, which is knowledge: "One should properly strive after knowledge of *ātman, deśa, kula, kāla, bala,* and *śakti* and serve people who are learned about that [knowledge]."[11] In his commentary Cakrapāṇidatta explains this statement in this way: "That knowledge [referred to] here is knowledge of medicine for mental illness."[12] The way to know *ātman, deśa, kula, kāla, bala,* and *śakti*, he further proposes, involves a process of detailed self-reflection and interrogation, which he models in his commentary with a series of questions and answers: "Who am I? What is good for me? Knowledge of *ātman*. What is *deśa*? What is appropriate in this [*deśa*]? Knowledge of *deśa*. In the same way, knowledge of *kāla* and so on should also be known."[13] The way that one chooses to read the compound listing the different types of knowledge in the *Caraka Saṃhitā*'s statement (*ātman, deśa, kula,* and so on) is important to determine exactly what the text intends by using the term *ātman* here. Commentators often parse such strings of words and suggest optimal ways to understand the syntax and word meanings in the root text, thereby aiding the modern reception and translation of these classical texts. Unfortunately, Cakrapāṇidatta does not analyze this compound. I therefore propose two possible readings here, following an earlier study that Brahmadathan and I published on Cakrapāṇidatta's *Āyurvedadīpikā*.[14]

One reading is to take the six terms as autonomous categories, each of which stands in a genitive relation to the term knowledge (*jñāna*). Parsed in this way the compound reads: knowledge of the self (*ātman*), knowledge of location (*deśa*), knowledge of family (*kula*), knowledge of time (*kāla*), knowledge of strength (*bala*), and knowledge of ability (*śakti*).[15] Grammatically this is an acceptable translation of the compound. However, this reading is unsuitable within the context of the text. Cakrapāṇidatta is interpreting a passage in the *Caraka Saṃhitā* about mental illness. Extreme feelings such as grief, envy, lust, euphoria, and jubilation underlie mental illness in this Āyurvedic discussion. These feelings have the power to disconnect people's perceptions of themselves from reality, to cloud their ability to think clearly about themselves and how they relate to others. About this passage in Cakrapāṇidatta's

Āyurvedadīpikā, Brahmadathan and I have argued that "[e]ven if the categories of knowledge listed here are vital to being human, which they no doubt are, if we interpret the *Caraka Saṃhitā* as presenting them as independent, non-interrelated categories of knowledge, then we must read this passage as inspiring people not to unify all areas of their self-knowledge, but rather to divide and isolate them."[16] Such a reading would seem to undercut the *Caraka Saṃhitā*'s approach to mental illness.

Another reading of the compound starts with Cakrapāṇidatta's self-reflexive analysis, "Who am I? What is good for me?" To the question "What is good for me?" Cakrapāṇidatta responds, "knowledge of the *ātman*." The term *ātman* here is not the transcendent self within all bodies that elsewhere in the *Caraka Saṃhitā* is identified with Brahman, the absolute reality.[17] Instead, *ātman* here is a reflexive pronoun meaning "oneself." It literally refers to a person's physical presence. So to the question "Who am I?" I answer, "an active living body." The specific knowledge of *ātman* that is good for me is knowledge of myself in relation to my physical capacities and surroundings. In this way the *Caraka Saṃhitā*'s proposal to cultivate knowledge of the *ātman* may be read as a prescription to be self-aware, paying special attention to one's physical presence and potential, which ultimately cannot be separated from one's relationships to others, the environment, and the world. Understood in this way, the *Caraka Saṃhitā*'s compound reads like this: knowledge of the *ātman* entails knowledge of one's strengths (*bala*) and abilities (*śakti*) with respect to one's location (*deśa*), one's family (*kula*), and one's time (*kāla*, in the sense of astrological and seasonal time as well as life cycle time).[18]

The term *ātman* in Cakrapāṇidatta's commentary designates the material body. It is the material flesh and bones of a person's anatomical self. It also designates a person's physical presence and aptitude within social and temporal contexts. And yet the term *ātman* in the Āyurvedic context means much more than this, for it is also often used to refer to the transcendent self that is identified with Brahman and that is regularly encountered in Hindu, Buddhist, and Jain philosophical discourses. The *Caraka Saṃhitā* includes several verses about the *ātman* as the transcendent self. For example, the text says that this self is independent of the material body, yet it is located in and motivates the body, and it is all-pervading and remains nonchanging throughout countless rounds of birth and death. Every person has the potential to realize the identity of the transcendent self with Brahman, which results in *mokṣa*, liberation from *saṃsāra*, the cycle of birth and death.[19] The *Caraka Saṃhitā*'s use of the term *ātman* in these passages is somewhat puzzling in view of the physicality conveyed by the same term in the text's treatment of mental illness. However, variable usage of the term *ātman* is not unique to classical Āyurvedic sources. The Āyurvedic understanding of *ātman* as both the body and the transcendent self resembles the semantic range of the term in Upaniṣads such as the Chāndogya Upaniṣad, in which the *ātman* is identified in turn with the physical body, dream consciousness, the bliss of deep sleep, and Brahman.[20]

While in the Sanskrit medical classics *ātman* may at times designate the physical body, the term is most widely used in the medical literature to designate the nonmaterial, transcendent self. As the nonmaterial self, standing apart from but always in relation to the material body, the characteristics of *ātman* help us make sense of the contours of the Āyurvedic tradition's notions of health, happiness, and *dharma*. To describe these important elements of the human condition, the classical Āyurvedic sources and their commentators typically use three distinct and occasionally overlapping concepts, which I will unpack in turn: person (*puruṣa*), fitness (*sātmya*), and happiness (*sukha*).

In the Sanskrit literature of Āyurveda, the individual person, *puruṣa*, is usually a kind of empirical homologue of the transcendent self.[21] The person is said to be unaffected by disease and detached from the material body. Even so, in the *Caraka Saṃhitā* the person is on occasion tantamount to the physical body (made up of the five gross elements that constitute all matter), while at other times it is clearly just the empirical self.[22] Further complicating the issue, the person is at times equated with consciousness, and in this capacity it acts as a kind of demi-*ātman*, a mediator between the body and the *ātman*, the transcendent self. In the *Caraka Saṃhitā*'s terminology, the person qua consciousness is the intermediary between the "field" (*kṣetra*) and the "knower of the field" (*kṣetra-jña*).[23] The field and the knower of the field are here, as they are in other genres of Sanskrit literature, common metaphors for the material body and the nonmaterial self.

In the fragmentary remnants of the *Bhānumatī*, his eleventh-century commentary on the Āyurvedic classic the *Suśruta Saṃhitā* (ca. second century CE), Cakrapāṇidatta deals with the complicated relationship between the body and the self by identifying the self with a person's somatic fitness (*sātmya*), or well-being. Fitness of a body, he says, is homologous with the self:

> Well-being, which constitutes health, can be obtained in a person who is well by preventing disorders which have not yet occurred, and in a person who is ill by the *sātmya* which

> cures the illness. And when one defines *sātmya* as that which is homologous with the nature of the *ātman*, that is the strict truth since, if there is conformity with the *ātman*, there is, on that very account, an absence of disorder.[24]

Here the notion of fitness (translated as "appropriateness" by Zimmermann[25]) evokes states of harmony and conformity. When there is fitness in the body, there is conformity between the body and the *ātman*, self. And when the body conforms with the self, there is "an absence of disorder," which in this case means physiological and mental well-being. Fitness must be sustained in healthy people to prevent the onset of disease, and in ailing patients it must be developed to establish well-being. Accord between the body and the self is an ontological state that results in fitness, which is a condition either to be sustained or established. Well-being, in this view, is an ever-changing and developing modal experience. It is the experience of a state of being-in-the-world in which the body and the self merge in the service of (to repair or to establish anew) complete "self-dependence," or *svāsthya*, which is the Sanskrit term most commonly translated in English as "health."

In the *Nibandhasaṃgraha*, Ḍalhaṇa's widely cited twelfth-century commentary on the *Suśruta Saṃhitā*, health is a condition that must be developed and sustained through activities of the human organism in an ever-changing environment, rather than merely an internal physiological state of the physical body. Ḍalhaṇa claims that "the term fitness (*sātmya*) means that which makes happiness (*sukha*)."[26] The term *sukha* is used here to designate "happiness." Following Monier-Williams's etymology, in classical Sanskrit literature *sukha* usually refers to a good or sound (*su*) aperture (*kha*), such as one of the nine openings in the human body (the mouth, the two eyes, the two ears, the two nostrils, the genitals, and the anus). Monier-Williams also suggests that in the older literature of Vedic Sanskrit, *sukha* is a quality of the axle hole of a chariot that enables the smooth rotational functioning of the chariot's wheels ("having a good axle hole").[27] Following these historical usages, Āyurvedic literature presents an example of rich semantic layering in which *sukha* qua happiness is interpreted in terms of sound bodily functioning. Following the rhetorical rule (*tantrayukti*) of *hetvārtha*, "the thing [implied] by its cause" (or simply "implication"), the notion of happiness in Āyurveda may be read as a metaphor for the smooth (*su*) movement of fluids and air through the body's many openings and spaces (*kha*s): blood coursing unobstructed through the veins, air moving freely through the mouth and nostrils, excretion leaving the body on a regular schedule, and so on. In this way so-called "good openings" certify happiness, which comes from being well, or health.[28] It may not be obvious how health, if understood only in terms of the physical body, leads to happiness, since the physical body does not express the modal aspect of health that is contingent on a person's actions and behavior in relation to other humans, animals, and nature. Predating Ḍalhaṇa's commentary on the *Suśruta Saṃhitā*, the compilers of the *Kāśyapa Saṃhitā*, a seventh-century Sanskrit text on women's and children's medicine, similarly characterize *sukha*, happiness, as agreement of one's physical body and embodied self, while also adding that this agreement is a human being's natural state (*prakṛti*): "sameness of body and self is happiness, and that is the natural state."[29]

The *Kāśyapa Saṃhitā*'s assertion that harmony between the body and the self is the human organism's natural state evokes a notion of microcosmic-macrocosmic homologues in classical Āyurveda, in which, as I will discuss later, the relationship between the self and the body parallels the relationship between the cosmic principles of *puruṣa* and *prakṛti*, pure consciousness and the ever-changing realm of nature or matter, in the Sāṃkhya philosophical system.[30] Health in Āyurveda is measured not only by a person's biophysiology but also by his or her social activity and relationship to the immediate environment and to the material world as a whole. Examples of this logic can be seen in Āyurvedic narrative etiologies of disease. In these stories the relative health of the physical body is a direct result of a person's knowledge of, and ability and willingness to uphold the demands of, his or her multifaceted *dharma*—the complicated set of social, legal, and ethical obligations with which he or she is confronted in life. These obligations range from private and public ritual activity to domestic and community relations.[31] When they are not adequately met, the result is an ailing body that does not function in the ways in which a person would like it to function, which often leads in turn to unhealthful and possibly indecorous behaviors and disrupts a person's effectiveness in the grander physiology of the environment and the cosmos as a whole. To this end, the *Caraka Saṃhitā* stresses that health undergirds not only the three aims mentioned earlier—*dharma*, *artha*, and *kāma*—but also the fourth and ultimate aim of human existence, *mokṣa*: "Health is the very root of *dharma*, prosperity, sexual pleasure, and liberation (*mokṣa*) from the cycle of birth and death."[32] Knowledge of what constitutes health is a pathway to bodily well-being, and the state of bodily well-being is in turn the *sine qua non* for the pursuit of the four *puruṣārtha*s, the four aims of human existence.

Wujastyk has recently observed that Āyurvedic physicians in premodern India at times "subordinated the quest for dharma to the quest for health."[33] I would modify this assertion and suggest that the quest for physical health in the Sanskrit medical classics does not involve a demotion of *dharma*, but rather *dharma* is fundamental to the quest for health in premodern Āyurveda. Āyurvedic literature adds to the quest for *dharma* a comprehensive obligation to take care of one's body. When this duty is not upheld, everything else in one's life is liable to come undone. This, I submit, is Āyurveda's unique articulation of the Indian cultural principle of *dharma*, or what I call "body *dharma*." Elaborated in such a comprehensive manner, across a diverse corpus of literature, an Āyurvedic body *dharma* may be understood as undergirding all other notions of *dharma* pertaining to a person's social, legal, and religious obligations and activities. In eight technical genres—internal medicine, ear-nose-throat medicine, surgery, toxicology, demonology, obstetrics and pediatrics, rejuvenation therapies, and sexual therapies—the Sanskrit medical classics establish the breadth and depth of *āyur-veda*, "knowledge for long life." (A Sanskrit grammatical rule regarding euphonic combination, *sandhi*, of final and initial letters turns *āyus* + *veda* into *āyur-veda*.) This *āyur-veda* establishes a framework both for knowing the self and for understanding one's somatic capacities in lived experience. Āyurveda is thus a type of knowledge that enables a person to experience life optimally. This includes resources necessary to cultivate, nourish, correct, and palliate the basic instrumental means—the body proper—with which any and all duties (*dharma*s) and actions (*karman*s) must begin and end.[34]

The Material Body and the Embodied Self

The relationship of the body to the classical Indian principle of *dharma*, especially as it is expressed in Hindu traditions, is articulated through the two body typologies in the medical classics that I mentioned earlier: the material body and the embodied self. These typologies are heuristic devices that address, respectively, biophysical aspects and dharmic aspects of the human condition. Attention to these two typologies—cultivation of the body and cultivation of the self—equally contribute to the fulfillment of a person's *dharma*, or the nexus of social, religious, and legal obligations that a person is expected to uphold. In proposing a twofold commitment to the body and the self, Āyurveda provides a unique somatic variation on the *dharma* principle. A person's ability to uphold an array of commitments (*dharmas*), including the performance of religious rituals, maintenance or avoidance of certain social relationships, and adherence to certain legal injunctions—all of which in the Dharmaśāstra literature are determined for each person according to multiple variables such as sex, age, class, caste, and profession—is contingent on a basic dharmic commitment to bodily upkeep. The classical sources posit the production of health in the body as a *dharma* as such. Āyurveda's body *dharma* is an obligation that befalls anyone who is able to implement the knowledge (*veda*) that leads to long life (*āyus*) that undergirds the classical tradition as we find it in the sources.

There are other ways to characterize these two body typologies in classical Āyurveda. For example, Steven Engler has identified two body types in the tradition, material and nonmaterial, which he reads, as do others, as reflective of a tension in the classical sources between medical science and brahmanical religion.[35] I opt not to join or perpetuate this debate about classical Indian science versus religion here, for I think it unnecessarily pulls apart a singular knowledge system that, despite its diversity of interests and specializations, is unified by an exhaustive pursuit to know, elaborate, and promote longevity of human life, the basis of which is the body. This pursuit covers a great deal of ground, and topics taken up in Āyurveda are also regularly taken up in nonmedical inquiries and debates in classical India. Questions about which came first in the classical Āyurvedic sources, the so-called scientific or the religious, do little to facilitate our understanding of Āyurvedic conceptions of the body and of human life, which is what I am after here. English-language categories like "religion" and "science" are part of the problem when it comes to grasping classical Āyurveda's expansive view of health, the body, and embodiment. Instead of attempting to separate out layers of science vis-à-vis layers of religion in the sources, we must learn how to read statements made by the premodern Indian authors as "facts of a special kind," as Shigehisa Kuriyama puts it, that "invite us to develop our sensibility in such a way as to discern the realities described."[36] The Sanskrit literature of Āyurveda is filled with expressions about the body, bodily well-being, and bodily dysfunction. Statements such as the assertion that the effects of one's social decisions and actions are critical to the upkeep of one's body present us with a "view"—what the Sanskrit pandits called *dṛṣṭi*—to be learned and cultivated so as to shape our experience and ways of knowing. The texts offer a structure for creating a somatic sensibility that enables us to see the body as a topography that is coterminous with, contingent upon, and formative in society and nature. This sensibility might run counter to a modern biomedical textbook's "anatomical body." Yet these contending perspectives need not result in the determination that one body vis-à-vis the other is false. In learning to read the Indian texts in context and with self-awareness of our intellectual predispositions and aims, we may come to appreciate the meaning of a text's assertions as "facts of a special kind" that need not be explained away, in an English-language idiom, as too religious to be medical or, conversely, as so strictly anatomical that they must be devoid of moral or social import.

As I conceive them here, the material body and the embodied self both entail a particular *pathology* pertaining to the origin, structure, and effects of disease in the body and a particular *ontology* pertaining to the internal (physiological) functioning and external (social) capacities and effects of the body. Of the two, the material body typology is more commonly represented in classical Āyurvedic literature. Discussions of the material body tend toward physiological reductionism in that the classical authors presuppose a discrete material body with an internally coherent composition that is entirely isolable from its exterior environment. The type of discourse used to describe this body is characteristic of Āyurveda's so-called internal medicine (*kāya-cikitsā*). Surface symptoms, afflictions, and social disabilities resulting from sickness and disease are generally considered epiphenomenal. Disease morphologies and pathologies are predominantly endogenous.[37] Nosological discussions present the material body as an enclosed, stationary, and dissectible space. Treatment of the material body therefore follows an objective and idealized view that similar symptoms in different bodies are treatable by similar therapies. Technical methods and medicines are designed to maintain congruence among the body's fluid and material components, including the humors (*doṣa*s), tissues, sinews, organs, and waste products.

Nearly any discussion of the material body in the Sanskrit classics, most notably in discussions of internal medicine, to some extent touches upon what is perhaps the most well-known aspect of Āyurveda today: *tridoṣa-vidyā*, the theory of the three *doṣa*s, or bodily humors, known as *vāta* (wind), *pitta* (bile), and *kapha* (phlegm). While the precise source of Āyurveda's doctrine of the *doṣa*s is uncertain, Hartmut Scharfe has argued that the classical Āyurvedic humoral theory of Caraka, Suśruta, and Vāgbhaṭa developed on the basis of Buddhist canonical sources.[38] The Sanskrit word *doṣa* literally means "fault" or "taint." In Āyurvedic sources the *doṣa*s are not merely conceptual entities or indexical measures for speculation on diseases and their origins. They are real, semi-fluid substances that circulate throughout the body. But unlike other substances that fill the material body, the *doṣa*s are pathogenic arbiters that constantly interact with the body's fluids, organs, tissues, and other substances. As they circulate their abundance and/or deficiency in any area can generate somatic dysfunctions and diseases of varying kinds and degrees. A *doṣa* is literally a "taint" or "fault" when it settles outside of its appropriate abode in the body, which in the case of *vāta* is the pelvic region; *pitta,* the stomach; and *kapha,* the head and chest.

The physiology of Āyurveda's internal medicine gives the impression that the body is a closed working unit. However, the tradition also articulates a number of notions that implicate social activity in the health and welfare of the human body. Another body typology emerges in those passages in the literature that emphasize how the operations of a person's body affect, while also being affected by, other people's bodies and the natural environment. This agentive social body illustrates the embodied self typology. Always changing and constantly engaged in social interactions, the embodied self typology asserts the primacy of the body in the state of being human. Beyond its substantial makeup as flesh and bones and fluids, the Āyurvedic embodied self underscores the ways in which—through social practices, religious activities, sexual engagements, and so on—the body actively participates in and is a product of the swarm of intersecting "modal states" that occupy our lives.[39] Following Geoffrey Samuel's notion of the multimodal framework, by modal states I mean nonsubstantive conditions and patterns of relationships that exist among humans and between humans and their environments. Humans may be conscious or unconscious of their conditions and relationship patterns, including moods, feelings, thoughts, and tastes; these conditions and patterns change from moment to moment and continuously affect human behavior and perception.[40] Modal states of an individual person and of human communities are neither reducible to one another nor entirely distinct from one another. They are interconnected derivatives of an ever-changing ecosystem.[41] The material body is part and parcel of the activity of the embodied self in this ecosystem, as a means for the embodied self to express itself and negotiate experience. Directing the material body through differing circumstances of human life, the embodied self exemplifies what Gerald Larson has identified as the sociobiological aspect of Āyurvedic medicine.[42]

In the embodied self typology there is thus a personal facet of human life that motivates the body to act. In addition to the self, the body of course houses a mind (*manas*). But the mind in Āyurveda accounts only for *how* a person acts and thinks; it does not explain *why* a person acts or thinks in certain ways. The purposive element of human life is the nonmaterial self, *ātman*. It is the conscious agent that motivates the mind to impel the material body to act. The mind has motional capacities, for it controls the sense organs and acts as the instrument of reasoning and analysis. The mind does not act of its own accord, however. It must be "endowed with action," as the *Caraka Saṃhitā* explains, by the agentive self, the *ātman*.[43] The embodied self is furthermore said to be the cause and the sustainer of consciousness (*cetanā*) and the agent that interfaces with the consciousness of other beings, both human and nonhuman.[44]

A person's self-expressions and interactions with other human and nonhuman beings and the environment impact the health of the material body. Diseases resulting from such activity are typically attributable to either mental or exogenous sources. Diseases of the mind, body, and sense organs do not impair the self, even though the self, the "ruler" (*vaśin*) of the material body aggregate, motivates the material body to act.[45] The ways in which the Sanskrit medical sources address health and illness ensuing from dharmic infringements are not as fixed or as clear-cut as biophysical treatments designed for the material body, such as those designed to recalibrate the three *doṣas*. To care for ailments of a dharmic nature, the *Caraka Saṃhitā* lays out a process of self-cultivation (*ātma-hita*). The Āyurvedic notion of self-cultivation underlies the logic connecting morality and illness in Āyurveda, in which a person's failure to uphold his or her dharmic obligations initiates the movement from a state of healthfulness to patienthood.

Self-cultivation

Time and again in the Sanskrit medical classics we are reminded that the material body is the foundational support of human life. An instructive passage in the *Caraka Saṃhitā* reiterates this position while at the same time emphasizing the body's fundamental role as a sustaining mechanism for something grander than its own structural frame. "At the cost of all other things," the *Caraka Saṃhitā* asserts, "the body should be preserved. Because in the death of that [body] there is total failure of the coming-to-be of humans."[46] The use of the term *bhāva*, "coming-to-be" or "becoming," suggests that something arises in the lives of people who achieve sound physical health of the body. Without a properly preserved body, that something does not emerge.

But what does *bhāva* mean here in the *Caraka Saṃhitā*? What does it mean to "come to be" in the world? Useful to this discussion is Matthew Kapstein's description of the dialectical program in a classical Buddhist text, Śāntarakṣita's *Tattvasaṃgraha* (eighth century CE). He interprets the work as a way of "bringing into being" or "coming-to-be" (*bhāvanā*, feminine derivative of the same verbal root, *bhū*, from which *bhāva* is derived). He suggests that Śāntarakṣita's critical assessment of Indian philosophical schools that deliberated "thatness" (*tattva*), the real nature of things, was not designed simply as a cognitive exercise in the apprehension of thought objects. Śāntarakṣita's *Tattvasaṃgraha* is a kind of "therapy," Kapstein explains,

> whereby one must challenge one's own self-understandings so as to disclose and finally uproot the misunderstandings that are concealed therein. This process involves equally the positive construction of a conceptual model of the Buddha's teaching and of the Buddha himself, a conceptual model that is to be progressively assimilated until, in the end, concept and being have merged. This is a self-transcending project, oriented toward that omniscient being who, as the very self of compassion, is oriented to benefit all beings.[47]

Self-cultivation in Āyurveda entails a process of coming-to-be akin to Śāntarakṣita's therapeutic program of self-transcendence in the *Tattvasaṃgraha*. In the *Caraka Saṃhitā*, for example, coming-to-be in the world concerns the preservation of the body, and by extension the promotion of health, by cultivating in one's life things that are "good for oneself," *ātma-hita*. This involves a comprehensive process of sustaining or reestablishing health by crafting a sound material body that is aligned with the self. This may be done, as we saw in Cakrapāṇidatta's reflection on mental disease, by learning the limits and potentialities of one's physicality in relation to one's social, religious, and legal responsibilities (*dharma*), to the environment, and to other goals in life. Somatic health and long life are essentially synonymous in this personal coming-to-be in the sense that freedom from disease and health of the body, barring any unforeseen accidents, produce long life, and long life in turn indicates bodily health.

Unlike Śāntarakṣita's program, in which the life and teachings of the Buddha provide a unified model that every person aspires to emulate, Āyurveda offers multiple ways to realize and preserve a healthy body. But the dharmic life of social, religious, and legal responsibilities that is to be forged in the process is comparatively less defined than in Śāntarakṣita's program and is arguably fluid from one classical medical source to the next. This has to do with the fact that the Āyurvedic classics are not concerned with a single sustained topic or paradigmatic life. While one work might deal specifically with embryology, obstetrics, and related issues of women's health (for example, *Kāśyapa Saṃhitā*), another might largely eschew discussions of embodiment and the place of *dharma* in the production of bodily health in favor of clinical questions of surgery and dissection (for example, *Śusruta Saṃhitā*). Other works, such as the *Caraka Saṃhitā* and its commentaries, frequently include psychological questions in their considerations of health, while still others promote lifestyle paradigms of a Buddhist character, evoking fundamental teachings such as the "middle way" as a means to achieve health (for example, *Aṣṭāṅgahṛdaya Saṃhitā*).[48] Whichever type of life is under inspection in the classical sources, there are generally clear authorial positions and expectations concerning the human agents who fall ill, especially concerning the principles of *dharma* and *karma*. Typically, we learn about the social, religious, and legal foundations of somatic well-being, about the effects of *dharma* and *karma* on the production of health, through examples of what *not* to do—a kind of *via negativa*. Through the lives and activities of diseased patients (*rogins*) as represented in the classical sources, we can discern the medical authors' views about how not to act in the world. Ill patients epitomize a lack of self-knowledge and a failure to cultivate certain dharmic qualities in their lives, which has the effect of bringing ruin to the physical body.

Surendranath Dasgupta has argued that the *Caraka Saṃhitā*'s notion of self-cultivation, *ātma-hita*, which he translates as "self-good," constitutes the classical medical tradition's basic therapy for acquiring self-knowledge so as to be able to act in the world with supreme conformity between the body and the self. His summary of *ātma-hita* brings together several of the concepts treated in the foregoing analysis—namely, happiness, well-being, and fitness of body and self:

> [Self-cultivation] is described as not only that which gives us pleasure and supplies the material for our comfort, ease of mind and long life, but also that which will be beneficial to us in our future life. Right conduct (*sad-vṛtta*) leads to the health and well-being of body and mind and secures sense-control (*indriya-vijaya*).[49]

Self-cultivation involves rigorous ethical weighing of consequences resulting from one's actions and a clearly defined conception of correct attention and conduct. Cakrapāṇidatta emphasizes that the *Caraka Saṃhitā* encourages people to avoid harmful acts and to perform advantageous ones.[50] This is basic consequentialism, or teleological ethics. The authors of the *Caraka Saṃhitā* advise people to start with goals rather than moral rules so that in every situation they judge the goodness or badness of their actions with respect to whether their actions will or will not further their goals. Self-cultivation also involves management of the sense organs so that they meet with their proper phenomenal objects. Self-cultivation ultimately requires that people reassess their self-understanding. The purpose of such a reassessment is to help people to eventually recognize that in the past they might have overestimated or undervalued—that is, generally misunderstood—their own capabilities and responsibilities. To wit, *ātma-hita* is achieved, the *Caraka Saṃhitā* declares,

> by effecting right actions after properly understanding what is to be perceived and not perceived through the connection of the sense organs with their appropriate objects and by admitting to acting wrongly with respect to qualities of place, time, and the body (*ātman*). Therefore, one absolutely wishing to make what is good for oneself should always observe good behavior in accordance with tradition (*smṛti*).[51]

My translation of the term *ātman* here as "body" follows Cakrapāṇidatta's commentary on this verse: "The word *ātman* refers to the understanding of physical constitution and bodily sickness."[52] Neither the *Caraka Saṃhitā*'s compilers nor Cakrapāṇidatta elaborate on the nod to tradition (*smṛti*) in this verse. Cakrapāṇidatta does say, however, that good behavior accords with dharmic activities like pacification and purification rites and the pursuit of the three aims of human life (*dharma, artha,* and *kāma*).[53]

Dasgupta likens the *Caraka Saṃhitā*'s notion of self-cultivation to "the old principle of the golden mean."[54] He thus recalls Aristotle's famous discourse on "the mean" in the *Ethics*, which suggests that the best path to take in any situation is the one in which extremes are avoided.[55] Dasgupta could just as well have cited Vāgbhaṭa's prescription in the *Aṣṭāṅgahṛdaya Saṃhitā* to "follow the middle way at every step in all dharmic endeavors."[56] In fact, Vāgbhaṭa's daily and seasonal regimens not only advance the ideals of self-control and temperance, they also provide a comprehensive ethic for attaining and sustaining the so-called good life. For Dasgupta it seems that self-cultivation in classical Āyurveda is concerned with maintaining a sense of balance or harmony between one's body and one's environment. In particular, he calls attention to a basic impulse that undergirds the human pursuit of what is good for oneself. It is a motivation that, to borrow Wujastyk's phrasing, underlies "a uniquely medical threesome of goals" found in Āyurveda: the desire for life; the desire for wealth; and the desire for the other world or pleasant future lives.[57] In the *Caraka Saṃhitā* the desire for life is a desire to preserve oneself for as long as possible, and this desire is primary among its "uniquely medical threesome of goals": "Of these desires, a person should above all secure the desire for life. Why? Because when life is abandoned, everything is gone. It can be preserved by following the healthy behavior of a healthy person and through attention to the healing of a patient's sickness."[58] According to Āyurveda in general, and the *Caraka Saṃhitā* in particular, one of the biggest obstacles to right conduct and thus the achievement of a long and healthy life is a misuse or violation of knowledge (*prajñāparādha*). The outright misapplication of knowledge in one's life—generally doing the opposite of what one knows to be conducive to somatic well-being—is a workable explanation in Āyurveda for why people become ill.

The successful practice of self-cultivation requires more than theoretical knowledge of the body and its place in the universe. The realization of what is good for oneself is a lifelong process, and it entails continual attention to one's embodied living. In his commentary on the *Caraka Saṃhitā*'s discussion of the three desires, Cakrapāṇidatta recognizes that the desire for enjoyment is implicit in the desire to live.[59] This is so, Wujastyk explains, because only "the person who is an engaged participant in the experience of life (*bhogārthipuruṣa*), not someone seeking ultimate liberation (*mokṣārthipuruṣa*)," would have a desire for life.[60]

The Cosmic Physiology

A person desirous of life, in the classical Āyurvedic view, manages to attain bodily health in large part because of his or her propensity to integrate with—or disconnect from where appropriate—the "cosmic physiology" of which the human physiology is a part. Before looking at the classical Āyurvedic conception of what I am calling here the "cosmic physiology," a word of warning is in order: any discussion of microcosmic and macrocosmic correspondences, or body-cosmos homologies, in Āyurveda must not lead us to mistake Āyurveda for astronomy or forget that Āyurveda's central focus is the human body. Āyurveda is by and large a clinically oriented knowledge system, alongside which we find a meaningful "rhetoric of cosmic harmonies," to borrow Kuriyama's expression.[61] Homologies of somatic and cosmic physiology are there to be sure, but this knowledge tends more toward the metaphorical and theoretical than the literal. In actual practice it is probable that notions of body-cosmos harmonies received little more than symbolic appreciation from practicing physicians in classical India.

The *Caraka Saṃhitā* leaves no stone unturned and states that every human being has a body. This body is an autonomous organism with a regular structure and standard working apparatuses that are at once a part of, and independent from, a far bigger cosmological body. The medical sage Punarvasu Ātreya comments on the relationship between these two bodies in this way:

> The individual is of the same measure as the universe. As much as there is elemental diversity in the universe, in equal measure there is elemental diversity in the individual. As much as there is elemental diversity in the individual, in equal measure there is elemental diversity in the universe.[62]

A person's body is a cosmos in miniature, the microcosmic counterpart of the macrocosmos. Classical Āyurvedic cosmologies are for the most part analogous to cosmologies in Sāṃkhya philosophy, although considerable parallels with Vaiśeṣika philosophy are also evident.[63] Āyurveda identifies associations among all worldly objects, including the human body, at the level of the five gross elements (*pañca-mahābhūtas*: earth, water, fire, wind, and space), the basic constituents of material things, the qualities that inhere in objects, and the all-pervading self (*ātman*). On the subject of the five gross elements that constitute the universe and the human body, for example, the *Caraka Saṃhitā*'s authors envision macro-micro correspondences in this way: "Earth constitutes the solid form of the human being. Water makes up the moisture. Fire is the heat. Wind constitutes the breath. Space constitutes the hollow parts. Brahman is the interior self."[64] This view of the body's five primary elements and assorted basic constituents may be traced back to the Garbha Upaniṣad of Pippālada, which is associated with the Atharva-Veda tradition and outlines the formation of the embryo from conception to full bodily development.[65] This short Upaniṣad offers a miniature view of a grander vision in the Sanskrit medical classics in which the internal milieu of a person's body is understood to interact with, and to be influenced by, environments external to it such as the biosphere, the family, and the larger society. The linkages of homologous elements across inner somatic and outer social fields are furthermore said to be critical determinants in the well-being of both the individual body and the body's external environments.

According to Sāṃkhya philosophy, everything in the universe is made up of two ontologically distinct principles: *puruṣa*, which is nonchanging pure consciousness, and *prakṛti*, which is ever-changing, nonconscious materiality.[66] The Sanskrit word *prakṛti* literally means "nature" or "matter," and Īśvarakṛṣṇa's *Sāṃkhyakārikā* uses the term *prakṛti* primarily to refer to the material world.[67] As mentioned earlier, the relationship between *prakṛti* and *puruṣa* in Sāṃkhya closely resembles the relationship between the material body and the *ātman* in the embodied self typology of Āyurveda.[68] Just as the transcendent self, *ātman*, is housed in and motivates the material body while in its essential nature it is eternally independent of the body, in the Sāṃkhyan system the *puruṣa* appears to be connected to and motivate the material world of *prakṛti* while in reality it is eternally distinct from *prakṛti*. The two principles, although ontologically distinct, are interdependent in that each serves to define the contours of the other. Hence Tracy Pintchman notes that *puruṣa*'s "presence is nevertheless a vital component [of the material world], for it is only in the presence of *puruṣa*, the principle of pure consciousness, that *prakṛti* can evolve."[69] All material phenomena come into existence on account of *prakṛti*, which is made up of three constituents termed *guṇa*s: *sattva* (purity), *rajas* (energy), and *tamas* (inertia). When the equilibrium of the *guṇa*s is broken, *prakṛti* unfolds in a series of twenty-three *tattva*s, elementary principles, that together constitute the stuff of material existence: intellect, ego, mind, five sense capacities, five action capacities, five subtle elements, and five gross elements. As long as a person is deluded by ignorance and is unaware of his or her true nature as *puruṣa*, which is eternally separate from the material realm of *prakṛti*, he or she falsely identifies with the material psychophysical organism that is constituted by the *tattva*s of *prakṛti*. Only by awakening to one's true identity as the nonchanging self, *puruṣa*, can a person be liberated from the fetters of *prakṛti* and its endless cycles of birth and death.[70]

The classical texts of Āyurveda invoke at times the Sāṃkhyan notion of the three *guṇa*s, while at the same time they formulate a second triad in the form of the three *doṣas*—*vāta*, *pitta*, and *kapha*—that mirrors the *guṇa* triad in certain ways while at the same time retaining its distinctive identity as a uniquely medical model. Just as the disruption of the equilibrium of the *guṇa*s of *prakṛti* causes the *tattva*s to unfold as the evolutes of primordial matter, in a similar way when the *doṣa*s are irritated (*prakupita*) or in a state of irregularity (*vaiṣamya*), disease materializes in the body. Each *doṣa* has specific properties that determine its influence on the seven *dhātus*, bodily tissues (chyle, blood, flesh, fat, bone, marrow, and semen). So, for example, *vāta* is dry, cool, light, and mobile; *pitta* is slightly oily, hot, light, and prickly; *kapha* is cold, slimy, heavy, and soft. While every phenomenon in the material world can be classified in Sāṃkhya philosophy according to the predominance of one or more of the *guṇas*, in a similar way specific bodily disorders and illnesses can be classified in Āyurveda according to the predominance of one or more of the *doṣas* in particular locations in a patient's body.

Each *doṣa* conveys one of the five gross elements as it circulates throughout the body—for example, *vāta* conveys air, *pitta* conveys fire, and *kapha* conveys water. Thus the stuff of the ground we walk upon and the air we breathe is the very same stuff as that which flows throughout our bodies. Zimmermann emphasizes that the same humors that are circulating in our bodies are also "circulating underground, in the water, in the air . . . everywhere around us and within us." However, he continues, "they are also forces, powers which foment disorders, pathogenic principles between which the doctor must establish justice."[71] The disorders and pathogenic principles that Zimmermann mentions constitute a kind of ontological pathology in Āyurveda, which incorporates the sociobiological dimensions of Āyurveda by taking into account ethical factors in a patient's life along with a diagnosis of any imbalances in the *doṣas*. To establish "justice" in the patient, the Āyurvedic physician uses knowledge of the Sanskrit sources to calculate a regimen that cultivates both the nonmaterial self and the material body of the patient. What is good for the patient not only rectifies imbalances in his or her *doṣas*, but it also harmonizes the patient's somatic physiology with the "flow of relatedness" between the individual body, humans and nonhumans, and the ecosystem.[72]

Every person in Āyurveda has permeable boundaries that are penetrated by a multitude of forces in a way that calls to mind McKim Marriott's proposal that the classical Indian perception of the human being is "dividual" rather than individual. Every person is understood to be continually engaged with other people and the natural world through the transference of what Marriott calls "substance-codes," which flow through food and water, alms, air, and the like in a web of interconnectedness.[73] Zimmermann suggests something very similar to Marriott's notion of "dividuality" in his characterization of the cosmic breadth of Āyurveda: "Through his food, habitat, and bodily techniques, the living being is influenced, penetrated, immersed in the system of the humors, flavors, and qualities that makes up the atmosphere, the climate, the landscape in which he takes root."[74] The critical idea that Zimmermann illuminates is that bodies in poor health, for one reason or another, are environmentally and cosmically crooked. In such cases the microcosmic physiology of the body is not compatible with the macrocosmic physiology of the immediate environment and of the universe as a whole. When an Āyurvedic physician treats a patient, he or she must therefore attempt to reestablish the lost balance between the somatic microcosmos of the patient and the macrocosmos.[75]

Dharma and Body

To bring the body and its environment into a state of efficacious balance, the compilers of the Sanskrit medical classics fashion a distinctively medical type of *dharma*, a body *dharma*. As I stated in the introduction, this *dharma* is foundational to all other *dharma*s in India's religious traditions. Despite its perceived importance to the compilers of Āyurvedic literature, body *dharma* is a category that often goes unnoticed in the secondary literature on religious and social *dharma* in Indian history. It is a type of *dharma* designed specifically for the body, and it is an essential element in the achievement of other types of *dharma* commonly found in the Dharmaśāstra literature, such as *svadharma* (one's own *dharma*) and *sādhāraṇa dharma* (universal norms of *dharma*).

The body *dharma* of Āyurveda is a kind of *svadharma* insofar as it applies to specific behaviors more than outlooks and dispositions, which tend to fall under the purview of *dharma* that is common to everyone.[76] The classics of Āyurveda lay out a comprehensive system for each person to follow to care for his or her body, which includes pharmaceutical remedies along with social, religious, and legal aids, so that every single body may function at its optimal capacity in carrying out the demands that are incumbent upon it. The baseline for Āyurveda's body *dharma* is the outlook expressed in the classical sources that, in Wujastyk's words, "ayurveda leads to health and health leads to dharma."[77]

Discourses on health and disease in Āyurveda attempt to bring to the conscious level a knowledge of *dharma* as a course of action, or more fundamentally a mode of being, through which people experience the world and attempt to achieve certain goals in life. In this way the prescriptions and proscriptions of Āyurveda constitute a foundational *dharma* of the body that must be attended to before all other obligations. This body *dharma* is meant to regulate everything a person does. As we have seen, there are striking instances in Āyurveda's classical literature that move beyond the inner workings of the material body and suggest that a breakdown in self-cultivation (*ātma-hita*) and lack of attention to what is good for oneself may lead to a breakdown of body *dharma*. This may result in the onset of sickness and bodily dysfunction, which in turn may compromise a person's ability to be a productive member of society and an active member of a religion or social community. While the disruption of body *dharma* leads to bodily illness, the fulfillment of body *dharma* leads to bodily health, and bodily health in turn sustains human existence and makes possible the achievement of the host of aims to which human beings aspire throughout their lives.

Notes

1. For example, the *Caraka Saṃhitā*, *Bhela Saṃhitā*, and *Kāśyapa Saṃhitā* each count the number of bones (*asthi*) in the human body (including teeth and nails) to be 360, while the *Suśruta Saṃhitā* lists just 300 (*Caraka Saṃhitā* Śārīrasthāna 7.6; *Suśruta Saṃhitā* Śārīrasthāna 5.18; *Bhela Saṃhitā* Śārīrasthāna 7.2; *Kāśyapa Saṃhitā* Śārīrasthāna 2). The *Caraka Saṃhitā* and *Bhela Saṃhitā* identify six layers of skin (*tvac*), while the *Suśruta Saṃhitā* identifies seven (*Caraka Saṃhitā* Śārīrasthāna 7.1–4; *Suśruta Saṃhitā* Śārīrasthāna 4.4; 5.6; *Bhela Saṃhitā* Śārīrasthāna 7.1).

2. Mazars 2006: 84–85. While the surgical skills of the physicians who compiled the *Suśruta Saṃhitā* were clearly far more advanced than the compilers of the other classical compendia, the accuracy of their conceptions of the human body should be viewed with the knowledge that they, like their contemporaries in classical India, had limited access to human bodies for dissection. Even physicians associated with the *Suśruta Saṃhitā*, the text explains, trained on nonhuman objects and bodies, such as animal carcasses, gourds, and the hollow trunks of plants, to prepare for surgery on humans.

3. Zimmermann 1979: 10.

4. Wujastyk 2002: 78; 2003: 70.

5. *Caraka Saṃhitā* Sūtrasthāna 11.45. All translations of Sanskrit passages are my own, unless otherwise indicated.

6. Wujastyk 2003: 31 n. 29.

7. Cerulli and Brahmadathan 2009: 102.

8. *Āyurvedadīpikā* on *Caraka Saṃhitā* Sūtrasthāna 11.45.

9. Cerulli and Brahmadathan 2009: 103.

10. The *trivarga* are the first three of the four *puruṣārthas*, aims of humankind, in classical Hindu traditions. As I will discuss later, the fourth aim is *mokṣa*, liberation from the cycle of birth and death.

11. *Caraka Saṃhitā* Sūtrasthāna 11.46.

12. *Āyurvedadīpikā* on *Caraka Saṃhitā* Sūtrasthāna 11.46.

13. *Āyurvedadīpikā* on *Caraka Saṃhitā* Sūtrasthāna 11.46.

14. Cerulli and Brahmadathan 2009.

15. In grammatical terms this reading consists of one copulative compound (*dvandva samāsa*) within the overall genitive compound (*ṣaṣṭhī tatpuruṣa samāsa*).

16. Cerulli and Brahmadathan 2009: 104.

17. *Caraka Saṃhitā* Śārīrasthāna 1.81. The *ātman* is said to exist "within all wombs" (*sarva-yoni-gata*)—that is, within the origin and initial place of development of the body.

18. In this reading the grammatical configuration of the compound *ātma-deśa-kula-kāla-bala-śakti-jñāna* consists of two copulative compounds (*dvandva samāsas*) syntactically related as a locative compound (*saptamī tatpuruṣa samāsa*) within the overall genitive compound. See also Cerulli and Brahmadathan 2009: 105.

19. *Caraka Saṃhitā* Śārīrasthāna 1.70–85; 5.11–12. The idea that *ātman* is identical with Brahman is perhaps the most widely known view of *ātman* today, due in large part to the popularity of Śaṃkara, the eighth-century philosopher of Advaita Vedānta, who espoused a monistic, or nondualist, philosophy founded on the assertion that the *ātman* is nondifferent from Brahman.

20. Kapstein 2003: 37–38, 55–59. See also Olivelle 1996: xlix.

21. *Caraka Saṃhitā* Śārīrasthāna 1.1–19; *Suśruta Saṃhitā* Sūtrasthāna 1.22.

22. Valiathan 2003: 184.

23. *Caraka Saṃhitā* Śārīrasthāna 1.8–9; 1.63–65.

24. *Bhānumatī* on *Suśruta Saṃhitā* Sūtrasthāna 35.39; cited in Zimmermann 1999: 23. The *Bhānumatī* is for all intents and purposes unavailable today. Meulenbeld (1999: vol. 1A, 374–375) states that the only portions of Cakrapāṇidatta's commentary on the *Suśruta Saṃhitā* that have been preserved pertain to the work's Sūtrasthāna. Otherwise, we know about the *Bhānumatī* through references to this work by later authors.

25. Zimmermann 1980.

26. *Nibandhasaṃgraha* on *Suśruta Saṃhitā* Sūtrasthāna 35.39.

27. Monier-Williams 1997, s.v. *sukha*.

28. Singh 1992: 420.

29. *Kāśyapa Saṃhitā* Sūtrasthāna 27.6.

30. Larson 1987: 249–250; Pintchman 1994: 86–87.

31. Cerulli 2012. For a general introduction to the roles of narrative in the Sanskrit medical classics, see esp. chapter 1 and chapter 7.

32. *Caraka Saṃhitā* Sūtrasthāna 1.15.

33. Wujastyk 2004: 838.

34. Here again there appears to be a parallel with the *ātman* of the Upaniṣads, where the *ātman*, interpreted by the commentators as "body," is called "the origin of all actions, for hence arise all actions" (Bṛhadāraṇyaka Upaniṣad 3.9.28; cited in Kapstein 2003: 55).

35. Engler 2003: 422–425. See also Chattopadhyaya 1986; Zimmermann 1999: 206–217; Zysk 1991: 118; Thapar 2002: 258.

36. Kuriyama 2007: 600.

37. See, for example, *Caraka Saṃhitā* Sūtrasthāna 11.45; *Aṣṭāṅgahṛdaya Saṃhitā* Sūtrasthāna 1.20–21.

38. Scharfe 1999.

39. Samuel 1990: 8–16, 70–71.

40. Samuel 1990: 74.

41. Samuel (1990) uses the term "social manifold" for what I am calling the "ever-changing ecosystem" in which the modal states of individuals and society interrelate.

42. Larson 1987: 256.

43. *Caraka Saṃhitā* Śārīrasthāna 1.75–76; cf. *Caraka Saṃhitā* Śārīrasthāna 1.54–57.

44. *Āyurvedadīpikā* on *Caraka Saṃhitā* Sūtrasthāna 11.13.

45. *Caraka Saṃhitā* Śārīrasthāna 1.78.

46. *Caraka Saṃhitā* Nidānasthāna 6.7.

47. Kapstein 2003: 15.

48. Of all the classical medical authors, Vāgbhaṭa, to whom both the *Aṣṭāṅgahṛdaya Saṃhitā* and the *Aṣṭāṅgasaṃgraha Saṃhitā* are often ascribed (although both sources were in all likelihood not written by the same person), is traditionally thought to have been the most influenced by Buddhist traditions. For instance, Vāgbhaṭa mentions the "middle way" in the *Aṣṭāṅgahṛdaya Saṃhitā* (*Aṣṭāṅgahṛdaya* Sūtrasthāna 2.30), and he refers to several names known in Buddhist literature and tradition, including his teacher Avalokita (*Aṣṭāṅgasaṃgraha* Sūtrasthāna 28.34; Cikitsāsthāna 2.144; Uttarasthāna 8.57; *Aṣṭāṅgahṛdaya* Uttarasthāna 5.50); Bhaiṣajyaguru (*Aṣṭāṅgasaṃgraha* Sūtrasthāna 27.12–13; *Aṣṭāṅgahṛdaya* Sūtrasthāna 18.17–18); Avalokiteśvara (*Aṣṭāṅgasaṃgraha* Sūtrasthāna 8.59); Ratnaketu (*Aṣṭāṅgasaṃgraha* Uttarasthāna 1.19); and others. Other indications that the works ascribed to Vāgbhaṭa are indebted to Buddhism include the use of the title *arhat* for Bhaiṣajyaguru in both the *Aṣṭāṅgasaṃgraha* and the *Aṣṭāṅgahṛdaya*; references to a healing figure (*dhāriṇī*) who prepares a collyrium paste meant to purify the three eyes (of *prajñā*, *jñāna*, and *vijñāna*) and who is also called a *tathāgata* and *samyak-sambuddha* (*Aṣṭāṅgasaṃgraha* Sūtrasthāna 58–61); and references to the Buddhist deity Tāra in both the *Aṣṭāṅgasaṃgraha* and the *Aṣṭāṅgahṛdaya* (*Aṣṭāṅgasaṃgraha* Cikitsāsthāna 21.135; *Aṣṭāṅgahṛdaya* Cikitsāstāna 19.98).

49. Dasgupta 1968: vol. 2, 405.

50. *Āyurvedadīpikā* on *Caraka Saṃhitā* Sūtrasthāna 8.17.

51. *Caraka Saṃhitā* Sūtrasthāna 8.17.

52. *Āyurvedadīpikā* on *Caraka Saṃhitā* Sūtrasthāna 8.17.

53. *Āyurvedadīpikā* on *Caraka Saṃhitā* Sūtrasthāna 8.17.

54. Dasgupta 1968: vol. 2, 405.

55. This discussion occurs in book 2 of the *Nicomachean Ethics* (Ostwald 1962).

56. *Aṣṭāṅgahṛdaya Saṃhitā* Sūtrasthāna 2.30. See also n. 48.

57. Wujastyk 2004: 838.

58. *Caraka Saṃhitā* Sūtrasthāna 11.4.

59. *Āyurvedadīpikā* on *Caraka Saṃhitā* Sūtrasthāna 11.3.

60. Wujastyk 2004: 838.

61. Kuriyama 2002: 267.

62. *Caraka Saṃhitā* Śārīrasthāna 5.3.

63. Larson 1987; Comba 2001.

64. *Caraka Saṃhitā* Śārīrasthāna 5.5.

65. Kapani 1989a, 1989b.

66. The following discussion of Āyurveda and Sāṃkhya also occurs, with some elaborations and expanded discussions, in Cerulli 2012: 27–29.

67. Larson 2005: 256 n. 3. For the Sanskrit text along with a translation of Īśvarakṛṣṇa's *Sāṃkhyakārikā*, see Larson 2005: appendix B.

68. A lot of ink has been spilled concerning which knowledge system, Āyurveda or Sāṃkhya, influenced the other on the subjects of cosmogony, cosmology, and the relationship between matter and the self. It is likely that the two systems were relatively coeval in Indian history, and as far as I can determine, there is no conclusive evidence to suggest which of the two systems had a greater influence on the other.

69. Pintchman 1994: 86.

70. Larson 1983: 307–312.

71. Zimmermann 1999: 31.

72. Samuel 1990: 56–66.

73. Marriott 1976: 110–111.

74. Zimmermann 1980: 101. Marriott was a co-translator of this article into English from its original rendering in French. Zimmermann has also dealt with Āyurvedic cosmology and the openness and boundedness of the body in Āyurveda elsewhere. See, for example, Zimmermann 1999: 218–223; 2004: 7–11.

75. White 1996: 15–23, 218–262.

76. O'Flaherty 1976: 96; Holdrege 2004: 238, 244–246.

77. Wujastyk 2004: 838.

References

Aṣṭāṅgahṛdaya Saṃhitā of Vāgbhaṭa. 2002 [1939]. *Aṣṭāṅgahṛdayam,* ed. Aṇṇā Moreśvara Kuṇṭe, Kṛṣṇaśāstrī Navare, and Hariśāstrī Parāḍakara. 9th ed. Includes the commentaries of Aruṇadatta and Hemādri. Varanasi: Chaukhambha Orientalia.

Aṣṭāṅgasaṃgraha Saṃhitā of Vāgbhaṭa. 1990 [1938–1940]. *Aṣṭāṅga Sangraha,* ed. Rāmacandraśāstrī Kiñjavaḍekara. 3 vols. Includes the *Śaśilekhā* of Indu. Reprint. Delhi: Sri Satguru Publications.

Bhela Saṃhitā. 2000. *Bhela-Saṃhitā*, ed. Priya Vrat Sharma. Includes English translation and commentary by K. H. Krishnamurthy. Varanasi: Chaukhambha Visvabharati.

Caraka Saṃhitā. 1992 [1941]. *Carakasaṃhitā of Agniveśa*, ed. Jādavjī Trikamjī. 5th ed. Includes the *Āyurvedadīpikā* of Cakrapāṇidatta. New Delhi: Munshiram Manoharlal.

Cerulli, Anthony. 2012. *Somatic Lessons: Narrating Patienthood and Illness in Indian Medical Literature*. Albany: State University of New York Press.

Cerulli, Anthony, and Brahmadathan U.M.T. 2009. "Know Thy Body, Know Thyself: Decoding Knowledge of the Ātman in Sanskrit Medical Literature." *Journal of Indian Medicine* 2, no. 3: 101–107.

Chattopadhyaya, Debiprasad. 1986. "Tradition of Rationalist Medicine in Ancient India: Case for a Critical Analysis of the *Caraka-saṃhitā*." In *Sanskrit and World Culture: Proceedings of the Fourth World Sanskrit Conference of the International Association of Sanskrit Studies, Weimar, May 23–30, 1979*, ed. Wolfgang Morgenroth, 85–115. Berlin: Akademie-Verlag.

Comba, Antonella. 2001 [1987]. "Carakasaṃhitā, Śārīrasthāna I and Vaiśeṣika Philosophy." In *Studies on Indian Medical History*, ed. G. Jan Meulenbeld and Dominik Wujastyk, 39–55. Reprint. Delhi: Motilal Banarsidass.

Dasgupta, Surendranath. 1968 [1932]. *A History of Indian Philosophy*. Vol. 2. Reprint. London: Cambridge University Press.

Engler, Steven. 2003. "'Science' vs. 'Religion' in Classical Ayurveda." *Numen* 50, no. 4: 416–463.

Holdrege, Barbara A. 2004. "Dharma." In *The Hindu World*, ed. Sushil Mittal and Gene Thursby, 213–248. New York: Routledge.

Kapani, Lakshmi. 1989a. "Note on the Garbha-Upaniṣad." In *Fragments for a History of the Human Body*, ed. Michel Feher, with Ramona Naddaff and Nadia Tazi, vol. 3, 180–196. New York: Zone Books.

Kapani, Lakshmi, trans. 1989b. "Upaniṣad of the Embryo." In *Fragments for a History of the Human Body*, ed. Michel Feher, with Ramona Naddaff and Nadia Tazi, vol. 3, 176–179. New York: Zone Books.

Kapstein, Matthew T. 2003 [2001]. *Reason's Traces: Identity and Interpretation in Indian and Tibetan Buddhist Thought*. Reprint. New Delhi: Oxford University Press.

Kāśyapa Saṃhitā. 1938. *Kāśyapasaṃhitā*, ed. Vaidya Jādavjī Trikamjī Āchārya and Somanāth Śarmā. Bombay: J. T. Acharya.

Kuriyama, Shigehisa. 2002 [1999]. *The Expressiveness of the Body and the Divergence of Greek and Chinese Medicine*. Reprint. New York: Zone Books.

Kuriyama, Shigehisa. 2007. "Pulse Diagnosis in the Greek and Chinese Traditions." In *Beyond the Body Proper: Reading the Anthropology of Material Life*, ed. Margaret Lock and Judith Farquhar, 595–607. Durham: Duke University Press.

Larson, Gerald James. 1983 [1980]. "Karma as a 'Sociology of Knowledge' or 'Social Psychology' of Process/Praxis." In *Karma and Rebirth in Classical*

Indian Traditions, ed. Wendy Doniger O'Flaherty, 303–316. Reprint. Delhi: Motilal Banarsidass.

Larson, Gerald James. 1987. "Āyurveda and the Hindu Philosophical Systems." *Philosophy East and West* 37, no. 3: 245–259.

Larson, Gerald James. 2005 [1969]. *Classical Sāṃkhya: An Interpretation of Its History and Meaning*. 2nd rev. ed. Reprint. Delhi: Motilal Banarsidass.

Marriott, McKim. 1976. "Hindu Transactions: Diversity without Dualism." In *Transaction and Meaning: Directions in the Anthropology of Exchange and Symbolic Behavior*, ed. Bruce Kapferer, 109–142. Philadelphia: Institute for the Study of Human Issues.

Mazars, Guy. 2006. *A Concise Introduction to Indian Medicine: La Médicine indienne*. Translated by T. K. Gopalan. Delhi: Motilal Banarsidass.

Meulenbeld, G. Jan. 1999–2002. *A History of Indian Medical Literature*. 5 vols. Groningen: Egbert Forsten.

Monier-Williams, Monier. 1997 [1872]. *A Sanskrit-English Dictionary*. Rev. ed. Reprint. Delhi: Motilal Banarsidass.

O'Flaherty, Wendy Doniger. 1976. *The Origins of Evil in Hindu Mythology*. Berkeley: University of California Press.

Olivelle, Patrick, trans. 1996. *Upaniṣads*. New York: Oxford University Press.

Ostwald, Martin, trans. 1962. *Nicomachean Ethics*. Indianapolis: Bobbs-Merrill.

Pintchman, Tracy. 1994. *The Rise of the Goddess in the Hindu Tradition*. Albany: State University of New York Press.

Samuel, Geoffrey. 1990. *Mind, Body and Culture: Anthropology and the Biological Interface*. Cambridge: Cambridge University Press.

Scharfe, Hartmut. 1999. "The Doctrine of the Three Humors in Traditional Indian Medicine and the Alleged Antiquity of Tamil Siddha Medicine." *Journal of the American Oriental Society* 119, no. 4: 609–629.

Singh, R. H. 1992. "Preventive and Social Medicine." In *History of Medicine in India: From Antiquity to 1000 AD*, ed. Priya Vrat Sharma. New Delhi: Indian National Science Academy.

Suśruta Saṃhitā. 2002. *Suśrutasaṃhitā of Suśruta*, ed. Jādavjī Trikamjī and Nārāyaṇa Rāma Ācārya. 7th ed. Includes the *Nibandhasaṃgraha* of Ḍalhaṇa and the *Nyāyacandrikā Pañjikā* of Gayadāsa on the Nidānasthāna. Varanasi: Chaukhambha Orientalia.

Thapar, Romila. 2002. *Early India: From the Origins to AD 1300*. London: Allen Lane.

Valiathan, M. S. 2003. *The Legacy of Caraka*. Chennai: Orient Longman.

White, David Gordon. 1996. *The Alchemical Body: Siddha Traditions in Medieval India*. Chicago: University of Chicago Press.

Wujastyk, Dominik. 2002. "Interpréter l'image du corps humain dans l'inde prémoderne." In *Images du corps dans le monde hindou*, ed. Véronique Bouillier and Gilles Tarabout, 71–99. Paris: CNRS Éditions.

Wujastyk, Dominik, trans. 2003 [1998]. *The Roots of Āyurveda: Selections from Sanskrit Medical Writings*. Rev. ed. New York: Penguin Books.

Wujastyk, Dominik. 2004. "Medicine and Dharma." *Journal of Indian Philosophy* 32, no. 5/6: 831–842.

Zimmermann, Francis. 1979. "Remarks on the Conception of the Body in Ayurvedic Medicine." *South Asian Digest of Regional Writing* 8: 10–26.

Zimmermann, Francis. 1980. "*Ṛtu-Sātmya*: The Seasonal Cycle and the Principle of Appropriateness." Translated by McKim Marriott and John Leavitt. *Social Science and Medicine. Part B: Medical Anthropology* 14, no. 2: 99–106.

Zimmermann, Francis. 1999 [1982]. *The Jungle and the Aroma of Meats: An Ecological Theme in Hindu Medicine*. Reprint. Delhi: Motilal Banarsidass.

Zimmermann, Francis. 2004. "'May Godly Clouds Rain for You!': Metaphors of Well-being in Sanskrit." *Studia Asiatica: International Journal for Asian Studies* 4/5: 371–382.

Zysk, Kenneth G. 1991. *Asceticism and Healing in Ancient India: Medicine in the Buddhist Monastery*. New York: Oxford University Press.

Chapter 3

Bodily Gestures and Embodied Awareness

Mudrā as the Bodily Seal of Being in the Trika Śaivism of Kashmir

KERRY MARTIN SKORA

This essay is a study of *mudrā* in the life-world of the Hindu tantric visionary Abhinavagupta (ca. 975–1025 CE), who lived in the vale of Kashmir approximately one thousand years ago. Abhinavagupta uses the term *mudrā* in two different senses: (1) *mudrā* as the bodily gestures that spontaneously manifest in the realized tantric master as the physical counterpart of his perfected state of nondual consciousness; and (2) the practice of *mudrā* as the formation of specific bodily gestures with the hands or other parts of the body in order to catalyze the realization of higher states of awareness. To evoke this intertwining of external gesture and internal states of awareness, I interpret *mudrā* as "bodily gesture that embodies awareness." Abhinavagupta's understanding of these bodily gestures shows that for him there is not a dualistic dichotomy between external bodily forms and internal states of awareness. The implication is that changes in awareness and processes of self-liberation are manifested in and through the body.

In this essay I will engage in a hermeneutical phenomenology in which I bring Abhinavagupta's understanding of *mudrā* into conversation with the phenomenology of the body articulated by the contemporary philosopher David Michael Levin in his notion of the "body's recollection of Being," which in turn builds on Maurice Merleau-Ponty's notion of the "lived body."[1] In the Trika Śaivism of Abhinavagupta, the Being that the body recollects in the highest state of realization is Śiva, the ultimate reality, which in its essential nature is infinite, unbounded, absolute consciousness. I will focus on a discussion of the thirty-second chapter of Abhinavagupta's magnum opus, *Tantrāloka* (Illumination of the Tantra), an encyclopedic synthesis of the discourse and practice of the Trika Śaivism of Kashmir, in which he lays out his understanding of *mudrā*s as gestures that embody awareness.[2] In this chapter Abhinavagupta focuses in particular on what he refers to as the most perfect of all *mudrā*s formed by the entire body, hands, speech, or mind, which empowers all other *mudrā*s: the *khecarī-mudrā*, or the "bodily gesture embodying the stance of flying through the void."[3] I will elucidate Abhinavagupta's understanding of embodied awareness as manifested by *mudrā* in two phases. In the first phase, I will focus on *mudrā* as mimetic image, which simultaneously reflects and gives rise to an awareness of Śiva-Who-Is-Being. In the second phase, I will examine the spontaneous *mudrā* of Abhinavagupta himself, his natural stance or manner of bearing, as depicted by his disciple Madhurāja (ca. 1000–1050 CE).

Mudrā as Mimetic Image

I will begin my analysis where Abhinavagupta begins: by ex-cave-ating, extracting from the deep void of the ground of reality, the layers and layers of meaning embodied in the term *mudrā*. I do this to emphasize my stance: to practice etymology (*nirvacana*) with Abhinavagupta is to recollect the embodied and sensuous nature of language. Levin presents etymology as bodily when he writes: "[W]hen words freely resonate, they are able to sublimate ego-logical sense and reactivate even their most ancient sensuous sense, an unconscious original sense full of creative powers."[4]

Other scholars who have written on *mudrā* have laboriously gone through the motions of reviewing the traditional etymologies associated with the term while not taking these etymologies seriously. Thus prior to deciphering etymologies of the term *mudrā*, including Abhinavagupta's, Dirk Jan Hoens dismisses their significance, telling his readers that these etymologies are both "incorrect" and "farfetched."[5] With a similar swipe, Jan Gonda, in his essay on *mudrā*, warns us that any etymologies of the term *mudrā* can only be false "pseudo-etymologies" that wither next to real "etymological," "semantic," and "historical" facts.[6] The hidden assumption of both Hoens and Gonda is that language is simply representational. Here I will take care to avoid superimposing this assumption on Abhinavagupta, who does not subscribe to such an analytical and conventional understanding of language. In Abhinavagupta's perspective language, rather than being analytical, is primordially poetic and revelatory, revealing the intertwining and interplaying of language and gesture, and gesture and reality, and is designed to lead others to deeper encounters with Being.[7]

The crux of the matter has been articulated by Levin. Do words simply represent or point to a reality out there that is completely separate from the words? Or might an "encounter" with language (and gesture, I suggest) evoke forceful experiences of reality, empowering us to "enter into an experience with truth"?[8] Unlike Hoens and Gonda, it is not Abhinavagupta's end to provide us with mere analytical representation in which words correspond in a conventional sense to the objects that they signify. Abhinavagupta's intention is rather to use language to empower each of his listeners in their flesh and bones to join him in the bodily experience of profound reality.

Such intention corresponds to Abhinavagupta's understanding of the revelatory nature of the Tantras.[9] The term *tantra,* from the Sanskrit root *tan,* "to extend or weave," evokes reality itself, a reality that is extensive or whose essence extends itself, continually repeating itself on different levels. The term *tantra* also evokes the image of "text," not only as a body of words but as something that is woven or con-structed and contains a deep structure. For Abhinavagupta *tantra* is the deep and text-ured reality-text, a great text-ile consisting of the warp and woof of consciousness and made up of layers upon layers of embodied meaning.[10] For Abhinavagupta the words and meanings of tantric discourses are revelations that flow directly from Śiva-Who-Is-Being and continue to participate in its power, enabling the resonant-hearted listener to recollect Being. Likewise, Abhinavagupta's own language is meant to empower the practitioner to move into deeper dimensions of reality.

Immediately at the beginning of the thirty-second chapter of the *Tantrāloka,* we enter the sensuous wordplay of Abhinavagupta, his playful and powerful use of language, as he moves both himself and his listener into a full-bodied awareness of Being. Abhinavagupta profoundly transforms ordinary discourse on the term *mudrā,* evoking the intertwining dynamics of gesture and awareness. This intertwining may be initially described as gesture giving rise to awareness and awareness giving rise to gesture.

Abhinavagupta, referring to the *Devyāyāmalatantra,* a Tantra that is no longer extant, first tells us that the nature of *mudrā* is *pratibimba,* "mimetic image." He then defines *pratibimba* as *bimbodaya,* a compound composed of two terms: *bimba,* "primordial image," and *udaya,* "arising." Abhinavagupta next unpacks the relationship between *pratibimba* and *bimba*, mimetic image and primordial image, in two different ways: "[T]he term *bimbodaya*, 'arising from the primordial image,' has two different meanings. [Thus] *mudrā* is *pratibimba* [in two different ways] because [1] it arises from the primordial image (*bimba*); [and] because [2] it [itself] is the source [the cause of arising] of the primordial image (*bimba*). . . ."[11] As mimetic image, on the one hand, *mudrā* arises out of authentic contact with Being, the primordial image. On the other hand, *mudrā* itself gives rise to an awareness of Being and is a source of return to the embodied recollection of Being. Thus *mudrā* as mimetic image evokes the intertwining dynamics of gesture as the authentic bodily response to Being and gesture as the catalyst that precipitates an awareness of Being. For Abhinavagupta *mudrā* is gesture that embodies awareness, where gesture and awareness are inextricably intertwined.

As a way of further emphasizing this intertwining relationship, in which *mudrā* as gesture embodies the awareness of Being out of which it arises and to which it returns, *mudrā* may also be interpreted as "bodily bearing of Being." With this phrase I want to evoke the layers of embodied meaning in the term "bearing" that Levin uncovers. The term "bearing," according to Levin, carries the sense of giving birth, gestating, bringing forth, and giving rise to. At the same time, the term "bearing" carries the sense of supporting and carrying. Levin's etymological excavation is part of his larger project that asks: How do our bodily motility and gestures bear Being? For Levin our gestures give birth to Being; they are the means of manifesting Being. At the same time, they carry, protect, and guard primordial Being. The sense here is that Being simultaneously precedes and depends on our gestures; our gestures are reflections of something deeper that is our very ground.[12]

Similarly, the implication of Abhinavagupta's formulation is that *mudrā* is the gesture that gives rise to an awareness of Being, while at the same time it is a reflection of Being, bearing its imprint. Abhinavagupta's understanding thus unpacks the deeper layers of meaning embedded in the literal sense of the term *mudrā*, which denotes a "seal" and which he interprets as the bodily seal that bears the impression of Being. Being's impression made on the body is what Levin refers to as the "call" or "claim" of Being. I would suggest that for Abhinavagupta *mudrā* bears the call of Being. The proper response of the individual is to guard, protect, and nurture this call. Being calls the individual precisely by means of the body, revealing itself through the process of "sealing" or marking the finite body with its imprint. In the paradoxical stance of Abhinavagupta's life-world, the finite body is called by the infinite Other, setting in motion the life-task of the individual to recollect Being.

In attempting to uncover the primordial roots of the human condition, Abhinavagupta thus reveals a dialectic between the finite body and the infinite Other.

The contemporary philosopher and Christian theologian Jean-Louis Chrétien, in his *The Call and the Response,* develops a theological phenomenology in which he poetically evokes the paradoxical relationship between the finite body and the infinite Other:

> When the entire body radiates and burns through this divine touch, it becomes song and word. Yet that which it sings with its entire being, collected whole and gathered up by the Other, is what it cannot say, what infinitely exceeds it—excess to which touch as such is destined, and which in the humblest sensation and least contact here below was already forever unsealed to us.[13]

Chrétien portrays the divine Other as being always already "unsealed" to us through the primordial touch of the divine.

Similarly, in Abhinavagupta's Trika Śaiva tradition, Śiva-Who-Is-Being "calls" the individual precisely by means of "touching" the body in the sense that it "unseals" or opens itself by "sealing" or binding the finite body with infinite consciousness. Thus Abhinavagupta's foremost disciple, Kṣemarāja (ca. 1000–1050 CE), recovers the meaning of *mudrā* as the "seal" or "stamp" that bears an impression. For Kṣemarāja *mudrā,* etymologically connected with the verb *mudrayati* (to seal, stamp, mark, impress, or imprint), means that which "seals" the universe, the phenomenal world of embodied forms, with the imprint of Being, infinite consciousness.[14] The implication here is that the finite body is claimed or called by Being. *Mudrā* is the bodily seal that bears the pattern of Being, while at the same time it unseals, opens up, or reveals. In this perspective the purpose of engaging in the practice of *mudrā* as a bodily technique is to precipitate bodily transformation, a new way of being in the body and comporting oneself in the body, thereby unsealing a dimension of reality that was previously hidden.[15] Such reality, according to Abhinavagupta, is in fact always already there, hidden in the body as a gift that the body is waiting to reveal. Thus Abhinavagupta tells us that *mudrā,* authentic gesture, gives the gift of the authentic Self by means of the body.[16]

For Abhinavagupta and the Trika Śaiva tradition, prior to and higher than any imprinting on the body by a hegemonic society—in particular, the brahmanical hegemony that sought to rule the body by means of purity laws involving "touch and touch-me-not"[17]—is the impression made on the body by Being, infinite consciousness. The human being is first claimed or called by Being, which marks itself on the very body of the individual. Thus the task of the tantric *sādhaka* (practitioner) is to take this impression seriously, to protect and guard this call, and to respond to the call by bodily recollecting Being's claim through the practice of *mudrā*, bodily gestures. Significantly, Abhinavagupta states in his final lines of the thirty-second chapter on *mudrā* that the practice of *mudrā* yields fruit and gives rise to higher states of awareness only when *mudrā*s are kept secret, well protected, or well guarded (*sugūḍha*).[18] By guarding and engaging the *mudrā*s, the *sādhaka* protects and nurtures Being, and in particular Being's call impressed on and through the body. Thus in both the opening and closing of his text on *mudrā*, Abhinavagupta evokes an intertwining relationship between gesture and awareness and between finite being and infinite Being.

These relationships form part of the pervasive nondual stance of Abhinavagupta's tradition and are connected in particular to the specific relationship between practice and goal, between individual effort and the supreme reality toward which effort is directed. In his eloquent essay on *mantra*, Harvey P. Alper points to Kṣemarāja's commentary on the *Śiva-Sūtra*,[19] where he cites a passage from the *Tantrasadbhāva*, a Tantra that is no longer extant, that evokes the intertwining relationship between the individual effort of the *sādhaka* and the reality that is his goal.

> Just as a hawk, hovering in the sky, notices his prey, my dear,
> And quickly, naturally, with a lunge, plucks it to himself (*akarṣayet*)
> A master yogi, in this very way, should send out (*vikarṣayet*) his mind to the foundation point (*bindu*);
> Just as an arrow placed on a bow flies [to its target] when it has been carefully shot (*yatnena ātāḍya*)
> So, Goddess, the foundation point flies [to the yogi] by means of his enunciation (*uccāra*) [of the mantra].[20]

Alper illuminates the "dialectical tact" of both this passage and Kṣemarāja's commentary on it: the *sādhaka* is not passive, yet at the same time his recitation of the *mantra* and other practices that form part of his *sādhana* are not determinative. Rather, as Alper suggests, the *sādhaka* elicits a response from the reality he seeks to realize. The practice of *mudrā*, like the practice of *mantra*, invites a bodily discipline of care, skill, and grace that is not ego-centered. Being precedes the practitioner, who moves toward Being, thus opening up a space for Being to reveal itself. In the passage cited by Kṣemarāja, we see that when the practitioner invokes the Goddess without calculation and without ego, she responds by flying to the practitioner.

For Abhinavagupta the relationship between bodily gesture and awareness is similarly circular. In Abhinavagupta's understanding of *mudrā*, bodily gestures are not merely external symbols that point to an inner state of awareness; rather, they body forth awareness as spontaneous manifestations of the internal state. Abhinavagupta's formulation resonates with the insights of the eco-philosopher David Abram, who elucidates Merleau-Ponty's understanding of gesture as the primordial language that bodies forth emotion into the world: "The gesture is spontaneous and immediate. It is not an arbitrary sign that we mentally attach to a particular emotion or feeling; rather, the gesture *is* the bodying-forth of that emotion into the world, it *is* that feeling of delight or of anguish in its tangible, visible aspect."[21]

While Abhinavagupta would concur with Abram's characterization of gesture as the bodying-forth of an internal state, in the final analysis his understanding of *mudrā* diverges from that of Abram, for he is not concerned with the bodying-forth of ordinary emotions. Rather, for Abhinavagupta *mudrā* is the bodying-forth of the perfected state of nondual consciousness, which finds spontaneous expression in the bodily comportment and gestures of the realized tantric master. It is these bodily gestures that are formalized and incorporated into the repertoire of *mudrā*s that are engaged by *sādhaka*s as part of their regimen of tantric practices on the path to realization. Paul Muller-Ortega comments:

> This understanding of spontaneously appearing mudrās provides us with what amounts to a Tantric theory of origin for mudrās. By implication, we can speculate that the strategic practice of mudrā appears to be the imitation of such gestures, stances, and poses. What had previously been observed in the posture and demeanor of the enlightened yogin as spontaneous manifestations of deep inner transformation are purposefully imitated by other yogins as a conscious stratagem for precipitating or reduplicating that very state of illuminated consciousness.[22]

Abhinavagupta's understanding of these two aspects of *mudrā*—(1) as the spontaneously manifested bodily gestures of a realized tantric master; and (2) as the strategic practice of imitating such bodily gestures in order to catalyze a state of consciousness comparable to that of the realized master—can be fruitfully compared to his understanding of the mechanisms of production and reception of a work of art by an inspired artist. Jan Gonda, in his classic work on the religious and artistic creative process, *The Vision of the Vedic Poets*,[23] connects Abhinavagupta's understanding of *dhyāna*, meditation, and *sahṛdayatva*, aesthetic sensibility, to the wider Indian understanding. Gonda emphasizes the importance of *dhyāna*, and more specifically meditative visualization, as essential to the artistic process.[24] According to the traditional Indian understanding of the visual arts, the ancient seers (*ṛṣis*) through their practice of meditation stationed their awareness in the heart (*hṛd* or *hṛdaya*), the innermost seat of consciousness, where they "saw" (root *dṛś*) the gods in their light-filled realms. They subsequently recorded their visions of the forms of the gods and thereby provided the paradigmatic models that visual artists who wish to create a sculpture or painting of a specific deity are expected to visualize while immersed in the depths of meditation. Through the process of meditative visualization, the inspired artist, like the ancient seers, establishes his awareness in the heart and attains a direct visionary experience in which he enters into communion with the deity who is the object of meditation. The artist then converts his visionary experience into an external work of art, thereby serving as a channel through which the deity finds manifest expression in a visible image.[25] The image of the deity in turn becomes an object of meditative visualization for the religious practitioner, serving as a basis through which he or she accesses the divine power originally experienced by the artist—a power not just represented but actually embodied as a *living presence* in the image. As Gonda notes, the work of art thus becomes a bearer of power.[26]

Gonda, in his analysis of the process of creation and reception of a work of art, explicitly invokes Abhinavagupta's understanding of aesthetics in which a person with aesthetic sensibility is called a *sahṛdaya*, one who is "possessed of heart" or who "has the same heart" as the inspired artist who produced the work of art and thus is able to identify with the artist's experience of the divine power that is embodied in the image. According to Abhinavagupta, the *sahṛdaya* encounters the external form that embodies the divine reality and thereby is able to access that reality.[27] I would emphasize here that such an encounter must naturally take place through the body and senses. In other words, the *sahṛdaya* uses both his external and internal bodily felt perception to tap into the heart of the artist and access the divine reality embodied in the image.

Gonda compares the process through which a work of art becomes a bearer of power with the mechanisms through which *mantras* become bearers of power. This is significant because for Abhinavagupta both *mantra* and *mudrā* embody power or vitality (*vīrya*). Just as a sculpted image is a bearer of power that can catalyze an awareness of the divine reality experienced by the original artist, *mudrā* as a strategic practice is a bearer of power that can catalyze an awareness of Being, nondual consciousness, experienced by the realized tantric master whose bodily gestures are being imitated.[28] What does it mean to say that gestures contain power? Such a notion is best interpreted phenomenologically, for the power of *mudrā* points to an experience in the body. Indeed, there is no *mudrā* without the body of a practitioner experiencing the *mudrā*. It makes no sense to posit a disembodied *mudrā*. *Mudrā* is phenomenological, not metaphysical, and thus self-realization for Abhinavagupta involves re-empowering the body and the senses. This re-empowerment is precisely what is effected by the power of external images and *mantras* used in ritual and in particular by the vitality of *mudrās*, bodily gestures. Abhinavagupta thus calls the practitioner back to the body: rather than disembodied concepts working on disembodied thinking and leading to disembodied beliefs, *mudrās* work at the preconceptual level of bodily felt sense. *Mudrās*, like *mantras* and other elements of tantric *sādhana*, are able to revitalize and liberate the very senses that have been previously deadened by enslavement to brahmanical laws of purity. *Mudrās* and *mantras* are efficacious because they are nondiscursive and work on the body directly and hence are able to effect transformations of awareness.[29] The vitality of *mudrās* and *mantras* awakens the senses of the practitioner, who ultimately recollects Being in the body. Thus Jayaratha (ca. 1225–1275 CE), in his famous commentary on the *Tantrāloka*, connects the vitality of the *khecarī-mudrā*—the most perfect of all bodily gestures in Abhinavagupta's perspective—with the vitality of *mantra*, both of which serve to catalyze an awareness of Being that is bodily felt in a variety of ways: "At the time of immersion in the *khecarī-mudrā*, . . . experiencing awareness, whose nature is [bodily felt] awareness, arises; such is the vitality of *mantra*, whose own nature is [bodily felt] awareness of the supreme resonance divided into eight kinds. . . ."[30]

I would like to conclude this section by recounting a story relevant to our understanding of the intertwining dynamics of gesture and awareness. This story is told by Lama Govinda in *The Way of the White Clouds*, his account of his famous pilgrimage to Tibet.[31] Govinda journeys to an ancient temple in order to trace its art frescoes of various Buddhas and Bodhisattvas and preserve them for posterity. He recounts his experience of tracing the frescoes:

> And as we traced . . . these frescoes . . . we began to experience the magic of these lines, which enshrined the heart-beat and the living devotion of the artists who had dedicated themselves to this work. Merely to trace these delicate lines accurately demanded the most intense concentration, and it was a strange sensation to relive the feelings and emotions of people who had lived almost a millennium before us. It was like entering their very bodies and personalities, their thoughts and feelings, and thus reliving their innermost life. It showed that not only inner emotion can be expressed by outer movement—be it in the form of brush-lines or in the movements of dance, gestures, *mudrās*, and *āsanas*—but that equally the faithful repetition of such outer movements could induce emotions and experiences similar to those which originally created those movements.[32]

In his account Govinda assumes the role of a religious *sahṛdaya* who not only visually relishes the frescoes of Buddhas and Bodhisattvas but also retraces the brushstrokes of the original artists, thereby becoming identified with the hearts of the artists and possessed, as it were, by their "bodies and personalities" and "thoughts and feelings." He suggests that the mode of being that he accesses through replicating their bodily movements is the very mode of being that was experienced by the original artists and that inspired their artistic visions. Govinda reveals the heart of the religious and artistic creative process as understood in the Indian tradition and as eloquently articulated by Abhinavagupta in particular.

Recollecting Abhinavagupta's Bodily Bearing

I turn now to a poem written by Madhurāja, a direct disciple of Abhinavagupta from the South Indian Śaiva center of Madurai. He was part of a tradition known as Anuttara, one of several systems taught by Abhinavagupta as part of the Trika Śaiva ensemble.[33] Through Abhinavagupta's description of *mudrā* we have seen that the practice of *mudrā* empowers one to enter a mode of being in communion with Śiva-Who-Is-Being. Inspired by Govinda, in this section I ask: How does Abhinavagupta's own disciple Madhurāja access the very body and personality, thought and feeling of Abhinavagupta, whom he revered as an incarnation of Śiva? How does his poetic evocation of Abhinavagupta's bodily bearing and gestures reflect the master's innermost life?

Madhurāja's poem, entitled *Dhyānaśloka* (Verses on Visualization [of Abhinavagupta]), consists of only four verses, yet it is detailed enough to have inspired an artist to recreate his vision of Abhinavagupta in the form of a painting. The painting itself became famous in circles of Abhinavagupta studies when it was included in the first edition of K. C. Pandey's foundational work *Abhinavagupta: An Historical and Philosophical Study*.[34] The poem is especially significant in giving us a sense of how one disciple experienced the embodied presence of his teacher, making Abhinavagupta come alive. In addition, the poem evokes an image of a perfected tantric master whose inner state of nondual consciousness is spontaneously manifested in his bodily demeanor, postures, and gestures.

In another text entitled *Gurunāthaparāmarśa* (Recollection of the Teacher-Lord), Madhurāja states that he came to master the universe following the practice of a system known as Anuttara.[35] Madhurāja's phrase "mastering the universe" is precise and not meant to be merely metaphorical. His word choice suggests, in accordance with Abhinavagupta's teaching, that enlightenment is not a disembodied cognitive process. For Madhurāja liberating transformation means gaining control of the powers, or *śakti*s, of the universe, through one's own bodily capacities and powers. Extending Merleau-Ponty, we can say that enlightened consciousness is not a matter of "I think that" but rather "I can."[36] In other words, for Madhurāja, as for his teacher Abhinavagupta, authentic awareness is not body-less cognition but rather is realized in/through/as one's very body.

Madhurāja's poem is the only writing we have that presents a vivid visualization of the great master Abhinavagupta. *Dhyāna*, meditative visualization, would have been a central practice for Madhurāja as an essential component of Abhinavagupta's system of *sādhana*, and it would have been performed in conjunction with *mantra* and *mudrā* practice. The practice involves meditative visualization of the body of a deity and is intended to culminate in identification with the deity in which the *sādhaka* comes to embody the deity's essential qualities. The centrality of *dhyāna* in Madhurāja's regimen of *sādhana* clearly suggests that he wrote the verses depicting the form of Abhinavagupta not merely to praise Abhinavagupta, nor simply as a way to preserve him in our visual memory, but rather to provide the basis for an extended meditation on the bodily comportment of the great master. Madhurāja's text provides a precise pattern for visualizing Abhinavagupta in meditation, as a means of embodying the essential qualities of Abhinavagupta, who is understood in turn as the very embodiment of Śiva. Thus the purpose of this text is to lead the practitioner of the meditative visualization to experience in his body nothing less than the presence of Śiva-Who-Is-Being manifesting as Abhinavagupta.

In the tantric practice of *dhyāna*, meditative visualization, exquisite attention is given to the bodily postures and hand gestures of the deity who is the object of meditation.[37] The *sādhaka* comes to embody the qualities of the deity through bodily mimesis, incorporating the deity's postures and gestures into his own body to the point of identifying with the body of the deity. The qualities of the deity, embodied in the deity's postures and gestures, are mimetically transferred to the body of the *sādhaka*, who comes to embody in his very postures and gestures the qualities of the deity.[38]

We are now in a position to fully appreciate the import of Madhurāja's poetic visualization of Abhinavagupta in which he tends properly to the lived body of his teacher. Like other seers and artists who are inspired by lived experience of the deep structures of reality and create forms to return one back to that experience, Madhurāja pays exquisite attention to the details of the postures and gestures of Abhinavagupta that are the externalized expressions of his nondual consciousness.[39]

In his poem *Dhyānaśloka*, Madhurāja describes a great religious gathering in an open arena, in the middle of a garden of grapes, where an overflowing ensemble of people come together to meet, dance, and listen to the words of the great Śaiva master Abhinavagupta.[40] He is their empowering center, sitting on a seat of gold, below which is soft ground and above which is a pearl-garlanded canopy. Abhinavagupta is surrounded by students led by his greatest disciple, Kṣemarāja, and all are gathered at Abhinavagupta's feet, with each student in a distinctive sitting position signifying an attentive heart. Men and women alike are gathered, and two female tantric partners are standing, flanking Abhinavagupta, each holding in one hand a vessel of the liquid bliss of Śiva (*śiva-rasa*)[41] and embracing with the other hand sweet limes and lotus blossoms.

Madhurāja's poem gives special attention to Abhinavagupta's facial expressions,[42] bodily appearance, and bodily attitude. Abhinavagupta's eyes are said to be subtly vibrating with joy. His forehead is marked by ashes with the three-lined symbol (*tilaka*) sealing him as a follower of Śiva, with one *rudrākṣa* bead radiating on his ear, a full head of hair entwined by flowers, and a long, full beard. His body is said to be illumined with a rosy, healthy glow. Interpreting this phenomenologically suggests that Madhurāja does not intend the references to light as mere metaphors. Abhinavagupta's presence is transmitted to Madhurāja as pure radiance that he experiences in his own body.[43]

Madhurāja's poem continues: Like blue-throated Śiva, Abhinavagupta's neck is a dark shining color, blessed with a fragrant ointment. He wears a sacred thread and is adorned in white silk that is dazzling like moonbeams. He simultaneously manifests restfulness and vitality, resting in *vīrāsana*, the yogic posture of the vital spiritual hero. The positions of Abhinavagupta's hands, down to his very fingertips, are also revealing for Madhurāja. One hand rests on his knee holding a rosary, manifesting the *mudrā* of embodying Śiva's direct awareness. The tip of the fingernail of his left hand vibrates, like a delicate flower blowing in the wind, and miraculously emits light as he gently plays the lute, striking it so as to make it resonate with the primordial hum of spontaneous resonance (*dhvani*). Finally, Madhurāja proclaims that this person is the very embodiment of Śiva, who has come to this particular place, the land of Kashmir, to bless others with his deep compassion. Śiva takes on bodily form in the person of Abhinavagupta so that those present can encounter him face-to-face, as Madhurāja says, right before their very own eyes.

Thus the bodily presence of his master is evoked by Madhurāja. The presencing of Abhinavagupta breaks down the distinction between external expression and internal awareness, for his bodily comportment is the manifest counterpart of his nondual consciousness. Madhurāja tends to the motility and stances of both Abhinavagupta and those who surround him, their locations, their physical presence and activities, and the objects they hold and embrace. The subtle vibrations and radiance emanating from Abhinavagupta's body; the manner in which he rests, sits, and sets down his hands and fingers; his position in the environment, orientation in relation to sky and earth, and poised stance of perfect equilibrium in the center—the details of Madhurāja's portrait converge to reveal that Abhinavagupta's very postures and gestures embody the attitude of enlightened consciousness. In Madhurāja's evocation Abhinavagupta's motility and gestures are centered, graceful, and compassionate—a spontaneous manifestation of his nondual consciousness in which he is none other than Śiva-Who-Is-Being.[44] Abhinavagupta's manner of carrying himself impresses Madhurāja, inspiring him to carefully and mimetically record, in bodily communion with Abhinavagupta, his vision of the bodily markings, postures, and gestures of the perfected tantric master who is none other than Śiva himself embodied in human form.

Notes

1. Levin's writings (1985, 1988, 1989) provide deep inspiration for my methodology. I emphasize that what Abhinavagupta has to say is unique and valuable in itself. Levin's work is helpful for approaching Abhinavagupta not because of any specific theory, worldview, or metaphysics, and not because of saying something that Abhinavagupta is unable to, but rather because his methodology aids us in accessing what Abhinavagupta has already been revealing and that otherwise might remain concealed if it were approached as an abstract metaphysics rather than as a phenomenology of experience. For further unpacking and justification of this Levinian methodology, see Skora 2007b.

2. For previous work on the thirty-second chapter of the *Tantrāloka*, see Padoux 1990; Muller-Ortega 2000. I am grateful to both of these brilliant scholars whose work has helped me in my own thinking about Abhinavagupta's life-world. Where I differ I believe is in employing a hermeneutical phenomenology to recover Abhinavagupta's understanding of the "lived body."

3. *Tantrāloka* 32.9b–10a: "*Mudrā* is fourfold, according to the divisions of body (*kāya*), hands (*karas*), speech (*vāc*), and mind (*citta*). I will describe just the *khecarī-mudrā*, its form being perfect among them."

4. Levin 1977: 234.

5. Gupta, Hoens, and Goudriaan 1979: 116.

6. Gonda 1972: 21.

7. See Kahrs 1998: 55–97 for a critique of scholarship that fails to appreciate the subtleties and creativity of the Indian tradition of semantic analysis and for an alternative appreciation of the powerful hermeneutics involved in Abhinavagupta's own practice of etymology.

8. Levin 1988: 422.

9. The rest of this paragraph is an abridgement and slight modification of a paragraph found in Skora 2001: 7–8.

10. Abhinavagupta's approach is not entirely his own. He is building on and elaborating a fundamentally Indic pattern. This is understood well by Calasso (1999) in his treatment of Hindu mythological material in which meaning is revealed through the crossing and overlapping of multiple layers and dimensions of narratives and images.

11. *Tantrāloka* 3.1a–2b.

12. Levin's creative etymology of "bearing" that I have summarized here is found in Levin 1985: 91. The etymology forms the basis of his thinking on

the intertwining of Being and the body that bears Being. See esp. his chapter "The Bearing of Thought" in Levin 1985: 90–166.

13. Chrétien 2004: 131.

14. I borrow the term "seal" from Singh 1990. This term happily evokes the dialectic of the two-way process of the finite-infinite encounter: the finite body going beyond itself toward the infinite Other, and the infinite Other coming out of itself to make its mark on the finite body. The finite is sealed, but it is sealed with a blessing of infinite consciousness revealing or unsealing itself. A similar dialectic between finite and infinite may be found in Tibetan Buddhist rDzogs-chen interpretations of *mudrā* (Tibetan *phyag-rgya*). See, for example, Guenther 1984: 127–132, 272 n. 21. See also Gonda 1972: 27 for a discussion of *mudrā* as a seal that opens up the hidden secret for initiates while closing out intruders.

15. See also Alper 1989: 276.

16. *Tantrāloka* 32.3.

17. Lannoy 1971: 54. For a discussion of Abhinavagupta's life-world as an embodied response to a brahmanical hegemony that attempted to contain the body and the senses, see Skora 2007b, 2009.

18. *Tantrāloka* 32, closing verse (not numbered).

19. The *Śiva-Sūtra* (ca. ninth century CE) is the foundational text of Abhinavagupta's Trika Śaiva tradition and is traditionally understood to have been revealed to the sage Vasugupta.

20. *Tantrasadbhāva* excerpt cited by Kṣemarāja in his *Śivasūtravimarśinī*, commentary on *Śiva-Sūtra* 2.2, trans. Alper 1989: 261; cf. 288 n. 31 (Sanskrit).

21. Abram 1996: 74.

22. Muller-Ortega 2000: 581.

23. Gonda 1963.

24. Such meditative visualization is as important to Abhinavagupta's tantric tradition as it is to the artistic traditions. In the tantric tradition *dhyāna* is performed in conjunction with both *mantra* practice and *mudrā* practice, and thus tantric performance is a full-bodied performance, involving a fusion of the senses of vision, hearing, and touching. On the fusion of the senses as essential to the tantric performance of the cosmic body (*kula-yāga*) and the embodied recollection attained therein, see Skora 2007b: 438–442. On *maṇḍala* practice as a multisensory and full-bodied performance, see Skora 2009.

25. The artist, by becoming a channel of the deity, thereby embodies the "otherness" of the divine power. See the discussions of "embodied otherness" by Csordas (2002: 82–83; 2001: 238–241), the noted anthropologist of the body.

26. Here I am summarizing and extending Gonda's insights in 1963: 61–64. While I often put his insights into my own language to connect to the rest of the essay, I have not changed the essence of his insights. For Gonda's discussion of the heart as the seat of consciousness in Indian thought, see 1963: 276–288. For a phenomenological approach to the phenomenon of the heart, see Strasser 1977.

27. See Gonda 1963: 63, 287–288.

28. For Abhinavagupta, who freely fuses together religious vision and artistic vision, the highest form of awareness is identification with Śiva-Who-Is-Being. Identification with Being requires the dissolving of boundaries between the finite self and infinite Other, the dissolution of ego-consciousness in order to enter into a state of nondual identity with Being. Regarding the intersections of Abhinavagupta's tantric vision and his philosophy of aesthetics, see Masson and Patwardhan 1969: 38–43, where they translate the *Dhyānaśloka* by Madhurāja that I will interpret in terms of the lived body in the next section of this essay. See also Gnoli 1968: xxvii–lii; Larson 1976; Wulff 1986; Goodwin 1995; Skora 2007a.

29. See Staal's (1989: 84) interpretation of *mantra* in terms of the lived body in response to brahmanical rigidity. The material in this paragraph is taken from Skora 2007b: 442–446, where I give a more extensive analysis of vitality as pertaining to the lived body.

30. Jayaratha, *Tantrālokaviveka*, commentary on *Tantrāloka* 29.158a.

31. Govinda 1970.

32. Govinda 1970: 237.

33. Sanderson 1990: 80.

34. Pandey 1963.

35. Sanderson 1990: 80.

36. Merleau-Ponty 1962: 137. Both Jackson (1996: 31–32) and Stoller (1998: 251–252) build on Merleau-Ponty's development of this insight in constructing their phenomenological anthropologies. See also Skora 2009.

37. For Gonda's comments on *dhyāna*, see 1963: 289–301. For examples of meditative visualizations of deities in Abhinavagupta's tradition, see Sanderson 1990.

38. See Taussig 1993; Csordas 2002; Skora 2009. In Skora 2009 I extend the creative "body work" of Taussig and Csordas, suggesting that tantric ritual involves the "mimetic transfer" of vitality, giving rise to a bodily felt experience in the disciple and substantially connecting him to his *guru* and to Śiva.

39. For a similar practice recently presented by the Tibetan Buddhist teacher Tarthang Tulku, which is designed to connect the lived body of the practitioner with the "living presence" of the master Longchenpa, see Tulku 2007: 34–35.

40. Here and in the following paragraphs I am presenting a paraphrase that encapsulates my interpretation of the *Dhyānaśloka*. This is based on my previous translation of the verses in Skora 2001: 11–13, which was partly inspired by the earlier translations of Pandey (1963: 21–22) and Masson and Patwardhan (1969: 38–39). The Sanskrit of the text may be found in Pandey 1963: 738.

41. This reference to *śiva-rasa* connects the gathering to a tantric ritual. For more on *śiva-rasa*, liquid bliss, see Skora 2001: 419–426.

42. According to Ekman, the world's foremost expert on facial expressions, the current Dalai Lama uses his facial expressions more fully and in a more complex manner than anyone else he has studied in forty years (Iyer 2008: 21–22). We would only find it natural that the Dalai Lama's facial expressions, like those of Abhinavagupta according to Madhurāja, correspond to a life dedicated to

developing wisdom and compassion. Ekman's research (2007) demonstrates the intimate relationship between, on the one hand, external facial movements and physiology, and, on the other hand, internal sensations and awareness.

43. On the luminous intensity of the teacher image in Tibetan Buddhism, see Guenther 1994: 36. On the Self as a body of light and the embodied experience of radiant beings and bodies, see Guenther 1994: 56–57; Levin 1988: 389–390, 447–453.

44. My remarks here are inspired by the bodily felt language of Levin. Especially relevant to my concluding remarks here is his discussion of the body in relation to individuation and his summary table relating the qualities of motility to development, personality, and encounters with Being (Levin 1985: 90–114).

References

Abram, David. 1996. *The Spell of the Sensuous: Perception and Language in a More-Than-Human-World*. New York: Vintage Books.

Alper, Harvey P. 1989. "The Cosmos as Śiva's Language-Game: 'Mantra' According to Kṣemarāja's *Śivasūtravimarśinī*." In *Mantra*, ed. Harvey P. Alper, 249–294. Albany: State University of New York Press.

Calasso, Roberto. 1999 [1998]. *Ka: Stories of the Minds and Gods of India*. Translated by Tim Parks. New York: Vintage International.

Chrétien, Jean-Louis. 2004 [1992]. *The Call and the Response*. Translated by Anne A. Davenport. New York: Fordham University Press.

Csordas, Thomas J. 2001. *Language, Charisma, and Creativity: Ritual Life in the Catholic Charismatic Renewal*. New York: Palgrave.

Csordas, Thomas J. 2002. *Body/Meaning/Healing*. New York: Palgrave Macmillan.

Ekman, Paul. 2007 [2003]. *Emotions Revealed: Recognizing Faces and Feelings to Improve Communication and Emotional Life*. New York: Henry Holt.

Gnoli, Raniero. 1968 [1956]. *The Aesthetic Experience According to Abhinavagupta*. 2nd ed. rev. Varanasi: Chowkhamba Sanskrit Series Office.

Gonda, J. 1963. *The Vision of the Vedic Poets*. The Hague: Mouton.

Gonda, J. 1972. "Mudrā." In *Ex Orbe Religionum: Studia Geo Widengren*, vol. 2, 21–31. Leiden: E. J. Brill.

Goodwin, Robert E. 1995. "The Play World of Sanskrit Poetry." In *The Gods at Play: Līlā in South Asia*, ed. William S. Sax, 50–86. New York: Oxford University Press.

Govinda, Anagarika Lama. 1970 [1966]. *The Way of the White Clouds: A Buddhist Pilgrim in Tibet*. Berkeley: Shambhala.

Guenther, Herbert V. 1984. *Matrix of Mystery: Scientific and Humanistic Aspects of rDzogs-chen Thought*. Boulder: Shambhala.

Guenther, Herbert V. 1994. *Wholeness Lost and Wholeness Regained: Forgotten Tales of Individuation from Ancient Tibet*. Albany: State University of New York Press.

Gupta, Sanjukta, Dirk Jan Hoens, and Teun Goudriaan. 1979. *Hindu Tantrism*. Leiden: E. J. Brill.

Iyer, Pico. 2008. *The Open Road: The Global Journey of the Fourteenth Dalai Lama*. New York: Alfred A. Knopf.

Jackson, Michael. 1996. "Introduction: Phenomenology, Radical Empiricism, and Anthropological Critique." In *Things as They Are: New Directions in Phenomenological Anthropology*, ed. Michael Jackson, 1–50. Bloomington: Indiana University Press.

Kahrs, Eivind. 1998. *Indian Semantic Analysis: The 'Nirvacana' Tradition*. Cambridge: Cambridge University Press.

Lannoy, Richard. 1971. *The Speaking Tree: A Study of Indian Culture and Society*. London: Oxford University Press.

Larson, Gerald James. 1976. "The Aesthetic (*Rasāsvāda*) and the Religious (*Brahmāsvāda*) in Abhinavagupta's Kashmir Śaivism." *Philosophy East and West* 26, no. 4: 371–387.

Levin, David Michael. 1977. "The Phenomenon and Noumenon of Language: The Twin Paths of *Mantra* (Perfect Speaking) and *Mudra* (Perfect Writing)." *TriQuarterly* 38: 229–255.

Levin, David Michael. 1985. *The Body's Recollection of Being: Phenomenological Psychology and the Deconstruction of Nihilism*. London: Routledge and Kegan Paul.

Levin, David Michael. 1988. *The Opening of Vision: Nihilism and the Postmodern Situation*. London: Routledge.

Levin, David Michael. 1989. *The Listening Self: Personal Growth, Social Change and the Closure of Metaphysics*. London: Routledge.

Masson, J. L., and M. V. Patwardhan. 1969. *Śāntarasa and Abhinavagupta's Philosophy of Aesthetics*. Poona: Bhandarkar Oriental Research Institute.

Merleau-Ponty, Maurice. 1962 [1945]. *Phenomenology of Perception*. Translated by Colin Smith. London: Routledge and Kegan Paul.

Muller-Ortega, Paul E. 2000. "On the Seal of Śambhu: A Poem by Abhinavagupta." In *Tantra in Practice*, ed. David Gordon White, 573–586. Princeton: Princeton University Press.

Padoux, André. 1990. "The Body in Tantric Ritual: The Case of the Mudrās." In *The Sanskrit Tradition and Tantrism*, ed. Teun Goudriaan, 66–75. Leiden: E. J. Brill.

Pandey, Kanti Chandra. 1963 [1935]. *Abhinavagupta: An Historical and Philosophical Study*. Varanasi: Chowkhamba Sanskrit Series Office.

Sanderson, Alexis. 1990. "The Visualization of the Deities of the Trika." In *Image Divine, Culte et Méditation dans l'Hindouisme*, ed. André Padoux, 31–88. Paris: Centre National de la Recherche Scientifique.

Singh, Jaideva, trans. 1990. *The Doctrine of Recognition: A Translation of Pratyabhijñāhṛdayam [by Kṣemarāja] with an Introduction and Notes*. Albany: State University of New York Press.

Skora, Kerry Martin. 2001. "Consciousness of Consciousness: Reflexive Awareness in the Trika Śaivism of Abhinavagupta." PhD diss., University of Virginia.

Skora, Kerry Martin. 2007a. "Abhinavagupta's Aesthetics of Touch: Synaesthetic Awareness and Lucid Dream-Play." Fifth Conference of the Dharma Association of North America. San Diego, November 16–18.

Skora, Kerry Martin. 2007b. "The Pulsating Heart and Its Divine Sense Energies: Body and Touch in Abhinavagupta's Trika Śaivism." *Numen: International Review for the History of Religions* 54, no. 4: 420–458.

Skora, Kerry Martin. 2009. "The Hermeneutics of Touch: Uncovering Abhinavagupta's Tactile Terrain." *Method and Theory in the Study of Religion* 21, no. 1: 87–106.

Staal, Frits. 1989. "Vedic Mantras." In *Mantra,* ed. Harvey P. Alper, 48–95. Albany: State University of New York Press.

Stoller, Paul. 1998. "Rationality." In *Critical Terms for Religious Studies,* ed. Mark C. Taylor, 239–255. Chicago: University of Chicago Press.

Strasser, Stephan. 1977. *Phenomenology of Feeling: An Essay on the Phenomena of the Heart.* Pittsburgh: Duquesne University Press.

Tantrāloka of Abhinavagupta. 1987 [1918–1938]. *The Tantrāloka of Abhinavagupta with the Commentary [Tantrālokaviveka] of Jayaratha,* ed. R. C. Dwivedi and Navajivan Rastogi. 8 vols. Delhi: Motilal Banarsidass.

Taussig, Michael. 1993. *Mimesis and Alterity: A Particular History of the Senses.* New York: Routledge.

Tulku, Tarthang. 2007. "Introduction: All Knowledge, All Light." In Longchenpa, *Now That I Come to Die: Intimate Guidance from One of Tibet's Greatest Masters,* 9–35. Berkeley: Dharma Publishing.

Wulff, Donna. 1986. "Religion in a New Mode: The Convergence of the Aesthetic and the Religious in Medieval India." *Journal of the American Academy of Religion* 54, no. 4: 673–688.

Chapter 4

Bodied, Embodied, and Reflective Selves

Theorizing Performative Selfhood in South Indian Performance

HARSHITA MRUTHINTI KAMATH

The presence, absence, or partial existence of the self has been the focus of much debate for cultural anthropologists and scholars of religion studying Hindu traditions in the South Asian context. Spanning from the classical formulations of Louis Dumont and McKim Marriott to the more recent research of Isabelle Nabokov, anthropologists studying the Indian subcontinent continue to ponder the topic of selfhood. When defining the self in the Indian context, Dumont (1970, 1986) deconstructs the possibility of individuality, Marriott (1976) suggests a notion of dividual personhood, and Nabokov (2000) posits a ritually fragmented self. More recently, Frederick Smith's (2006) extensive analysis of possession in South Asia contributes to this discussion by distinguishing the self as ontologically separate from personhood.

In this essay I engage with such scholarly constructions of the self, specifically by utilizing the lenses of body and performance. I will analyze the ways in which performance demonstrates the presence of the self by asking, Does the self of the performer exist during the performative moment, and, if so, how does this self influence the body of the performer? In order to answer these questions, I will examine two case studies of South Indian performance: possession in the Tamil ritual context and the genre of South Indian classical dance, specifically focusing on the forms of Kathakali and Kuchipudi. Through analyses of these performative contexts, I will argue for the presence of a lingering self during South Indian performance that paradoxically constructs and is constructed by the body of the performer.

Scholarly Constructions of the Self

Before turning to an analysis of my own theory of performative selfhood, I will briefly highlight the contributions of Dumont, Marriott, Nabokov, and Smith to scholarly reflections on the self in South Asia.

According to the classical articulations of Dumont, the concept of selfhood in Western society is that of an individual self. In contrast, due to the hierarchical relationality of the caste system, such notions of individuality are significantly absent within the Indian framework. Thus, in an early essay on Indian religions, Dumont argues:

> To say that the world of caste is a world of relations is to say that the particular caste and the particular man have no substance: they exist empirically, but they have no reality in thought, no Being. . . . I regard it as fundamental and would therefore firmly posit, at the risk of being crude, that on the level of life in the world the [Indian] individual is not.[1]

In later discussions on the same topic, Dumont describes India as a hierarchically defined, holistic society that "valorizes the social whole and neglects or subordinates the human individual."[2] For Dumont, a person existing within the hierarchical caste-driven framework of Indian society lacks the capacity for individual selfhood.

As an alternative approach to understanding the Indian self, Marriott argues for the notion of "dividual" personhood. He formulates his notion of dividual as part of his transactional model of caste interactions that involves the transfer of bodily substance-codes through the exchange of food, services, and women in marriage.

> It appears that persons are generally thought by South Asians to be "dividual" or divisible. To exist, dividual persons absorb heterogeneous material influences. They must also give out from themselves particles of their own coded substances—essences, residues, or other active influences—that may then reproduce in others something of the nature of the persons in whom they have originated. Persons engage in transfer of

bodily substance-codes through parentage, through marriage, and through other kinds of interpersonal contact.[3]

In *Religion Against the Self: An Ethnography of Tamil Rituals*, Nabokov attempts to counter both Dumont's and Marriott's claims through her work on ritual possession in the South Indian state of Tamil Nadu. By analyzing possession in the Tamil context, Nabokov argues that while the individual person within Tamil society does exist, ritual functions to split apart a holistic notion of this person's selfhood. For Nabokov, the "fundamental subject of Tamil religion is identity. . . . [However], far from integrating or reintegrating people, Tamil rituals may fragment them to the point of splitting them apart."[4]

My concern with all three of these theorists is that they effectively deconstruct the possibility for individual selfhood within the South Asian context. With respect to Dumont and Marriott, both scholars participate in the essentializing project of positing individualism as somehow unique to modern Western discourses and thereby antithetical to an Indian worldview. Dumont defines the individual as "the independent, autonomous *moral* and, thus, essentially non-social being, as encountered first of all in our modern ideology of man and society."[5] Similarly, Marriott states that "persons—single actors—are not thought in South Asia to be 'individual,' that is indivisible, bounded units, as they are in much of Western social and psychological theory as well as in common sense."[6] These essentializing notions of the individual self as inextricably Western in nature preclude the possibility of selfhood in the Indian context. As a result of this essentialism, Dumont is unable to grant the Indian person individual existence, while the most Marriott can bestow is a dividual reality.[7]

Nabokov critiques both Dumont and Marriott for their "ethnocentric" and "essentialist" claims. She depicts Dumont's research as "plain wrong, as contemporary writers have found that the very people who had been the focus of Dumont's extensive ethnographic research apparently do recognize individuality as an essential feature of ordinary life."[8] Nabokov critiques Marriott's notion of dividual personhood by stating that "such a volatile person remains within the legacy of Western assumptions about bounded, united, and essentialist selves. For he or she strives to retain a sense of wholeness or absolute identity by means of ritual action."[9] Even in light of such critiques, Nabokov herself falls into the trap of essentialism by essentializing Tamil ritual practice as inherently violent toward the self. She describes the relationships constructed through Tamil rituals as "dangerously encroaching, even physically threatening, to the Tamil self."[10] Due to Nabokov's preoccupation with ritual violence, she ultimately fails to recognize the resilience possible within the Tamil selves she studies. She overlooks the possibility that although some Tamil possession rituals may threaten divisiveness, they may not always succeed in fragmenting the self.

In Smith's extended study of possession, *The Self Possessed: Deity and Spirit Possession in South Asian Literature and Civilization,* he proposes a useful distinction between the notions of the person and the self in the South Asian context by arguing that while the person is culturally constructed, the self is internally realizable. For Smith, "the culturally constituted Indic notion of selfhood is of a self that is not culturally constructed; it is of a preobjective self that is free of cultural constructions of the world."[11] In this context he frames Marriott's notion of bodily substance-codes as pertaining to the realm of personhood rather than to the self. Central to Smith's analysis of selfhood is his use of the indigenous categories of *puruṣa/puruṣottama* and *ātman/brahman.* He argues that personhood finds salience in the distinction of *puruṣa/puruṣottama,* while selfhood is articulated through the philosophical concepts of *ātman/brahman*. Drawing on Sanskrit literary sources, Smith defines *puruṣa* as "man" or "person" and *puruṣottama* as the "highest person" who encompasses all of materiality. Through the dyad of *puruṣa/puruṣottama,* Smith argues that personhood in the Indian context "is a manifestation of form, attribute, substance, and materiality."[12] In contrast to this materially based interpretation of personhood, Smith utilizes the indigenous categories of *ātman/brahman* to justify an autonomous notion of Indian selfhood. In line with Upaniṣadic interpretations, Smith defines *ātman* as the "thumb-sized person" that resides in the heart and *brahman* as the "absolute macrocosmic" principle. Smith goes on to argue that although *ātman* is tied to the body, it "is separate from substance and substantiality. It is free and autonomous."[13] The notion of *ātman,* which is the microcosmic counterpart of the macrocosmic *brahman,* exemplifies for Smith the Indian conception of the self.

Smith's nuanced analysis of the distinction between person and self is illuminating for our discussion of selfhood in the South Asian context. This essay builds on Smith's analysis by examining the distinction between person and self through the lens of performance. It is important to note that while Smith utilizes the person/self distinction as an analytical framework to examine possession within the South Asian context, he maintains that possession "directly engages and affects the person"[14] and only indirectly touches on the realm of the self. For Smith, possession functions within the sphere of the person, not the realm of the self, and he is therefore "careful to keep discussion of possession within the domain of personhood."[15] It is with reference to this latter claim that I depart from Smith's work. Instead of marginalizing the notion of selfhood in the performance of possession, as well as other performative contexts in India, my analysis foregrounds the role of the self during the moment of performance. Moreover, by focusing on the role of the body, I reframe Smith's person/self distinction as a body/self dichotomy, which I suggest is a more fruitful lens through which to examine selfhood within the performative realm. In what follows I hope to demonstrate the existence of selfhood within Indian performance by providing an extended analysis of the self's relationship to the body.

A Theory of Performative Selfhood: Beyond *Rasa* Theory

I propose a theory of performative selfhood that can provide a useful analytical framework for examining the interactions of body and self in South Indian performance. Integral to my theory of performative selfhood are three categories: the bodied self, the embodied self, and the reflective self. I define the *bodied self* as a visual selfhood expressed through the physical body of the performer. The characteristics that mark the performer's bodied self include, but are not limited to, costume, makeup, and bodily gestures. The second category is the *embodied self*, or the constellation of psychoemotional faculties residing within the corporeal form of the bodied self. This embodied self can utilize the physical aspects of the bodied self as a medium for expression, as in the cases of possession and classical dance that I will discuss in the following sections of this essay. Finally, the third category is the *reflective self*, or the self-conscious faculty that exists independent of the performer's body but has the ability to observe, reflect upon, and control both bodied and embodied selves. By examining all three categories of performative selfhood together, we can trace a path from outward to inward realms: selfhood transitions from external bodied appearance, to internal embodied psychoemotional states, to the reflective self beyond embodiment.

Before turning to the specific case studies in which these three categories find meaning, it is important to distinguish my theory of performative selfhood from the categories of Indian aesthetics. Bharata's *Nāṭya-Śāstra* (ca. early centuries CE), the foundational text of Indian aesthetics, describes the dramaturgical implications of the concept of *rasa*. *Rasa*, aesthetic enjoyment, according to Bharata, is the primary objective of dramatic performance, which arises in the audience members when accomplished actors successfully reproduce on stage the particular *sthāyi-bhāva*, abiding emotion, that the dramatist intends to evoke through the play. Bharata enumerates the eight fundamental types of emotions, or *sthāyi-bhāva*s, as love (*rati*), humor (*hāsa*), sorrow (*śoka*), anger (*krodha*), courage (*utsāha*), fear (*bhaya*), disgust (*jugupsā*), and wonder (*vismaya*). The eight corresponding *rasa*s are erotic (*śṛṅgāra*), comic (*hāsya*), tragic (*karuṇa*), furious (*raudra*), heroic (*vīra*), terrifying (*bhayānaka*), disgusting (*bībhatsa*), and wondrous (*adbhuta*).

In a well-known passage from the *Nāṭya-Śāstra*, Bharata mentions the key aesthetic components that the master dramatist combines in order to evoke a particular *sthāyi-bhāva*, abiding emotion, and elicit the corresponding *rasa*, which is savored by sensitive audience members as the distilled essence of the emotion: "From the combination of the *vibhāva*s, the *anubhāva*s, and the *vyabhicāribhāva*s, *rasa* is created."[16] The *vibhāva*s are the stimulants, such as the qualities of the hero and heroine and the time frame and setting of the play, that serve to enliven the audience members' appreciation of the *sthāyi-bhāva*. The *anubhāva*s are the bodily manifestations, including speech, gestures, and movements, through which the performer suggests the presence of the *sthāyi-bhāva*. The *vyabhicāri-bhāva*s are transitory emotions, such as confusion or envy, that may accompany the *sthāyi-bhāva*. Through the skillful deployment of the *vibhāva*s, *anubhāva*s, and *vyabhicāri-bhāva*s, the performer is able to foster in the audience members an appreciation of the *sthāyi-bhāva* and an experience of the *rasa*, the distilled essence of the emotion.[17]

As suggested by Bharata's articulation of *rasa* theory, the *anubhāva*s are the physical expressions that are externally enacted by the performer's body; the *sthāyi-bhāva*s and *vyabhicāri-bhāva*s are the emotions, whether abiding or transitory, that are experienced internally within the performer's body; and the savoring of the *rasa* is a distilled experience of the *sthāyi-bhāva* that transcends bodily experience.[18] This progression in classical Indian aesthetics corresponds to the progression in my theory of performative selfhood: the bodied self of the performer expresses the physical characteristics of the corporeal, the embodied self reflects the performer's internal emotions within the corporeal, and the reflective self transcends such corporeal constraints.

Despite these resonances, my theory of performative selfhood is distinct from Indian aesthetic theories of *rasa* with regard to two important issues: the location of aesthetic experience and the role of individual subjective experience. With regard to the first issue, a great deal of commentary has been dedicated to answering the question, Where is *rasa* located during the moment of performance? Although Bharata himself suggests in the *Nāṭya-Śāstra* that the experience of *rasa* is limited to refined audience members, Bhaṭṭa Lollaṭa, the ninth-century commentator on the *Nāṭya-Śāstra,* maintains that *rasa* is located in the accomplished actor who is able to identify completely with the character he or she is embodying during the performance.[19] Abhinavagupta, the eminent eleventh-century exponent of Kashmir Śaiva traditions who is acclaimed as the principal spokesman of the dominant school of Indian aesthetics, counters this possibility in his *Dhvanyāloka-Locana* by limiting the experience of *rasa* to *sahṛdaya*s, sensitive persons of refined taste who view the performance. David Haberman observes:

> Abhinavagupta refuses to grant the aesthetic experience of *rasa* to the actor. The actor is too close, too technically involved, for Abhinava to permit him to have the experience of *rasa*. . . . Abhinava is insistent . . . that only the spectator who has the proper "artistic distance" and can truly let go of the ordinary world, can experience the mysterious delight of *rasa*. Though he never states so directly, his theory that *rasa* exists only in art implies that the original character, along with the actor, is also denied the experience of *rasa*.[20]

Due to Abhinavagupta's significant influence on Indian aesthetic theories, many later theorists limit the experience of *rasa* to refined audience members. Haberman argues against this overarching impact of Abhinavagupta by raising the example of Viśvanātha Kavirāja, the fourteenth-century author of the *Sāhitya-Darpaṇa*. Viśvanātha agrees with Abhinavagupta that the actor does not traditionally experience *rasa*. However, if the actor realizes the meaning of the drama and becomes completely immersed in the role being performed, he or she may also relish the *rasa*.[21] Both Viśvanātha's take on Abhinavagupta and Bhaṭṭa Lollaṭa's earlier position demonstrate the complexities of locating *rasa* within aesthetic theories of performance. My theory of performative selfhood, in contrast, does not engage these debates about the location of *rasa* but focuses instead on the experience of the performer without explicit reference to the category of *rasa* and without examining the experience of the audience members who view the performance.

The second issue that distinguishes my theory of performative selfhood from theories of *rasa* concerns the role allotted to individual subjective experience. According to Abhinavagupta's classical formulation of *rasa* theory, the ultimate goal of the performance is to generate a state in which the *sahṛdaya* moves beyond mundane subjective emotions and relishes the universal essence of the *sthāyi-bhāva* in the transcendental state of *rasa*, which is experienced as pure impersonal joy beyond the ego-bound concerns of the individual.[22] In the case of the actor as well, theories of *rasa* tend to emphasize the distinction between the mundane emotions that constitute the actor's individual subjective experience and the performed emotions that he or she enacts on stage. Thus Richard Schechner writes:

> In the rasic system, there are "artistically performed emotions" which comprise a distinct kind of behavior. . . . These performed emotions are separate from the "feelings"—the interior, subjective experience of any given performer during a particular performance. There is no necessary and ineluctable chain linking these "performed emotions" with the "emotions of everyday life." In the rasic system, the emotions *in the arts, not in ordinary life* are knowable, manageable, and transmittable.[23]

In contrast to most *rasa* theories, which tend to abandon the interior realm of individual subjectivity, my theory of performative selfhood emphasizes the performer's individual subjective experience. Rather than requiring the performer to hold in abeyance his or her distinctive interior life, my theory of performative selfhood explores how a person's internal emotions help to construct the subjective self.

Even in light of these differences, performative selfhood does not preclude the performer from experiencing *rasa*, just as Indian aesthetics may not prevent the actor from maintaining some level of individual selfhood during the performative moment. However, my goal in articulating a distinctive notion of performative selfhood is to uncover new possibilities within the analytical framework of Indian performance that may fall beyond the boundaries of classical *rasa* theory. By shifting the discourse on Indian performance from a focus on the impersonal aesthetic enjoyment of the refined audience member to the individual subjective experience of the performer, I hope to expand Indian performance theory beyond an investigation of the dynamics of aesthetic experience to an excavation of the multilayered roles of the self in performance.

Effects of Possession on the Bodied, Embodied, and Reflective Selves

With these notions of performative selfhood in mind, I will now ground my theory in an analysis of two case studies of South Indian performance: ritual possession in Tamil Nadu and the classical dance forms of Kathakali and Kuchipudi. For the first case study, I will focus on one type of possession discussed in Nabokov's book *Religion Against the Self*, specifically possession by spirits of deceased relatives.[24]

Nabokov tells the story of Leila, a Tamil woman in her mid-twenties whose husband, Ramesh, had died prematurely. According to Leila, after the sixteenth-day ceremony that officially marked her status as a widow, her husband Ramesh came to her through a possession experience and revealed that he would continue to protect her even in death. Following this event, Ramesh's spirit began to come to Leila once every month, but soon the possession events increased in frequency. Leila describes her discomfort at these numerous possessions:

> He began to come on me outside our home. As soon as I would hear the *pampai* drum I would go out in the street to dance. I would dance so hard that my sari slipped off my shoulder. I was ashamed. I went to the [goddess temple] . . . and talked to my husband. I said, "Not only you made me into a widow but you shame me in public. Please don't make me dance in the streets!"[25]

Leila's description of possession reveals her lack of bodily control within the performative moment: when Ramesh's spirit comes upon her, Leila seems to forget societal prescriptions concerning female bodily propriety and dances in the street with unkempt garments. Moreover, as implied by Leila's shame, it is her husband, and not she herself, who spurs such seemingly inappropriate behavior.

Kathleen Erndl describes a similar lack of bodily control, particularly the loosening of bound hair, in her discussion of goddess possession in northwest India:

> When a woman is possessed, the Goddess is said to take on a "wind form," enter her, and "play" within her. Her hair, no matter how tightly bound, is said to come undone and fly freely in response to the force of the wind (*pavan*). The state of possession is characterized by glazed eyes, a change in voice,

> and the whirling around of the head, with hair flying loose. Under normal circumstances, a respectable woman's hair is tied up and braided, not allowed to hang loose.[26]

The temporary suspension of control over bodily movements, clothing, and hair, as described in both Erndl's study of goddess possession and Nabokov's observations regarding Leila's experience of spirit possession, suggests a broader grammar of possession in the Indian context.

How does this relate to the topic of selfhood? If we examine Leila's speech through the lens of performative selfhood, it seems that Ramesh's spirit initially gains control over Leila's internal embodied self, specifically her psychoemotional faculties. Following this initial moment of possession, Ramesh's presence within Leila's embodied self affects her external bodied self, as demonstrated by Leila's slipping sari and dancing gestures. In light of Ramesh's possession of Leila's bodied and embodied selves, we may ask, What becomes of her reflective self, which functions as an independent self-conscious faculty? Because Leila cannot control her bodied and embodied selves during possession, we may be tempted to conclude that Ramesh's spirit also penetrates and overcomes her reflective self.

Such a perspective would seem to support Nabokov's notion of ritual possession as enacting violence against the self and also to accord with other scholarly interpretations of possession, which Ann Grodzins Gold characterizes as "any complete but temporary domination of a person's body and the blotting out of that person's consciousness, by a distinct alien power of known or unknown origin."[27] The depiction of possession as exemplifying "temporary domination," loss of consciousness, and even ritual violence would appear at first glance to undermine my theory of performative selfhood, which argues that reflective self-awareness continues during the possession performance. However, at least in the case of Tamil ritual possession, the fact that Leila is able to remember and recount the possession experience *after* the event demonstrates her reflective self's capacity for self-awareness *during* the event. While possession manipulates the gestures of Leila's bodied self and penetrates the internal psychoemotional faculties of her embodied self, it does not exert complete control over the memory capabilities of Leila's reflective selfhood. Although Tamil possession rituals may penetrate and even violently impinge upon some aspects of selfhood, the reflective self escapes such destruction and continues to linger during the moment of performance.[28]

Training the Performing Self in South Indian Classical Dance

In light of Leila's inability to control her bodied and embodied selves, is it possible for the reflective self not only to maintain self-consciousness but also to exert control over the other two aspects of selfhood during performance? In order to address this question, I will now turn to the second case study of classical dance in South India. I will focus more specifically on the styles of Kathakali and Kuchipudi, two performance genres that, unlike possession, prescribe the deliberate control of the body by the reflective self.

Kathakali and Kuchipudi are considered to be "classical" South Indian dance forms, along with their well-known counterpart, Bharata Natyam.[29] One factor that defines these dance forms as "classical" in nature is their purported reliance on Bharata's *Nāṭya-Śāstra*. According to the accounts of contemporary practitioners, these dance forms utilize Bharata's rules concerning performative techniques, including his prescriptions for appropriate hand, foot, and face gestures, as the foundational framework for training the performer.

This emphasis on the performer's training and experience is explicit in Phillip Zarrilli's book, *Kathakali Dance-Drama: Where Gods and Demons Come to Play*, which describes the intensive training processes necessary to becoming a seasoned Kathakali artist. Young boys undergo daily rigorous training of the body for a period of six to ten years in order to perfect their performative technique.[30] Zarrilli maintains that over time this training becomes internalized in the dancer's body: "[T]he external 'forms' of training have been gradually encoded into the neophyte's bodymind through repetition and drill to a point where they become part of his performative 'body-consciousness' and as such are ready-at-hand to be used 'unthinkably.'"[31] Following this bodily internalization process, the experienced Kathakali actor shifts his focus from bodily precision to complete absorption in performance. Zarrilli describes the mental processes of this advanced state of performance:

> The master performer is eventually freed from the flux of the normative, everyday psychomental stream of consciousness for the performative moment. He is freed from "consciousness about" for a state of "concentratedness" in and for the task at hand—fully embodying and engaging himself in psychophysiological actions through which his character is created in time.[32]

Zarrilli goes on to state that when the Kathakali actor attains "concentratedness" in the performative moment, the best acting is seen to occur, specifically when "the actor becomes the character . . . or the actor becomes one with the character."[33]

In light of Kathakali's prescriptions for complete absorption in a particular role, we can ask with reference to my theory of performative selfhood, What becomes of the performer's bodied, embodied, and reflective selves in this performative process? The initial phase of Kathakali training focuses attention on perfecting the bodied self of the performer. In support of this corporeal primacy, the master Kathakali dancer M. P. Sankaran Namboodiri succinctly states, "First, the perfection of the body is most important."[34] Once this technical training is repeated often enough to become inscribed in the bodied self, the master performer shifts his focus to the embodied self, particularly "concentratedness" in a particular character or role. During this state of psychoemotional focus, the embodied self of the seasoned Kathakali dancer "becomes one with the character" and loses "consciousness about" the world around him; as a result, the performer's embodied self becomes absorbed in the character or role being performed.

What, then, becomes of the reflective self? It is tempting to view Kathakali as mirroring the processes of Tamil ritual possession discussed earlier, in which the performer's reflective self retains some level of self-consciousness but cannot exert control over the bodied and embodied selves. However, unlike Tamil possession, the highly stylized performance tradition of Kathakali prescribes that the performer must maintain deliberate control during the performative moment itself. According to one Kathakali actor, "It is not right to have real tears on stage; it does not fit our stylized type of theater. But the emotion must be there and it will affect the audience. As an actor, you must always use your emotions, knowing that you are onstage."[35] In light of this onstage awareness, it seems that while the emotions of the embodied self may become absorbed in a particular role, the reflective self must consciously restrain this emotional expression.

In addition to controlling the psychoemotional states of the embodied self, the reflective self must also exert control over the bodied self, specifically by ensuring that the performer's physical body adheres to the formalized technical training previously encoded within the corporeal form. Alongside this strict adherence to technical body knowledge, Zarrilli also describes the mathematical precision inherent in the performative structure of Kathakali itself:

> [Kathakali] allows the actor little if any freedom from their structured, set scoring. Actors and connoisseurs describe [Kathakali] as "rigidly structured" or having a structure in performance which is inviolable. Kathakali actor Balasubramaniam described the [performances] as having a "mathematical accuracy" which "only allows the actor to do what has been taught in the classroom and nothing more."[36]

As evident in Zarrilli's description, the reflective self must restrict the bodied self to a doubly precise performative paradigm: the dancer's reflective self ensures that the bodied self strictly performs the specific stylized movements encoded within the corporeal and also strictly adheres to the broader inviolable structure found in Kathakali performance itself.

In stark contrast to the case of Tamil ritual possession, Kathakali mandates that the reflective self exercise self-conscious control over the bodied and embodied selves. Whereas in the case of Tamil possession Leila's reflective self, although lingering, is overshadowed and thus her bodied self dances inappropriately on the streets with unkempt garments, the strict precision and stylized framework of Kathakali mandates that the performer's reflective self restrict the bodied self from exhibiting such uncontrolled gestures. And although both ritual possession and Kathakali allow the performer's embodied self to merge, respectively, with the possessing spirit or the character being performed, the reflective self of the Kathakali actor actively restrains and controls this absorption process. The Kathakali performer's reflective self utilizes the stylized framework and training of classical dance to exert complete control over both the bodied and embodied selves.

In light of the antithetical relationship of ritual possession and classical dance as demonstrated by the Kathakali tradition, we might be led to assume that these modes of performance can never coexist during a single performative moment. However, in my second example of South Indian classical dance, I will examine the case of a Kuchipudi dancer whose performative experiences collapse the polarity between uncontrolled possession and stylized classical performance.

With the aim of understanding the performative experiences of a trained classical dancer, in November 2006 I interviewed in Atlanta, Georgia, Sasikala Penumarthi, a Kuchipudi teacher and performer in Atlanta who spent fifteen years training in Chennai under the well-known Kuchipudi master Vempati Chinna Satyam.[37] Sasikala has taught

Kuchipudi dance in the Atlanta area since 1991 and currently trains a group of approximately seventy female and male students.[38] I began my interview by asking questions related to Sasikala's personal experiences with training and performance in the Kuchipudi tradition. I first raised the issue of education and asked Sasikala whether Kuchipudi training requires less time than the six- to ten-year training period characteristic of the Kathakali dance form. In response Sasikala stated:

> It is not less in Kuchipudi. For a dancer to be completely on her own, like individually performing solos and ballets, to get all the technique of the dance and reach that level of skill, I think it takes that amount of time, like eight to nine years of training to reach that level.[39]

As part of this extensive training process, Sasikala said that expertise "comes over the years of practicing and experiencing the [dance form]. . . . As you experience it more and more, practicing it more and more number of times, you actually take it into your body." Sasikala further elaborated upon her own training experiences:

> Maybe in the beginning when I [danced], probably I would have done exactly what [my teacher] taught me or what I saw [the senior dancers do], I used to imitate what it is. But over a period of time, I don't know, now I feel like it comes out of me. I don't feel like I am acting now. It comes without thinking. When the song is going on, it automatically comes to me.

Sasikala's language here concerning her Kuchipudi education mirrors Kathakali's notions of bodily inscription: both dance genres seem to suggest that once technical training is repeated often enough, it becomes inscribed in the dancer's corporeal form.

Following this initial discussion of Kuchipudi training, I questioned Sasikala about the transformative processes necessary for playing a specific character. In particular, I asked her to comment on the experience of enacting the role of Satī in the Kuchipudi dance-drama *Haravilāsam*.[40] Before turning to Sasikala's own responses, I will briefly analyze her enactment of Satī's immolation in a staged performance of the *Haravilāsam* drama in Orlando, Florida, in 1994.[41]

The fourth scene of the *Haravilāsam* dance-drama opens with Dakṣa, the mind-born son of the creator Brahmā, conducting a Vedic sacrifice (*yajña*) in his heavenly abode. Although many gods, goddesses, and sages are seated around the sacrificial fire to witness the auspicious event, Dakṣa's daughter, the goddess Satī, and her husband, the god Śiva, are significantly marked by their absence. While the Vedic rites are proceeding, Satī conspicuously enters the scene, having previously heard the news of her father's sacrifice from the peripatetic sage Nārada. Looking deeply pained at her father's oversight, Satī interrogates Dakṣa regarding his reasons for neglecting to invite her and her husband, Śiva, to the sacrifice. Dakṣa, rising from the sacrificial arena, angrily responds to Satī by critiquing her husband for his lack of proper lineage and origins. Dakṣa further denigrates Śiva by stating: "He wanders around naked, without any proper clothes. He smears ash on his forehead instead of camphor. He eats from skulls instead of using proper plates. He rides on a bull instead of an actual vehicle (*vāhana*). You call him my son-in-law?!"[42] Continuing to hurl abuses at his daughter, Dakṣa grabs Satī's hand and angrily throws her to the ground. Satī, shocked and humiliated by her father's words and actions, shakily stands up. She attempts to garner support by pleading with the gods and sages who have come to witness Dakṣa's sacrifice. However, the guests, looking embarrassed at this public spectacle, leave the sacrificial arena, refusing to listen to Satī's plight. As a result of this lack of sympathy, Satī's humiliation quickly turns into fury, and she angrily vows to end her life through self-immolation in the sacrificial fire. The scene ends climactically with Dakṣa appearing aghast and grief-stricken as Satī's body is consumed by the flames of the sacrificial arena.

A performance analysis of this scene of Satī's self-immolation demands that we focus on the external corporeal manifestations of the characters' internal psychoemotional states. Dakṣa's anger, Satī's humiliation, and the guests' embarrassment are visually manifested through vigorous gestures, clenched hands, and downcast looks. Moreover, these emotions seem to be conveyed through two distinct sets of actions. First, the characters utilize stylized, choreographed hand and foot gestures that follow the musical lyrics explicitly. For example, Dakṣa, when criticizing Śiva's inappropriate use of ash in the place of camphor, mimetically smears ash across his forehead with his right hand while angrily striding across the stage. In addition to such explicit actions, the characters also convey emotions through unchoreographed, yet still stylized, movements. For example, while Satī listens to her father's disparagement of Śiva, she repeatedly shakes her head, covers her ears with her hands, and opens her mouth in surprise. Both sets of stylized bodily actions—choreographed and unchoreographed—succeed in externally expressing the characters' internal pyschoemotional states. These corporeal manifestations of internal states become most apparent in the final moments of the scene leading up to Satī's immolation. While the guests awkwardly file out of the sacrificial arena, Satī's emotional shift from humiliation to anger becomes clear as her pleading words and surprised looks transform into declarative statements and abrupt hand movements. If we analyze this scene utilizing the rhetoric of performative selfhood, it seems simple enough to state that the character Satī's embodied self is marked on her corporeal bodied form. However, what becomes of the bodied, embodied, and reflective selves of Sasikala, the performer who is enacting the character Satī?

In order to examine the relationship between Satī the character and Sasikala the performer, during my interview in November 2006 I asked Sasikala to comment on the transformative processes necessary for playing such a powerful role.[43] Sasikala related that by focusing on the narrative elements underlying Satī's character, she was able to reimagine herself within Satī's worldview. She observed:

> If you really understand the story and the situation there, you automatically transform yourself into the Satī role and you become Satī. . . . What happens when I go there, I become Satī and [I think of] what Satī would have felt at that point. During that time, everybody insults [her]—her father insults her in front of all the sisters and the guests, invited guests. She is uninvited there, and [I think of] how she feels.

As a result of this technique of narrative contemplation, Sasikala revealed that not only did she become the character of Satī, but she also became "possessed" by Satī's character. Sasikala elaborated:

> I imagine all that in mind and kind of I go to that level of possession, I think. I don't even realize myself sometimes. I just go. And when I come there, it takes a while for me to control myself from that state to the normal state. . . . It takes time for me to get back to normal, because I really go there. I go there and my body shivers and I kind of become furious there. . . . She becomes angry there and immolates herself into the fire, and so I get that emotion there, and after that it takes a while for me to control my emotion there, to calm myself.

Sasikala's rhetoric of possession suggests that we must rethink our earlier depiction of South Indian classical performance as prescribing total performative control. If we were to take Sasikala's words to their logical conclusion, then we might surmise that the Indian classical dancer can attain complete character involvement through a paradigm of uncontrolled possession, which lies outside the traditional framework of classical dance. However, countering such an interpretation, Sasikala indicated that she retained some element of control during the performative moment:

> I can't jump off the stage with my anger. At the same time, I am controlling my body. Part of my body is acting too, because I am controlling my body [right]? At the same time, I am taking my emotion to that level of . . . what happened to Satī. So I am going through that, controlling my body also at the same time.

By espousing complete character absorption through a rhetoric of possession along with deliberate bodily control through a discourse of classical dance, Sasikala seems to construct a paradox when speaking of her performance as Satī. This paradox can be resolved through the theory of performative selfhood by suggesting that Sasikala's reflective self only exerts influence over her bodied self while relinquishing such control over her embodied selfhood. Sasikala's bodied self performs the stylized gestures of classical dance without "jumping off the stage," while her embodied self completely merges with Satī and experiences the emotional anguish of the self-immolation narrative. Due to the coexistence of Sasikala's stylized bodied self and immersed embodied self, she is able to perform within a paradigm of what I term "classical possession": Sasikala's bodied self dances within precise classical conventions, while her embodied self is possessed through immersion in the psychoemotional states of the character Satī. In positing a notion of "classical possession," I hope to illustrate the fluidity of the self that is possible in highly stylized performance genres such as Kuchipudi, in which individual expression can manifest through multilayered expressions of selfhood.

Conclusion: Constructing the Lingering Self

Through my analysis of constructing the self through various forms of South Indian performance, I have sought to show that the model of performative selfhood can account for a spectrum of interactions between a performer's bodied, embodied, and reflective selves. In the case of Tamil ritual possession, the performer's bodied and embodied selves are possessed by the spirit of a deceased relative, while the reflective self passively observes and remembers this possession process. In the case of classical dance, the Kathakali performer's reflective self exerts complete control over the bodied and embodied selves and thereby prevents the performer from total character absorption, whereas the Kuchipudi dancer's reflective self exerts control over the bodily performance while allowing for complete character immersion on the level of the embodied self, thereby exemplifying a paradigm of "classical possession."

The theory of performative selfhood, as explicated in this essay, analyzes the roles of the reflective self, which can passively observe or actively control the bodied and embodied selves of the performer. Due to the significant presence of the reflective self during the moment of performance, my theory of performative selfhood seeks to overturn the deconstruction of the individual self in the South Asian context as posited by Dumont, Marriott, and Nabokov. Instead of undermining selfhood, this theory constructs the possibility of a "lingering self" that influences how the performer relates to the possessing spirit or the character being performed. While this lingering self is the primary source of control over the performer, a paradox arises when we realize that the lingering reflective self remains inextricably tied to both bodied and embodied selves. As a result of the interconnectedness between these three aspects of the self, my theory of performative selfhood ultimately suggests that the lingering reflective self of the performer paradoxically constructs and is constructed by both bodied and embodied domains.

Notes

1. Dumont 1970: 42.

2. Dumont 1986: 279. It is important to note that Dumont (1970: 45) does grant individuality to the Indian renunciant. Dumont distinguishes the renunciant from the rest of Indian society by stating, "He thinks as an individual, and this is the distinctive trait which opposes him to the man-in-the-world and brings him closer to the western thinker."

3. Marriott 1976: 111.

4. Nabokov 2000: 15.

5. Dumont 1986: 279.

6. Marriott 1976: 111.

7. For further critiques of Dumont's essentializing discourse, see Nabokov 2000: 13.

8. Nabokov 2000: 13.
9. Nabokov 2000: 15.
10. Nabokov 2000: 182.
11. Smith 2006: 20.
12. Smith 2006: 21.
13. Smith 2006: 21.
14. Smith 2006: 22.
15. Smith 2006: 22.
16. *Nāṭya-Śāstra* 6.31, cited in Raja 1963: 286.
17. See Holdrege 2015, chapter 2.
18. It is important to note that although the *vyabhicāri-bhāvas* are emotions experienced internally within the body, they can be visibly manifested on the body.
19. Haberman 1988: 23.
20. Haberman 1988: 24.
21. Haberman 1988: 25.
22. See Holdrege 2015, chapter 2. Patnaik (2004: 52) describes the experience of *rasa* as involving "a forgetting of both ordinary time and space; and once one loses oneself in the experience, time and space (depicted) in the work are also forgotten."
23. Schechner 2001: 32.
24. For a more general discussion of possession in the Tamil context, see Smith 2006: 127–133.
25. Nabokov 2000: 107.
26. Erndl 2006: 162.
27. Gold 1988: 35 n. 1. See also Erndl 2006: 162.
28. It is important to note that my analysis in this section does not aim to generalize about possession in all South Asian contexts but specifically concerns possession in the Tamil ritual context.
29. For a discussion of the complicated history of the classicization of South Indian dance, particularly the forms of Bharata Natyam and Kuchipudi, see Soneji 2010; Putcha 2011.
30. Zarrilli (2000) notes that in order to train full time, young boys are taught in formal Kathakali dance institutions, where they live and spend their days learning the art form. Furthermore, Zarrilli emphasizes that full-time Kathakali training is restricted to men, although women may be taught the dance style through private, part-time lessons. For a more detailed discussion of women's participation in Kathakali dance, see Daugherty and Pitkow 1991.
31. Zarrilli 2000: 92.
32. Zarrilli 2000: 92.
33. Zarrilli 2000: 62.
34. Zarrilli 2000: 66.
35. Zarrilli 2000: 90.
36. Zarrilli 2000: 84.

37. I have taken Kuchipudi dance classes with Sasikala since 1998, and due to my familiarity with her performative techniques and experiences, I chose to interview her for this essay. This interview was conducted mostly in English and partly in Telugu, the South Indian language of Andhra Pradesh.

38. It is important to emphasize that Sasikala's case cannot be generalized as representing the experiences of all Kuchipudi dancers, much less all South Indian classical dance performers. However, although Sasikala's statements in this interview reflect her own personal experiences with Kuchipudi dance, her experiences serve as noteworthy alternatives to the examples of Kathakali dance outlined by Zarrilli's research.

39. All statements by Sasikala Penumarthi quoted in this section are from my interview with her in Atlanta in November 2006.

40. Kuchipudi, like Kathakali, utilizes the genre of dance-dramas, or "ballets," when staging public performances. For both Kuchipudi and Kathakali, a dance-drama consists of an extended play that usually focuses on a Hindu mythological narrative and combines shorter dance pieces with longer acting segments. The dance-drama *Haravilāsam* was composed and choreographed by Sasikala's teacher, Vempati Chinna Satyam, but stems directly from the Purāṇic myth of Dakṣa's sacrifice.

41. This analysis is based on a videotaped recording of the *Haravilāsam* dance-drama performed by the Kuchipudi Art Academy in Orlando, Florida, in 1994. The recording itself was commissioned by the Sri Venkateswara temple in Pittsburgh, Pennsylvania.

42. Please note that this is my own translation of the Telugu lines sung by Dakṣa. Also, it is important to emphasize that in the Kuchipudi tradition the dancers themselves do not sing the lines on stage. Rather, they mouth the lyrics that are sung by musicians who are seated offstage throughout the duration of the performance.

43. Sasikala has played Satī in several staged performances of *Haravilāsam*, beyond the single videotaped performance that I discuss in this essay. Therefore, her comments do not reflect any single performance of *Haravilāsam* but rather pertain to her overall performative experience of enacting the character of Satī.

References

Daugherty, Diane, and Marlene Pitkow. 1991. "Who Wears the Skirts in Kathakali?" *The Drama Review* 35, no. 2: 138–156.

Dumont, Louis. 1986. *Essays on Individualism*. Chicago: University of Chicago Press.

Dumont, Louis. 1970. *Religion/Politics and History in India: Collected Papers in Indian Sociology*. Paris: Mouton.

Erndl, Kathleen M. 2006. "Possession by Durga: The Mother Who Possesses." In *The Life of Hinduism*, ed. John Stratton Hawley and Vasudha Narayanan, 158–170. Berkeley: University of California Press.

Gold, Ann Grodzins. 1988. "Spirit Possession Perceived and Performed in Rural Rajasthan." *Contributions to Indian Sociology* 22, no. 1: 35–63.

Haberman, David L. 1988. *Acting as a Way of Salvation: A Study of Rāgānugā Bhakti Sādhana*. New York: Oxford University Press.

Holdrege, Barbara A. 2015. *Bhakti and Embodiment: Fashioning Divine Bodies and Devotional Bodies in Kṛṣṇa Bhakti*. New York: Routledge.

Marriott, McKim. 1976. "Hindu Transactions: Diversity without Dualism." In *Transaction and Meaning: Directions in the Anthropology of Exchange and Symbolic Behavior*, ed. Bruce Kapferer, 109–142. Philadelphia: Institute for the Study of Human Issues.

Nabokov, Isabelle. 2000. *Religion Against the Self: An Ethnography of Tamil Rituals*. Oxford: Oxford University Press.

Nāṭya-Śāstra of Bharata. 2002–2003. *The Nāṭyaśāstra: A Treatise on Ancient Indian Dramaturgy and Histrionics Ascribed to Bharata-Muni*, ed. and trans. Manomahan Ghosh. 4 vols. Varanasi: Chowkhamba Sanskrit Series Office.

Patnaik, Priyadarshi. 2004. *Rasa in Aesthetics: An Application of Rasa Theory to Modern Western Literature*. New Delhi: D. K. Printworld.

Putcha, Rumya. 2011. "Revisiting the Classical: A Critical History of Kuchipudi Dance." PhD diss., University of Chicago.

Raja, K. Kunjuni. 1963. *Indian Theories of Meaning*. Madras: Adyar Library and Research Centre.

Schechner, Richard. 2001. "Rasaesthetics." *The Drama Review* 45, no. 3: 27–50.

Smith, Frederick M. 2006. *The Self Possessed: Deity and Spirit Possession in South Asian Literature and Civilization*. New York: Columbia University Press.

Soneji, Davesh, ed. 2010. *Bharatanatyam: A Reader*. New Delhi: Oxford University Press.

Zarrilli, Phillip B. 2000. *Kathakali Dance-Drama: Where Gods and Demons Come to Play*. New York: Routledge.

Part 2

Divine Bodies and Devotional Bodies

Chapter 5

Observations on the Bodies of the Gods in the Mahābhārata

KENDALL BUSSE

The Mahābhārata provides important glimpses into the religious and cultural contexts of the period from the second century BCE to the second century CE, a time of important transition and change in Indian history.[1] Some of the earliest available Indian sculptural remains have been roughly dated to the beginning of the second century BCE, and, although these remains need not support a date for the inception of sculpted images in India, they can help mark the beginning of a shifting attitude toward divine embodiment, an attitude that becomes dominant by the second century CE and onward when images are found in profusion. Art historians have scrutinized the Mahābhārata for textual evidence to prove the existence of sculpted images during this period, but such an approach can provide only the bare beginnings of a substantive understanding of divine embodiment. This approach has tended to neglect Indian classifications of divine bodies and has reduced our categorization of modes of embodiment to binaries—such as Āryan/indigenous or iconic/aniconic. Perhaps most importantly, excessive attention to sculpted images has distracted scholars from carefully attending to the epic's representations of the ways in which the gods, *devatās* or *devas*, are embodied, whether sculptural or not. Scholars who have approached the Mahābhārata looking for clues of sculpted images have been left to speculate on ambiguous phrases such as *tatra viśveśvaram dṛṣṭvā,* "having seen the god there."[2] Under close scrutiny such references do not use any of the Sanskrit terms that later come to mean a sculpted image—in particular, *pratimā, arcā, bimba, vigraha,* or *mūrti*—although most of these words appear in the epic in other contexts.[3] This essay will explore constructions of divine embodiment in the Mahābhārata by providing an attentive mapping of the semantics of divine embodiment employed within the text.

A survey of the critical edition of the Mahābhārata shows that the terms that clearly denote a sculpted image are incredibly rare. Although there is evidence in the epic of the worship of *devatās*, pilgrimages, and visits to *tīrthas* (sacred sites), these instances rarely use the terms that later come to mean a sculpted image. Some of these terms, such as *arcā,* are never used in the epic to designate an image and are found only in verbal forms. The term *pratimā* retains the Vedic sense of "counterpart" in the epic, and in one of the few places that it does denote a sculpted image, it refers to a human image and not to a divine image. The Pāṇḍava hero Bhīma is saved from his uncle Dhṛtarāṣṭra's curse when Kṛṣṇa quickly replaces Bhīma with an iron replica (*pratimā*) so that the statue is crushed instead of Bhīma.[4] This is one of the few times in which any of the terms that in the post-epic period come to mean a sculpted image is clearly used in the epic to refer to an image—although in this case the reference is to a sculpted human image, not a divine image. The terms *vigraha* and *mūrti* are found fairly frequently in the Mahābhārata, both in their possessive forms (*vigrahavant* and *mūrtimant*) and as nouns. However, neither term is ever used to designate a sculpted image, although both terms are used to refer to divine bodies. I will focus on the terms *vigraha* (human-like bodies that the gods take on) and *mūrti* (diverse bodies that the gods manifest by means of their powers of *yoga*), which I argue are critical to understanding the new modes of divine embodiment in the epic.

The Visual Accessibility and Multiplicity of the Gods' Bodies

A close analysis of the terms *vigraha* and *mūrti* must be prefaced by a brief discussion of two general trends articulated in the Mahābhārata: the visual accessibility of the gods' bodies, and the multiplicity of the gods' bodies. As Charles Malamoud has emphasized, Vedic texts provide only formulaic allusions to the gods' bodies and do not give detailed descriptions of their corporeal forms.[5] However, the Mahābhārata is full of descriptive details concerning the forms of *devatās* as well as of *rākṣasas* (demons) and semi-divine beings such as *yakṣas* (chthonic spirits). For example, the Pāṇḍava hero Arjuna, the brother of Bhīma, is said to have seen "standing on a dam an odd-eyed, big-bodied Yakṣa, tall as a palm, fiery like fire and sun, unconquerable and mountainous," who was speaking to him in a voice "as deep as a thunderclap."[6] In another passage the *rākṣasas* protecting the Pāṇḍavas' *sabhā* (assembly hall) are described as "sky-going, terrifying, gigantic, powerful, red-eyed and yellow-eyed, with ears of mother-of-pearl."[7]

The Mahābhārata includes many passages that depict the gods assuming forms on the earthly plane. Although some deities are visible to the human eye, others are said to reveal themselves only to those who are worthy. For example, the *loka-pālas*, or world guardians, address Arjuna, "[B]ehold us! The World Guardians have assembled. We bestow on you eyesight, for you are worthy of seeing us. You are the mighty ancient seer Nara, of measureless spirit."[8] In a similar episode, Arjuna comes upon a mountain man who is the bull-bannered deity Śiva in disguise. After a short battle that leaves Arjuna like a ball of flesh, Śiva decides that Arjuna is worthy to "set eyes on" him and states, "I shall give you eyesight."[9] This last example is highly instructive and suggests that there are some gods who assume bodily guises that are easily seen, while their "own forms" (*sva-rūpas*) can only be seen through divine sight (*divya-darśana*). One might see a god, but with ordinary human sight one might not even be aware of the true identity of the god. There are other examples in the epic in which the gods are said to be displeased with people seeing them and following them around, and they consequently render an area inaccessible so that only those who have practiced austerities can access their abodes.[10] More commonly, however, the gods interact with human actors who are oblivious to their divine status unless provided special vision to see the gods' celestial forms. Moreover, the particularized descriptions of the bodies of the gods who are accessible through divine sight further emphasize the importance of the visual mode of apprehension.

There are numerous emic approaches that explain the changes in the visual accessibility of the gods over time. According to the Śatapatha Brāhmaṇa, a Vedic text that predates the Mahābhārata, "Gods and men, and the Fathers as well, drank together (at the sacrifice): it was their communal feast. Formerly, they could be seen when they came to the feast; today they still attend, but now they are invisible."[11] The text recognizes that at one time the gods and the ancestors were seen at the sacrifice. However, while acknowledging the present invisibility of the gods—and by extension perhaps the lesser powers of those who can now no longer see them—this is not the primary focus of the passage. The visual accessibility of the gods seems to have little bearing on the effectiveness of the sacrifice or on the authenticity of the presence of the gods, both of which are strongly affirmed by this text. Although no longer visible, their presence at the sacrifice is not in question. This passage pairs well with other Vedic material that suggests that the gods may not want to be seen; it is simply their presence that is important.[12]

The Purāṇas, in contrast, which postdate the Mahābhārata, emphasize that "the gods were visible in the first age of the cosmic cycle, and that there were at that time neither images of nor temples to them. In the second and third ages, it was possible to see the gods both directly and in their images. In the fourth age, our own times, only the images remain."[13] In contrast to the Śatapatha Brāhmaṇa passage, the Purāṇic authors assume the importance of the visual accessibility of the gods for each cosmic age (*yuga*) and thus are concerned with how a vision of the gods was attained in each age, whether through images or not. In the Purāṇic perspective sight is important as a means of accessing and experiencing the divine presence.

Both the Brāhmaṇas and the Purāṇas recognize that whereas in earlier ages human beings had the capacity to see the gods directly, in more recent times their ability to see the gods has diminished or the necessary faculty of supranormal sight is lacking. The ability to have direct visionary experience is ascribed to the ancient Vedic seers, or *ṛṣis*, the forefathers of humankind, in the beginning of creation. Cognition, both visual and oral-aural, of the gods by the *ṛṣis* allowed them direct access to the abodes of the gods and an intimate knowledge of creation: "Having gone 'in their minds' to the heavenly abodes of the gods, having stationed their awareness on those celestial planes where the gods dwell, the *ṛṣis* directly 'see' with their mind's eye the deities riding in their chariots, seated on their heavenly thrones, or engaged in various types of activities."[14] The Vedic seers are described as having access to the heavenly realms, and the gods are seen directly in their heavenly abodes.

In the Mahābhārata, as in Vedic texts, divine sight is portrayed as an extraordinary faculty. The Vedic *ṛṣis* are held to have attained their visionary experiences through the practice of *tapas*, and in the epic such visions are also represented as resulting from austerities. However, whereas the *ṛṣis* "saw" (root *dṛś*) the gods directly in their heavenly abodes, the epic's sages and heroes are generally shown a bodily form of the gods on earth. For example, the goddess Gaṅgā shows herself in bodily form (*mūrtimant*) to King Bhagīratha after he has engaged in severe austerities, living off of fruits and roots, for a divine millennium.[15] Yudhiṣṭhira, the eldest of the five Pāṇḍava brothers, is similarly represented as performing arduous austerities as a means of propitiating Sūrya, the god of the sun. Sūrya subsequently appears before Yudhiṣṭhira and shows him his "own body" (*sva-vapus*), which is "ablaze like a flaming fire."[16] It would seem that in such cases austerities are performed for the very purpose of ensuring not only the deity's presence but also his or her visual manifestation. Unlike the Śatapatha Brāhmaṇa passage discussed earlier, in the epic the visual manifestation of the deity is necessary to authorize and confirm the divine presence.

Another example of the primacy accorded to the sense of sight in the epic is the visionary experience of the divine form of Sūrya by Kuntī, the maiden who subsequently married King Pāṇḍu and gave birth to three of the five Pāṇḍava heroes, Yudhiṣṭhira, Bhīma, and Arjuna. The visual relationship established between Kuntī and Sūrya due to the manifestation of his divine body results in the boon of the child Karṇa. First she sees the sun shining in the sky with its thousand rays, but then with her divine sight (*divya-darśana*) she sees his divine form:

> Her eyesight became divine [*divya-darśana*], and she saw the God of divine aspect [Sūrya], accoutred with armor and adorned with earrings. . . . His complexion was honey-yellow, his arms were large, his neck grooved like a conch shell. He seemed to laugh, he wore upper arm bracelets, and appeared to set fire to space. By his [*yoga*] he had split himself in two, and thus came there and went on shining in the sky.[17]

The text makes clear that the form seen by Kuntī is not the visible form of the sun normally seen abiding in the sky. The form Kuntī sees with divine sight comes to her on earth, where she is. Moreover, in contrast to the formulaic and nonspecific allusions to the bodies of the gods found in Vedic texts, this passage provides a detailed description of the divine form of Sūrya. Sūrya's form is human-like and at the same time beyond human; it is this perfected form that is visually accessible. And yet, upon Sūrya's request, the text elaborates that Kuntī's divine sight also allows her to look up into heaven to see "the Thirty Gods, all comfortable in their proper spheres, and that mighty luminous God who gave forth light like the sun itself."[18] It seems fair to assume that Kuntī's vision of Sūrya is of a divine form found outside its "proper sphere," namely, within the human sphere—a point that is made clear by the contrast between, on the one hand, Sūrya who is standing before her and, on the other hand, the gods, including Sūrya, seen in their proper spheres.

As the Vedic *ṛṣis* cognized the gods in their subtle material forms abiding in their highest heavenly abodes, so Kuntī is afforded a similar vision, placing her and other epic heroes with divine sight on the level of the *ṛṣis*. However, in contrast to the epic's heroes, the Vedic *ṛṣis* are represented as in constant contact with the gods and as having the ability to station their awareness on the celestial planes of the gods where they can access at will, with their "mind's eye," the subtle forms of the deities.[19] Kuntī and the epic heroes do not have such free access to the celestial realms of the gods, but rather, through the boons of particular deities, they are granted temporary glimpses of the gods' subtle forms while remaining on earth.

Together these examples provide a variety of insights. First, the greater attention given in the epic to particularized descriptions of a wide range of bodies of celestial beings—whether the bodies of *yakṣas* easily seen with ordinary human sight or the divine bodies of *devatās* only seen with the boon of divine sight—demonstrates the increasing importance of visual modes of apprehension. Second, representations of divine bodies in the epic continue the logic developed in earlier Vedic texts that gods possess multiple gross material and subtle material bodies. However, despite this shared assumption, there are substantive differences between Vedic and epic perspectives. The gross material bodies of the gods in Vedic texts are generally ritual bodies that are constituted by concrete materials. For example, in Vedic rituals the deity Agni is embodied in the flames of fire that convey the ritual oblations to the gods; in *soma* rituals the deity Soma is embodied in the *soma* plant whose juice is ritually extracted and ingested during the course of the ritual; in the *agnicayana* ceremony the creator Prajāpati is embodied in the brick fire altar that is ritually constructed as his gross material form.[20] By definition these ritual bodies are accessible to human sight. These modes of divine embodiment in the Vedic period are "mesocosmic forms"—to use Barbara Holdrege's term—or "intermediate structures that mediate between the transcosmic absolute body and the microcosmic human body by serving as vehicles through which human beings can access and engage the [deity]."[21] Although ultimately divine bodies, the fire, *soma* plant, and brick fire altar are mesocosmic modes of embodiment in that they can be engaged and manipulated on earth through human actions. The sculpted images of the gods that emerge in the post-epic period are also mesocosmic modes of divine embodiment. However, the forms of the gods found in the epic are hardly mesocosmic because human beings cannot manipulate or control them. Moreover, whereas the materiality of divine bodies in the Vedic period allows for ritual engagement with these divine forms, the materiality of divine bodies in the epic is framed in terms of visual modes of engagement.

I will now turn to an examination of the distinctive modes of divine embodiment articulated in the epic's representations of *vigraha*s and *mūrti*s.

Vigraha: Gods and Human Bodies

Many of the terms that in post-Vedic texts come to mean "image" are originally found in the Vedic ritual context. P. K. Agrawala has traced the use of the term *vigraha* to the later Vedic period.[22] In the Taittirīya Saṃhitā the related term *vigrahaṇa* is a verse that accompanies a ritual oblation and supports the offering to various deities,[23] and thus in its original context this term has an oral rather than a visual component. The term *vigraha* is similarly used in a ritual context to designate a partial offering or an offering divided into several portions, from the root *grah + vi,* "to divide, distribute, separate."[24] In *Darśan: Seeing the Divine Image in India,* Diana Eck cites the common Purāṇic etymology for the term *vigraha* that emphasizes an alternative meaning of the root *grah + vi,* "to grasp, take hold of," and thus, according to Eck, a *vigraha* is "that form which enables the mind to grasp the nature of God." She characterizes *vigraha*s more specifically as images of the gods that "are not 'likenesses' of any earthly form. They are fantastic forms, with multiple heads and arms, with blue, green or vermillion coloring, or with part-animal bodies. They are not intended to 'represent' earthly realities, but rather to present divine realities."[25] In the epic, however, the picture is very different. Here *vigraha*s are not images of the gods that facilitate human beings' ability to grasp the nature of divinity, but rather they are the very human-like bodies that the gods themselves "grasp" or "take on" in order to interact with human beings on the earthly plane and to influence human events.

In the Mahābhārata when the earth seeks refuge with the creator Brahmā, Brahmā tells the gods, "Be born among men with parts of yourselves, in the fashion that pleases you."[26] These portions (*aṃśa*s) of the gods play an important part in the narrative layers of the epic. The fact that the epic's heroes are also ascribed the status of "portions" of the gods lends cosmic significance to their actions as part of the greater cosmic drama to reestablish *dharma*. Although André Couture emphasizes the connection between these "portions" and *avatāra*s, there seems to be some connection with *vigraha*s as well. According to Couture, *aṃśāvataraṇa*—"the descent of the gods with a part of themselves"—predates the use of the term *avatāra,* which is used only once in the epic.[27] Although the gods descend with parts (*aṃśa*s or *bhāga*s) of themselves, it is the term *vigraha* that is employed to refer to the actual form that is assumed. For example, Draupadī, the young maiden who was destined to become the wife of the five Pāṇḍava brothers, is portrayed as the human form (*mānuṣa-vigraha*) through which the goddess Śrī manifests on earth: "Thereupon a young maiden arose from the center of the altar, the well-favored and beautiful Daughter of the Pāñcālas, heart-fetching, with a waist shaped like an altar. She was dark, with eyes like lotus petals, her hair glossy black and curling—a lovely Goddess who had chosen a human form [*mānuṣa-vigraha*]."[28] The reference here is not to the human Draupadī but to Draupadī as a portion, a "divided form," of the goddess Śrī. The connection of Draupadī to Śrī is referred to numerous times throughout the epic and is introduced in the chapter following Brahmā's order to the gods to be born on earth with a part of themselves: "A part of Śrī was born here on earth for the sake of love as a blameless virgin, from the middle of an altar in the house of Drupada. She was neither too small nor too tall, and fragrant like the blue lotus; her eyes were long and lotus-like, her hips well-shaped, her hair long and black."[29] Draupadī's perfectly shaped form is understood as evidence that this body was the chosen form of the goddess.

In another passage the goddess Gaṅgā takes on a human form (*mānuṣa vigraha*): "And the divinely lovely [*divya-rūpa*] Goddess herself, Gaṅgā the river who travels her three journeys, in the lustrously human form [*mānuṣa vigraha śrīmat*] she had assumed [root *kṛ*] became the obedient wife of a man whose love ripened with his fortunes."[30] One could revise J. A. B. van Buitenen's translation of *divya-rūpa* as "divinely lovely" and render it as a *bahuvṛhi* compound, "one with divine form." This revision draws attention to the contrast set up in this passage between Gaṅgā's divine form (*divya-rūpa*) and her human form (*mānuṣa vigraha*). This human form is assumed by the divine form. These examples demonstrate the importance of divine agency in the epic: it is the gods who "take on" these *vigraha*s through their own powers.

My argument that *vigraha* is best understood as an individual, human-like form that a deity chooses and manifests according to his or her will is further supported in the episode in which the Pāṇḍava brothers and Draupadī head toward the mountains undertaking the *dharma* of *yoga.* They come across the deity Agni, who demands that Arjuna give up his divine weapon. "There they saw Agni, placed like a mountain before them, obstructing the road, presented in the individual form of a man [*puruṣa-vigraha*]."[31] In this example van Buitenen's translation of *vigraha* as "individual form" adheres closely to the root meaning of *vigraha* as "division or separation."

Interestingly, in its epic use the term *vigraha* is reserved solely for the bodies of gods and is only used to refer to human bodies when drawing attention to their true identity as a portion of a god or goddess. This emphasizes that a *vigraha* is not a physical body of an ordinary human being but a body of a god who appears on earth as human. The gods' *vigrahas* are human-like bodies, although they are never solely human. The cases of Gaṅgā and of Śrī embodied as Draupadī point to the suprahuman qualities of human-like bodies, which, when assumed by deities as a portion of themselves, display a degree of corporeality and materiality. The form of Draupadī, although sometimes radiant like a goddess, is still very material, corporeal, and human, and the same may be assumed about the form of Gaṅgā when she descends to become the wife of a human being.

In these examples the gods manifest bodies for themselves. Frederick M. Smith, in his book *The Self Possessed: Deity and Spirit Possession in South Asian Literature and Civilization,* makes the useful distinction between, on the one hand, deceptive, coercive, and unexpected possession by gods and, on the other hand, more "benign and natural" modes of possession, which he terms possession-as-incarnation or possession-as-temporary vehicle. The similarity between these two modes is that the gods are in control—a feature that we see highlighted with *vigrahas*. Smith argues that incarnation and embodiment are articulated through the theme of possession in the Upaniṣads, a theme that he sees carried forward in the epic.[32] I would argue that an understanding of *vigraha* as possession-as-incarnation allows for greater insight into the epic's understanding of the term than the later Purāṇic interpretations in which it is a form that the human mind is able to grasp.

Mūrti: Condensed Presence

An etymology of the term *mūrti* that has been advanced by a number of scholars suggests its relationship to the terms *mūra* or *mūra-devas*, meaning "senseless like stones" or "those who worship images, which are lifeless objects."[33] However, as in the case of *vigraha*, the tendency of some scholars to delimit the meaning of the term *mūrti* to the post-epic sense of "sculpted image" does not do justice to the multilayered significations of the term in Vedic and epic contexts. The closely related terms *mūrta* and *amūrta* are found frequently throughout the Upaniṣads and provide a better basis for understanding the use of the term *mūrti* in the epic.

Mūrti is generally held to be derived from the root *murch*, "to become solid, congealed, formed." When the adjective *mūrta* or the noun *mūrti* are found in the Upaniṣads, these forms signify something with a congealed or formed shape. In a description of Ātman creating the world, the Aitareya Upaniṣad says, "He then thought to himself: 'Now that these worlds and their keepers are in place, I had better create food for them.' So he incubated [root *tap* + *abhi*] the waters. When the waters were incubated, there emerged from them something solid [*mūrti*]. And the solid thing [*mūrti*] that emerged was food."[34] A *mūrti* in this context is something with a definite, fixed shape that emerges from the amorphous waters of creation. There is a sharp contrast here between the fixed, delimited, and contained shape of food and the liquid formlessness of the waters of creation. Moreover, as is the case in the later epic usage, a *mūrti* is a shaped form specifically related to the process of heating—here the heating of the primordial waters at creation.[35]

Another reason to give priority to the terms *mūrta* and *amūrta* when investigating the Vedic antecedents of *mūrti* is that these terms are invoked in Upaniṣadic representations of divine embodiment. In the early Upaniṣads these terms are used to describe the qualities of Upaniṣadic gods and more specifically the two aspects of the ultimate reality, Brahman, which is represented as both *mūrta* and *amūrta*, with a fixed shape and without a fixed shape. The following passage from the Bṛhadāraṇyaka Upaniṣad describes the *mūrta* and *amūrta* aspects of Brahman: "There are, indeed, two visible appearances [*rūpa*s] of Brahman—the one has a fixed shape [*mūrta*], and the other is without a fixed shape [*amūrta*]; the one is mortal, and the other is immortal; the one is stationary, and the other is in motion."[36] The parallel to the creation of food in the primordial waters is clear. That which is *mūrta* is fixed, stationary, and mortal, while that which is *amūrta* is mobile and without shape like the primordial waters themselves. A hierarchy is not established here. Rather, Brahman has two aspects, both of which are forms (*rūpa*s) of the ultimate reality. Malamoud's definition of *mūrti* evokes the Upaniṣadic contrast between *mūrta* and *amūrta*: "a corporeal form enclosed or frozen within a set limit, a condensed presence, an arrested movement. . . . [T]he *mūrti* serves as a matrix for the concretization of a divine fluidity that cannot be grasped."[37] This contrast with divine fluidity is established in the pair *mūrta*/*amūrta*; thus it is not surprising that these terms are usually not found alone but as a pair in the Upaniṣads.

Whereas the Upaniṣads employ *mūrta* and *mūrti* in order to illuminate the distinction between the immanent and transcendent aspects of Brahman, the epic employs these terms because of its increased interest in the gross material and subtle material forms of the gods. Similar to the Upaniṣadic use of *mūrta/amūrta,* in the Mahābhārata the *pitṛ*s are often described as both embodied and unembodied (*mūrtyamūrti-dhara*). However, the term *mūrti* is most commonly found in the Mahābhārata as a possessive form, *mūrtimant* (literally, "having a bodily form"), which is not found in the early Upaniṣads. For example, the term *mūrtimant* is used with reference to the bodily form that the goddess Gaṅgā manifests to King Bhagīratha. As mentioned earlier, after he had practiced austerities for a divine millennium, "the great River Ganges showed herself in bodily form [*mūrtimant*]."[38] The *mūrtimant* through which Gaṅgā shows herself to Bhagīratha appears to be different from the *vigraha* that she is said to assume when she takes on a human form. The context is ambiguous, so we can only surmise that hers is an embodied form of some sort. The term *mūrtimant* is also used with reference to King Daśaratha, the father of Rāma, who at a critical juncture in the epic's recounting of the story of Rāma appears in the sky along with hosts of gods and other celestial beings. King Daśaratha is described as appearing "in a divine and luminous bodily form [*divya-bhāsvara-mūrtimant*], riding a precious and resplendent chariot that was yoked with wild geese."[39] As he is described riding in a chariot, it seems likely that his form is human-like, while the divine luminosity of his form that shines forth in the sky would seem to suggest a subtle material body. However, in both of these examples it is unclear whether one can see these forms with ordinary human sight. On initial investigation one might hypothesize that while the term *vigraha* is used to refer to gross material human-like bodies that the gods assume, the term *mūrtimant*—as these examples suggest—is used to designate subtle material bodies that seem to be less specific in shape.

However, when the term *mūrti* is used in the nominal rather than the possessive form, it frequently designates multiple bodies. For example, when Agni is cursed to consume anything put into his flames, he responds by saying, "I am no less capable of cursing you, but I must honor the Brahmins. I shall now assert the matter clearly before you, albeit you know the truth. Now hear it. By my [*yoga*] I divide myself into many parts and reside in many [embodiments] [*mūrti*s]—in *agnihotra*s, in *sattra*s, and in other rituals and ceremonies."[40] In this passage Agni refers to his multiple bodies, which exist simultaneously in the various sacrifices as distinct *mūrti*s. Agni is a particularly interesting example because, as the god of fire, by practical and ritual necessity he must have multiple gross material bodies as distinct fires that can exist simultaneously, along with his subtle material divine form that continues to exist even when the gross material bodies are extinguished. In the same way that Agni is able to embody himself in multiple gross and subtle material forms, other gods are also able to embody themselves in numerous forms across time and space. These manifold bodies are termed *mūrti* by the epic, pointing to the fact that the materiality of a *mūrti* can be either gross or subtle.

As in the example of Agni, the term *mūrti* is often used to designate the multiple forms of a god that are visible to ordinary human vision. When the monkey-god Hanumān reveals himself to Bhīma, he says, "This is as much of my body [*mūrti*] as you can stand seeing, prince sans blame. I can grow bigger than this, as big as I want, Bhīma, and in an encounter with my enemies my body grows immense by my own power."[41] It would seem that in this example Hanumān's *mūrti*s, like those of Agni, are less fixed and that the term *mūrti* designates a changeable form that can be seen with ordinary human vision. In the Mahābhārata the gods as well as the demons create and control *mūrti*s by means of their own power. This is even clearer in a passage in which the sage Dhaumya destroys a *rākṣasa*:

> Meanwhile the powerful Dhaumya, before the Pāṇḍavas' eyes, exorcised the ghastly apparitions of the demon with the various spells that are designed to kill demons and that he employed accurately. His [*yoga*] destroyed, the brawny fiend, who could assume any shape [*mūrti*] at will, appeared before them with eyes widened in fury, like Time the Destroyer himself.[42]

These examples clearly point to the ability of human beings to see these forms with ordinary human sight as forms that exist "before the eyes."[43]

Mūrti and *Yoga*

A close connection is established in the Mahābhārata between *mūrti* and *yoga*. It is by means of *yoga* that Agni attains his many embodied forms (*mūrti*s) in the various rituals. It is also by means of *yoga* that Sūrya divides himself into two so that he can appear in his form as the sun in the sky and at the same time manifest his divine form to Kuntī. Likewise, the *rākṣasa* destroyed by Dhaumya assumes various forms (*mūrtis*) through *yoga*. Human yogic practice may result in a vision of the god's form, but it is specifically the *yoga* practiced by gods that produces *mūrtis*.

As a noun *mūrti* suggests a particular mode of divine embodiment, and in nearly every instance in which *mūrti* refers specifically to a divine body the term *yoga* is also invoked, pointing to a technical use of the term *mūrti* as one type of divine embodiment that is achieved through *yoga*. The compound *yoga-mūrti* is at times used to designate a body generated by means of *yoga*, or a yogic body. For example, when Kuntī calls on the god Dharma to help her conceive a child, it is with his *yoga-mūrti*, yogic body, that he appears: "The queen at once brought offerings to Dharma and solemnly muttered the spells that Durvāsas had given her. She lay with Dharma, who had assumed a yogic body [*yoga-mūrti-dharaṇa*], and the buxom woman received a son who would be the greatest of all breathing creatures. . . ."[44] As discussed earlier, in a passage describing a similar event the god Sūrya is said to appear before Kuntī: "[H]e wore upper arm bracelets, and appeared to set fire to space. By his [*yoga*] he had split himself in two, and thus came there and went on shining in the sky."[45] Although the term *mūrti* is not used in this passage, it is still said that by means of *yoga* Sūrya divides himself, existing simultaneously as the gross material sun in the sky and as a divine form appearing to Kuntī's divine sight on the earthly plane.

That Kuntī's encounter with Dharma does employ the term *yoga-mūrti* is especially interesting when viewed in relation to Dharma's other embodiments in the epic, specifically Yudhiṣṭhira. The term *vigrahavant* is used with reference to Yudhiṣṭhira, who is described as like Dharma incarnate (*dharmo vigrahavān iva*).[46] There is clearly a difference between Dharma's manifestation in his *yoga-mūrti* and his embodiment in the human form (*vigrahavant*) of Yudhiṣṭhira, although the epic does not elaborate on the difference. Similarly, there is clearly a difference between the *mūrtis* of Agni when he manifests as multiple fires in various sacrifices and the *puruṣa-vigraha* of Agni when he appears to the Pāṇḍavas as an imposing mountain of a man.

If anything is clear about the use of the term *mūrti* in the Mahābhārata, it is that a *mūrti* is not a likeness, a reflection, or a symbol of the god. It is a particular body that the god assumes—a manifestation, a concentrated presence of the deity. More specifically, *mūrtis* are the varied and multiple bodies that deities are able to manifest by means of *yoga*. Although at least some of these *mūrtis* have a substantial degree of materiality, they are not sculpted images, nor are they inert, passive, or lifeless. These bodies are not mesocosmic forms that human beings construct and manipulate in the way that a sculpted image is fashioned by an artisan and enlivened through ritual means. While epic heroes may be able, through engaging in austerities, to summon a deity into their presence, it is through the deity's own yogic powers that its form is manifested.[47]

The term *yoga,* when invoked in the passages in the Mahābhārata that I have been discussing, has often been translated by van Buitenen and other scholars as "wizardry." The assumption underlying such an understanding is that this "magical" *yoga* is subordinate to the "true" *yoga,* which subsumes such magical powers within a philosophical framework as subsidiary powers attained on the path to the ultimate goal of *mokṣa,* or liberation. E. Washburn Hopkins identifies these two traditions within the epic as "popular" and "philosophical":

> Here the popular Yoga parts from philosophical Yoga. The ordinary saint or ascetic of the epic is acquainted only with Yoga as a means to the attainment of magical powers. All he cares for is to become a wizard of this sort in life and to continue after death as a superior god-compelling wiseacre, as dreaded in heaven as he is in earth.[48]

Hopkins admits to the prevalence of "popular" yogic traditions in the epic and argues that the Mahābhārata does not put forth a formal "philosophical" system of *yoga.*

Among previous studies of the relationship between *yoga* and *mūrti* in the Mahābhārata, a number of scholars have tended to impose on the epic material the values of the later philosophical system of classical Yoga articulated in the Yoga-Sūtras of Patañjali (ca. 400–500 CE) and to relegate any practices that are not directly aimed at liberation to the domain of "wizardry" or "magic." Moreover, several of these scholars not only invest the term *yoga* in the epic with the post-epic valences of Pātañjala Yoga, but they also invest the term *mūrti* with the post-epic valences of sculpted images. For example, the art historian T. A. Gopinatha Rao seeks to illuminate the relationship between *yoga* and *mūrti* in the epic by appealing to Pātañjala Yoga's definition of *dhāraṇā* as "the process of fixing the mind on some object well defined in space"[49] and arguing that an image (*mūrti*) can be employed as a locus of *dhāraṇā* in order to focus the mind in meditation. However, while forms of the root *dhṛ,* "to hold, bear," are sometimes found with *yoga-mūrti* in the epic, the forms that are used, such as *dharaṇa,* which means "bearing," do not convey the same semantic sense as the technical term *dhāraṇā* that is used in Patañjali's classical system of Yoga. In the case of *yoga-mūrti*, it is the god who "bears" or "assumes" a yogic body, while in Rao's analysis of classical Yoga it is the *yogin* who manipulates the image, or *mūrti*, to concentrate the mind. Thus the relationship between *yoga* and *mūrti*s in the epic does not align itself with the classical Yoga of Patañjali. Similar to Rao, Jitendra Nath Banerjea argues that "the last constituent of the act of *pūjā*"—which Banerjea understands as meditation on an image—"has got special bearing on the history of the evolution of the icons."[50] He cites sources such as the later *Śukranītisāra* that suggest that the artist should create an image that is conducive to *dhyāna-yoga*, the *yoga* of meditation, which for Banerjea is why early images of the Buddha and *jina*s are shown in the yogic pose of seated meditation.[51] However, in the epic the *mūrti*s of the gods are not objects of meditation, and there is little if any evidence that they are seen through meditative visions. Rather, those who see the gods' *mūrti*s are generally engaged with the deity in a variety of activities. It is thus clear from the evidence in the Mahābhārata that an analysis of the relationship between classical Yoga and sculpted images does not serve to illuminate the relationship between *yoga* and *mūrti* in the epic. Such an analysis might help us to understand post-epic yogic activities involving meditation on images but not epic portrayals of the yogic activity of the gods in manifesting *mūrti*s as modes of divine embodiment.

Another dominant scholarly approach has tended to impose on the epic material the pre-epic values of Vedic traditions by equating *yoga* with earlier Vedic practices, particularly with reference to the concepts of *māyā* and *tapas*. For example, Hopkins, along with other scholars, equates *yoga* with *tapas* and argues that "Yoga here [in the Mahābhārata] is not philosophical Yoga at all, but only Vedic asceticism."[52] However, *yoga* as it relates to divine *mūrti*s employs a particular type of power—namely, the power to manifest multiple bodies. Consequently, the relationship between *yoga* and the concepts of *māyā* and *tapas* in the epic context needs to be reconsidered.

One of the powers of Vedic gods is their *māyā*, their "capacity for creating multiple identities for themselves and others, and . . . their power to structure reality."[53] According to Teun Goudriaan, this power manifests through the gods' ability to simultaneously materialize in multiple forms.[54] Thus in the Upaniṣads the gods' many forms (*rūpa*s) are attained through *māyā*: "Indra by his wizardry [*māyā*] travels in many forms [*puru-rūpa*]."[55] One might be tempted to argue that in the same way that the gods achieve many *rūpas* through *māyā*, they achieve their many *mūrtis* through *yoga*. *Māyā* is the power of shape-shifting, which certainly seems at first glance to resonate with the epic's understanding of *mūrti*. However, Goudriaan points to the fact that *māyā* is often understood in the Mahābhārata as the power that veils. For example, the term *māyā* is used when discussing the many forms that Indra assumes to trick and seduce women. Rather than a mode through which the god reveals himself to human sight, *māyā* is frequently a mode of concealment.[56] Indra's manifold *rūpas*—whether he dons the form of a god, demon, king, bird, bee, or mosquito—are not the god's true identity in the epic. Thus, not surprisingly, although *māyā* is frequently used in the epic alongside *rūpa*, it is rarely found with *mūrti*. In contrast, the forms that a god manifests through *yoga* often require divine sight, such as Kuntī's vision of Sūrya, in which she gains the ability to see the god's divine form. Even when a god's *mūrti* is seen by ordinary human sight, such a form is not understood negatively but is rather treated as one of the god's embodiments. When Hanumān tells Bhīma that he is showing him as much of his *mūrti* as he can stand seeing, the implication is not that Hanumān is appearing in a false form, but rather he is manifesting all of his actual body that can be seen with ordinary human vision. If Bhīma had the capacity of divine sight, the implication is that he would see more, rather than see something entirely different, as in the case of Indra's guises. The epic authors thus suggest something important about the multiple bodies of the gods by evoking the term *yoga* in such contexts: in contrast to the forms generated through *māyā*, divine bodies manifested through *yoga* are not produced through mere "wizardry."

Another scholarly approach has been to argue that *tapas* and *yoga* are synonymous in the Mahābhārata. In the Brāhmaṇas and Upaniṣads the gods attained their divine status via *tapas*, and it is easy to extend the meanings of the term *yoga* to include the supranormal feats of the gods.[57] There are numerous epic passages that state that the gods attained their sovereignty because they possessed the power of *yoga*. But what is gained by equating *yoga* and *tapas*? What is *tapas*? Hopkins refers to the Kuntī passage discussed earlier in order to argue that there is no difference between *tapas* and *yoga* in the Mahābhārata,[58] because in his perspective both are ascetic practices.[59] A similar argument advanced by Mircea Eliade suggests that *yoga* was assimilated to *tapas* because of their similar methods—for example, fasting, breathing exercises, and various other ascetic practices that focus on restraint of the senses and meditation.[60] However, it is important to note that the Mahābhārata passages that discuss *yoga-mūrtis* do not refer specifically to any of these ascetic practices, and thus equating *yoga* with *tapas* in the sense of ascetic regimens does little to account for the role of *yoga* in generating multiple divine bodies in the epic. In attempting to assess the relationship between *tapas* and *yoga* in the epic, we must first critically examine the changing matrix of meanings in which *tapas* is used and also look closely at the particular yogic powers of the gods.

According to Walter Kaelber, *tapas,* as both process and product, is ultimately heat, or a "heated passage." In the context of the Vedic sacrifice this passage is the external passage of the ascetic endeavors of the *yajamāna* (sacrificial patron), whereas in the Upaniṣads it is an internal passage through meditative practices.[61] Neither of these meanings of *tapa*s seems suitable to the specific instances in which we find *yoga-mūrti*s in the Mahābhārata. Perhaps the strongest parallel is found in the Upaniṣadic notion that the heating (root *tap*) of the waters of creation results in a solid form, or *mūrti,* which is food. Through creative heat one is able to construct material forms. The creative power of *tapas* is a common theme in the Brāhmaṇas, in which the creator Prajāpati practices *tapas* in order to generate the multiple forms and phenomena of the material creation.

The earlier scholarly attempts to understand the relationship between *yoga* and *tapas* in the epic do not generally take into account popular *yoga* traditions. It is important to consider how the term *tapas* may have been assimilated to this alternative understanding of *yoga*. Interestingly, it is in popular *yoga* that the concern for the body, and even multiple bodies, is most evident. Hopkins notes this emphasis on the body in popular *yoga*: "[To practitioners of *yoga*] physical exercises are not ascetic mortifications [but] are conceived of as 'perfections' (*siddhi*s). Indeed, what is sought after through development of the body is 'altered states' but not 'of consciousness' (as in contemporary Western adaptations), but of the body."[62]

David Gordon White's recent studies of *yoga* have brought to light a popular tradition of *yoga* found throughout the Mahābhārata that has received relatively little attention in previous studies.[63] White draws attention to the term *yoga-yukta* as well as to the terminology of yogic possession and argues for a different understanding of *yoga*. He contends that the most systematic and technical uses of the term *yoga* in the Mahābhārata are found in descriptions of the death of the hero who, "yoked to *yoga*" (*yoga-yukta*) on the battlefield, penetrates the sun and attains the immortal realm. The procedure for obtaining the highest course, the sun, as recounted in the Harivaṃśa, the appendix to the Mahābhārata, is described by Hopkins:

> One faces the east, sitting on *kuśa* grass, in a place that is level and clear; then in accordance with the Śāstras and in accordance with rule, one who knows the proper order puts his soul in all the limbs, beginning with the feet, in regular succession, drawing in his hands and feet.[64]

The epic's *yogin* actualizes through his own practice the Upaniṣadic cosmological vision of release from the physical world, as portrayed, for example, in the Chāndogya Upaniṣad:

> Just as a long highway traverses both the villages, the one near by and the one far away, so also these rays of the sun traverse both the worlds, the one down here and the one up above. Extending out from the sun up there, they slip into these veins [of the heart] here, and extending out from these veins [of the heart] here, they slip into the sun up there.[65]

According to White, the epic's *yogin*, following the example of the Upaniṣadic sages, yokes himself to these rays and travels to the immortal realm beyond the sun.

White extends the analysis of *yoga-yukta* to other forms of *yoga* found throughout the Mahābhārata, and more specifically to possession of human bodies by those who are endowed with *yoga-bala*, the power of *yoga*. When Vidura possesses Yudhiṣṭhira by means of *yoga*, he fixes his sight on him eye to eye, enters (root *viś*) with his limbs into Yudhiṣṭhira's limbs, with his breath into Yudhiṣṭhira's breath, and with his senses into Yudhiṣṭhira's senses. Similarly, the *yogin* yokes himself to the rays of the eyes and possesses the bodies of others. White draws attention to a passage in the Mahābhārata that suggests that the power of the *yogin* is his power to possess other bodies:

> [P]ractitioners of Yoga who are without restraints and endowed with the power of yoga (*yogabalānvitāḥ*) are (so many) lords (of yoga), who enter into (the bodies of) the Prajāpatis, the sages, the gods, and the great beings. Neither Yama nor angry Antaka nor death of terrible prowess has dominion over the Yogi who is possessed of immeasurable splendor.[66]

In this passage, like many others in the epic, we get the sense that the *yogin* is able to enter and shed bodies in the same way that one clothes oneself in a garment that one subsequently sheds. The body is merely a shell that the *yogin* enters with his *prāṇa* (breath). White mentions other examples of this type of possession in the epic, such as Vipula possessing the body of his *guru*'s wife and Sulabhā obtaining a beautiful body and possessing the body of King Janaka.

Looking closely at the various strands of *yoga* woven throughout the Mahābhārata, I would argue that it is not a concern for ascetic practices that unites them. Rather, one factor that unites many of these strands is that they tend to share a concern for attaining (new) bodies by means of *yoga*—a concern that has pre-epic roots in the Upaniṣads. The Śvetāśvatara Upaniṣad states, "When earth, water, fire, air, and ether have arisen together, and the body made up of these five becomes equipped with the attribute of yoga, that man, obtaining a body tempered by the fire of yoga, will no longer experience sickness, old age, or suffering."[67] Although the broader context of this passage involves the practice of meditation and breathing exercises, these practices are nonetheless directed toward obtaining a new yogic body. Even the more philosophical *yoga* found in the Mokṣadharma section of the Mahābhārata, with its heightened interest in liberation, expresses an interest in transforming the human body. Through the practice of *yoga* a new, pure body is cultivated and attained. Ascetic practices are assimilated to the yogic concern for attaining new bodies by making such practices a way of cultivating a body. I would suggest that in those examples in the epic that connect *yoga* and *mūrti*, it would be best to understand *yoga* as a way of yoking—in a variety of ways—bodies. As many examples show, *yoga* is about manifesting and cultivating new bodies as well as harnessing other bodies for the *yogin*. While human *yogin*s are concerned with new bodies, the gods' *yoga* is directed at manifesting multiple bodies. Although the Mahābhārata does not describe the mechanisms by which gods manifest their *mūrti*s through *yoga*, it does provide descriptions of human *yogin*s obtaining other bodies through *yoga*. In the same way that yogic practices are the means through which human *yogin*s attain new bodies, it is often by means of *yoga* that the gods attain manifold bodies.[68]

Concluding Remarks

This examination of constructions of divine embodiment in the Mahābhārata reveals that while the terms *mūrti* and *vigraha* do not yet convey the meaning of a sculpted image in the epic, they are nonetheless critical to attaining a more complete understanding of divine embodiment during this pivotal period in Indian history. A comparison between Vedic and epic modes of embodiment points to the increasing importance of visual modes of apprehension in the epic period and the corresponding shifting understandings concerning the materiality of divine bodies. Whereas Vedic notions of embodiment tend to emphasize mesocosmic forms of the gods, such as the brick fire altar, that human beings can engage and manipulate through rituals, in the Mahābhārata both *mūrti*s and *vigraha*s are bodies that the gods manifest through their own powers, and thus human beings are limited in their ability to access and manipulate them. Specifically, I have shown that the term *vigraha* is used to refer to the human-like bodies that the gods assume on the earthly plane in order to interact with human beings and to influence human events. The term *mūrti* is used to refer to the multiple bodies that the gods manifest, while *yoga-mūrti* is a technical term for the bodies that the gods attain by means of *yoga*.

In this essay I have suggested that we redirect our scholarly inquiries and, rather than focusing on the question of whether or not sculpted images existed in the epic period, we give priority instead to attaining a better understanding of the terms that are used in the Mahābhārata to designate modes of divine embodiment. I have also challenged the usefulness of applying the classical system of Pātañjala Yoga to understand the epic material and have argued that popular understandings of *yoga* may provide a more useful framework for understanding the connections between *yoga* and *mūrti*s in the Mahābhārata.

Notes

The title of this essay was inspired by Malamoud's (1996) exploration of divine bodies in his essay "Bricks and Words: Observations on the Bodies of the Gods in Vedic India."

1. Some scholars date oral redactions of the Mahābhārata as early as 400–200 BCE. Van Buitenen (1973–1978) estimates 400 BCE for the earliest portions of the epic and 400 CE for the later, didactic portions. Hiltebeitel (2001) suggests the mid-second century BCE to the year zero as dates for the epic's composition. Most scholars have generally accepted 200 BCE–200 CE as the most likely dates for its composition.

2. Ambiguous phrases such as this one contribute little to our understanding of sculpted images. Chapter 82 of the Vana-Parvan is particularly rich with such allusions to the presence of deities at particular sites. The emphasis of this chapter generally seems to be about "seeing" (root *dṛś*) and "approaching" (root *gam* + *abhi*) a centralized and consolidated divine presence (*saṃnihita*). Although such examples convey much about the nature of sacred space and the abodes of

the gods in the epic, none of the examples use any of the terms that later come to mean a sculpted image—although these are the very instances in which we might expect these terms to be used.

3. Banerjea (2002) presents a variety of textual examples that he argues prove the existence of images in the epic period. However, only one of Banerjea's examples employs the term *mūrti* or any other specific term for image. He cites the following verse, which he identifies as Mahābhārata 13.25.21: "*nandīśvarasya mūrtiṃ tu dṛṣṭvā mucyeta kilviṣaiḥ*" (Banerjea 2002: 88). It is unclear from his notes and bibliography in what edition(s) this verse is found, and after searching the apparatus of the critical edition, I was unable to locate this verse. I also searched the critical edition using the versification of the Bombay, Calcutta, Kumbhakonam, and Madras editions, but to no avail. Thus the verse cited by Banerjea raises many unanswered questions about its date, in how many texts it occurs, and from what region it derives.

4. Mahābhārata 11.11.27.

5. Malamoud 1996: 223.

6. Mahābhārata 3.297.20–23. The translations of passages from the Mahābhārata, unless otherwise indicated, are from van Buitenen 1973–1978. In every case I have consulted the original Sanskrit text and have at times inserted in brackets relevant Sanskrit terms or other minor revisions to van Buitenen's translations.

7. Mahābhārata 2.3.25.

8. Mahābhārata 3.42.17–18.

9. Mahābhārata 3.40.53.

10. Mahābhārata 3.109.10–15.

11. Śatapatha Brāhmaṇa 3.6.2.26, cited in Malamoud 1996: 207.

12. See Malamoud 1996: 207–208. The Vedic seers, or *ṛṣis*, are held to have cognized the Vedas and preserved their cognitions in the form of the Vedic *mantras*, the recitation of which during the performance of Vedic sacrificial rituals is ascribed the power to make present the gods at the sacrifice. For an analysis of the mechanisms of the *ṛṣis*' cognitions, see Holdrege 1996: chapter 3.

13. Malamoud 1996: 325. Malamoud cites Viṣṇudharmottara Purāṇa 3.93.1–6 as an example of this Purāṇic perspective.

14. Holdrege 1996: 231.

15. Mahābhārata 3.107.14.

16. Mahābhārata 3.3.12–15; 3.4.1.

17. Mahābhārata 3.290.5–10.

18. Mahābhārata 3.290.20

19. See Holdrege 1996: 231.

20. See Malamoud 1996.

21. Holdrege 2008: 31. For an analysis of the function of mesocosmic forms in Kṛṣṇa *bhakti* (devotional) traditions, see Holdrege's essay (chapter 6) in the present volume as well as her extended study (Holdrege 2015).

22. In the early Vedic Saṃhitās and Brāhmaṇas, the root *grah* is used in the sense of "to take, hold, assume." Agrawala 2002b: 298.

23. Agrawala 2002b: 298.

24. Agrawala 2002b: 298.

25. Eck 1998: 38.

26. Mahābhārata 1.58.48.

27. See Couture 2001. The epic's use of the term *vigraha* seems to suggest something different from the Purāṇic use of the term *avatāra*, because *vigraha* is used to designate anthropomorphic or human-like forms and not the theriomorphic or animal-like forms that are associated with certain *avatāra*s of the deity Viṣṇu in the Purāṇas.

28. Mahābhārata 1.155.41–42.

29. Mahābhārata 1.61.95.

30. Mahābhārata 1.92.39.

31. Mahābhārata 17.1.33.

32. Smith 2006: 259.

33. See Banerjea 2002: 65.

34. Aitareya Upaniṣad 1.3.1–2. The translations of passages from the Upaniṣads, unless otherwise indicated, are from Olivelle 1998. In every case I have consulted the original Sanskrit text and have at times inserted in brackets relevant Sanskrit terms or other minor revisions to Olivelle's translations.

35. Agrawala 2002a: 186.

36. Bṛhadāraṇyaka Upaniṣad 2.3.1.

37. Malamoud 1996: 209.

38. Mahābhārata 3.107.14.

39. Mahābhārata 3.275.19.

40. Mahābhārata 1.7.6.

41. Mahābhārata 3.149.9.

42. Mahābhārata 3.12.20.

43. There seems to be a pattern in the frequency with which *yakṣas*, *rākṣasas*, and other subtle beings are described as *mūrtimant*, or as having *mūrtis*.

44. Mahābhārata 1.114.2–3. With reference to this episode with Dharma and Kuntī, Agrawala (2002a: 195–196) identifies *yoga-mūrti* as a technical term found in the epic, which he defines as a "spiritual embodiment" or "subtle image." However, he provides little to help us understand what he means by this translation. If a *yoga-mūrti* is a subtle image, does this imply that divine sight is necessary to see such *mūrtis*? In the episodes in which *yoga-mūrti* is used, it is not clear that divine sight is necessarily required. If anything, the preponderance of evidence suggests that *mūrtis* are frequently accessible to ordinary human sight.

45. See Mahābhārata 3.290.5–10, cited earlier.

46. Mahābhārata 1.45.7.

47. The term *yoga-mūrti* appears throughout the Mahābhārata, most prevalently in the first three Parvans. However, the occurrence of *yoga* and *mūrti* together, specifically with reference to divine bodies, is noticeably absent from the Śānti-Parvan, and particularly from the Mokṣadharma section (Mahābhārata 12.168–353), which is generally considered a later addition. There are instances in which the possessive form *mūrtimant* is used to describe kings as the

embodiments of Dharma, and it is also used in other contexts that are common throughout the epic. However, the specific meaning of *mūrti* as a body that a deity manifests by means of *yoga* is completely absent. Rather, the Mokṣadharma primarily employs *mūrti* to refer to human bodies. Thus a group of people mourning a boy who has died is approached by a vulture who says, "Understand the unpleasant fate that accompanies those with bodies [*mūrti*s]" (Mahābhārata 12.149.32). Here the parallels to the Upaniṣadic tradition of *mūrta/amūrta* are clear. The purely physical, material, and inert qualities of human *mūrti*s are emphasized. The Bṛhadāraṇyaka Upaniṣad passage, discussed earlier, that describes the two aspects of Brahman as *mūrta* and *amūrta* goes on to assert that the human body is *mūrta*, while *prāṇa* (breath) is *amūrta* (Bṛhadāraṇyaka Upaniṣad 2.3.1; 2.3.4–5). The Chāndogya Upaniṣad characterizes the physical body (*śarīra*) and its relationship to the *amūrta prāṇa* as follows: "This body [*śarīra*], Maghavan, is mortal; it is in the grip of death. So, it is the abode of this immortal and non-bodily self [Ātman]. One who has a body is in the grip of joy and sorrow, and there is no freedom from joy and sorrow for one who has a body. . . . The lifebreath [*prāṇa*] is yoked [*yukta*] to this body, as a draught animal to a cart" (Chāndogya Upaniṣad 8.12.1; 8.12.3). Although this passage does not use the term *mūrti* for body as the epic passage does, it interestingly employs the language of yoking, specifically the yoking of *prāṇa* to the body. It seems to be an extension of the Upaniṣadic distinction between *mūrta* and *amūrta* to call the material body to which the *amūrta prāṇa* is yoked a *mūrti*. As I will discuss later, in those passages in the epic that connect *yoga* and *mūrti*, *yoga* can be understood as a means of "yoking" bodies—more specifically, of manifesting multiple bodies, in the case of the gods, or cultivating new, pure bodies, in the case of human *yogins*.

48. Hopkins 1901: 337.

49. Rao 1985: vol. 1, 1.

50. Banerjea 2002: 79.

51. Banerjea 2002: 78–79.

52. Hopkins 1901: 368.

53. Malamoud 1996: 220.

54. Goudriaan 1978: 4.

55. Bṛhadāraṇyaka Upaniṣad 2.5.19, citing a verse that derives from Ṛg-Veda 6.47.18.

56. Goudriaan 1978: 18–19.

57. Eliade 1958: 150.

58. Hopkins 1901: 376–377.

59. See Hopkins 1901: 368, cited earlier.

60. Eliade 1958: 108–109.

61. Kaelber 1989: 141.

62. Cited in Smith 2006: 583.

63. See White 2003–2004, 2009.

64. Hopkins 1901: 361.

65. Chāndogya Upaniṣad 8.6.2.

66. Mahābhārata 12.289.24–26, cited in White 2003–2004: 619.

67. Śvetāśvatara Upaniṣad 2.12.

68. In his study of the discourse of possession throughout Indic history, from the Vedic period to the modern period, Smith argues that embodiment is repeatedly articulated through the rubric of possession. By drawing attention to the emic category of possession, Smith identifies a variety of modes of embodiment that fall under the paradigm of possession, including shapeshifting, incarnation, and transfer of essence. If, as Smith argues, "the territory of possession is the assumption of a multiplicity of bodies" (2006: 198), then one fruitful avenue of investigation might be to consider to what extent *yoga*, as the means through which the gods manifest multiple bodies, can be understood as a strategy of possession.

References

Agrawala, P. K. 2002a. "Mūrti." In *Kalātattvakośa: A Lexicon of Fundamental Concepts of the Indian Arts*, vol. 5, *Form/Shape: Ākāra/Ākṛti*, ed. Ramesh Chandra Sharma, 181–236. New Delhi: Indira Gandhi National Centre for the Arts; Delhi: Motilal Banarsidass.

Agrawala, P. K. 2002b. "Vigraha." In *Kalātattvakośa: A Lexicon of Fundamental Concepts of the Indian Arts*, vol. 5, *Form/Shape: Ākāra/Ākṛti*, ed. Ramesh Chandra Sharma, 295–332. New Delhi: Indira Gandhi National Centre for the Arts; Delhi: Motilal Banarsidass.

Banerjea, Jitendra Nath. 2002. *The Development of Hindu Iconography*. 5th ed. New Delhi: Munshiram Manoharlal.

Couture, André. 2001. "From Viṣṇu's Deeds to Viṣṇu's Play, or Observations on the Word Avatāra as a Designation for the Manifestations of Viṣṇu." *Journal of Indian Philosophy* 29, no. 3: 313–326.

Eck, Diana L. 1998. *Darśan: Seeing the Divine Image in India*. 3rd ed. New York: Columbia University Press.

Eliade, Mircea. 1958. *Yoga: Immortality and Freedom*. New York: Pantheon Books.

Goudriaan, Teun. 1978. "The Māyā of the Gods." In his *Māyā Divine and Human: A Study of Magic and Its Religious Foundations in Sanskrit Texts, with Particular Attention to a Fragment on Viṣṇu's Māyā Preserved in Bali*, 1–55. Delhi: Motilal Banarsidass.

Hiltebeitel, Alf. 2001. *Rethinking the Mahābhārata: A Reader's Guide to the Education of the Dharma King*. Chicago: University of Chicago Press.

Holdrege, Barbara A. 1996. *Veda and Torah: Transcending the Textuality of Scripture*. Albany: State University of New York Press.

Holdrege, Barbara A. 2008. "Body." In *Studying Hinduism: Key Concepts and Methods*, ed. Sushil Mittal and Gene Thursby, 19–40. New York: Routledge.

Holdrege, Barbara A. 2015. *Bhakti and Embodiment: Fashioning Divine Bodies and Devotional Bodies in Kṛṣṇa Bhakti*. New York: Routledge.

Hopkins, E. Washburn. 1901. "Yoga-Technique in the Great Epic." *Journal of the American Oriental Society* 22: 333–379.

Kaelber, Walter O. 1989. *Tapta Mārga: Asceticism and Initiation in Vedic India.* Albany: State University of New York Press.

Mahābhārata. 1933–1972. *The Mahābhārata,* ed. Vishnu S. Sukthankar, S. K. Belvalkar, and P. L. Vaidya. 19 vols. Pune: Bhandarkar Oriental Research Institute.

Malamoud, Charles. 1996 [1989]. "Bricks and Words: Observations on the Bodies of the Gods in Vedic India." In his *Cooking the World: Ritual and Thought in Ancient India,* 207–225. Translated by David White. New Delhi: Oxford University Press.

Olivelle, Patrick, ed. and trans. 1998. *The Early Upaniṣads: Annotated Text and Translation.* New York: Oxford University Press.

Rao, T. A. Gopinatha. 1985 [1914]. *Elements of Hindu Iconography.* 2 vols. Reprint. Delhi: Motilal Banarsidass.

Smith, Frederick M. 2006. *The Self Possessed: Deity and Spirit Possession in South Asian Literature and Civilization.* New York: Columbia University Press.

van Buitenen, J. A. B., trans. and ed. 1973–1978. *The Mahābhārata.* 3 vols. Chicago: University of Chicago Press.

White, David Gordon. 2003–2004. "Early Understandings of Yoga in the Light of Three Aphorisms from the Yoga Sūtra of Patañjali." *Studia Asiatica: International Journal for Asian Studies* 4–5: 613–629.

White, David Gordon. 2009. *Sinister Yogis.* Chicago: University of Chicago Press.

Chapter 6

Bhakti and Embodiment

Bodies of Devotion and Bodies of Bliss in Kṛṣṇa *Bhakti*

BARBARA A. HOLDREGE

The term *bhakti*, from the root *bhaj*, "to share, partake of," is first and foremost about relationship. Among the earliest occurrences of the term, in Pāṇini's *Aṣṭādhyāyī* (ca. 500–400 BCE)[1] and the Mahābhārata (ca. 200 BCE–100 CE) the term *bhakti* is at times used to refer to a relationship of loyalty, service, and homage to a king or military leader, while in the Śvetāśvatara Upaniṣad (ca. 400–200 BCE)[2] and the Bhagavad-Gītā (ca. 200 BCE) the meaning of the term is extended to include service, reverence, love for, and devotion to a deity. In later *bhakti* traditions the term is also at times extended further to include the *guru* as the object of *bhakti*. *Bhakti*, as a term concerning a relationship with a deity, connotes sharing in, partaking of, and participating in the deity as Other. The various traditions that constitute themselves in relation to the category *bhakti* tend to posit an initial duality between the *bhakta* as subject and the divine Other as object and then delineate a path by means of which the *bhakta* can overcome the state of separation and engage in an increasingly intimate relationship with the divine Other conceived of as a personal God. This relationship finds fruition in the ultimate goal of union with the deity, which is variously represented, ranging from a state of union-in-difference to a state of undifferentiated unity without duality. *Bhakti*, as a term connoting partaking of and participation in the deity, is thus at times invoked as both a means and an end, as constitutive of the path as well as of the goal.[3]

In the first part of this essay I will explore the connections between *bhakti* and embodiment and will be concerned more specifically with the role that discursive representations and practices pertaining to divine bodies and devotional bodies assume in the construction of *bhakti* traditions. In the second part of the essay I will ground my general reflections on *bhakti* and embodiment in an analysis of the discourse of Kṛṣṇa *bhakti* developed by the Gauḍīya Vaiṣṇava tradition, an important *bhakti* tradition inspired by Caitanya (1486–1533 CE) in the sixteenth century CE in the northeastern region of India that is now known as Bengal, which can serve as a case study to illustrate how issues of embodiment are grappled with in a specific discursive framework.[4]

Bhakti and Embodiment

In order to illuminate the connections between *bhakti* and embodiment and to highlight more specifically the various factors that tend to distinguish highly embodied traditions and less embodied traditions, I would like to briefly examine the role of embodiment in the emergence of *bhakti* traditions.

The period between 200 BCE and 200 CE marks the transition from the Vedic period to the post-Vedic period in which a new brahmanical synthesis—that "federation of cultures popularly known as Hinduism"[5]—emerged, which attempted to bring together and reconcile diverse strands of Indian thought and practice. Although certain proto-*bhakti* currents may be found in Vedic traditions, it is only in the period between 200 BCE and 200 CE that we see the emergence of popular *bhakti* movements. The *bhakti* stream, the underground currents of which may have been gathering force for centuries, suddenly bursts forth in certain areas of the Indian subcontinent in the last centuries before the Common Era, finding expression in the rise of sectarian devotional movements centering on the deities Viṣṇu and Śiva and in the upsurge of multiform vernacular traditions venerating a panoply of goddesses at the local village level.

The historical shift from Vedic traditions to post-Vedic *bhakti* traditions is accompanied by a shift from abstract, translocal notions of divinity to particularized, localized notions of divinity and a corresponding shift from aniconic to iconic traditions and from temporary sacrificial arenas to established temple sites. A. K. Ramanujan has provided a succinct encapsulation of a number of features that define this historical shift:

> This shift [from Vedic to bhakti traditions] is paralleled by other religious shifts: from the noniconic to the iconic; from the nonlocal to the local; from the sacrificial-fire rituals (*yajña* and *homa*) meant to be performed only by Vedic experts to worship (*pūjā*) by nearly all; from rituals in which a plot of ground is temporarily cordoned off and made into sacred space by experts in a consecration rite—to worship in temples, localized, named, open to almost the whole range of Hindu society. These changes are accompanied by a shift away from the absolute godhead, the non-personal Brahman of the Upaniṣads, to the gods of the mythologies, with faces, complexions, families, feelings, personalities, characters. Bhakti poems celebrate god as both local and translocal, and especially as the nexus of the two.[6]

I would argue that the various transformations that characterize this historical shift from Vedic traditions to post-Vedic *bhakti* traditions are a direct consequence of newly emerging discourses of the body in *bhakti* traditions in which constructions of *divine embodiment* proliferate, celebrating the notion that a deity, while remaining translocal in his or her essential nature, can appear in manifold corporeal forms and assume various types of concentrated presence in different times and different localities on different planes of existence.[7] These new constructions of divine embodiment can be distinguished from earlier Vedic formulations in seven ways.

Particularized divine bodies. In contrast to Vedic texts, which make formulaic allusions to the bodies of gods and goddesses while eschewing individualized descriptions of their corporeal forms, *bhakti* traditions develop elaborate and particularized descriptions of the bodies of the deities.[8] The rise of *bhakti* traditions is accompanied by the elaboration of iconographic and mythological traditions in which each of the major deities becomes associated with a standardized repertoire of particularized forms, with distinctive postures, gestures, and emblems.

Embodiment of the divine in time. The emergence of *bhakti* traditions is accompanied by the development of post-Vedic notions of "divine descent"—designated by the terms *avatāra, avataraṇa,* or other substantive forms derived from the root *tṝ* + *ava,* "to descend"—in which certain deities are represented as descending from their divine abodes to the material realm periodically and becoming embodied in manifest forms—whether divine, human, animal, or hybrid forms—in different cosmic cycles.[9]

Embodiment of the divine in place. In Vedic *yajñas*, sacrificial rituals, a sacrificial arena is temporarily cordoned off and particular deities are invoked to become present at the seat of sacrifice and to receive the oblations offered into the sacrificial fire, after which the deities are invited to depart and the sacrificial arena is destroyed. In contrast to the temporary constructions of sacred space and translocal notions of divinity associated with Vedic traditions, *bhakti* traditions foster locative discourses and practices centering on sacred sites, or *tīrthas* (from the root *tṝ*, "to cross over"), that function as "crossing-places" in which deities become embodied in particular locales. As the counterpart of the notion of *avatāra*, the concept of *tīrtha* encompasses the multiple places on earth to which deities descend from their divine abodes, assuming localized forms in particular geographic features such as rivers, mountains, forests, rock outcroppings, and caves, or infusing their divine presence in the landscape of an entire region. *Tīrthas*, as centers of concentrated divine presence associated with particular deities, are variously represented as manifestations of the deity, parts of the deity's body, special abodes (*dhāmans*) of the deity, or sites of the deity's divine play (*līlā*). *Bhakti* communities develop a variety of means to visibly mark such places as sacred—in particular, through building architectural structures such as temples and shrines to mark the sites of divine presence and then investing these built structures with the status of *tīrthas*. In addition, *tīrtha-yātrā*, pilgrimage to *tīrthas*, is ascribed primacy of place in the emerging complex of *bhakti* practices as a ritual alternative to Vedic *yajñas* that is in principle open to people at all levels of the socioreligious hierarchy.[10]

Embodiment of the divine in image. In contrast to the aniconic orientation of the Vedic tradition,[11] in *bhakti* traditions the notion of *avatāra*, divine descent in time, and the notion of *tīrtha*, divine instantiation in place, converge in conceptions of image-incarnations in which ritual images (*mūrtis* or *arcās*) are revered as localized embodiments of the deity.[12]

Embodiment of the divine in name. Vedic conceptions of language, in which the names (*nāmans*) contained in the Vedic *mantras* are held to be the sound correlates that contain the subtle essence and structure of the forms (*rūpas*) that they signify, are extended and recast in *bhakti* formulations concerning divine names (*nāmans*) in which the name is extolled as the sonic form of the deity.[13]

Embodiment of the divine in text. Vedic constructions of scripture, in which the body of the creator Prajāpati or the body of Brahman-Ātman is held to be constituted by the Vedic *mantras*, are appropriated and reinterpreted in *bhakti* traditions with reference to their own sacred texts.[14] In certain *bhakti* reformulations the deity is celebrated as becoming embodied in a variety of different kinds of sacred texts, ranging from Sanskritic *smṛti* texts that emulate the paradigmatic Veda to vernacular hymns that are revered as text-embodiments of the deity. Moreover, the notion of divine embodiment is extended beyond oral texts to include written texts as well, in which the concrete book is viewed as an incarnate form of the deity that is to be worshiped accordingly.

Embodiment of the divine in human form. Bhakti traditions foster a variety of notions in which the deity assumes corporeal form in a human body. In such conceptions certain human beings—in particular, realized *gurus*, poet-saints, and exalted *bhaktas*—are revered as localized embodiments of the deity. The deity is also held to descend and become temporarily instantiated in particular human bodies through a variety of embodied practices, including ritual possession, dance, and dramatic performances.

This constellation of notions pertaining to divine bodies—along with the associated practices through which devotional bodies are constituted in relation to these modes of divine embodiment—is configured in a variety of ways in early *bhakti* traditions. A number of these notions and practices are found in incipient form in the Mahābhārata (ca. 200 BCE–100 CE)—the first great textual monument to *bhakti*—and are further crystallized and expanded in the Harivaṃśa (ca. 200 CE), the appendix to the Mahābhārata, and in the early Purāṇas that derive from the Gupta Period (ca. 320–550 CE). Certain epic and Purāṇic traditions pertaining to these various modes of divine embodiment are in turn selectively appropriated and reimagined in the earliest full-fledged *bhakti* movements for which we have textual witness in the form of devotional poetry: the Tamil Vaiṣṇava poet-saints known as the Āḻvārs and their Tamil Śaiva counterparts, the Nāyaṉārs and Māṇikkavācakar, who flourished in the Tamil-speaking areas of South India between the sixth and ninth centuries CE.

An exploration of the connections between *bhakti* and embodiment can thus serve to illuminate a number of the transformations that characterize the historical shift from Vedic traditions to post-Vedic *bhakti* traditions. Moreover, I would suggest that such an investigation is critical to our understanding of the myriad forms that *bhakti* has historically assumed up to the present time, for embodiment is integral to the oral-aural and performative dimensions of devotional practices through which *bhaktas* engage the deity in his or her various embodied forms: *tīrtha-yātrā*, pilgrimage to the sacred places in which the deity's presence is held to be instantiated; *pūjā*, ritual offerings to the image-incarnations of the deity in temples and shrines; *nāma-kīrtana*, singing of the divine names as a means of engaging the sonic forms of the deity; *paṭhana*, recitation of the scriptures and devotional hymns that are revered as text-embodiments of the deity; *līlā-kīrtana*, singing and recounting the stories of the divine play of the deity in various bodily forms; and *rāsa-līlā* and *nṛtya*, dramatic and dance performances in which the performers are revered as living forms (*svarūpa*s), or temporary instantiations, of the deity. All of these practices are *embodied* practices—practices through which the bodies of *bhakta*s engage the embodied forms of the deity. Karen Pechilis Prentiss, in her study of Tamil Śaiva *bhakti* from the seventh to fourteenth centuries CE, has argued that *bhakti* functions as a "theology of embodiment" for Tamil Śaivas and for *bhakti* traditions generally.[15] More recently, Christian Novetzke, building on Prentiss's insights, has emphasized that embodiment has not only assumed a critical role in the sociocultural construction of particular *bhakti* communities but, more broadly, constitutes the "very epicenter" of what he terms the "publics of *bhakti*."

> Just as the public sphere requires literacy, the publics of *bhakti* in South Asia require "embodiment," the human as medium. This very useful notion of "embodiment" does not simply exist as a trope of literature, but is deeply engaged in the performance of the discourse of *bhakti*. By "discourse" I mean the manifestation of *bhakti* not only in performance through song or literacy, but also through all those actions and bodily displays that make up *bhakti* in the broadest sense, such as . . . pilgrimage, *pūjā*, *darśan*, the wearing of signs on the body, and so on. Embodiment, then, is not so much a technique of *bhakti* as its very epicenter: *bhakti* needs bodies.[16]

I would suggest that an investigation of embodiment as the "very epicenter" of *bhakti* can illuminate correlations among the array of ontologies, devotional modes, goals, and practices found in *bhakti* traditions. In this context I would posit, as a heuristic device, a spectrum of *bhakti* traditions characterized by varying degrees of embodiment, with highly embodied traditions at one end of the spectrum and less embodied traditions at the other end. Highly embodied *bhakti* traditions tend to be correlated with ontologies that celebrate the manifold forms of the Godhead, modes of *bhakti* that favor more passionate and ecstatic expressions of devotion, and formulations of the goal of life that emphasize the state of union-in-difference in which the *bhakta* savors the embrace of the deity in eternal relationship. Exemplars of highly embodied traditions include the Āḻvārs Nammāḻvār and Āṇṭāḷ (ca. ninth century CE), the Bhāgavata Purāṇa (ca. ninth to tenth century CE), and Caitanya (1486–1533 CE) and his Gauḍīya followers. Less embodied *bhakti* traditions tend to be correlated with ontologies that emphasize the formlessness of the Godhead in its essential nature, modes of *bhakti* that favor more contemplative forms of devotion, and formulations of the goal of life that emphasize the state of undifferentiated unity without duality in which the *bhakta* merges with the deity. Among the exemplars of less embodied traditions, I would single out Kabīr (ca. 1398–1448 CE) in particular.[17]

The Gauḍīya Discourse of Embodiment

In the remainder of this essay I will focus on the discourse of embodiment developed by the Gauḍīya Sampradāya (school) in the sixteenth century, which provides a striking example of the multileveled models of embodiment and systems of bodily practices that are integral to many *bhakti* traditions. Caitanya himself did not leave a legacy of devotional poetry or other literary expression beyond eight verses, termed *Śikṣāṣṭaka*, that are traditionally ascribed to him. He is represented in hagiographic narratives as charging a group of his disciples, who came to be known as the "six Gosvāmins of Vṛndāvana," with the task of developing a formal system of theology and practice to perpetuate the *bhakti* movement inspired by him. The six Gosvāmins are credited with formulating a *bhakti-śāstra*, formal discourse of *bhakti*, together with the associated regimen of practices termed *sādhana-bhakti* that define the distinctive tradition-identity of the Gauḍīya Sampradāya.[18] In the following analysis I will seek to illuminate the critical defining feature that distinguishes the Gauḍīya discourse of *bhakti* from contending discourses in the Indian religiocultural landscape: its function as a *discourse of embodiment*.

The Gauḍīya discourse of embodiment is elaborated by Rūpa Gosvāmin (ca. 1470–1557 CE) and Jīva Gosvāmin (ca. 1516–1608 CE), the principal architects of the Gauḍīya theological edifice, in their most important works: Rūpa's *Bhaktirasāmṛtasindhu*,[19] *Ujjvalanīlamaṇi*, and *Laghubhāgavatāmṛta*,[20] and Jīva's six-volume *Bhāgavata Sandarbha*.[21] The key elements of this discourse are encapsulated and expanded on by Kṛṣṇadāsa Kavirāja (ca. 1517–1620 CE), the Gosvāmins' acclaimed disciple, in his Bengali compendium *Caitanya Caritāmṛta*.[22] This discourse includes a robust discourse of divine embodiment pertaining to the manifold forms of Kṛṣṇa and an equally robust discourse of human embodiment pertaining to the devotional bodies of Kṛṣṇa *bhaktas*. While the early Gauḍīya authorities ground their discursive representations and practices pertaining to both divine bodies and human bodies in the canonical authority of the Bhāgavata Purāṇa, at the same time they invest the Bhāgavata's teachings with new valences by reframing Kṛṣṇa devotion in light of Indian theories of aesthetics and generating a distinctive new discourse of *bhakti* founded on the category of *bhakti-rasa* that I term an "embodied aesthetics of *bhakti*."

The Gauḍīya discourse of divine embodiment celebrates the deity Kṛṣṇa as *ananta-rūpa*, "he who has endless forms," his limitless forms encompassing and interweaving the transcosmic, macrocosmic, and microcosmic planes of existence. In addition, this discourse includes a number of intermediary forms that I term "mesocosmic" modes of divine embodiment in that they function in Gauḍīya formulations as mediating forms through which *bhaktas* can access, engage, and experience the concentrated presence of the deity in localized forms on the gross material plane. The Gauḍīya discourse of divine embodiment has its counterpart in a discourse of human embodiment that is concerned with fashioning devotional bodies by means of *sādhana-bhakti*, an elaborate system of embodied practices that comprises two forms of devotional discipline: *vaidhī-bhakti* and *rāgānugā-bhakti*. In *vaidhī-bhakti* the practitioner, or *sādhaka*, performs external bodily practices with the *sādhaka-rūpa*, the material psychophysical complex, and engages in a regimen guided by scriptural injunctions (*vidhis*) that is designed to purify and transform the psychophysiology, reconstituting the karmically constructed body of bondage as a body of devotion in which the mental faculties, sense organs, and organs of action are all oriented toward one-pointed worship of Kṛṣṇa. In *rāgānugā-bhakti*, an advanced form of *sādhana-bhakti* characterized by passionate love (*rāga*), the *bhakta* engages in a regimen that combines internal meditative practices with external bodily practices in order to realize a *siddha-rūpa*, a perfected devotional body that is an eternal, nonmaterial body of bliss.

In a separate study I have provided an extended analysis of the Gauḍīya discourse of embodiment pertaining to both the divine bodies of Kṛṣṇa and the devotional bodies of Kṛṣṇa *bhaktas*.[23] In the following analysis I will focus on three categories that are pivotal to this discourse—*ananta-rūpa*, *sādhaka-rūpa*, and *siddha-rūpa*—and the associated regimens of practice for fashioning a devotional body.

Ananta-rūpa: The Limitless Forms of Kṛṣṇa

The Gauḍīya discourse of divine embodiment constructs a number of hierarchical taxonomies that classify and rank the multifarious divine forms of Kṛṣṇa as *ananta-rūpa*.[24]

Brahman, Paramātman, and Bhagavān

The most important of the Gauḍīya taxonomies involves a hierarchical assessment of the three aspects of the supreme Godhead, from lowest to highest: Brahman, Paramātman, and Bhagavān. As we shall see, in allotting the highest place in their ontological hierarchy to Bhagavān, who is represented as a personal Godhead endowed with an absolute body, infinite qualities, and innumerable *śakti*s (energies), the early Gauḍīya authorities engage in a polemic that challenges the contending ontologies of two rival philosophical schools: the monistic ontology of Advaita Vedānta, which identifies the ultimate reality with the impersonal, formless Brahman, and the dualistic ontology of Pātañjala Yoga, which posits a plurality of nonchanging, formless *puruṣa*s as the highest reality.

To provide a scriptural basis for this hierarchical assessment, the early Gauḍīya authorities invoke Bhāgavata Purāṇa 1.2.11 and interpret the order of terms in the verse as indicating increasing ontological importance: "The knowers of reality declare the ultimate reality to be that which is nondual knowledge. It is called Brahman, Paramātman, and Bhagavān." In Gauḍīya formulations these three aspects of the Godhead are associated with different dimensions of embodiment. Brahman, the lowest aspect of the Godhead, is the impersonal, formless, attributeless, and undifferentiated ground of existence that is beyond *prakṛti*, primordial matter, and is the radiant effulgence of the absolute body of Bhagavān. Paramātman, the intermediary aspect of the Godhead, is the indwelling Self, who on the macrocosmic level animates the innumerable universes, or cosmos bodies, and on the microcosmic level resides in the hearts of all *jīva*s, embodied beings. Bhagavān, the highest aspect of the Godhead, is transcosmic—beyond both the macrocosmos and the microcosmos—and is personal, endowed with an absolute body (*vigraha*), replete with infinite qualities (*guṇa*s), and possessed of innumerable *śakti*s. Bhagavān is ascribed the status of the Godhead in his complete fullness (*pūrṇa*), who encompasses within himself Brahman and Paramātman and is at the same time beyond both.[25] The early Gauḍīya authorities invoke the declaration in Bhāgavata Purāṇa 1.3.28 that "Kṛṣṇa is Bhagavān himself (Bhagavān *svayam*)" as the *mahā-vākya*, authoritative scriptural utterance, that establishes Kṛṣṇa's supreme status as *pūrṇa* Bhagavān, the full and complete Godhead.[26]

Bhagavān's Self-Referral Play with His Śaktis

The Gauḍīya discourse of divine embodiment emphasizes that Bhagavān is *śaktimat*, the possessor of innumerable *śakti*s, energies or powers. The three principal types of *śakti* are the *svarūpa-śakti, māyā-śakti,* and *jīva-śakti*. The *svarūpa-śakti* operates on the transcosmic level as the *śakti* that is intrinsic (*antar-aṅga*) to Bhagavān's essential nature (*svarūpa*), comprising three aspects: *saṃdhinī-śakti*, the power of *sat*, being; *saṃvit-śakti*, the power of *cit*, consciousness; and *hlādinī-śakti*, the power of *ānanda*, bliss. The *māyā-śakti* operates on the macrocosmic level as the *śakti* that is extrinsic (*bahir-aṅga*) to Bhagavān and that is responsible for manifesting and regulating the material realm of *prakṛti* and for subjecting *jīva*s, individual living beings, to the bondage of *saṃsāra*, the cycle of birth and death. The *jīva-śakti* operates on the microcosmic level as the intermediary (*taṭasthā*, literally, "standing on the border") *śakti* that constitutes *jīva*s as, on the one hand, an *aṃśa*, or part, of Bhagavān in the *svarūpa-śakti* and, on the other hand, subject to the binding influence of the *māyā-śakti*.[27]

The Gauḍīya discourse of divine embodiment, as explicated by Jīva Gosvāmin, is concerned in particular with the structures and dynamics of the *svarūpa-śakti*. The *svarūpa-śakti* assumes two forms: the *svarūpa*, which is Bhagavān himself in his essential nature and absolute body; and the *svarūpa-vaibhava*, which includes his transcendent abode, *dhāman*, and his eternal associates, *parikara*s or *pārṣada*s. The *svarūpa-śakti* also includes Kṛṣṇa's *līlā*, divine play, as *svayaṃ* Bhagavān, which is represented as the spontaneous expression of the *hlādinī-śakti*, the bliss that is intrinsic to Bhagavān's essential nature. The transcendent *dhāman* is called Kṛṣṇaloka and is the domain where Kṛṣṇa engages eternally in his *līlā*. Kṛṣṇaloka is subdivided into three *dhāman*s. The innermost *dhāman* of Kṛṣṇaloka is the transcendent Vraja-*dhāman*, Goloka-Vṛndāvana, which is the transcosmic prototype of the earthly region of Vraja in North India.[28]

Jīva, building on the formulations of Rūpa Gosvāmin, seeks to establish that Kṛṣṇa's *līlā*, which is recorded in narrative form in the tenth book of the Bhāgavata Purāṇa, occurs on both the manifest (*prakaṭa*) and unmanifest (*aprakaṭa*) levels. The Bhāgavata Purāṇa portrays Kṛṣṇa as descending to the material realm and unfolding his *līlā* on earth at a particular time and place in history: in the terrestrial region of Vraja in North India at the end of Dvāpara Yuga in the current *manvantara* (interval of Manu) known as Vaivasvata Manvantara in approximately 3000 BCE. In a hermeneutical turn that is critical to the Gauḍīya discourse of divine embodiment, Jīva interprets this earthly *līlā* as the manifest counterpart of the *aprakaṭa līlā,* unmanifest *līlā,* that goes on eternally within Bhagavān in Kṛṣṇaloka, beyond the material realm of *prakṛti* and beyond Brahman. He also ascribes an eternal status to the cowherds (*gopa*s), cowmaidens (*gopī*s), and other companions of Kṛṣṇa who are the key characters in the Bhāgavata Purāṇa's literary account of the divine drama in Vraja. Kṛṣṇa's foster parents Nanda and Yaśodā, attendants, cowherd friends, and cowmaiden lovers are represented as his eternal associates, *parikara*s or *pārṣada*s, eternally perfect beings who participate in his essential nature as part of the *svarūpa-śakti* and engage with him eternally in the unmanifest *līlā* in his transcendent Vraja-*dhāman*.[29] Jīva is concerned to illumine more specifically the relationship between Kṛṣṇa and the *gopī*s, the cowmaidens of Vraja, portrayed in the *rāsa-pañcādhyāyī,* chapters 29 to 33 of the tenth book of the Bhāgavata Purāṇa, which celebrates in lavish detail Kṛṣṇa's love-play with the *gopī*s, culminating in the *rāsa-līlā,* the circle dance of Kṛṣṇa with his cowmaiden lovers.[30] Jīva argues that the *gopī*s are the eternal expressions of the *hlādinī-śakti,* the blissful aspect of the *svarūpa-śakti,* and the unmanifest *līlā* of Kṛṣṇa with the *gopī*s is thus interpreted in terms of the inner dynamics of the Godhead as self-referral play within Bhagavān in which he revels eternally with the blissful impulses of his own nature.

When Kṛṣṇa descends to earth at the end of Dvāpara Yuga, the *gopī*s and the other eternal associates are represented as descending with him to the terrestrial region of Vraja in North India, where he displays his manifest *līlā*. The *līlā* is thus understood as a process of self-disclosure through which Kṛṣṇa revels on the unmanifest plane in the rapturous delights of his own divine play and expresses himself on the manifest plane in a series of episodes that display different aspects of the divine nature.

While the Gauḍīya discourse of divine embodiment centers on the *svarūpa-śakti,* the discourse of human embodiment centers on the *jīva-śakti* and the mechanisms of liberation from the binding influence of the *māyā-śakti.* The ultimate goal of human existence is represented as the attainment of a state of realization in which the *jīva* is liberated from the bondage of the *māyā-śakti* and awakens to the reality of Kṛṣṇa as *svayaṃ* Bhagavān and to its true identity as an *aṃśa* of Bhagavān in the *svarūpa-śakti.* The *jīva* attains direct experiential realization of its eternal relationship with Bhagavān in *acintya-bhedābheda,* inconceivable difference-in-nondifference. Having cast off the last vestiges of bondage to material existence, the realized *jīva* reclaims its distinctive role in the transcendent Vraja-*dhāman* as a participant in the unmanifest *līlā* and enjoys the bliss of *preman*, all-consuming love for Kṛṣṇa, in the eternal embrace of the supreme Godhead.

The Absolute Body of Bhagavān

One of the most striking claims of the Gauḍīya discourse of divine embodiment is its insistence that—contrary to the ontologies of competing philosophical schools that claim that the ultimate reality in its essential nature is formless—the highest aspect of the Godhead, Bhagavān, is not without form (*nirākāra*) but rather is endowed with an absolute *body* with distinctive bodily features that is at the same time nonmaterial (*aprākṛta*), unmanifest (*avyakta*), eternal (*nitya*), and self-luminous (*svaprakāśa*). This absolute body is designated by the term *vigraha*. The early Gauḍīya authorities emphasize that Bhagavān's *vigraha*, like his *svarūpa*, essential nature, consists of being (*sat*), consciousness (*cit*), and bliss (*ānanda*). Thus in Bhagavān there is no distinction between body and essence, *vigraha* and *svarūpa*, for the body (*deha*) and the possessor of the body (*dehin*) are nondifferent.[31] Indeed, in the Gauḍīya discourse of divine embodiment, the term *svarūpa* is used at times to refer to Bhagavān's essential nature and at other times to refer to his essential form, which in the final analysis are considered identical.

The Gauḍīyas assert the paradoxical notion that Bhagavān's absolute body, in its *svayaṃ-rūpa* or *svarūpa*, essential form, is the two-armed form of Gopāla Kṛṣṇa, who is extolled in the tenth book of the Bhāgavata Purāṇa as descending to earth and carrying out his *līlā* in the form of a *gopa*, cowherd boy, in the area of Vraja in North India. It is the beautiful youthful form (*kiśora-mūrti*) of the cowherd Kṛṣṇa—with its distinctive blue-black color, body marks, dress, ornaments, and characteristic emblems such as the flute—that is celebrated by the Gauḍīyas as the absolute body, *vigraha*, that exists eternally in the transcendent Vraja-*dhāman*, Goloka-Vṛndāvana. Rūpa Gosvāmin gives the following description of Kṛṣṇa's *svayaṃ-rūpa*:

> The sweet form (*mūrti*) of the enemy of Madhu [Kṛṣṇa] brings me intense joy. His neck has three lines like a conch, his clever eyes are charming like lotuses, his blue-black limbs are more resplendent than the tamāla tree, . . . his chest displays the Śrīvatsa mark, and his hands are marked with the discus, conch, and other emblems. . . . This lover has a beautiful

> body (*aṅga*) and is endowed with all auspicious marks, radiant, luminous, powerful, eternally young.[32]

The Source and Container of Avatāras

The early Gauḍīya authorities emphasize that Kṛṣṇa, while maintaining the integrity of his *vigraha,* absolute body, simultaneously assumes innumerable forms (*sarva-rūpa-svabhāvatva*) on the transcosmic, macrocosmic, and microcosmic planes of existence. In their recasting of Purāṇic theories of *avatāra,* they emphasize that Kṛṣṇa, as *svayaṃ* Bhagavān, is not himself an *avatāra,* but rather he is the *avatārin* who is the source and container of all *avatāra*s, descending to the material realm periodically and assuming a variety of forms in different cosmic cycles.[33] The Bhāgavata Purāṇa's account of twenty-two *avatāra*s, which culminates in the *mahā-vākya* that "Kṛṣṇa is Bhagavān *svayam,*" is invoked as scriptural evidence to ground this claim: "O brahmins, the *avatāra*s of Hari, who is the ocean of being, are countless, like thousands of streams flowing from an inexhaustible lake. . . . All these are portions (*aṃśa*s) or fractions of portions (*kalā*s) of the supreme Person, but Kṛṣṇa is Bhagavān himself (Bhagavān *svayam*)."[34]

Building on the language and imagery of the Bhāgavata, the Gauḍīyas maintain that Kṛṣṇa, the inexhaustible plenitude of being, sends forth an endless stream of *avatāra*s, which are partial manifestations—whether *aṃśa*s, portions, or *kalā*s, fractions of portions—of his absolute body consisting of *sat-cit-ānanda.*

> Kṛṣṇa is the highest Īśvara, *svayaṃ bhagavān,* the container of *avatāra*s, and the chief cause of everything. The infinite Vaikuṇṭha and the infinite *avatāra*s, the infinite Brahmā-worlds—he is the receptacle of all of these. He is Vrajendranandana [the son of Nanda the lord of Vraja], whose body is *sat, cit,* and *ānanda;* he possesses all majesty, all *śakti*s, and is full of all *rasa.*[35]

The Gauḍīya Challenge to Advaita Vedānta and Pātañjala Yoga

The early Gauḍīya authorities deploy their discourse of divine embodiment as the distinguishing feature of what I term their "theology of superordination," in which they attenuate the challenges posed by competing philosophical schools and *bhakti* traditions by selectively appropriating and accommodating elements of those traditions' teachings and integrating them into an encompassing hierarchical system that ultimately serves to domesticate and subordinate the competition. In particular, by allotting the highest place in their ontological hierarchy to Bhagavān, who is represented as a personal Godhead endowed with an absolute body, and relegating Brahman and Paramātman to subordinate positions as partial aspects of Bhagavān, they engage in a polemic that is aimed both implicitly and explicitly at challenging the contending ontologies of two rival philosophical schools: the monistic ontology of Advaita Vedānta, which identifies the ultimate reality with the impersonal, formless Brahman, and the dualistic ontology of Pātañjala Yoga, which posits a plurality of nonchanging, formless *puruṣa*s as the highest reality.[36]

Classical Advaita Vedānta, as expounded by Śaṃkara (ca. 788–820 CE), is based on a monistic ontology that identifies the ultimate reality with Brahman, an impersonal unitary reality that in its essential nature is *nirguṇa*, completely devoid of attributes, and as such is described as undifferentiated (*nirviśeṣa*), nonactive (*niṣkriya*), and formless (*nirākāra*). In refutation of the Advaitins' characterizations of the ultimate reality, the early Gauḍīya authorities assert that, on the contrary, the highest aspect of the Godhead is personal, replete with infinite qualities (*saguṇa*), differentiated (*saviśeṣa*), possessed of innumerable *śakti*s (*śaktimat*), and endowed with an absolute body (*vigraha*) that is nonmaterial (*aprākṛta*). Moreover, in opposition to the Advaitin ontological hierarchy in which the personal God is identified with *saguṇa* Brahman, Brahman with attributes, and is associated with the domain of *māyā* (illusion) as a lower manifestation of the impersonal *nirguṇa* Brahman, the Gauḍīyas maintain that the impersonal Brahman is itself subsumed within the supreme personal Godhead as an incomplete manifestation (*asamyag-āvirbhāva*) of Bhagavān. In the Gauḍīya perspective Brahman is simply the effulgence that shines forth from the self-luminous absolute body of Bhagavān (*tanu-bhā* or *aṅga-prabhā*). Moreover, they assert that the joy that arises from realization of the impersonal, formless Brahman is as insignificant as a tiny puddle of water contained in a cow's hoofprint when compared to the pure ocean of bliss (*āhlāda-viśuddhābdhi*) that arises from direct visionary experience (*sākṣāt-kāra*) of Bhagavān's absolute body.[37]

The early Gauḍīya authorities also provide a critical assessment of the dualistic ontology advanced by the advocates of Pātañjala Yoga, which is first articulated in the Yoga-Sūtras of Patañjali (ca. 400–500 CE) and builds upon the ontology and epistemology of Sāṃkhya. In their hierarchical assessment of contending ontologies, the Gauḍīyas allot a higher place to the dualistic ontology of Pātañjala Yoga than to the monistic ontology of Advaita Vedānta. In the Gauḍīya perspective the Pātañjala Yoga goal of *kaivalya*, absolute isolation or separation, in which the *yogin* awakens to the reality of the nonchanging Self, *puruṣa*, as distinct from the material realm of *prakṛti* and from other *puruṣa*s, is a higher state of realization than the Advaitin goal of *mokṣa*, liberation, in which the liberated sage awakens to the reality of the universal Self, Ātman, as identical with the distinctionless unitary reality, Brahman. The Gauḍīyas understand the Pātañjala Yoga goal of realization of *puruṣa* as pointing to the realization of *saviśeṣa* (differentiated) Paramātman, which they assert is a higher state than the realization of *nirviśeṣa* (undifferentiated) Brahman. However, while the advocates of Pātañjala Yoga are viewed as avoiding the Advaitin extreme of absolute unity, they are critiqued for indulging in the opposite extreme of absolute separation. While they are applauded for maintaining the distinctions among the plurality of *puruṣa*s—which the Gauḍīyas term *jīva*s—they are chided for failing to recognize that the individual *jīva*s are themselves parts (*aṃśa*s) of a greater all-encompassing totality: Bhagavān, who is Puruṣottama, the supreme Puruṣa, and who subsumes within himself both *saviśeṣa* Paramātman and *nirviśeṣa* Brahman as partial aspects of his totality.

The Gauḍīya critiques of Advaita Vedānta and Pātañjala Yoga are articulated as a contestation among paths (*mārga*s) to realization in which the *bhakti-mārga*, the path of devotion, emerges victorious as the supreme path that surpasses both the *jñāna-mārga*, the path of knowledge advocated by the Advaitins, and the *yoga-mārga*, the path of *yoga* advocated by the exponents of Pātañjala Yoga. The Gauḍīyas maintain that although those who follow the *jñāna-mārga* may realize their identity with *nirviśeṣa* Brahman, the lowest aspect of Kṛṣṇa, and those who follow the *yoga-mārga* may experience *saviśeṣa* Paramātman, the intermediary aspect of Kṛṣṇa, neither the *jñānin* nor the *yogin* realizes the highest aspect of Kṛṣṇa as Bhagavān, the supreme personal Godhead, who is attained through the *bhakti-mārga* alone.[38] Invoking the canonical authority of the Bhāgavata Purāṇa, the Gauḍīyas declare that *jñāna* and *yoga*, when devoid of *bhakti*, are barren paths that cannot yield the highest fruit of realization in which one awakens to Kṛṣṇa as *svayaṃ* Bhagavān: "The *śāstra*s say: abandon *karma* and *jñāna* and *yoga*. Kṛṣṇa is controlled by *bhakti*, and by *bhakti* he should be worshiped. . . . 'Only that very powerful *bhakti* toward me [Kṛṣṇa] is able to compel me; I am not [compelled by] *yoga*, *sāṃkhya*, *dharma*, Vedic study, *tapas*,[39] or renunciation.' "[40]

The Gauḍīyas' hierarchical analysis provides a striking example of their theology of superordination in that, in contrast to a theology of supersessionism, the Gauḍīyas do not claim to *exclude* or *replace* the contending models of realization propounded by the exponents of Advaita

Vedānta and Pātañjala Yoga, but rather they posit a model of realization that *incorporates* and *domesticates* the Advaitin and Pātañjala Yoga models by recasting them as lower levels of realization of their own all-encompassing Godhead.

The Gauḍīya critiques of Advaita Vedānta and Pātañjala Yoga thus encompass not only the nature of their respective paths but also their formulations of the goal of human existence. For the Gauḍīyas *acintya-bhedābheda*, inconceivable difference-in-nondifference, is not simply an abstract ontological formulation but is the highest goal of realization in which the *jīva* awakens to the reality of its union-in-difference with Bhagavān. As part of their theology of superordination, they relegate to subordinate positions as lower levels of realization both the goal of absolute unity or identity with Brahman advanced by the Advaitins and the goal of absolute separation or isolation (*kaivalya*) advanced by the exponents of Pātañjala Yoga. In this context they provide a critique of the formulations of liberation, *mokṣa* or *mukti*, propounded by both schools.

Invoking the Bhāgavata Purāṇa as their scriptural authority, the Gauḍīyas assert that true *bhakta*s do not desire any form of liberation but rather cherish *bhakti*, selfless devotion to Kṛṣṇa, as the highest end of human existence.[41] Among the various types of liberation, they disparage in particular *ṣāyujya*, in which one attains undifferentiated unity with the deity, for they consider it to be synonymous with the Advaitin goal of absolute unity in which the realized sage merges with the impersonal Brahman like a drop merging with the ocean.[42] In the Gauḍīya hierarchy of models of realization, the ultimate goal is not nonduality but rather union-in-difference in which some distinction between the subject (*āśraya*) and the divine object of devotion (*viṣaya*) is maintained so that the *bhakta* can enjoy eternally the bliss of *preman*, the fully mature state of supreme love for Kṛṣṇa. Having realized its true identity as an *aṃśa* of the supreme Godhead, the *jīva* savors the exhilarating sweetness of *preman* in eternal relationship with Bhagavān. Consistent with the principle of superordination, the Gauḍīyas assert that the realized *bhakta* who has attained Kṛṣṇa-*preman* is the "crest-jewel of *mukta*s,"[43] for although liberation is not the goal of the *bhakta*, it is the natural byproduct of the perfected state of *preman*.

Mesocosmic Forms of Kṛṣṇa

The Gauḍīya discourse of divine embodiment, as mentioned earlier, represents Kṛṣṇa, *svayaṃ* Bhagavān, as maintaining the integrity of his *vigraha*, absolute body, while simultaneously assuming limitless divine forms on the transcosmic, macrocosmic, and microcosmic planes of existence. In addition, Kṛṣṇa is represented as becoming embodied in a number of intermediary forms that I term "mesocosmic" modes of divine embodiment, which I argue are critical to our understanding of the Gauḍīya hermeneutics of embodiment. These mesocosmic forms mediate between the transcosmic absolute body and the microcosmic human body by serving as concrete means through which human beings can access, encounter, engage, and experience the concentrated presence of the Godhead in localized forms on the gross material plane.

According to the Gauḍīya theory of *avatāra*s, when Kṛṣṇa descends to the material realm periodically in different cosmic cycles, he assumes the forms of various kinds of living beings—whether divine, human, animal, or hybrid forms—on the macrocosmic plane in order to accomplish specific tasks for a delimited period of time, after which his *avatāra*s return to their transcendent abodes. In the case of the mesocosmic forms, in contrast, Kṛṣṇa descends to the material realm and becomes embodied in particular configurations of language—as *śāstra,* scripture, and as *nāman,* name—and in visible forms associated with particular locales—as *dhāman,* geographic place, and as *mūrti,* ritual image. The notion of *avatāra* is extended in this context to include Kṛṣṇa's divine descents in four types of mesocosmic forms that—in contrast to the time-bound descents of the macrocosmic *avatāras*—he "leaves behind" on earth as enduring modes of divine embodiment that human beings can access and engage over time: (1) *grantha-avatāra,* Kṛṣṇa's *avatāra* in the form of a scriptural text, *grantha* or *śāstra,* that is identified more specifically as the Bhāgavata Purāṇa, the sovereign of all *śāstras;* (2) *nāma-avatāra*s, Kṛṣṇa's *avatāra*s in the form of divine names, *nāman*s, that are ultimately held to be identical with Kṛṣṇa's essential nature (*svarūpa*) and absolute body (*vigraha*); (3) Vraja-*dhāman,* Kṛṣṇa's embodiment in the form of a geographic place, *dhāman,* that is celebrated as the manifest counterpart of his transcendent abode; and (4) *arcā-avatāras,* Kṛṣṇa's *avatāra*s in the form of ritual images, *arcā*s or *mūrti*s, that are venerated as his localized embodiments in temples and shrines.

Rūpa Gosvāmin ascribes "inconceivable power" (*acintya śakti*) to these four mesocosmic forms—Bhāgavata Purāṇa, *nāman,* Vraja-*dhāman,* and *mūrti*—as "transmundane (*alaukika*) forms" that are in the final analysis nondifferent from Kṛṣṇa and are therefore efficacious not only in arousing Kṛṣṇa-*rati,* love for Kṛṣṇa, in the hearts of *bhakta*s but also in manifesting the object of this love—Kṛṣṇa himself—on the gross material plane: "The inconceivable power (*acintya śakti*) of these transmundane (*alaukika*) forms is such that it will manifest the *bhāva* [of Kṛṣṇa-*rati*] and its object [Kṛṣṇa] at the same time."[44]

Invoking the semiotic terminology of Charles Sanders Peirce, we could say that in the Gauḍīya hermeneutics of embodiment these mesocosmic forms are not understood as "symbols" that *represent* the deity, pointing beyond themselves to a transcendent referent, but rather they function as "iconic signs" that *manifest* the deity, disclosing the deity's living presence through a localized form—whether the form of a text, a name, a geographic place, or a ritual image.[45]

Śāstra. Kṛṣṇa is celebrated as becoming embodied in *śāstra*, scripture, in the Bhāgavata Purāṇa, which is extolled as a *grantha-avatāra*, text-*avatāra*. Jīva Gosvāmin asserts the special status of the Bhāgavata Purāṇa as the "representative embodiment (*pratinidhi-rūpa*) of Kṛṣṇa," and he invokes the Bhāgavata itself to establish that it is this text-*avatāra* that Kṛṣṇa leaves behind when, at the onset of Kali Yuga, he departs the earth and returns to his transcendent abode: "Now that Kṛṣṇa has departed for his own abode (*sva-dhāman*) along with *dharma*, knowledge, and so on, this Purāṇa has risen like the sun for the sake of those who are bereft of sight in Kali Yuga."[46] As an oral-aural collection of recited narratives, the Bhāgavata Purāṇa is revered as an embodiment of Kṛṣṇa in the form of reverberating speech, while in its written-visual mode it is venerated as a ritual icon in the form of a concrete book.[47]

Nāman. Kṛṣṇa's embodiment in language is not limited to the reverberating speech of the Bhāgavata Purāṇa but also includes his manifestation in the seed-syllables that constitute his *nāman*s, divine names, which are revered as *nāma-avatāra*s, name-*avatāra*s, or *varṇa-avatāra*s, sound-*avatāra*s. The name is held to be a concentrated form of *sat-cit-ānanda* and thus is considered identical with Kṛṣṇa's *svarūpa*, essential nature, and his *vigraha*, absolute body. Kṛṣṇadāsa Kavirāja asserts, "The name, the *vigraha*, and the *svarūpa*, these three are one *rūpa*; there is no division among the three; the three are the *cidānanda svarūpa*. There is no division in Kṛṣṇa between the body and the possessor of the body, nor between the name and the possessor of the name."[48]

Dhāman. Kṛṣṇa is also extolled as becoming embodied in *dhāman*, place, and more specifically in Vraja-*dhāman*. As we have seen, Vraja is represented in the Gauḍīya tradition both as a transcendent space, which is the abode of Kṛṣṇa's absolute body and the domain of the unmanifest *līlā*, and as a geographic place, which is the abode of his *svayaṃ-rūpa*, essential form, and the site of the manifest *līlā* during his sojourn on earth as Gopāla Kṛṣṇa. The earthly Vraja-*dhāman* is held to be the manifest counterpart of the unmanifest Vraja-*dhāman*, Goloka-Vṛndāvana, which is simultaneously immanent and transcendent, and therefore from this perspective Kṛṣṇa does not cease to dwell in the terrestrial Vraja even after he departs from the earth. His instantiation in the sacred geography of Vraja in North India is understood in three different senses. First, the earthly Vraja is revered as the place where Kṛṣṇa appeared at the end of Dvāpara Yuga in his essential form as a cowherd boy, and the entire landscape is held to be imprinted with his footprints, marking the *līlā-sthala*s, the sites of his playful exploits, during his earthly sojourn. Second, the earthly Vraja is extolled as the terrestrial manifestation of the transcendent Vraja-*dhāman* where Kṛṣṇa eternally abides, and thus the landscape is held to be infused with his divine presence at all times—before, during, and after his earthly sojourn. Third, the entire sacred geography of Vraja is celebrated as the body of Kṛṣṇa, with the twelve forests and other important pilgrimage sites identified with specific body parts.[49]

Mūrti. Kṛṣṇa's instantiation in place is not limited to the sacred geography of Vraja but also includes his embodiment in *mūrti*s, ritual images, in which he assumes localized forms in temples and shrines throughout the Indian subcontinent. The Gauḍīyas emphasize that Kṛṣṇa, out of his grace, descends and dwells in *mūrti*s, ritual images, which are also termed *arcā*s, *arcā-vigraha*s, and *pratimā*s. Moreover, they assert that these *arcā-avatāra*s, image-*avatāra*s, are nondifferent from Kṛṣṇa and that those adepts who are advanced in the practice of *bhakti* have the ability to perceive the living presence of Bhagavān within the *mūrti*.[50]

Sādhaka-Rūpa: Fashioning a Body of Devotion

The mesocosmic forms of Kṛṣṇa are ascribed a pivotal role not only in the Gauḍīya discourse pertaining to divine bodies but also in the discourse pertaining to devotional bodies. The path to realization advocated by the early Gauḍīya authorities engages both the external (*aṅga*) and internal (*antar-aṅga*) aspects of the psychophysiology[51] and involves fashioning a devotional body in two phases corresponding to the two forms of *sādhana-bhakti* mentioned earlier: *vaidhī-bhakti* and *rāgānugā-bhakti*. In *vaidhī-bhakti*, the initial phase of *sādhana-bhakti*, the *bhakta* performs external bodily practices with the *sādhaka-rūpa*, the sexually marked material body that the *jīva* enters at the time of birth and that is constructed by the residual karmic impressions (*saṃskāra*s) accumulated from the *jīva*'s previous births. The regimen of *vaidhī-bhakti* is designed to refigure the karmically constructed biological body as a body of devotion that is entirely dedicated to Bhagavān. The defective material body born through biological reproduction and delimited by brahmanical markers of *ascribed identity*—sex, social class (*varṇa*), and caste (*jāti*)—is born anew out of the ritual womb of *vaidhī-bhakti* and reconstituted as a "devotionally informed body" that—evoking Bourdieu's notion of a "socially informed body" (*habitus*)—is *inscribed* with the socioreligious taxonomies of the *bhakta-saṅgha*, the Gauḍīya community of *bhaktas*.[52] In *rāgānugā-bhakti* the *bhakta* engages in an advanced regimen that combines internal meditative practices with external bodily practices in order to attain an embodied state of realization in which he or she ceases to identify with the karmically bound biological body and realizes a *siddha-rūpa*, a perfected devotional body that is eternal and nonmaterial.[53]

Re-figuring the Psychophysiology

Rūpa Gosvāmin, in his discussion of *sādhana-bhakti*, repeatedly emphasizes the embodied nature of devotional practices. He defines *bhakti* as "service with the senses (*hṛṣīka*) to the Lord of the senses (Hṛṣīkeśa),"[54] and he characterizes the sixty-four practices of *vaidhī-bhakti* as "forms of worship (*upāsanas*) for the physical body (*kāya*), senses (*hṛṣīka*), and mental faculties (*antaḥ-karaṇa*)."[55] Through these practices the *bhakta* re-figures the psychophysiology by focusing all aspects of the *sādhaka-rūpa*, the material psychophysical complex, on Bhagavān, including the mind, the sense organs (ears, sense of touch, eyes, tongue, and nose), and the organs of action (mouth, hands, feet, limbs, and so on). Rūpa and Kṛṣṇadāsa Kavirāja both invoke the Bhāgavata Purāṇa's description of the embodied practices of the paradigmatic *bhakta*:

> He engaged his mind on the lotus-feet of Kṛṣṇa, his words in recounting the virtues of Vaikuṇṭha, his hands in cleaning the temple of Hari, his ears in hearing glorious stories about Acyuta, his eyes in seeing the images and temples of Mukunda, his sense of touch in touching the bodies of his servants, his nose in smelling the fragrance of the *tulasī* leaves placed at his lotus-feet, his tongue in tasting the food that had been offered to him, his feet in traveling by foot to the holy places of Hari, his head in bowing to the feet of Hṛṣīkeśa, and his desire in serving him. . . .[56]

Engaging Kṛṣṇa's Mesocosmic Forms

Among the sixty-four practices of *vaidhī-bhakti*, five are singled out by Rūpa and Kṛṣṇadāsa as most important for cultivating *prema-rasa*, the fully mature state of supreme love for Kṛṣṇa: (1) hearing (*śravaṇa*) the Bhāgavata Purāṇa and savoring (*āsvāda*) its meanings; (2) singing (*kīrtana* or *saṃkīrtana*) the names (*nāman*s) of Kṛṣṇa; (3) residing (*sthiti* or *vāsa*) in Mathurā-*maṇḍala*, the "circle of Mathurā," that encompasses the entire region of Vraja; (4) worship (*sevana*) of ritual images (*mūrti*s) of Kṛṣṇa; and (5) association (*saṅga*) with holy persons (*sādhus*).[57] Four of the five fundamental practices—as well as many of the other *vaidhī-bhakti* practices—thus involve engaging the four types of mesocosmic forms that, as discussed earlier, Rūpa extols as "transmundane (*alaukika*) forms" invested with the "inconceivable power" (*acintya śakti*) to manifest Kṛṣṇa on the gross material plane: Bhāgavata Purāṇa, *nāman*, Vraja-*dhāman*, and *mūrti*.[58]

Each of these modes of divine embodiment is associated with a distinct sensorium, or perceptual world, in which a particular "ratio of the senses"[59] dominates. In two of these mesocosmic forms Kṛṣṇa is embodied in language—as *śāstra*, the Bhāgavata Purāṇa, or as *nāman*, name—and therefore the principal modes of reception are *śravaṇa*, hearing; *paṭhana*, recitation; and *kīrtana*, singing. These practices are then extended through a variety of cognitive and corporeal modalities. On the one hand, they are internalized through meditative practices such as *dhyāna*, meditation; *smaraṇa*, contemplative recollection; or *japa*, silent repetition. On the other hand, they are externalized through bodily performances such as *rāsa-līlā*s, dramatic performances, or *nṛtya*, dance. In the other two mesocosmic forms Kṛṣṇa is embodied in place in visible forms—as the sacred geography of Vraja-*dhāman* or as the *mūrti* enshrined in the temple—and in these cases the principal perceptual modalities are *darśana*, seeing, and *sparśana*, touching. The associated bodily performances involve ritual negotiation of sacred space through *tīrtha-yātrā*, pilgrimage, or the carefully choreographed postures and gestures of *mūrti-sevā*, service to the *mūrti*.

*Bhāgavata Purāṇa. Bhakta*s engage the Bhāgavata Purāṇa through hearing (Bhāgavata-*śravaṇa*) and recitation (Bhāgavata-*paṭhana*). More specifically, they engage the text through hearing about (*śravaṇa*), singing about (*kīrtana*), meditation on (*dhyāna*), and contemplative recollection of (*smaraṇa*) the world of Kṛṣṇa that is enshrined in his text-*avatāra*, including not only his *līlā* but also his names (*nāman*s), forms (*rūpa*s), and qualities (*guṇa*s). They savor (*āsvāda*) the meanings (*artha*) of the Bhāgavata and drink (*pāna*) from its inexhaustible supply of ambrosial nectar (*amṛta* or *rasa*), reveling in its bliss-bestowing stories of Kṛṣṇa's *līlā*.[60] They also relish the enactment of the Bhāgavata's stories of Kṛṣṇa's *līlā* in dramatic performances, *rāsa-līlā*s, in which the actors who embody

Kṛṣṇa and Rādhā are revered during the performance as *svarūpas*, living forms, of the deity and his eternal consort.[61] In addition, they venerate the concrete book as a ritual icon that is a text-incarnation of Kṛṣṇa.

Nāman. *Bhaktas* engage the *nāman* through singing (*nāma-kīrtana*), hearing (*nāma-śravaṇa*), contemplative recollection (*nāma-smaraṇa*), and silent repetition in meditation (*mantra dhyāna* or *japa*) of the divine names of Kṛṣṇa, invoking his *nāma-avatāras* to experience the divine presence. They also inscribe their bodies with the letters of the divine name (*nāmākṣara*) as a means of embodying Kṛṣṇa in their own flesh.[62] During *nāma-saṃkīrtana*, communal singing of the divine names, the pulsating reverberations of the divine name at times overflow from the speech into the limbs, inspiring *bhaktas* to dance and whirl in ecstatic celebration of the *nāman*.[63]

Dhāman. *Bhaktas* engage the *dhāman* through residing (*sthiti* or *nivāsa*) in the land of Vraja and through pilgrimage (*tīrtha-yātrā*), which serve as means of encountering Kṛṣṇa's divine presence instantiated in the sacred geography of Vraja-*dhāman*, the most celebrated of all *tīrthas*. As pilgrims circumambulate the network of *līlā-sthalas*, the sites where Kṛṣṇa's playful exploits are held to have occurred, they obtain *darśana* of Kṛṣṇa embodied in the landscape; touch (*sparśana*), roll in, and ingest the dust that has been consecrated by his feet; and embrace the sacred ground through full-body prostrations (*daṇḍavat-praṇāmas*).[64] Advanced *sādhakas* incorporate meditative practices (*dhyāna* or *smaraṇa*) into their daily regimen as a means of attaining direct experiential realization of Kṛṣṇa in his transcendent Vraja-*dhāman*.

Mūrti. *Bhaktas* venerate the *mūrti* through seeing (*darśana*), touching (*sparśana*), and worshiping Kṛṣṇa's image-*avatāra* with ritual offerings (*upacāras*) and *mantras* in *arcana*, *pūjā*, and other forms of *mūrti-sevā*. They also engage in various forms of bodily service through circumambulating (*parikrama*), prostrating (*daṇḍavat-nati*), singing (*kīrtana* or *stavana*), and dancing (*tāṇḍava* or *nṛtya*) before the *mūrti*. In addition, through partaking of the *prasāda*, the remnants of the ritual offerings that are suffused with the deity's blessings, they enliven and cultivate the various sense faculties. More importantly, they invest their own bodies with the qualities of the deity's form through relishing (*svāda*) the food offered to him, savoring (*svāda*) the water used to wash his feet, smelling (*āghrāṇa*) the sweet fragrance of the incense and flowers enjoyed by him, and adorning their own bodies with the clothing, ornaments, and flower garlands blessed by the touch of his form.[65]

The *bhakta* thus fashions a devotional body through invoking, hearing, seeing, touching, tasting, smelling, and embracing the various mesocosmic forms in which Kṛṣṇa is embodied on the gross material plane. Through engaging and partaking of Kṛṣṇa's mesocosmic forms, the *bhakta*'s own psychophysiology is gradually suffused with the qualities and substance of Kṛṣṇa's absolute body (*vigraha*), which consists of *sat-cit-ānanda*, being, consciousness, and bliss.[66]

Siddha-Rūpa: Realizing a Body of Bliss

In *rāgānugā-bhakti* the *bhakta* engages in an advanced regimen of practices in order to realize a *siddha-rūpa*, a perfected devotional body that is eternal (*nitya*), nonmaterial (*aprākṛta*), and consists of *cit* and *ānanda*, consciousness and bliss. The practices of *rāgānugā-bhakti* are represented as the means to catalyze the *bhakta*'s shift from the *inscribed identity* of a devotionally informed material body to the *re-membered identity* of a perfected nonmaterial body that is *like* (*tulya*)—but at the same time eternally distinct from—the absolute body of Kṛṣṇa.

In *rāgānugā-bhakti* the advanced *sādhaka* enters into an intimate relationship with Kṛṣṇa characterized by passionate love (*rāga*). This form of *bhakti* is achieved through emulating the eternally perfect associates (*parikara*s or *pārṣada*s) who reside with Kṛṣṇa in the transcendent Vraja-*dhāman*, Goloka-Vṛndāvana, and who are called *rāgātmikā bhakta*s because their very essence (*ātman*) is spontaneously absorbed in passionate, all-consuming love (*rāga*) for Kṛṣṇa.[67] According to Rūpa Gosvāmin's definition, "That [*bhakti*] is called *rāgānugā* which emulates the *rāgātmikā-bhakti* that shines forth clearly in those who reside in Vraja."[68] The process of emulation involves cultivating one of the four principal *rasa*s, modes of devotional relationship, that are embodied by the paradigmatic *rāgātmikā bhakta*s: *dāsya-rasa*, the mode of service, exemplified by the attendants of Kṛṣṇa; *sakhya-rasa*, the mode of friendship, exemplified by Kṛṣṇa's cowherd friends; *vātsalya-rasa*, the mode of parental love, exemplified by Nanda and Yaśodā and other elders; and *mādhurya-rasa*, the mode of erotic love, exemplified by Kṛṣṇa's cowmaiden lovers.

Two Bodies: Sādhaka-Rūpa and Siddha-Rūpa

Rūpa suggests that the *rāgānugā sādhaka* should seek to realize the *rasa* that accords with his or her unique inherent nature (*svarūpa*)—whether that of a servant, friend, elder, or lover—by emulating a corresponding *rāgātmikā bhakta* of the transcendent Vraja "with both the *sādhaka-rūpa* and the *siddha-rūpa*."

> One should dwell (*vāsa*) continually in Vraja, absorbed in various stories (*kathā*) about it, remembering (root *smṛ*) Kṛṣṇa and his beloved associates whose devotional mode accords with one's own. One who wishes to realize a particular devotional mode (*bhāva*) should perform devotional service (*sevā*) emulating the residents of Vraja with both the *sādhaka-rūpa* and the *siddha-rūpa*.[69]

Although Rūpa himself does not elaborate on the nature of these two bodies, in his commentary Jīva Gosvāmin renders the term *rūpa* as *deha*, "body," and glosses *sādhaka-rūpa* as the "body as it is" (*yathāvastitha-deha*) and *siddha-rūpa* as an "internal meditative body (*antaś-cintita-deha*) that is suitable for one's intended devotional service (*sevā*) to Kṛṣṇa."[70] Kṛṣṇadāsa Kavirāja suggests that the *sādhaka*'s emulation of the *rāgātmikā bhakta*s with both the *sādhaka-rūpa* and the *siddha-rūpa*—which he terms the *sādhaka-deha* and the *siddha-deha*—entails becoming identified with the chosen *rāgātmikā bhakta* on two levels: first, by emulating the chosen *rāgātmikā bhakta* through performing external bodily practices such as *śravaṇa* and *kīrtana* with the *sādhaka-rūpa* that engage Kṛṣṇa and his *līlā*; and, second, by cultivating a state of inner absorption in the *aprakaṭa līlā*, unmanifest *līlā*, of the transcendent Vraja through internal meditative practices such as *līlā-smaraṇa* and *dhyāna*, which culminates in the realization of a perfected devotional body, *siddha-rūpa*.

> This *sādhana* has two parts: external and internal. External is the performance of *śravaṇa* and *kīrtana* with the body of the *sādhaka* [*sādhaka-deha*]. In their minds [these *sādhaka*s] mentally construct their own perfected bodies [*siddha-deha*s], and day and night they serve Kṛṣṇa in Vraja. . . . Following after one who is beloved of Kṛṣṇa, . . . in their inner minds they serve him eternally.[71]

This passage presents the difference between the *sādhaka-rūpa* and the *siddha-rūpa* in terms of different forms of practice: the physical body utilized in external bodily practices and the meditative body constructed through internal mental practices. However, in other contexts the distinction between the *sādhaka-rūpa* and the *siddha-rūpa* is presented as an ontological distinction between two categories of embodiment: the material (*prākṛta*) psychophysical complex that is subject to the binding influence of Kṛṣṇa's *māyā-śakti* in the material realm of *prakṛti*, and the eternal, nonmaterial (*aprākṛta*) body that participates in Kṛṣṇa's *svarūpa-śakti* in the transcendent Vraja-*dhāman*. In this perspective every *jīva* possesses a *siddha-rūpa*, an eternal body, which is an *aṃśa* of the self-luminous effulgence (*jyotir*) of Bhagavān and, like the absolute body (*vigraha*) of Kṛṣṇa himself, is constituted of *cit* and *ānanda*.[72] Due to the binding influence of the *māyā-śakti*, the *jīva* becomes deluded by ignorance (*avidyā*), mistakenly identifies with the material psychophysical complex, and forgets its true identity as an *aṃśa* of Bhagavān. Moreover, the *jīva* forgets its unique inherent nature (*svarūpa*), which determines its distinctive role as an eternal protagonist in the unmanifest *līlā* and the corresponding form of its *siddha-rūpa* in the transcendent Vraja-*dhāman*. The goal of *rāgānugā-bhakti* is to awaken the *jīva* from the sleep of ignorance so that it can realize its *svarūpa*, unique inherent nature, and the particular form of its *siddha-rūpa*, nonmaterial body, which is eternally gendered in relation to the male Godhead, Kṛṣṇa, as either female—a female lover or maternal elder—or male—a male friend, paternal elder, or male attendant.[73]

Līlā-Smaraṇa and Realization of the Siddha-Rūpa

The Gauḍīya discourse of human embodiment emphasizes the role of the *guru* and of meditative practices such as *līlā-smaraṇa* and *dhyāna* as two critical components in the *rāgānugā sādhaka*'s realization of the *siddha-rūpa*. The realized *guru*, who has attained the status of a *samprāpta-siddha*, perfected *bhakta*, and continually delights in the unmanifest *līlā* of the transcendent Vraja-*dhāman*, Goloka-Vṛndāvana, is ascribed a role in revealing or confirming to the *sādhaka* the identity of his or her particular *siddha-rūpa*.[74] The practice of *līlā-smaraṇa*—contemplative recollection of the *līlā* of Kṛṣṇa and his eternal associates in Vraja—along with other forms of *smaraṇa* and *dhyāna* then serve as the means through which the *sādhaka* can gain direct experiential realization of the *siddha-rūpa* and reclaim his or her distinctive role as an eternal protagonist in the unmanifest *līlā*.

Rūpa provides the basis for the practice of *līlā-smaraṇa* by instructing practitioners of *rāgānugā-bhakti* to dwell continually in Vraja by remembering (root *smṛ*) Kṛṣṇa and his beloved companions.[75] Jīva elaborates on Rūpa's instruction by providing an extended analysis of *smaraṇa*, which he defines as contemplative recollection of the names (*nāmans*), forms (*rūpas*), qualities (*guṇas*), eternal associates (*parikaras*), service (*sevā*), and playful activities (*līlās*) of Kṛṣṇa. He distinguishes five stages of *smaraṇa*: (1) *smaraṇa*, thinking about Kṛṣṇa in any manner; (2) *dhāraṇā*, withdrawal of the attention from external sense objects and focusing the mind on Kṛṣṇa; (3) *dhyāna*, meditation on the forms and other aspects of Kṛṣṇa;

(4) *dhruvānusmṛti*, a more advanced stage of meditation in which consciousness flows in an unbroken stream toward Kṛṣṇa; and (5) *samādhi*, the most advanced stage of meditation in which the *sādhaka* attains a state of complete absorption that culminates in a direct cognition of Kṛṣṇa and his unmanifest *līlā*.[76] In his analysis of the five-stage meditative practice of *smaraṇa*, Jīva deploys the principle of superordination by appropriating three terms that are central to the practice of yogic meditation in *aṣṭāṅga-yoga*, the eight-limbed Yoga of Patañjali—*dhāraṇā*, *dhyāna*, and *samādhi*—and embedding them in a devotional framework that reinscribes them as stages in the Gauḍīya practice of meditation on Kṛṣṇa. He explicitly distinguishes his understanding of the highest form of *samādhi*, in which the *bhakta* attains a direct cognition of the self-luminous absolute body of Bhagavān, from the yogic ideal of *asamprajñāta samādhi*, which he frames as a lower form of *samādhi* in which the *yogin* attains an objectless state of absorption in the impersonal, formless Brahman. Moreover, he suggests that those *yogins* who take up the purely meditative form of *bhakti* known as *śānta-rasa*, in which they are intent on experiencing Kṛṣṇa as an object of meditation but do not seek an intimate emotional relationship with him, do not attain the highest form of *samādhi* in which direct experience of Kṛṣṇa's unmanifest *līlā* is attained. Direct experiential realization of Kṛṣṇa's *vigraha*, absolute body, and his unmanifest *līlā* is available only to *rāgānugā sādhaka*s who seek to realize one of the four modes of passionate (*rāga*) loving relationship with Kṛṣṇa as *pūrṇa* Bhagavān: *dāsya-rasa*, *sakhya-rasa*, *vātsalya-rasa*, or *mādhurya-rasa*.[77] Jīva allots a pivotal role to the meditative practices of *smaraṇa* and *dhyāna* as means to attain the highest stages of realization in *rāgānugā-bhakti*.[78]

Building on the insights of Rūpa and Jīva, Kṛṣṇadāsa and later Gauḍīya authorities developed the practice of *līlā-smaraṇa* into complex meditation techniques in which the *rāgānugā sādhaka* visualizes in elaborate detail the *aṣṭa-kālīya-līlā*, the eight periods of Kṛṣṇa's daily *līlā* that goes on eternally in the transcendent domain of Vraja. As part of these meditation techniques, the *sādhaka* visualizes the *svayaṃ-rūpa*, the beautiful two-armed cowherd form of Kṛṣṇa's absolute body; the eternal forms of the *gopī*s, *gopa*s, and other residents of Vraja; the spatial arrangement of the transcendent Vraja-*dhāman*, Goloka-Vṛndāvana, including the specific locale of each *līlā* activity; and the time of day in which the *līlā* activity occurs. The *sādhaka* also constructs a mental image of his or her own *siddha-rūpa* and visualizes this meditative body interacting with the eternal residents of Vraja in particular *līlā* activities. For example, if the *guru* has revealed or confirmed the identity of the *siddha-rūpa* to be that of a particular *gopī*, then the *sādhaka* visualizes his or her *gopī* body in all its particularity, including the *gopī*'s name, age, appearance, dress, place of residence, mode of service, and so on.[79] The implication of the Gauḍīyas' analysis is that regular meditation involving visualization of the mentally constructed *siddha-rūpa* serves to catalyze an awakening in which the *jīva re-members* (*smaraṇa*) its eternal *siddha-rūpa* and reclaims its distinctive role as an eternal participant in the unmanifest *līlā*. Established in the highest state of realization as a member of Kṛṣṇa's transcendent entourage, the *jīva* savors the exhilarating sweetness of *prema-rasa* in eternal relationship with Bhagavān.

The Physical Signs of Enraptured Devotion

The *samprāpta-siddha*, perfected *bhakta*, is represented in the Gauḍīya discourse of human embodiment as enjoying an embodied state of realization in which he or she remains inwardly identified with the *siddha-rūpa*, while outwardly the *sādhaka-rūpa* manifests as a transformed material body that is marked with the physical signs of enraptured devotion. The internal ecstatic state saturates all the senses and the organs of action and erupts in spontaneous bodily manifestations such as perspiration, trembling, bristling of body hair, tears, faltering voice, and change of color, which are termed *sāttvika-bhāva*s in the rhetoric of *bhakti-rasa* theory.[80]

> It is the nature of *prema* to agitate the body and mind. . . . By the nature of *prema* the *bhakta* laughs, and cries, and sings and being mad he dances and runs here and there. Sweat, trembling, thrilling, tears, choking, pallor, madness, sadness, composure, pride, happiness, humility—in all these *bhāva*s does *prema* cause the *bhakta* to dance; he floats in the sea of the nectar of *ānanda* of Kṛṣṇa.[81]

The early Gauḍīya authorities emphasize that while the realized *bhakta*'s consciousness, immersed in the ocean of Kṛṣṇa's *ānanda*, reverberates with the exhilarating waves of the nectar of *prema-rasa*, the physical body also thrills with the "divine madness" (*divyonmāda*) of devotion. The transformed material body, infused with bliss, manifests an array of involuntary physical symptoms, *sāttvika-bhāva*s, that are considered the externalized manifestations of the internal ecstatic state.[82]

In the Gauḍīya discourse of *bhakti* the human body is thus a site of central significance on three levels: first, as the material psychophysical complex that is to be cultivated on the path to realization; second, as the eternal, nonmaterial body that is to be attained in the highest state of realization; and, third, as the transformed material body that is the external counterpart of the eternal body of bliss. In refutation of contending discourses—in particular, the discourse of *jñāna* propounded by the exponents of Advaita Vedānta and the discourse of *yoga* promulgated by the exponents of Pātañjala Yoga—the exponents of the Gauḍīya *bhakti-śāstra* insist that the body is not simply an instrument to be disciplined on the path to realization and then dispensed with once the goal is reached. Rather, embodiment constitutes the critical defining feature of the Gauḍīya discourse of *bhakti*—indeed, its "very epicenter"—with both human and divine bodies ascribed pivotal roles not only on the *path* but also as integral parts of the *goal* of realization.

Notes

1. See *Aṣṭādhyāyī* 4.3.83–100, cited in Hardy 1983: 25–26.

2. Śvetāśvatara Upaniṣad 6.23.

3. Among studies of the category of *bhakti*, see in particular Hardy 1983; Sharma 1987; Ramanujan 1993; Prentiss 1999; Lorenzen 2004; Hawley 2005; Holdrege [2017a]. See also Hawley 2007; Narayanan 2007; Novetzke 2007; and the other essays in the special issue of the *International Journal of Hindu Studies* on *The Bhakti Movement—Says Who?* (2007). For more recent collections of essays, see the special issues of the *Journal of Hindu Studies* on *Mughal Bhakti* (2013) and on *Bhakti in Hindu Cultures* (2013). For bibliographic essays reviewing scholarship on a range of *bhakti* traditions, see Lutgendorf 2003; Coleman 2011.

4. For an extended study of the connections between *bhakti* and embodiment, see Holdrege 2015.

5. Bose 1951: 113.

6. Ramanujan 1993: 135–136.

7. For a collection of essays exploring diverse forms of divine embodiment in a variety of *bhakti* contexts, see Waghorne and Cutler 1985.

8. For an illuminating analysis of Vedic perspectives on divine corporeality, see Malamoud 1996.

9. In his study of the development of the concept of *avatāra*, Hacker (1960) provides an analysis of the terminological antecedents that are used in the Mahābhārata and early Purāṇas to designate manifestations of a deity on earth, including the term *prādur-bhāva* (appearance), which is gradually replaced by the term *avatāra*. In a more recent study Couture (2001: 313) suggests that Hacker "fails to deal adequately with the original context of the word *avatāra*," and he seeks to fill this lacuna by providing a careful analysis of the semantic valences of the verb *ava-tṝ* and its substantive derivations *avataraṇa, avatāraṇa,* and *avatāra* in the Mahābhārata and the Harivaṃśa, the appendix to the epic.

Couture (2001: 313–314) notes that the terms *avatāra* and *avatāraṇa* only appear once in the critical edition of the Mahābhārata (in 3.146.33 and 1.2.34, respectively), with the epic favoring the substantive form *avataraṇa*. The earliest texts to regularly use the terms *avatāra* and *avatāraṇa* are the Brahma Purāṇa and the Viṣṇu Purāṇa. Regarding the terminology used to designate the manifestations of Viṣṇu and Kṛṣṇa in particular, see Hardy 1983: 23–25. For an extended study of the relationship between Viṣṇu and Kṛṣṇa as reflected in the theories of *avatāra* presented in the Harivaṃśa, Viṣṇu Purāṇa, and Bhāgavata Purāṇa, see Matchett 2001.

10. For analyses of the complex network of significations associated with the term *tīrtha*, see Eck 1981; Bhardwaj and Lochtefeld 2004. For a survey of representations of *tīrtha*s in epic and Purāṇic sources, see Bhardwaj 1973. For a critical assessment of secondary studies of Hindu pilgrimage traditions, see Bhardwaj and Lochtefeld 2004: 486–488. For an extended study of the sacred geography of India, see Eck 2012.

11. Malamoud (1996: 208) remarks: "The India of the Vedas is . . . 'aniconic.' To be sure, there exists neither any rule nor any account condemning the manufacture of divine images. It remains the case, however, that Vedic India has left no vestige whatsoever that might bear witness to the prior existence of sculpted or painted effigies. . . . [T]here is no mention whatsoever—in this enormous agglomeration of hymns, prayers, aetiological narratives and prescription, bearing on the most minute details of worship—of objects depicting the gods." Malamoud emphasizes the links between Vedic aniconism and the perspectives on divine corporeality propounded in Vedic texts. It is important to note that we do find some evidence of *aniconic*—as opposed to iconic—representations in the Vedic period. For example, the bird-shaped fire altar in the *agnicayana* ceremony is understood to be a representation of the body of the creator Prajāpati.

12. The notion of an image-incarnation is formalized in Pāñcarātra traditions, where it is ascribed the status of one of the five modes of manifestation of the deity and is termed an *arcā-avatāra*, a divine descent in the form of a ritual image (*arcā* or *mūrti*). The Śrīvaiṣṇavas appropriated and recast Pāñcarātra constructions in their own theological formulations, in which they allot a pivotal role to *arcā-avatāra*s as the most accessible of Viṣṇu's five modes of manifestation. As we shall see, the early Gauḍīya authorities also revere *mūrti*s as image-*avatāra*s and may have been directly influenced in this context by Śrīvaiṣṇava formulations.

13. For an analysis of the Vedic antecedents of *bhakti* formulations concerning divine names, see Holdrege 2015, chapter 4.

14. For a discussion of relevant Vedic notions, see Holdrege 1996: 30–70.

15. See Prentiss 1999: esp. 6, 9, 153–154.

16. Novetzke 2007: 261. See also Novetzke 2008.

17. For an extended analysis of the range of ontologies, devotional modes, and goals found in *bhakti* traditions, see Holdrege [2017a].

18. For an overview of the history and works of the six Gosvāmins—Sanātana Gosvāmin, Rūpa Gosvāmin, Gopāla Bhaṭṭa Gosvāmin, Raghunāthadāsa

Gosvāmin, Raghunātha Bhaṭṭa Gosvāmin, and Jīva Gosvāmin—see De 1961: 111–165.

19. According to Haberman (2003: xxxiii), the *Bhaktirasāmṛtasindhu* was completed in 1541 CE. The *Bhaktirasāmṛtasindhu,* "The Ocean of the Nectar of *Bhakti-Rasa,*" is divided into four quarters (*vibhāgas*)—Eastern, Southern, Western, and Northern—each of which is subdivided into chapters called "waves" (*laharīs*). References in the notes to the *Bhaktirasāmṛtasindhu* indicate quarter (*vibhāga*), chapter (*laharī*), and verse(s). Among recent studies of Rūpa Gosvāmin's works, see Haberman 1988, 2003; Delmonico 1990, 1998.

20. References in the notes to the *Laghubhāgavatāmṛta* indicate section (*khaṇḍa*), chapter (*pariccheda*), and verse(s).

21. According to Brzezinski (1992: 20), the *Bhāgavata Sandarbha* was composed between 1555 and 1561 CE. The *Bhāgavata Sandarbha* is also called *Ṣaṭ Sandarbha,* since it comprises six *Sandarbhas*: *Tattva Sandarbha, Bhagavat Sandarbha, Paramātma Sandarbha, Kṛṣṇa Sandarbha, Bhakti Sandarbha,* and *Prīti Sandarbha*. For brief overviews of the contents of the six *Sandarbhas*, see Gupta 2007: 201–207; Dasa 2007: 373–387. References in the notes to the *Sandarbhas* indicate section (*anuccheda*). Among recent studies of Jīva Gosvāmin's works, see Brzezinski 1992, 2007; Gupta 2007.

22. According to Dimock (1999: 31–32), the *Caitanya Caritāmṛta* was most likely completed around 1615 CE and Kṛṣṇadāsa Kavirāja died between 1615 and 1620. References in the notes to the *Caitanya Caritāmṛta* indicate section (*līlā*), chapter (*pariccheda*), and verse(s) and follow the numbering convention adopted in Dimock's (1999) translation, *Caitanya Caritāmṛta of Kṛṣṇadāsa Kavirāja,* which is based on the Bengali edition of the *Caitanya Caritāmṛta,* edited by Rādhāgovinda Nātha (3rd ed., 1948–1952). Among recent studies of Kṛṣṇadāsa Kavirāja's *Caitanya Caritāmṛta,* see Dimock 1999; Stewart 2010.

23. See Holdrege 2015.

24. For an extended analysis of these taxonomies, see Holdrege 2015, chapter 1.

25. In the first seven sections (*anucchedas*) of the *Bhagavat Sandarbha,* Jīva Gosvāmin introduces the three aspects of the Godhead, Brahman, Paramātman, and Bhagavān. He then provides an extended analysis of the nature of Bhagavān in the remaining sections of the *Bhagavat Sandarbha* and an extended analysis of the nature of Paramātman in the *Paramātma Sandarbha*. He insists that it is not necessary to devote a separate *Sandarbha* to an analysis of Brahman because the *Bhagavat Sandarbha,* by providing a full explication of the nature of Bhagavān, simultaneously serves to clarify the nature of Brahman as an incomplete manifestation (*asamyag-āvirbhāva*) of Bhagavān. Kṛṣṇadāsa Kavirāja provides an overview of the three aspects of the Godhead—Brahman, Paramātman, and Bhagavān—in *Caitanya Caritāmṛta* 1.2.2–18; 2.20.134–137; 2.24.57–60.

26. After expounding the three aspects of the Godhead in the *Bhagavat Sandarbha* and *Paramātma Sandarbha,* Jīva Gosvāmin's principal concern in the *Kṛṣṇa Sandarbha* is to establish Kṛṣṇa's supreme status as *pūrṇa* Bhagavān, the full and

complete Godhead. For an analysis of the arguments used by Jīva in the *Kṛṣṇa Sandarbha* to establish the indisputable authority of Bhāgavata Purāṇa 1.3.28 as the *mahā-vākya* of all the *śāstras*, see De 1961: 316–325. Bhāgavata Purāṇa 1.3.28 appears at the end of the Bhāgavata's account of twenty-two *avatāras* and is invoked not only by Jīva but also by Rūpa Gosvāmin and Kṛṣṇadāsa Kavirāja to establish that Kṛṣṇa, as *svayaṃ* Bhagavān, is not himself an *avatāra* but is rather the *avatārin* who is the source and container of all *avatāras*.

27. Jīva introduces the three principal types of *śakti* in the *Bhagavat Sandarbha* and then focuses on the *svarūpa-śakti* that is intrinsic to Bhagavān's essential nature. In the *Kṛṣṇa Sandarbha*, after establishing that Kṛṣṇa is *svayaṃ* Bhagavān, he further explicates the *svarūpa-śakti* through an extended analysis of Kṛṣṇa's essential nature (*svarūpa*), absolute body (*vigraha*), transcendent abode (*dhāman*), and eternal associates (*parikaras* or *pārṣadas*). He provides an analysis of the functions of the *māyā-śakti* and the *jīva-śakti* in relation to Paramātman in the *Paramātma Sandarbha*.

28. The two outer *dhāmans* of Kṛṣṇaloka are called Mathurā and Dvārakā and are the transcosmic prototypes of the earthly cities of Mathurā and Dvārakā.

29. For extended analyses of the category of *līlā* in the Gauḍīya tradition, see Haberman 1988; Holdrege 2015.

30. For a recent translation and study of the *rāsa-pañcādhyāyī*, see Schweig 2005. Schweig's illuminating study draws on the works of Rūpa Gosvāmin, Jīva Gosvāmin, and Kṛṣṇadāsa Kavirāja, as well as later Gauḍīya commentators such as Viśvanātha Cakravartin (seventeenth to eighteenth century CE).

31. See, for example, *Laghubhāgavatāmṛta* 1.1.12–13; 1.5.341–342; 1.5.400; 1.5.402; 1.5.423; *Bhaktirasāmṛtasindhu* 2.1.38; 2.1.187; *Kṛṣṇa Sandarbha* 93, 99, 104, 106, 150, 153; *Caitanya Caritāmṛta* 2.17.127–128; 2.6.150; 3.5.117–118, with *śloka* 5.

32. *Bhaktirasāmṛtasindhu* 2.1.22–23. All translations of Sanskrit texts are my own. In this passage Rūpa Gosvāmin uses the term *svarūpa* rather than *svayaṃ-rūpa* to refer to Kṛṣṇa's essential form.

33. Among Gauḍīya assertions that Kṛṣṇa is the source and container of all *avatāras*, see, for example, *Bhaktirasāmṛtasindhu* 2.1.40; 2.1.202–203; 2.1.249–250; *Caitanya Caritāmṛta* 1.2.57; 1.2.74–76; 1.2.82; 1.2.91,93–97; 1.5.3; 1.5.111–115; 2.8.106–107. For an extended analysis of the hierarchical system of *avatāras* and other divine manifestations delineated by Rūpa Gosvāmin in the *Laghubhāgavatāmṛta* and expanded on by Kṛṣṇadāsa Kavirāja in the *Caitanya Caritāmṛta*, see Holdrege 2015, chapter 1. See also De 1960; Dimock 1999: 142–143.

34. Bhāgavata Purāṇa 1.3.26,28. Both Rūpa Gosvāmin and Jīva Gosvāmin draw on the Bhāgavata's list of twenty-two *avatāras* in their discussions of the various categories of *avatāras*. The principal concern of Jīva in the *Kṛṣṇa Sandarbha* is to establish that Kṛṣṇa is *svayaṃ* Bhagavān and that, in his supreme status as the cause of all causes, he is the *avatārin* who is the source of all *avatāras*. In this context he invokes Bhāgavata Purāṇa 1.3.28 as the *mahā-vākya* that provides the authoritative proof text around which he constructs his arguments.

35. *Caitanya Caritāmṛta* 2.8.106–108. All translations of the *Caitanya Caritāmṛta* are from Dimock 1999. I have at times inserted Bengali terms in brackets into Dimock's translations in order to call attention to specific terminology used by Kṛṣṇadāsa Kavirāja.

36. In the *Caitanya Caritāmṛta* Kṛṣnadāsa Kavirāja recasts this polemic in the form of explicit debates in which Caitanya is portrayed as disputing and refuting exponents of Advaita Vedānta, Sāṃkhya, Pātañjala Yoga, and other philosophical schools: "The philosophers and Mīmāṃsikas and followers of the Māyāvāda [Advaitins], and Sāṃkhyas and Pātañjalas, and followers of *smṛti* and the *purāṇas* and *āgamas*—all were vastly learned in their own *śāstras*. Prabhu [Caitanya] examined them critically and faulted the opinions of all of them. Everywhere Prabhu established the Vaiṣṇava doctrines, and no one was able to fault the doctrines of Prabhu. Being defeated one after the other, they accepted Prabhu's opinions" (2.9.36–39; cf. 2.25.42–48).

37. *Bhaktirasāmṛtasindhu* 1.1.39, citing *Haribhaktisudhodaya* 14.36; *Caitanya Caritāmṛta* 2.24.29, with *śloka* 9; 3.3.184, with *śloka* 13. In addition to countering Advaitin perspectives on the nature of the ultimate reality, the early Gauḍīya authorities also develop arguments to refute their doctrines of *māyā* and ignorance (*avidyā*) and their claims regarding the identity of the *jīva* with Brahman. Jīva Gosvāmin develops a number of arguments in refutation of Advaitin doctrines in *Tattva Sandarbha* 32–45 and then elaborates on these arguments in the *Paramātma Sandarbha*. Among the critiques of Advaitin doctrines in the *Caitanya Caritāmṛta*, see in particular 1.7.38–145, which portrays Caitanya engaging in a debate with a group of Advaitin *saṃnyāsins* (renunciants) in Kāśī (Vārāṇasī) in which he refutes Śaṃkara's interpretation of the Brahma-Sūtras. For an analysis of the critiques of Śaṃkara's teachings in this passage, see Chilcott 2006: 75–79.

It is important to emphasize that although the early Gauḍīya authorities reject the radically nondualist form of classical Advaita Vedānta expounded by Śaṃkara, they were directly influenced by certain *bhakti*-inflected forms of Advaita Vedānta that began to circulate from the fourteenth century CE on. For a discussion of the Gauḍīyas' contrasting attitudes toward the divergent forms of Advaita Vedānta that they encounter in classical Advaitin texts and in the Indian landscape, see Holdrege 2015: 40–43.

38. See, for example, *Caitanya Caritāmṛta* 2.20.134–137; 2.24.57–60; 1.2.2–18. In the *Bhakti Sandarbha* Jīva Gosvāmin discusses at length the defining characteristics and practices of *bhakti* and its relationship to other paths such as the *jñāna-mārga* and the *yoga-mārga*. See, for example, *Bhakti Sandarbha* 326–328.

39. The term *tapas* (literally, "heat") is a multivalent term that refers to the meditative practices and austerities by means of which one accumulates spiritual and creative power.

40. *Caitanya Caritāmṛta* 2.20.121, with *śloka* 13, which cites Bhāgavata Purāṇa 11.14.20. See also *Caitanya Caritāmṛta* 1.17.71, with *śloka* 5; 2.22.14–16. Jīva Gosvāmin invokes Bhāgavata Purāṇa 11.14.20 in *Bhakti Sandarbha* 327 in support of his

arguments regarding the supremacy of the path of *bhakti* over the paths of *jñāna* and *yoga*.

41. The Gauḍīyas' critical assessment of *mukti* includes an analysis of five types of liberation, which they recast from a theistic perspective as five modes of realization of the deity: *sālokya*, in which one resides in the world (*loka*) of the deity; *sārṣṭi*, in which one enjoys the powers of the deity; *sāmīpya*, in which one lives near the deity; *sārūpya*, in which one assumes a form (*rūpa*) like that of the deity; and *sāyujya*, in which one attains undifferentiated unity with the deity. In support of their position the early Gauḍīya authorities invoke the following verses from the Bhāgavata Purāṇa: "The distinguishing characteristic of unqualified *bhakti-yoga* is declared to be that devotion (*bhakti*) to the supreme Puruṣa [Kṛṣṇa] which is without motive and ceaseless. Even if *sālokya*, *sārṣṭi*, *sāmīpya*, *sārūpya*, and *ekatva* (unity) are offered, devotees do not accept anything except worship (*sevana*) of me. This very thing called *bhakti-yoga* is declared to be the highest end" (Bhāgavata Purāṇa 3.29.12–14; cf. 9.4.67). These verses are invoked by Rūpa Gosvāmin as part of his extended discussion of the glories of *bhakti* over the quest for *mukti* in *Bhaktirasāmṛtasindhu* 1.1.13–17; 1.2.22–57. Regarding the five types of *mukti*, see *Bhaktirasāmṛtasindhu* 1.1.13–15; 1.2.28; 1.2.38; 1.2.55–57; *Bhakti Sandarbha* 234; *Prīti Sandarbha* 10; *Caitanya Caritāmṛta* 2.6.236–242, with *śloka* 23; 2.9.243, with *śloka*s 24–26; 1.4.172, with *śloka*s 34–37; 2.19.149–150, with *śloka*s 22–25; 2.24.119, with *śloka* 66; 3.3.177, with *śloka* 12; 1.3.15–16. In the opening sections of the *Prīti Sandarbha*, Jīva Gosvāmin provides a critical assessment of the various types of *mukti* in relation to the ultimate goal (*prayojana*) of human existence: *prīti*, or *preman*, supreme love for Kṛṣṇa.

42. See, for example, *Caitanya Caritāmṛta* 2.6.236–242; 1.3.15–16; 1.5.27.

43. *Caitanya Caritāmṛta* 2.8.203.

44. *Bhaktirasāmṛtasindhu* 1.2.244. The transmundane realities to which Rūpa Gosvāmin refers in this verse are the Bhāgavata Purāṇa, *nāman*, Vraja-*dhāman*, and *mūrti*, along with Kṛṣṇa *bhakta*s, which he described in the five preceding verses, *Bhaktirasāmṛtasindhu* 1.2.239–243, as the focal points for the five most important practices of *vaidhī-bhakti*. I will discuss these five practices in a later section of this essay.

45. For Peirce's theory of signs, see Peirce 1955: 98–119.

46. *Tattva Sandarbha* 26, citing Bhāgavata Purāṇa 1.3.45.

47. For an extended analysis of the role of the Bhāgavata Purāṇa in the Gauḍīya discourse of embodiment, see Holdrege 2015, chapter 3.

48. *Caitanya Caritāmṛta* 2.17.127–128. The identity between Kṛṣṇa and his name is also emphasized in *Bhaktirasāmṛtasindhu* 1.2.233–234, with Jīva Gosvāmin's commentary. For a discussion of the theology of the name that undergirds the central Gauḍīya practice of *nāma-kīrtana*, singing of the divine names, see Hein 1976. For an extended analysis of the role of *nāman* in the Gauḍīya discourse of embodiment, see Holdrege 2015, chapter 4.

49. Jīva Gosvāmin provides an extended analysis of Kṛṣṇa's transcendent and terrestrial *dhāman*s in *Bhagavat Sandarbha* 60–78; *Kṛṣṇa Sandarbha* 106–116. For

an extended analysis of the role of Vraja in the Gauḍīya discourse of embodiment, see Holdrege 2015, chapter 5. For studies of Vraja (Hindi Braj) as a literary construction and a major pilgrimage center, see Entwistle 1987; Haberman 1994; Corcoran 1995.

50. See, for example, *Bhakti Sandarbha* 286. For a recent study of the theology and practice of *mūrti-sevā* in the Gauḍīya tradition, see Valpey 2006.

51. *Bhaktirasāmṛtasindhu* 1.4.4–5.

52. My notion of a "devotionally informed body" draws on Bourdieu's (1977, 1990) notion of a "socially informed body" in which the sociocultural taxonomies of a particular social field are inscribed in the body through the "logic of practice."

53. The two forms of *sādhana-bhakti*, *vaidhī-bhakti* and *rāgānugā-bhakti*, are discussed in *Bhaktirasāmṛtasindhu* 1.2–1.4; *Bhakti Sandarbha* 235–340; *Caitanya Caritāmṛta* 2.22.55–96.

54. *Bhaktirasāmṛtasindhu* 1.1.12.

55. *Bhaktirasāmṛtasindhu* 1.2.94. In *Bhaktirasāmṛtasindhu* 1.2.72, before enumerating the sixty-four practices of *vaidhī-bhakti*, Rūpa Gosvāmin acknowledges his indebtedness to the *Haribhaktivilāsa*, the Gauḍīya ritual compendium that is ascribed to Gopāla Bhaṭṭa Gosvāmin.

56. See *Bhaktirasāmṛtasindhu* 1.2.266–268; *Caitanya Caritāmṛta* 2.22.78, with *śloka*s 59–61. Both passages cite these verses from the Bhāgavata Purāṇa (9.4.18–20).

57. For Rūpa Gosvāmin's enumeration of the five practices, see *Bhaktirasāmṛtasindhu* 1.2.90–93, which in turn provides the basis for Kṛṣṇadāsa Kavirāja's enumeration in *Caitanya Caritāmṛta* 2.22.74–75. See also Rūpa's discussion of the five practices in *Bhaktirasāmṛtasindhu* 1.2.225–244.

58. See *Bhaktirasāmṛtasindhu* 1.2.244, quoted earlier.

59. This expression derives from Ong 1981, 1982.

60. *Bhaktirasāmṛtasindhu* 1.2.240; 1.2.170–173; 1.2.145–148; 1.2.37; 1.2.178–181; 1.2.91; 1.2.226–227; 1.2.210; *Bhakti Sandarbha* 248–275, esp. 260–262, 275.

61. For extended studies of *rāsa-līlā* performances, see Hein 1972; Hawley 1981, 1983: 181–257, 1995, 1999.

62. *Bhaktirasāmṛtasindhu* 1.2.92; 1.2.230–234; 1.2.145–146; 1.1.21; 1.2.170–171; 1.2.242; 1.2.177; 1.2.85; 1.2.149–150; 1.2.185; 1.2.84; 1.2.123–124; *Bhakti Sandarbha* 262–265, 271–274, 248, 128, 276.

63. See, for example, *Caitanya Caritāmṛta* 1.7.90–93, with *śloka* 4, which cites Bhāgavata Purāṇa 11.2.40.

64. *Bhaktirasāmṛtasindhu* 1.2.92; 1.2.235–237; 1.2.243; 1.2.88–89; 1.2.211–213; *Bhakti Sandarbha* 283, 286.

65. *Bhaktirasāmṛtasindhu* 1.2.90; 1.2.225; 1.2.239; 1.2.81; 1.2.84–87; 1.2.118; 1.2.125–129; 1.2.134–143; 1.2.159–169; 1.2.185; *Bhakti Sandarbha* 283–303. For an extended analysis of the practice of *mūrti-sevā* in the Gauḍīya tradition, with particular emphasis on the Rādhāramaṇa temple in Vṛndāvana, see Valpey 2006.

For an analysis of the ritual and aesthetic traditions that ground contemporary Gauḍīya practices of ornamentation of Kṛṣṇa's *mūrti*s in the Rādhāramaṇa temple and the Govindadeva temple in Jaipur, see Packert 2010: 28–73, 123–175.

66. See, for example, *Caitanya Caritāmṛta* 2.22.43; 3.4.183–185.

67. Rūpa Gosvāmin provides an overview of the progression from *rāgānugā-bhakti* to *prema-bhakti* in *Bhaktirasāmṛtasindhu* 1.2.270–1.4.21. See also Jīva Gosvāmin's discussion of *rāgānugā-bhakti* in *Bhakti Sandarbha* 310–340 and of *prema-bhakti*, or *prīti*, in the *Prīti Sandarbha*. For an extended analysis of *rāgānugā-bhakti*, see Haberman 1988.

68. *Bhaktirasāmṛtasindhu* 1.2.270.

69. *Bhaktirasāmṛtasindhu* 1.2.294–295.

70. Jīva Gosvāmin's commentary on *Bhaktirasāmṛtasindhu* 1.2.295.

71. *Caitanya Caritāmṛta* 2.22.89–91. This passage invokes *Bhaktirasāmṛtasindhu* 1.2.294 and 1.2.295 as illustrative *śloka*s (*śloka*s 70 and 69, respectively).

72. See, for example, *Prīti Sandarbha* 10; *Caitanya Caritāmṛta* 3.4.183–185. For a discussion of Gauḍīya conceptions of the *siddha-rūpa*, see Haberman 1988: 86–93.

73. For an extended analysis of the Gauḍīya framing of the sex/gender distinction, see Holdrege [2017b].

74. Regarding the central importance of the *guru* in the Gauḍīya tradition, see *Bhaktirasāmṛtasindhu* 1.2.74; 1.2.97–99, in which Rūpa Gosvāmin describes the first three practices among the sixty-four practices of *vaidhī-bhakti* as (1) taking refuge (*āśraya*) at the feet of a *guru*, (2) receiving initiation (*dīkṣā*) and instruction (*śikṣaṇa*) regarding Kṛṣṇa from the *guru*, and (3) serving (*sevā*) the *guru* with confidence. For Kṛṣṇadāsa Kavirāja's enumeration of these three practices, see *Caitanya Caritāmṛta* 2.22.61, with n. 61. See also *Bhakti Sandarbha* 202–203, 206–213, 237, in which Jīva Gosvāmin discusses the roles of the *śikṣā-guru* and the *dīkṣā-guru* and emphasizes that taking refuge (*śaraṇāpatti*) in a realized *guru* is the critical foundation of the Gauḍīya path of *sādhana-bhakti*.

75. *Bhaktirasāmṛtasindhu* 1.2.294. See also *Bhaktirasāmṛtasindhu* 1.2.87 and 1.2.175–177, in which Rūpa Gosvāmin includes *smṛti*, remembering, as one of the sixty-four practices of *vaidhī-bhakti*.

76. *Bhakti Sandarbha* 275–279.

77. *Bhakti Sandarbha* 278–279. See also *Bhaktirasāmṛtasindhu* 3.1.4–10, in which Rūpa Gosvāmin similarly suggests that although adherents of *śānta-rasa* may experience Kṛṣṇa's four-armed form as Vāsudeva, or Viṣṇu, they do not experience his mind-captivating *līlā*.

78. For an extended analysis of the repertoire of Gauḍīya meditative practices developed by Jīva Gosvāmin, see Holdrege 2015, chapter 6.

79. See in particular Kṛṣṇadāsa Kavirāja's *Govindalīlāmṛta*, the authoritative guidebook for the practice of *līlā-smaraṇa* visualization. Kṛṣṇadāsa's 2,488-verse poem provides an extended account of the *aṣṭa-kālīya-līlā*, the eight periods of Kṛṣṇa's *līlā*, which builds on Rūpa Gosvāmin's eleven-verse formulation in the

Aṣṭakālīyalīlāsmaraṇamaṅgalastotra. For an analysis of the role of *līlā-smaraṇa* in Gauḍīya traditions, along with a translation of Rūpa's *stotra*, see Haberman 1988: 123–133, 161–163.

80. In the Gauḍīya theory of *bhakti-rasa*, the *sāttvika-bhāvas* are the eight forms of involuntary bodily manifestations through which the *bhakta*'s internal devotional state is marked on the external body: stupefaction, perspiration, bristling of body hair, faltering voice, trembling, change of color, tears, and loss of external consciousness. Rūpa Gosvāmin discusses the *sāttvika-bhāvas* in the third chapter of the Southern Quarter of the *Bhaktirasāmṛtasindhu* (2.3). The eight *sāttvika-bhāvas* enumerated by Rūpa in *Bhaktirasāmṛtasindhu* 2.3.16 correspond to the standard list of eight *sāttvika-bhāvas* given in *Nāṭya-Śāstra* 6.22. For analyses of Rūpa's theory of *bhakti-rasa* and its relationship to the theories of *rasa* propounded by the dominant schools of Indian aesthetics, see Delmonico 1990, 1998; Haberman 2003: xxxvi–lxvii; Holdrege 2015, chapter 2.

81. *Caitanya Caritāmṛta* 1.7.84–87; cf. *Bhaktirasāmṛtasindhu* 1.2.241.

82. For a study of the role of *divyonmāda*, the divine madness of *bhakti*, in the Gauḍīya tradition, see McDaniel 1989: 29–85.

References

Aṣṭakālīyalīlāsmaraṇamaṅgalastotra of Rūpa Gosvāmin. 1961 [1942]. *Smaraṇamaṅgalaikādaśam*, ed. Sushil Kumar De, in his *Early History of the Vaisnava Faith and Movement in Bengal*, 673–675. 2nd ed. Calcutta: K. L. Mukhopadhyaya.

Bhāgavata Purāṇa. 1983. *Bhāgavata Purāṇa of Kṛṣṇa Dvaipāyana Vyāsa*, ed. J. L. Shastri. Includes the commentary of Śrīdhara Svāmin. Delhi: Motilal Banarsidass.

Bhāgavata Purāṇa. 1996–2002. *Śrībhāgavatam: Śrīmad Bhāgavata Mahāpurāṇam*, ed. H. G. Shastri, B. K. Shelat, and K. K. Shastri. 4 vols. Ahmedabad: B. J. Institute of Learning and Research.

Bhāgavata Sandarbha of Jīva Gosvāmin. 1951. *Śrīśrībhāgavatasandarbha*, ed. Purīdāsa Mahāśaya. 6 books in 2 vols. Vrindavan: Haridāsa Śarma.

Bhāgavata Sandarbha of Jīva Gosvāmin. 1982–1986. *Śrībhāgavatasandarbha*, ed. and trans. (Hindi) Haridāsa Śāstrī. 6 vols. Vrindavan: Śrīgadādharagaurahari Press.

Bhakti in Hindu Cultures. 2013. Special issue, *Journal of Hindu Studies* 6, no. 2.

The Bhakti Movement—Says Who? 2007. Special issue, *International Journal of Hindu Studies* 11, no. 3.

Bhaktirasāmṛtasindhu of Rūpa Gosvāmin. 1946. *Śrīśrībhaktirasāmṛtasindhu*, ed. Purīdāsa Mahāśaya. Vrindavan: Haridāsa Śarma.

Bhaktirasāmṛtasindhu of Rūpa Gosvāmin. 1981. *Śrībhaktirasāmṛtasindhu*, ed. and trans. (Hindi) Śyāmdās Hakīm. Includes the commentaries of Jīva Gosvāmin and Viśvanātha Cakravartin. Vrindavan: Harināma Press.

Bhaktirasāmṛtasindhu of Rūpa Gosvāmin. 2003. *The Bhaktirasāmṛtasindhu of Rūpa Gosvāmin*, ed. and trans. David L. Haberman. New Delhi: Indira Gandhi National Centre for the Arts; Delhi: Motilal Banarsidass.

Bhardwaj, Surinder Mohan. 1973. *Hindu Places of Pilgrimage in India (A Study in Cultural Geography)*. Berkeley: University of California Press.

Bhardwaj, Surinder M., and James G. Lochtefeld. 2004. "Tīrtha." In *The Hindu World*, ed. Sushil Mittal and Gene Thursby, 478–501. New York: Routledge.

Bose, Nirmal Kumar. 1951. "Caste in India." *Man in India* 31, nos. 3–4: 107–123.

Bourdieu, Pierre. 1977 [1972]. *Outline of a Theory of Practice*. Translated by Richard Nice. Cambridge: Cambridge University Press.

Bourdieu, Pierre. 1990 [1980]. *The Logic of Practice*. Translated by Richard Nice. Stanford: Stanford University Press.

Brzezinski, J. K. 1992. "Jīva Gosvāmin's Gopālacampū." PhD diss., University of London, School of Oriental and African Studies.

Brzezinski, Jan. 2007. "Jiva Goswami: Biography and Bibliography." *Journal of Vaishnava Studies* 15, no. 2: 51–80.

Caitanya Caritāmṛta of Kṛṣṇadāsa Kavirāja. 1948–1952. *Caitanyacaritāmṛta*, ed. Rādhāgovinda Nātha. 3rd ed. 6 vols. Calcutta: Sādhanā Prakāśanī.

Chilcott, Travis. 2006. "Appropriation and Subordination of Vedic Authority in the Gauḍīya Vaiṣṇava Tradition." *Journal of Vaishnava Studies* 15, no. 1: 71–86.

Coleman, Tracy. 2011. "Bhakti." *Oxford Bibliographies: Hinduism*, ed. Alf Hiltebeitel. New York: Oxford University Press.

Corcoran, Maura. 1995. *Vṛndāvana in Vaiṣṇava Literature: History, Mythology, Symbolism*. Vrindavan: Vrindaban Research Institute.

Couture, André. 2001. "From Viṣṇu's Deeds to Viṣṇu's Play, or Observations on the Word Avatāra as a Designation for the Manifestations of Viṣṇu." *Journal of Indian Philosophy* 29, no. 3: 313–326.

Dasa, Satyanarayana. 2007. "The Six Sandarbhas of Jiva Gosvami." In *Krishna: A Sourcebook*, ed. Edwin F. Bryant, 373–408. New York: Oxford University Press.

De, Sushil Kumar. 1960 [1943]. "The Doctrine of Avatāra (Incarnation) in Bengal Vaiṣṇavism." In his *Bengal's Contribution to Sanskrit Literature and Studies in Bengal Vaisnavism*, 143–153. Calcutta: K. L. Mukhopadhyaya.

De, Sushil Kumar. 1961 [1942]. *Early History of the Vaisnava Faith and Movement in Bengal*. 2nd ed. Calcutta: K. L. Mukhopadhyaya.

Delmonico, Neal Gorton. 1990. "Sacred Rapture: A Study of the Religious Aesthetic of Rupa Gosvamin." PhD diss., University of Chicago.

Delmonico, Neal. 1998. "Sacred Rapture: The Bhakti-Rasa Theory of Rūpa Gosvāmin." *Journal of Vaiṣṇava Studies* 6, no. 1: 75–98.

Dimock, Edward C., Jr., trans. 1999. *Caitanya Caritāmṛta of Kṛṣṇadāsa Kavirāja*. Edited by Tony K. Stewart. Cambridge: Harvard University Press.

Eck, Diana L. 1981. "India's Tīrthas: 'Crossings' in Sacred Geography." *History of Religions* 20, no. 4: 323–344.

Eck, Diana L. 2012. *India: A Sacred Geography*. New York: Harmony Books.

Entwistle, A. W. 1987. *Braj: Centre of Krishna Pilgrimage*. Groningen: Egbert Forsten.

Govindalīlāmṛta of Kṛṣṇadāsa Kavirāja. 1977–1981. *Śrīśrīgovindalīlāmṛta*, ed. and trans. (Hindi) Haridāsa Śāstrī. 3 vols. Vrindavan: Śrīgadādharagaurahari Press.

Gupta, Ravi M. 2007. *The Caitanya Vaiṣṇava Vedānta of Jīva Gosvāmī: When Knowledge Meets Devotion*. New York: Routledge.

Haberman, David L. 1988. *Acting as a Way of Salvation: A Study of Rāgānugā Bhakti Sādhana*. New York: Oxford University Press.

Haberman, David L. 1994. *Journey through the Twelve Forests: An Encounter with Krishna*. New York: Oxford University Press.

Haberman, David L., trans. 2003. *The Bhaktirasāmṛtasindhu of Rūpa Gosvāmin*. New Delhi: Indira Gandhi National Centre for the Arts; Delhi: Motilal Banarsidass.

Hacker, Paul. 1960. "Zur Entwicklung der Avatāralehre." *Wiener Zeitschrift für die Kunde Süd- und Ostasiens und Archiv für indische Philosophie* 4: 47–70.

Hardy, Friedhelm. 1983. *Viraha-Bhakti: The Early History of Kṛṣṇa Devotion in South India*. New Delhi: Oxford University Press.

Haribhaktivilāsa of Gopāla Bhaṭṭa Gosvāmin. 1986. *Śrī Haribhaktivilāsa*, ed. and trans. (Hindi) Haridāsa Śāstrī. Vrindavan: Śrīgadādharagaurahari Press.

Harivaṃśa. 1969–1971. *The Harivaṃśa*, ed. Parashuram Lakshman Vaidya. 2 vols. Poona: Bhandarkar Oriental Research Institute.

Hawley, John Stratton, in association with Shrivatsa Goswami. 1981. *At Play with Krishna: Pilgrimage Dramas from Brindaban*. Princeton: Princeton University Press.

Hawley, John Stratton. 1983. *Krishna, the Butter Thief*. Princeton: Princeton University Press.

Hawley, John Stratton. 1995. "Every Play a Play within a Play." In *The Gods at Play: Līlā in South Asia*, ed. William S. Sax, 115–130. New York: Oxford University Press.

Hawley, John Stratton. 1999. "Govardhan Pūjā, When Krishna Worships Krishna." In *Festivals*, special issue, *Journal of Vaiṣṇava Studies* 7, no. 2: 37–63.

Hawley, John Stratton. 2005. *Three Bhakti Voices: Mirabai, Surdas, and Kabir in Their Time and Ours*. New Delhi: Oxford University Press.

Hawley, John Stratton. 2007. "Introduction." In *The Bhakti Movement—Says Who?*, special issue, *International Journal of Hindu Studies* 11, no. 3: 209–225.

Hein, Norvin. 1972. *The Miracle Plays of Mathurā*. New Haven: Yale University Press.

Hein, Norvin J. 1976. "Caitanya's Ecstasies and the Theology of the Name." In *Hinduism: New Essays in the History of Religions*, ed. Bardwell L. Smith, 15–32. Leiden: E. J. Brill.

Holdrege, Barbara A. 1996. *Veda and Torah: Transcending the Textuality of Scripture*. Albany: State University of New York Press.

Holdrege, Barbara A. 2015. *Bhakti and Embodiment: Fashioning Divine Bodies and Devotional Bodies in Kṛṣṇa Bhakti*. New York: Routledge.

Holdrege, Barbara A. [2017a]. "Interrogating *Bhakti*." *International Journal of Hindu Studies* 21.

Holdrege, Barbara A. [2017b]. "Alternative Bodily Identities in Gauḍīya Vaiṣṇava Discourse: From Karmically Constructed Sexed Bodies to Eternally Gendered Nonmaterial Bodies." In *Sex, Gender, and Alternative Bodily Identities in Hindu Traditions*, ed. Barbara A. Holdrege, special issue, *International Journal of Hindu Studies* 21.

Kṛṣṇa Sandarbha of Jīva Gosvāmin. 1986. *Śrīkṛṣṇasandarbha and Its Critical Study*, ed. Chinmayi Chatterjee. Calcutta: Jadavpur University.

Laghubhāgavatāmṛta of Rūpa Gosvāmin. 1995. *Śrī Laghubhāgavatāmṛtam*, ed. and trans. (Bengali) Bhakti Vilāsa Tīrtha. Mayapur: Caitanya Maṭha.

Lorenzen, David N. 2004. "Bhakti." In *The Hindu World*, ed. Sushil Mittal and Gene Thursby, 185–209. New York: Routledge.

Lutgendorf, Philip. 2003. "Medieval Devotional Traditions: An Annotated Survey of Recent Scholarship." In *The Study of Hinduism*, ed. Arvind Sharma, 200–260. Columbia: University of South Carolina Press.

Mahābhārata. 1933–1972. *The Mahābhārata*, ed. Vishnu S. Sukthankar, S. K. Belvalkar, and P. L. Vaidya. 19 vols. Poona: Bhandarkar Oriental Research Institute.

Malamoud, Charles. 1996 [1989]. "Bricks and Words: Observations on the Bodies of the Gods in Vedic India." In his *Cooking the World: Ritual and Thought in Ancient India*, 207–225. Translated by David White. New Delhi: Oxford University Press.

Matchett, Freda. 2001. *Kṛṣṇa: Lord or Avatāra? The Relationship between Kṛṣṇa and Viṣṇu*. Richmond, Surrey, UK: Curzon Press.

McDaniel, June. 1989. *The Madness of the Saints: Ecstatic Religion in Bengal*. Chicago: University of Chicago Press.

Mughal Bhakti. 2013. Special issue, *Journal of Hindu Studies* 6, no. 1.

Narayanan, Vasudha. 2007. "'With the Earth as a Lamp and the Sun as the Flame': Lighting Devotion in South India." In *The Bhakti Movement—Says Who?*, special issue, *International Journal of Hindu Studies* 11, no. 3: 227–253.

Nāṭya-Śāstra of Bharata. 2002–2003. *The Nāṭyaśāstra: A Treatise on Ancient Indian Dramaturgy and Histrionics Ascribed to Bharata-Muni*, ed. and trans. Manomahan Ghosh. 4 vols. Varanasi: Chowkhamba Sanskrit Series Office.

Novetzke, Christian Lee. 2007. "*Bhakti* and Its Public." In *The Bhakti Movement—Says Who?*, special issue, *International Journal of Hindu Studies* 11, no. 3: 255–272.

Novetzke, Christian Lee. 2008. *Religion and Public Memory: A Cultural History of Saint Namdev in India*. New York: Columbia University Press.

Ong, Walter J. 1981 [1967]. *The Presence of the Word: Some Prolegomena for Cultural and Religious History*. 2nd ed. Minneapolis: University of Minnesota Press.

Ong, Walter J. 1982. *Orality and Literacy: The Technologizing of the Word*. New York: Methuen.

Packert, Cynthia. 2010. *The Art of Loving Krishna: Ornamentation and Devotion*. Bloomington: Indiana University Press.

Peirce, Charles Sanders. 1955 [1940]. *Philosophical Writings of Peirce*. Edited by Justus Buchler. Reprint. New York: Dover Publications.

Prentiss, Karen Pechilis. 1999. *The Embodiment of Bhakti*. New York: Oxford University Press.

Ramanujan, A. K., trans. 1993 [1981]. *Hymns for the Drowning: Poems for Viṣṇu by Nammālvār*. New Delhi: Penguin Books.

Schweig, Graham M., trans. 2005. *Dance of Divine Love: The Rāsa Līlā of Krishna from the Bhāgavata Purāṇa, India's Classic Sacred Love Story*. Princeton: Princeton University Press.

Sharma, Krishna. 1987. *Bhakti and the Bhakti Movement: A New Perspective. A Study in the History of Ideas*. New Delhi: Munshiram Manoharlal.

Stewart, Tony K. 2010. *The Final Word: The Caitanya Caritāmṛta and the Grammar of Religious Tradition*. New York: Oxford University Press.

Ujjvalanīlamaṇi of Rūpa Gosvāmin. 1954. *Ujjvalanīlamaṇi*, ed. Purīdāsa Mahāśaya. Vrindavan: Haridāsa Śarma.

Ujjvalanīlamaṇi of Rūpa Gosvāmin. 1985 [1932]. *Ujjvalanīlamaṇi*, ed. Durgāprasāda Dvivedi. Includes the commentaries of Jīva Gosvāmin and Viśvanātha Cakravartin. Delhi: Chaukhamba Sanskrit Pratishthan.

Upaniṣads. 1958. *Eighteen Principal Upaniṣads*, ed. V. P. Limaye and R. D. Vadekar. Vol. 1. Poona: Vaidika Saṃśodhana Maṇḍala.

Upaniṣads. 1998. *The Early Upaniṣads*, ed. and trans. Patrick Olivelle. New York: Oxford University Press.

Valpey, Kenneth Russell. 2006. *Attending Kṛṣṇa's Image: Caitanya Vaiṣṇava Mūrti-Sevā as Devotional Truth*. New York: Routledge.

Viṣṇu Purāṇa. 1882. *Vishnupurana*, ed. Jibananda Vidyasagara. Calcutta: Saraswati Press.

Viṣṇu Purāṇa. 1997–1999. *The Critical Edition of the Viṣṇupurāṇam*, ed. M. M. Pathak. Vadodara: Oriental Institute.

Waghorne, Joanne Punzo, and Norman Cutler, in association with Vasudha Narayanan, eds. 1985. *Gods of Flesh/Gods of Stone: The Embodiment of Divinity in India*. Chambersburg: Anima.

Chapter 7

To Body or Not to Body

Repulsion, Wonder, and the Tamil Saint Kāraikkāl Ammaiyār

Karen Pechilis

This essay delineates the creative space between a sixth-century female author of devotional poetry and her twelfth-century male biographer, contrasting the poet's creation of a devotional subjectivity toward the body of Śiva with her biographer's emphasis on the poet's own bodily transformation as the site of her devotion. Both of the authors, Kāraikkāl Ammaiyār and Cēkkiḻār, respectively, are claimed by the Tamil tradition of Śaiva *bhakti*—she as a poet who wrote about love for God and he as an author who created life stories of the sixty-three Tamil Śaiva Nāyaṉārs (pl. in Tamil *nāyaṉmār*), whom he celebrates as "servants" (*toṇṭar*) of Śiva, which were instrumental in establishing them as "saints" in the tradition.[1] The two hymns and two poems attributed to Kāraikkāl Ammaiyār were canonized; they are included with sundry other devotional texts in the eleventh volume of the Tamil Śaiva *bhakti* canon, the *Tirumuṟai* (Sacred Collection). However, Cēkkiḻār's work is the sole content of the twelfth and final volume and thus is positioned in the canon as the culminating "last word." His *Periya Purāṇam* (Great Story) was designed to be an authoritative, influential text, and it succeeded. Today it mediates knowledge of the Tamil Śaiva *bhakti* saints and provides a framework for understanding the works of those who were authors, especially the hymnists. In the case of Kāraikkāl Ammaiyār, the biographic narrative has greatly overshadowed her own work. Her story is very widely known in Tamil Nadu today, but it is rare to encounter a person who is knowledgeable about her compositions.[2] Cēkkiḻār's representation of her largely constitutes the Tamil public imagination of her. This essay argues that the two authors' distinctive treatments of the body in their works reveal their different priorities for defining and promoting the path of *bhakti*. In particular, this essay reclaims the female poet's voice in her distinctive use of language to promote an exploratory modality for humankind in the world, including women, a perspective that was contradicted and occluded by her later biographer.

Biography (and its subgenre hagiography)[3] foregrounds the body as the vehicle of public memory.[4] The body is the Wittgensteinian "picture" that makes the discourse of biography intelligible, eliding the genre's paradoxical thesis that the mortal body can be made eternal, that the life of an individual remains present even in death. The body does not itself have to be affirmed by biography, as two classic life stories in Tamil—perhaps the earliest two if one restricts the genre to an account of the full life of the subject, from birth to death—illustrate by their contrasting perspectives on the body: the tenth-century Jain *Cīvakacintāmaṇi* (Cīvakaṉ, the Wish-Fulfilling Gem), which validates renunciation from the world, and the *Periya Purāṇam,* which validates action in the world.[5] In biography the presumed shared humanity—embodiment—of the subject and the audience ensures the accessibility and the popularity of the genre, although clearly the message of a given biographical text is enmeshed in the self-creation or affirmation of distinctive communities. For reasons I discussed in my earlier work, Tamil Śaiva *bhakti* endows the body with positive nuances insofar as it promotes devotional action in the world.[6]

Given the accessibility of the biographical genre, it is understandable that members of the Tamil populace and scholars read Kāraikkāl Ammaiyār through Cēkkiḻār's lens, without attention to possible differences between their perspectives.[7] What this kind of popular reading elides is the poet's focus, which deserves to be examined on its own terms with respect to its role in the making of tradition. That there is a contrast between the poet and her biographer is clear. In addition to the contrast between the status of Kāraikkāl Ammaiyār and Cēkkiḻār in the public memory and imagination, we can add literary contrasts, including first person/third person, mimesis/diegesis, and poetry/narrative; historical contrasts, including some six hundred years that separate the two authors; and the contrast of gender, including the genders of the female poet and her male biographer as well as their narrative constructions of gender. In keeping with the emphasis on embodiment in *bhakti* and the body as the theme of this volume, I will argue a particular type of contrast in this essay: the nature of her poetic works is "to subject," while the nature of his narrative is "to body."

Both authors promote active engagement in service to Lord Śiva, whom they celebrate as the supreme deity. In Kāraikkāl Ammaiyār's works, she only obliquely thematizes the human body, in contrast to the three major male poet-saints of the Tamil Śaiva *bhakti* tradition—Campantar, Appar, and Cuntarar—who lived a century or so later. However, she shares with other *bhakti* authors, both within and outside her own tradition, many prominent characteristics, such as a focus on language, especially "singing the body of God."[8] Thus her focus is on the speaking subject, especially as such a subject can describe and reflect on the Lord's body. Also, her *bhakti* discourse is constituted by multiple meanings of "subject." There is the "I" of a speaking subject, who is the observer and the director of the gaze toward the Lord's body, which is inscribed in her poetry. There is her desire to subject herself (submission) to the gaze of her object, Śiva, whose autonomous subjectivity she presumes. Furthermore, she approaches him not only by constituting his subjectivity through praise but by subjecting him (confrontation) to questions about his identity and powers. Understood by devotees and scholars alike to be the first saintly author of devotional poetry in Tamil Śaiva *bhakti*, she created a devotional subjectivity that was emulated by later *bhakti* poets within her tradition.

Cēkkiḻār, Kāraikkāl Ammaiyār's biographer, is involved in a related but distinctive project: his project is "to body" her, as well as the other Śaiva *bhakti* saints, and thus his focus is on the human body. Cēkkiḻār tends toward excess in his emphasis on the body, offering dramatic and detailed portrayals of the saints actively performing their devotion in the world as a unifying theme in a narrative that seeks to comprehensively define devotion. Through their bodies he "fleshes out" the nature of *bhakti* and, in the case of the saints who are poets, he offers perspectives on how to interpret their poetry.[9]

The emphases of Kāraikkāl Ammaiyār and Cēkkiḻār are thus different. The female poet acknowledges the necessity of the human body for sight, speech, and intersubjectivity, but her focus is on the Lord's divine body, while the male biographer's focus is on the human bodies of the saints within the context of a narrative in praise of Śiva, who bodily appears to the saints in most of their stories. And yet there is a striking similarity in the two authors' representations of the body, for they both portray the body as a locus of repulsion in their works.

That devotion is made, in the sense of being defined in relation to other discourses, is an argument that I advanced in my earlier work analyzing the claims made for a devotional body by Tamil Śaiva *bhakti* proponents in relation to the competing claims about embodiment promulgated by other groups, such as brahmins, *saṃnyāsin*s (renunciants), non-Hindu religious, kings, ritual specialists, and philosophers.[10] The body has long been a topic of interest in Hindu traditions and the academic study of Hindu traditions.[11] Recent studies have illuminated the contested nature of the body in various historical contexts and sectarian circles, revealing indigenous typologies of the body and related argumentation on and across types. Katherine Zubko has identified discourses, such as cosmological-philosophical, theological, and social-communal, as well as bodily technologies, such as martial arts, *yoga*, and healing.[12] Gavin Flood has discussed the tantric body, the ascetic body, and the Vedic body, locating them in relation to texts, the physical body, cosmology, and each other.[13] Barbara Holdrege has discussed various discourses pertaining to the ritual body, the ascetic body, the purity body, the devotional body, and the tantric body.[14] What these studies make clear is that Hindu discourses privilege different texts and are distinguished by meaningful contrasts, such as that between the ritual body and the ascetic body, convincingly illustrating that such discourses of the body are central to the creation of different types of identities.[15] In particular, the ritual body, with its claims to Vedic status, is the paradigmatic body to which other discourses of the body compare themselves, from its rejection by the ascetic body discourse to its appropriation by the purity body discourse.

Bhakti traditions generally challenge the ritual body and its associations with purity and rote repetition in favor of an argument that the total devotion of one's heart and mind to the Lord is the only real necessity.[16] The leitmotif of the repulsive body in Kāraikkāl Ammaiyār's poetry and in Cēkkiḻār's biographic narrative participates in this challenge in a way that promotes the distinctiveness of Śaivism as a tradition whose classical myths celebrate frightful images of the supreme deity, Śiva. Kāraikkāl Ammaiyār imbues such images of the Lord with the challenge of creating a devotional subjectivity. Cēkkiḻār's emphasis on the repulsive human body resonates with renunciant tendencies in Hindu, Buddhist, and Jain traditions, but his is not a rejection of the body; instead, the repulsive human body marks the uncompromisingly devotional subject.

What She Said

The poet said she would explore God herself.[17] The way she said this was to compose four poetic works dedicated to Lord Śiva of varying length, with a total number of 143 verses. Two of her works are hymns set to music; each is eleven verses long, and they both purport to describe the scene of Śiva's dance at the town of Tiruvālaṅkāṭu. Two of her works are poems with 20 verses and 101 verses, respectively. Both poems are in the *antāti* style, which was popular in early Tamil *bhakti* compositions, with Kāraikkāl Ammaiyār as well as the contemporaneous first three Āḻvārs of the Tamil Vaiṣṇava *bhakti* tradition using it in their compositions.[18] Her work is also quite distinctive and pioneering; her shorter poem in particular is groundbreaking in its alternation by verse of two meters.[19] Both poems share a focus on descriptions of God's body, praise of him, and portrayals of the poet's interactions with him, the latter of which are often expressed through questions of practical and philosophical import. In the following discussion, I give priority to the longest of Kāraikkāl Ammaiyār's poems, now known as *Aṟputat Tiruvantāti* (Sacred Linked Verses of Wonder), which, at five times the length of her two Tiruvālaṅkāṭu hymns and five times the length of her other poem, constitutes her magnum opus.

Kāraikkāl Ammaiyār does not overtly thematize her own body in her creation of a devotional subjectivity in her poetic works. She uses the first-person singular and plural pronouns in her two poetic works, although such self-reference is conspicuously absent from her two Tiruvālaṅkāṭu hymns. The final verses of her two hymns and of her longest poem are signature verses in which "Kāraikkāl Pēy" is presented as the author of the works; however, this signature verse is absent from her shorter poem.[20] Neither the "I/we" nor the reference to *pēy* (ghoul, a multivalent term that I will discuss later) reveal anything about her gender, family, class, caste, or other markers of identity. The title "Kāraikkāl Ammaiyār," which means the "mother/lady/saint (of the town of) Kāraikkāl," clearly connotes gender, but this title is suggested only by Cēkkiḻār.

In some sense, then, the poet chooses not "to body" beyond assuming characteristics common to all human bodies, as she indicates in the first verse of her longest poem, *Aṟputat Tiruvantāti*:

Birth in this body
enabled me to express
my overflowing love
through speech,
and I reached
your sacred henna red feet.

And now I ask,
oh, lord of the gods
  whose neck shimmers black,
when will the afflictions
that birth in this world also enables ever end?[21]
  Aṟputat Tiruvantāti v. 1[22]

The poet's love for God is embodied. She informs us that she has a body, for she was born, she speaks, and she experiences love. These features are located in an individual, the "I" of the inflected verb, and yet her allusions to the human body are universal: she speaks of the birth from which her body emerged, she highlights the materiality of language in human learning and expression in speaking, and she describes the intersubjectivity of emotion that decenters the individuality of the body. It is the Lord's body that has singularity: his feet, naturally the auspicious hue of red, are her goal. "Reaching the Lord's feet" is a common trope in Tamil *bhakti* poetry, indicating the subordination of the devotee, who aspires to share in the Lord's presence at merely the lowest level of his body. The poet identifies and in effect names the Lord by an epithet that indexes one of his heroic deeds recounted in the mythological narrative of the churning of the ocean of milk: Śiva's neck "shimmers black" due to his swallowing of the poison that comes forth from the ocean of milk when the gods and demons churn its primordial waters. This is a universal, all-powerful form of the Lord, and yet the verse ties this form to the poet's particularity as a human speaker. She speaks directly to God and asks a spiritually informed question about ending "afflictions" (*iṭar*), which suggests the problem of embodiment. From her vantage point at the feet of the Lord, the poet can see both sides of human embodiment: it enables love and language, but it also permits suffering. Her embodiment of subordination is the context for her emotional and intellectual demand for release. There is thus a dialectic at work in the poem between the universal and the particular, type and singularity, and subordination and demand.

The devotional subjectivity that the poet creates in the poem pushes the boundaries of what is known by the speaking subject and her culture from the inherited Sanskrit mythology and emerging iconography of Śiva by describing, and creating knowledge of, exploratory interactive possibilities with her Lord beyond established ritual.

Was it not by grace
that I long ago achieved
the precious status of servant
to the lord who rules?

It was indeed grace
from the lord as majestic as a golden mountain

that bears the pure waves of the Gaṅgā
and streaming flames of fire.
Aṟputat Tiruvantāti v. 8[23]

She knows that she is a "servant" to God. She knows that she has been transformed by the Lord's grace, which is a salvific bestowal from him to her. This deeply personal, interactive knowledge is seamlessly joined with knowledge about the Lord's appearance, indexing established mythological narratives and emerging iconographic images of Śiva. Here intersubjective knowledge of Śiva—the shared public consciousness of his powers and his appearance—is framed by the active engagement of the speaking subject with Śiva as a servant who offers appreciation. Alternating with this articulation of what is known are expressions of a desire to know what she does not, especially the conditions of human embodiment and the possibility of salvation (as in v. 1), as well as the ways in which humankind should understand the Lord's embodiment. *That* Śiva is embodied serves as a vehicle for devotional praise; *understanding* his embodiment is a way for the speaking subject to interact with him in an interrogatory fashion. In this manner, she decenters the public lexicon of what is known from mythology and iconography, as in the following examples:

Oh, lord whose gaze reduced
the powerful god of love to ashes
and who resides in thoughts that are clear:
Tell us why
though your mouth imbibed the glossy poison
it was only your throat that darkened.
Aṟputat Tiruvantāti v. 89[24]

I became your servant
though I had not seen
your sacred form;
even today, I have not seen it.

So what will I answer
to those who repeatedly ask,
"Which is the form of your lord?"

What exactly is your true form?
Aṟputat Tiruvantāti v. 61[25]

In the first example, the poet asserts that clarity of thought characterizes the Lord, which inspires her to demand that he explain what appears to be a logical inconsistency in his appearance, about which the mythological story of Śiva swallowing the poison that emerges from the ocean of milk (referenced earlier in v. 1) is silent. Instead of using effusive praise to occlude discomfort, rupture, and puzzlement, she calls attention to details and inquires about them as a means of establishing intimacy with her Lord. In her poetry, interrogation is a valid form of active engagement with God; in the process, the public lexicon of what the Lord is like is decentered. When, in the second example, she asks to know about Śiva's ultimate form, this demand is once again an act of intimacy. She implies a contrast between the known mythological forms of the Lord, which she describes in other stanzas, and her expectation that he possesses another, ultimate form that he will reveal directly to her. Her demand is further contextualized with reference to other observers. The "those who repeatedly ask" of the second example are not specified, but the marker "your Lord" seems to distinguish them from the poet. Both the poet and her Lord are subject to the questioning gaze of others.

Along with representing the heroic deeds of Śiva, the poet describes him as a dancer at the cremation ground, an image that appears in the second verse of her longest poem and is invoked periodically throughout the later verses:

> Even if he would not cure my afflictions
> even if he would not pity me
> even if he would not tell me the right way,
>
> the love in my heart
> for our lord
> bedecked with bones
> as he dances on the flames
> at the burning ground
> will never cease.
>
> *Aṟputat Tiruvantāti* v. 2[26]

> His fullness is unknown to anyone,
> yet we can glimpse our lord's design
> when he joyfully dances on the flames
> adorned with skulls
> and accompanied by grim ghouls
> in the middle of the night.
>
> *Aṟputat Tiruvantāti* v. 30

Should I obtain a blessed view
of his highest form,
I would not wish for anything else
even if I was entitled;
the lord with the third eye
has granted me some knowledge
and I have joined his loyal band of ghouls.
Arputat Tiruvantāti v. 86[27]

For a poet who is concerned to push the boundaries of knowledge, invoking the form of Śiva as the dancer of destruction at the cremation ground is a fitting gesture toward the furthermost limit. As I discuss more fully elsewhere, the origin of this image has been something of a puzzle, and the innovation of the poet is an early, documented instance of its transformational development.[28] Unlike other images of Śiva alluded to in her poetry, such as the Lord who destroyed the triple cities and the Lord who swallowed poison, there was no developed story of the dance of Śiva for her to index, in no small part because the dance *qua* dance was not considered one of his "eight heroic deeds" in the traditional Sanskrit epic and Purāṇic literature.[29] According to recent scholarship, the famous image of Śiva as the dancer of creation (Naṭarāja) was developed in Tamil Nadu and did not appear before the tenth century CE.[30] As Padma Kaimal has demonstrated, forms of Śiva's dance other than the dance of creation were portrayed in sculptures across India prior to the tenth century, including at the Kailāsanāth temple in Kāñcīpuram (ca. 700–728 CE), where there is an image that seems to match the image of Śiva lifting his leg straight up that Kāraikkāl Ammaiyār mentions in one of the verses in the first of her Tiruvālaṅkāṭu hymns.[31] Kāraikkāl Ammaiyār is an early author whose works bring together images of Śiva as a fearsome force and as a dancer, coalescing into the potent image of Śiva as the Lord of time. She brings together and transforms several threads of inherited Śaiva tradition, including Sanskrit mythological stories that portray Śiva's dance as a victory related to specific heroic deeds, such as Śiva's killing of the demon Andhaka and his destruction of the triple cities; iconographic features that convey Śiva's fearsome ascetic persona, such as his serpent necklaces, bone adornments, skull begging bowl, and the cremation-ground setting of his dance; and images of violence and the goddess from Tamil sources, including Caṅkam-era poetry, the *Cilappatikāram* epic, and local place legends (Sthala-Purāṇas).[32]

Given her consistent references to Śiva in his frightful aspect, the poet's aesthetic is exploratory insofar as something that repulses the mind—as distinct from something that the mind can readily assimilate such as beauty—in its capacity as confrontational and memorable, is equally constitutive of devotional subjectivity. In what seems akin to a modernist project, she decenters the facile attraction and acceptance of beauty. Her references to the cremation ground and to bones and skulls suggest the abject, which is an existential challenge insofar as it forces the subject to confront his or her abhorrence and rejection of his or her own death—a confrontation that "disturbs identity, system, order."[33] Through engagement with the frightful appearance of the Lord, consciousness is "othered," since it is no longer concerned to uphold conventional boundaries that maintain the self, such as beauty and repulsion, life and death, purity and pollution. The cremation ground serves as an apt theater, since society views it as beyond the pale of human desire and thus socially uncontested.[34]

The fearsome body is a controversial body, and Kāraikkāl Ammaiyār's poetry preserves examples of challenging perspectives with regard to this form, in part due to the perceptions of others (as in v. 61).

All those who do not understand
the lord's true meaning reject him:
Outsiders see his form only as
a fear-inducing ghoul bearing skulls,
instead of the beauteous body
he has coated with sacred ash.
Arputat Tiruvantāti v. 29[35]

The beautiful lady
adorned with half plait and bangles
who shares your body
should not be brought along
when you dance on the flames
accompanied by ghouls
at the cremation ground
in the middle of the night,
your anklets ringing.
Arputat Tiruvantāti v. 51[36]

The *pēy* (ghouls) are part of the Lord's host at the cremation ground, known in Sanskrit by the term *bhūta*, which is "a close synonym for Tamil *pēy*."[37] The poetry of Kāraikkāl Ammaiyār seems largely to treat them as observers of Śiva's dance at the cremation ground, except in verse 29, when she suggests that the Lord himself appears to be a *pēy* (ghoul) to "outsiders" who do not understand his true meaning. This verse implies a very basic comparison that suggests that for those who know him, the frightening form *is* beauty—the fragrant body, covered with a sacred substance—whereas the ignorant respond with scorn. Verse 51 further nuances the point by specifying that conventional beauty is not part of the cremation scene. Those who know Śiva intimately do not require the domesticating influence of conventional beauty—revealingly identified in the verse with the feminine—in order to embrace his frightful appearance.

The interlocking of beauty and repulsion suggested in her poems takes on a graphic, experiential dimension in her two hymns on Tiruvālaṅkāṭu, each verse of which describes Śiva as dancing amid the gruesome elements of the cremation ground.

> The bushes are scorched
> the thicket is blackened
> the skulls ooze liquid
> and the chaparral has withered
> amid the tall trees.
>
> In this smoldering burning ground,
> clothed with the hide of the spotted deer
> and caped with the pelt of a tiger,
> the lord makes his home and performs his dance.
> *Tiruvālaṅkāṭṭut Tiruppatikam* 2 v. 5

The eyewitness observer whose view is described in these verses is not participating in a scripted ritual but in an unscripted, exploratory encounter in which both the frightful and the beautiful simultaneously coexist and are experienced as such.[38] While the scene of the cremation ground is not a habitable one in the social view, the signature verse tells us that "Kāraikkālpēy of the blazing mouth and teeth thrives at this burning ground" (*Tiruvālaṅkāṭṭut Tiruppatikam* 2 v. 11). Whether or not Kāraikkāl Ammaiyār herself takes on the body of a ghoul (*pēy*) is left open in her hymns, although her description of "a female *pēy*" in the first verse of her first Tiruvālaṅkāṭu hymn is generally taken to be a self-portrait and historically has informed her iconography in stone temple sculptures and bronze ritual images. Notably, this poetic description is in the third person, limning a female *pēy* at the cremation ground who is emaciated, with shriveled skin revealing the contours of her bones, and she is howling as the Lord dances. *If* it is a self-portrait, her use of the third person may provide a protective distance from the controversy of training a detailed descriptive gaze on a body that is human, female, and her own. But the larger point is that Kāraikkāl Ammaiyār does not train a descriptive gaze on her own body in her poetic corpus; she speaks generally of the human body as that which allows the experience of both painful afflictions and sublime love.

The sophistication of the devotional subjectivity described by Kāraikkāl Ammaiyār is at variance with her own portrait of ghouls at the cremation ground, which draws on earlier classical Tamil Caṅkam poetry. In several of these Caṅkam poems, poets describe the grisly scene of the cremation ground, specifically describing female ghouls (*peṇpēy*) as erratic, instinct-based creatures.[39] In evoking—and transforming—the classical Caṅkam poetry's imagining of the cremation ground and its characteristics, Kāraikkāl Ammaiyār *may* be describing herself as a *pēy*, and the ambiguity speaks to the centrality of the frightful to her devotional subjectivity. But through her appropriation and transformation of Caṅkam images, she is also clearly identifying herself as a *poet* in the Tamil tradition. The difference is that a poet is a speaking subject. As a speaking subject who speaks for herself to the Lord, notably in an interrogatory mode, and emphasizes a form of the divine that instantiates the abject and its possibilities, the poet has created a distinctive devotional subjectivity that urges transformation of one's own perspective though exploring challenges to the order, aesthetics, and propriety of the social order and the ritual body as its emblem.

What He Said

The biographer Cēkkiḻār authoritatively sealed Kāraikkāl Ammaiyār's reputation as a paradigmatic *bhakta*: she was one who embodied exemplary devotion. His project was "to body" the sixty-three Tamil Śaiva *bhaktas*, giving them all the status of Nāyaṉārs, "leaders," of their tradition. In one of the many paradoxes of Cēkkiḻār's biographic narratives in the *Periya Purāṇam*, he provides selective, although detailed, descriptions of the bodies of all sixty-three of the Tamil Śaiva *bhakti* saints, including gender, caste, occupation, and devotional actions, in order to advance his argument that none of these details are constitutive of the devotional subjectivity that is widely shared by them. For Cēkkiḻār the "servants" (*toṇṭar*) of Śiva are born, not made. Their stories are diverse, but they have in common an emphasis on the prior religiosity of the subject—whether due to the *bhakta*'s past births as a devotee of Śiva, or present birth to devout parents who practiced austerities, or birth in a town and community whose devotion to Śiva has spanned generations. Cēkkiḻār's theological perspective thus serves to marginalize the specific type of body one possesses in favor of the authenticity of one's heart or mind (both connoted by the Tamil word *maṉam*). Moreover, his suggestion that all body types are appropriate for the practice of *bhakti* is a significant argument against the brahmanical tradition's constructions of the ritual body, which impose limitations on the gender, caste, occupation, and actions of those who are qualified to participate in certain rituals. In advancing his thesis, Cēkkiḻār tells us over and over again that any given *bhakta*'s actions were based on love (*aṉpu*); it is this inner state shared by the sixty-three Tamil Śaiva *bhakta*s that serves as the real subject of his biographic narratives. His perspective resonates with what Cressida Heyes describes as

> a model of subjectivity in which the concepts of the authentic inner and often deceptive outer are incorporated into the structure of the self . . . so the discourse of the somatic individual relies on a distinction between the inner and outer in which the former is conceptually prior to the latter, and an a priori truth about the individual.[40]

In Cēkkiḻār's rendering, the heart is the same across bodies, but the classifications of individual bodies (occupation, caste, gender, and so forth) do affect the way in which the story of each *bhakta* is told, in part due to the real or imagined resources that would or would not have been available to the *bhakta*. In his biographic narrative of Kāraikkāl Ammaiyār in the *Periya Purāṇam*, Cēkkiḻār places a pronounced emphasis on social propriety.[41] Examples of his emphasis on social propriety are as follows.

In the beginning of her story, her body is described as not merely "normal" but as perfect. The biographer tells us that her original name was Puṉitavati—literally, "pure one." She was born into a successful merchant family and was wealthy, devout, and as beautiful as an incarnation of the goddess Lakṣmī (v. 2).[42] She had a marriage proposal from a suitable boy as soon as she came of age; although she did not leave the house after puberty, reports of her legendary beauty reached her suitor.[43] Once married, she and her husband settled in a house built by her father for them on his own property (v. 12), a detail that forecloses questions of propriety when her husband later abandons her. In the face of questions from her husband demanding to know from where she obtained a sublimely sweet mango, she is cautious not to say anything that might contradict his perspective (v. 27). She does not leave her marital duties to become a full-time *bhakta* until she is granted her husband's permission (v. 47). And, most revealingly, while she had been a devotee all of her life, her exemplary status as such is initiated by her rejection of her beautiful body in favor of the body of a *pēy*. Moreover, as a female *bhakta* separated from husband and family, she is alone and no longer supervised by society, and an unattractive body thus serves to foreclose questions of impropriety (v. 49).

Puṉitavati's beautiful body is not an obstacle to devotion until her husband forces the issue. As a wife, her domestic and devotional actions are undertaken with ever-increasing love (*aṉpuṟukātal*, v. 14), simplicity or innocence (*maṭavār*, v. 17), and modesty (*kaṟpuṭaiya*, v. 22). When her husband confronts her about the source of the mango, she responds with discipline and principle (*cīlattār*, v. 28). But when her husband does not believe her explanation that Śiva's grace is the source of the mango (her explanation is intimated but not described in the text), in response to his demand she secures yet another mango by praying to the Lord and thereby becomes a fear-inducing "other" in her husband's eyes, foreshadowing her transformation into a *pēy*. His "perplexed" mind views her as "some kind of a local goddess" (*vēṟu ōr aṇaṅku*, v. 31).[44] Because he is afraid of his wife, Puṉitavati's husband leaves their home and sails elsewhere under the duplicitous pretense that he is simply venturing on another trading enterprise.

The *Periya Purāṇam* holds in tension competing perceptions of Puṉitavati: after her husband remarries and has an infant daughter, he changes his mind and views her as a benevolent deity sacred to the family (*teyva*, v. 38), even naming his daughter after her; when Puṉitavati's relatives come to tell her of her husband's new life, she is represented as a fearsome goddess (*aṇaṅkaṉār*, v. 41); and when she steps into the palanquin to travel to her husband, she is once again likened to Lakṣmī (*tiru*, v. 42). This tension is only resolved when she is brought into her husband's presence. Once she arrives at her husband's new home, to her kin's astonishment her husband publicly prostrates himself before her, calling her a benevolent goddess (*teyvam*, v. 47). Her husband's assertion regarding her divine status precipitates her response, which begins with her praise of the Lord, leads her to request the Lord to release her from her body, and ends with her bodily transformation, a visible sign of her complete devotion to Śiva. The *Periya Purāṇam* recounts the story of her transformation into a *pēy* as follows:

48. As soon as he spoke, her relatives stood exclaiming, "What is this?" But when the lady of the fragrant hair heard the words of the merchant, she praised the ankleted feet of the Lord whose matted locks bear the *ko<u>n</u><u>r</u>ai* flower; achieving great knowledge through her singular focus (*cintai o<u>n</u><u>r</u>iya nōkkil mikka uṇarvukoṇṭu*), she proceeded to speak.

49. Bowing to the feet of the highest Lord, she said: "I request that you remove this sack of flesh that bears my beauty only for the sake of [my husband]. Instead, give to me, your servant, the form of the ghouls (*pēy*) who venerate your sacred feet."

50. At that moment, by the grace of the Lord who dances in the hall she fully realized the spiritual path and obtained what she desired: she shed all of her beauty that her fleshly body possessed and became a body of bones in the form of a ghoul (*pēy*) that is venerated by all on heaven and earth.

51. Flowers rained down and the sound of a heavenly drum reverberated everywhere; the celestials and sages rejoiced; celestial groups broke into dance; but her many relations, who stood before her, made reverential gestures and then departed in fear.

52. Then, united with the divine wisdom (*ñā<u>n</u>am*) that had arisen [within her], she gracefully composed the *Sacred Linked Verses of Wonder* (*A<u>r</u>putat Tiruvantāti*) in praise of the Lord who has Umai [Umā], which she lovingly sang, thinking, "I have truly become one of the fine group that praises his beautiful red lotus-like feet!"

Kāraikkāl Ammaiyār's self-affiliation with the dancing Śiva and his ghoulish host (*pēy*) that is expressed in her poetry is reflected in Cēkki<u>l</u>ār's narrative, but he contextualizes her choice with a social drama of bodily rejection in favor of a spiritual path. The rationale in the narrative for her choice of the form of a *pēy* is that her undesired beauty is now useless excess. Her desire to assume a ghoulish form could also speak to her rejection of the beauty and interactive responsibilities of a benevolent goddess, in the sense that she would prefer to be the subject who submits rather than the subject to whom others submit—but this is not explored in the story. A female poet's desire to approach Śiva by joining the *pēy*, his attendant-observers, is represented as creating a social rupture; there is no social status that would enable such a poet to continue to live in the ordinary social world.

That the social resolution in this story excludes Kāraikkāl Ammaiyār challenges the *bhakti* premise of action in the world, and, not surprisingly, such social exclusion is a feature of two stories in the *Periya Purāṇam* that are about "limit" cases: the one story about a woman that is told in more than a handful of verses (Kāraikkāl Ammaiyār), and the one story about an "untouchable" man (Tirunāḷaippōvār).[45] To my knowledge, these are the only two stories in the *Periya Purāṇam* that portray the saints as undergoing full bodily transformation.[46] In contrast, the text abounds in stories of the less-than-total bodily change of male saints, whether impoverished farmers or kings, who cut or burn themselves or others—with the implied or explicit comparison with cutting or burning *karma*—and all of the victims of the harm are represented as being restored in one way or another.[47] The revealing exception to the theme of restoration is that women are not represented as being restored when they are cut.[48] In addition, when a male *bhakta* of a particular caste assumes what others may view as a problematic appearance, it does not matter. For example, Cākkiya, who temporarily became a Buddhist before he rejected that teaching, continued to wear his monastic robes even after becoming a devotee of Śiva, since only his meditation on the feet of the Lord mattered.

The different ways in which bodies are treated in the *Periya Purāṇam* suggest that, in Cēkkiḻār's view, the devotional heart is "the same" no matter the body, and any body can house such a devotional heart. However, not all bodies are ascribed "the same" status socially. Devotional actions are undertaken in caste-inflected situations and locations (in a court, in a forest, and so forth), but they are not treated as caste duties as in the Bhagavad-Gītā. By calling attention to the social responses to bodies, Cēkkiḻār can be read as affirming social distinctions, and yet at the same time he reveals the patterns—the "fiction," as Gayatri Spivak has translated the term *māyā*—through which society constructs and evaluates gender and caste.[49]

Another implication of Kāraikkāl Ammaiyār's bodily transformation is that it displaces the poet's emphasis on the fearsome form of the Lord onto the body of the poet herself. Cēkkiḻār scrupulously avoids mentioning the frightful form and cremation-ground setting of Śiva so prominent in Kāraikkāl Ammaiyār's two hymns and longest poem.[50] He represents her second composition after her bodily transformation as her shorter poem, to which he gives a literary title, *Irattai Mālai Antāti*, or *The Double Garland of Linked Verses*, in reference to her alternation of meters. In his chronology her composition of this poem precipitates her pilgrimage to Mount Kailāsa to see Lord Śiva directly, where she again makes demands on him (however politely expressed, as in the case of her requests pertaining to the mango and her bodily transformation).[51] Cēkkiḻār's representation of Kāraikkāl Ammaiyār as undertaking the bodily challenge of pilgrimage draws on Nampi Āṇṭār Nampi's earlier brief biography of her, and it evokes the pilgrimages of the three most famous poet-saints in the Tamil Śaiva tradition—Campantar, Appar, and Cuntarar—to which they allude in their poetry and on which Cēkkiḻār elaborates in relating their stories.[52] Both biographers tell us that Kāraikkāl Ammaiyār "walked on her head, with her two legs high above" to ascend the mountain where her Lord resided. She sees the Lord in his majestic aspect, whom she calls "Father"; he responds by calling her "Mother."

As Anne Monius has discussed, "Śiva the Father" is a major motif in the *Periya Purāṇam* and is a critical component of the theological rhetoric deployed by Cēkkiḻār in response to Vaiṣṇava and Jain satirizing of the frightening forms of Śiva. She notes elements from the story of Kāraikkāl Ammaiyār in illustration of her argument: for example, her birth as a result of her father's practice of austerities; the "chaste" images of the saint as an incarnation of Lakṣmī; the calling of Śiva "Father" and the saint "Mother"; and her transformation into a fleshless, nonsensual, and nonsexual "body of bones."[53] We can add to this list the observation that, when Cēkkiḻār describes Kāraikkāl Ammaiyār's composition of her two Tiruvālaṅkāṭu hymns at the very end of her story, he makes no mention whatsoever of a cremation ground, instead describing the locale as an "excellent place" (v. 62). Nor does he mention any of the fearsome iconography of Śiva that she relishes, instead describing the Lord as "adorned with honeyed *koṉrai* blossoms" (v. 64), and his dance as that which "lovingly protects the earth" (v. 63) and is composed of "graceful movements in time with the drumbeat" (v. 64)—not at all the strenuous dance of destruction. In fact, his description of the dance as "graceful" uses most, but not all, of the words of a refrain to the first verse of her second Tiruvālaṅkāṭu hymn. Revealingly, Cēkkiḻār's story leaves out the hymn's reference to goblins.[54]

As Monius argues, the violent images in Cēkkiḻār's text were written against the Jain *Cīvakacintāmaṇi*. He replaced the "aesthetics of disgust" of the Jain text, in which violent acts encouraged renunciation, with images of "heroic" love on the part of the Śaiva *bhakta*s acting in the world, with their violent acts constituting "play" between a loving Lord and his "children."[55] Kāraikkāl Ammaiyār's story is not considered one of the violent ones in the *Periya Purāṇam*, so it encourages a more nuanced understanding of Cēkkiḻār's emphasis on the beautiful, keeping in mind Sara Ahmed's argument that emotions such as disgust have a powerful ability to maintain social hierarchies and modalities of power in their placement of people as above or below.[56] It seems convincing that Cēkkiḻār was at least in part responding to the vicious satire of other Hindu and non-Hindu groups when he disregarded Kāraikkāl Ammaiyār's version of the aesthetics of repulsion in which the fearsome image of Śiva is embraced as beautiful—and in fact she herself records such controversies in her poems, in terms of others' misunderstanding of the fearsome image of the divine and their ridicule of the devotees of that image. The *Periya Purāṇam* addresses these concerns by having saints act heroically on behalf of Śiva and his devotees, including the story of the saint Cakki, who cut out the tongues of those who disparaged Śaiva *bhaktas*. The image of a fearsome Śiva is represented in Cēkkiḻār's narrative at least once, although the father image is predominant in the biography as a whole.[57]

Even Cēkkiḻār's representation of Kāraikkāl Ammaiyār's consciousness highlights the Lord's beauty. First, the form of *pēy* indicates the beautiful and desirable state of God-consciousness. Kāraikkāl Ammaiyār is represented as in an enlightened state of consciousness when she requests the *pēy* form, and immediately after the transformation of her body she begins to compose poetry. Through this connection of *pēy* to poetry, Cēkkiḻār suggests that *pēy* indexes a state of God-consciousness, a meaning that was embodied by the Tamil Vaiṣṇava *bhakti* poet-saints who were contemporaneous with Kāraikkāl Ammaiyār.[58] This meaning of *pēy* was also explored in the post-Cēkkiḻār Tamil Śaiva *bhakti* tradition.[59] Second, the title that Cēkkiḻār gives to the first composition that Kāraikkāl Ammaiyār publicly utters, *Aṟputat Tiruvantāti*, or *Sacred Verses of Wonder*, is revealing. Significantly, she herself does not use the term "wonder" (*aṟputam*) in her poetry. The term represents her biographer's attempt to locate her poetry within aesthetic theory by appealing to a recognized category: *adbhuta*, wonder, which is one of the eight principal *rasas* of Sanskrit Indian aesthetics.[60]

In his recent elegant study of the aesthetics of wonder, Philip Fisher suggests that there are several characteristics that are especially constitutive of wonder.[61] First and foremost, it is related to knowing. Fisher describes a "poetics of wonder" that provides "a map of the features of thinking that guide us to satisfaction and a feeling of intelligibility within experience. . . . The local feeling of intelligibility is what we call . . . the feeling of 'getting it.'" Event-moments of wonder that we encounter in ordinary experience attract our attention: "The path from the puzzling to the feeling of intelligibility raises, among other questions, the issue of just why certain things puzzle us. Not everything that we do not know or cannot ever know puzzles us and draws us into thinking about it in an attempt to explain it to our satisfaction."[62] Kāraikkāl Ammaiyār's biographer informs us that the best way to understand her poem is in terms of the experience of wonder—both on the part of the author and the hearer. Viewed through this lens, Cēkkiḻār's designation of wonder underscores the poet's attempts to understand the Lord, through both her descriptions of him and her questions to him; she attempts to "get it," and to share it, in her poetry. He also captures the visual nature of her poetry in his appeal to the category of wonder to characterize her perspective.[63] However, wonder is first and foremost connected to the beautiful, since attraction and fascination provide the impetus to explore. As Fisher notes, the classic example of wonder is the rainbow, and it has fascinated philosophers from Aristotle to Descartes.[64] Cēkkiḻār's appeal to wonder is matched by his nearly exclusive emphasis on the majestic Śiva.

Concluding Remarks

Both the poet Kāraikkāl Ammaiyār and her biographer Cēkkiḻār interpret *bhakti* as a challenge to the social script by their emphasis on the repulsive body, but they deploy different ideas of embodiment and the voice suited to it. Kāraikkāl Ammaiyār is much more radical in this regard, since her insistence on the simultaneity of human attraction (beauty) and repulsion (death) in response to the body of Śiva, as well as in the bodily experience of witnessing his dance at the cremation ground, gives rise to a visceral transformation of consciousness toward a devotional subjectivity. Across her poetic works, a devotional subjectivity is an ongoing, productive tension between the desired and the abhorred, beginning with what tradition considers to be her first verse, in which she describes the human body as the means of both love and affliction. Her biographer Cēkkiḻār, on the other hand, draws a sharp line between beauty and the repulsive, by representing Kāraikkāl Ammaiyār as undergoing an irreversible bodily transformation from young woman to ghoul (*pēy*) and by completely exorcising the frightful aspect of Śiva found in her own poetry. The poet's holistic approach also contrasts with her biographer's emphasis on divisions when one examines their common underlying argument that devotional participation is a universal. In focusing on the human body generally instead of her own specific body, Kāraikkāl Ammaiyār speaks in a voice that presumes a universal stance: a woman's experience can represent a universally applicable devotional subjectivity. Her compositions destabilize the patriarchal formula that represents female as limited and male as universal. In his promotion of *bhakti* as a universal path, Cēkkiḻār strives to include one of everything—including one young unmarried woman, Puṉitavati/ Kāraikkāl Ammaiyār—in his depiction of the sixty-three Śaiva *bhakti* saints. He reinscribes her image in a narrative that betrays a patriarchal view of women: it reifies gendered expectations even as it sees through them. In the poet's vision, *bhakti* is a recognizable and realistic oscillation between poles of human affective experience, a somatic and thoughtful exploration of the intertwining of love and repulsion, certainty and fear, knowing and not knowing; in theory, this would have been the more accessible path, and perhaps her compositions were canonized in part on that basis. However, it is her biographer's vision of *bhakti* as a gendered story of the tension between marriage and devotion that is religiously—but not socially—resolved by the dramatic and singular miracle of her bodily transformation that remains the dominant voice between this pair of *bhakti* authors.[65] For her, through *bhakti* a woman as a human being could live in the world in an exploratory fashion; for him, a human being as a woman could not.

Notes

1. This essay is related to my book on Kāraikkāl Ammaiyār, *Interpreting Devotion: The Poetry and Legacy of a Female Bhakti Saint of India* (Pechilis 2011). Many of the perspectives I offer in this essay have received a much more detailed treatment in the book, including issues of the historicity of Kāraikkāl Ammaiyār. For a contextual discussion of Tamil Śaiva *bhakti,* see Prentiss 1999. For a translation of the story of Kāraikkāl Ammaiyār in Cēkkiḻār's *Periya Purāṇam,* see Pechilis 2006b, revised in Pechilis 2011. For an analysis of the story of Kāraikkāl Ammaiyār through a feminist lens, see Pechilis 2008 and 2014.

2. I base this comment on my discussions with a variety of people in Tamil Nadu over the past twenty years. Kāraikkāl Ammaiyār's hymns are publicly sung at an annual festival commemorating her liberation at the temple in Tiruvālaṅkāṭu near Chennai, but otherwise they are not much heard. The 1973 film *Kāraikkāl Ammaiyār* by director A. P. Nagarajan and starring the singer K. B. Sundarambal features cine-songs, not the saint's compositions. A striking recent example of the public performance of her hymns was the drama troupe Devi

Kalaikoodam's performance of "Karaikkal Ammaiyar" starring C. Devijarrina at the Narada Gana Sabha in Chennai on March 11, 2015, sponsored by the Tamil Nadu Eyal Isai Nataka. Ms. Devijarrina and her director husband Chand Basha had consulted with the *ōtuvār* (professional hymn singer) Sargurunathan of Mylapore's Kapaleeshwarar temple on the correct tunes (*paṉ*).

3. I use the term "biography" rather than "hagiography" in my discussion of Cēkkiḻār's work for several reasons. One is that he attempts to construct individuality, especially in his longer life stories. Another is that his work is not best understood as "uncritical endorsement" of his subject matter, but instead, as I argue in this essay and elsewhere (Pechilis 2011: 82–105, 2014), he presents a critical social stance on gender in his story of Kāraikkāl Ammaiyār. I also do not think that it serves the study of religion in the humanities to sequester its subject matter in a specialized category. See Pechilis 2011: esp. 3, 18–21; Jorgensen 2002: esp. 86–91.

4. In his recent essay on memory, Novetzke (2008b: 240) provocatively states: "I would argue that one finds in *bhakti* the longest, most sustained, most heterogeneous collective exploration of memory in South Asia." In Tamil Śaiva *bhakti*, Cēkkiḻār's emphasis on the body looms large in all of his stories of the saints, and in the case of Kāraikkāl Ammaiyār more specifically, it overshadows her own compositions. The creative space between poet and biographer is an example of the heterogeneity noted by Novetzke, as is the series of interpretations of *bhakti* within Tamil Śaiva *bhakti* discussed in Prentiss 1999.

5. Monius 2004a provides a comprehensive comparison of these two texts.

6. Prentiss 1999.

7. Many of the studies in English on Kāraikkāl Ammaiyār adopt this view—for example, Sasivalli 1984; Jagadeesan 1989 to some extent; Ramaswamy 1997; Craddock 2007, 2010; Mahalakshmi 2011. Other studies—such as my own (Prentiss 1999; Pechilis 2006b, 2008, 2011, 2014); Mahalakshmi 2000; and Pāskar 2006—tend to be more concerned with locating differences in perspectives and noting ruptures. More widespread is the tendency to conflate the embodiment and persona of Kāraikkāl Ammaiyār with the poet's description of a female *pēy* (ghoul), as I briefly discuss later in this essay and more fully in Pechilis 2011.

8. Recent publications that foreground various aspects of devotional singing are Kelting 2001; Hopkins 2002 and its companion volume, Hopkins 2007; Pechilis 2006a; Novetzke 2008a; Sanford 2009; DeNapoli 2014; and Shukla-Bhatt 2014.

9. I provide an example of Cēkkiḻār's interpretation of a hymn by Appar in Prentiss 1999: 72–75, 126–128.

10. Prentiss 1999: 64–76, 101–108, 123–133, passim.

11. See, for example, Zubko 2010; Holdrege 2008; Flood 2006: 20–24; Doniger 1997.

12. See, for example, the discussion and sources in Zubko 2010.

13. Flood 2004, 2006: 31–47.

14. Holdrege 2008: 20. Her essay invokes McKim Marriott's emphasis on the transactional nature of Hindu traditions in his studies from the 1960s and

1970s. Other essays in the Mittal and Thursby volume in which Holdrege's essay appears also draw on Marriott's work.

15. The discussions of course implicate caste but, refreshingly, look to other ways of characterizing discourses of the body in Hindu traditions.

16. The *bhakti* saints of India can be arranged on a spectrum ranging from acceptance to rejection of temple rituals. For example, the Tamil Śaiva and Vaiṣṇava *bhakti* saints tended to accept ritual worship, whereas saints such as Kabīr and Basavaṇṇa castigated it. Cutler (2003: 149) notes that a historical argument can in part explain the contrast in these positions: "Whereas in Tamilnadu the emergence of *bhakti* coincided with the origins of temple worship (ca. sixth century CE), proponents of some of the later *bhakti* traditions viewed temples as an established religious institution which had lost its vitality." Holdrege's study (2008) identifies ritual body discourse with the Vedic Saṃhitās and the Brāhmaṇas. However, by the time of the Tamil Śaiva *bhakti* saints, the discourse of the ritual body includes Āgamic Śaiva Siddhānta formulations, which also defined themselves in response to Vedic formulations (Prentiss 2001).

17. Readers familiar with classical Tamil literature will understand that I am playfully using the headings, such as the one that precedes this section, that traditional commentators bestowed on Caṅkam poetry, although, as Ali (2000: 175) has discussed, *bhakti* poetry replaces the unnamed characters in the classical poetry with a named deity and a named author.

18. Note that the first reference to titles for her poems is in Cēkkiḻār's *Periya Purāṇam*. As Cutler (1987: 38 n. 15) explains, the verses of works in the *antāti* style "are joined 'end to end' by means of a prosodic device called *antāti* (a Tamilization of the Sanskrit compound *anta*, 'end' + *ādi*, 'beginning'). According to the rules of *antāti*, the last syllable or several syllables of a verse in a multistanzaic poem must be identical to the first syllable or several syllables of its successor." As I explain in Pechilis 2011, the two hymns make use of an older style of *antāti*.

19. The poem, which is Kāraikkāl Ammaiyār's shorter poem, alternates verses in two different meters (*veṇpā* and *kaṭṭaḷaik kalit tuṟai*); regarding it, Gopala Iyer (1996: 352) notes, "Of the available works of this kind, Kāraikkāl Ammaiyār's *Tiruviraṭṭai Maṇi Mālai* is the earliest work."

20. The shorter poem is also different since it has an even number of verses (20), as distinct from the two hymns (11 each) and the longer poem (101). It is intriguing that the shorter poem alone lacks a signature verse among Kāraikkāl Ammaiyār's compositions. In the longer poem the signature verse is linked to the first verse in keeping with the *antāti* style. In the shorter poem the last verse (which is not a signature verse) is linked to the first verse in keeping with the *antāti* style, which strongly suggests that it never had a signature verse.

21. "love" (*kātal*). As discussed subsequently, Śiva's neck is black because, according to Śaiva mythology, he swallowed poison at the primordial churning of the ocean of milk.

22. All translations of her poetry and biography are my own, and most are found as in Pechilis 2011, although I have here modified some of the trans-

lations. I primarily used *Patinonrān Tirumurai* 1995 (poetry) and Cēkkilār 2000 (biography); for comparative purposes, I also used Kāraikkāl Ammaiyār 1982 and Ramachandran 1993.

23. "servant" (*āl*); "grace" (*arul*). In traditional Śaiva mythology and iconography, the Gaṅgā River flows forth from Śiva's hair, and he bears fire in one of his palms.

24. "resides in thoughts that are clear" (*telivulla cintaiyinir cērvāy*).

25. "true form" (*ninruruvam ētu*). The term *uruvam* is repeated in the poem. "Your" (*num*) follows commentators; "true" (*ētu*) connotes source or origin.

26. "burning ground" (*eri*, literally, "fire"); "love" (*anpu*).

27. The first-person plural inclusive form "we" is used in the first line of the poem (*namakku*) and in the fourth line (*nām*). However, it is possible to translate these forms as first-person singular.

28. Pechilis 2013 and 2016b.

29. See Peterson 1989: 342–348 for summaries of the eight heroic deeds and other myths of Śiva found in the Mahābhārata, Purāṇas, and Tamil sources. Smith 1996: 186 also provides a list from the Tamil text *Tirumantiram* (possibly dated to the tenth century CE, although much disputed), which constitutes the tenth volume of the *Tirumurai* canon. Śiva's dancing pervades his mythology. See Gaston 1982: 47–48, 133–139, 144–148, 152–169, 175–176.

30. See Kaimal 1999; Smith 1996; Younger 1995; Shulman 1980.

31. Kaimal 1999: 394, 415 n. 14. This image, both in her poetry and in iconography, is understood by tradition to allude to a dance competition between Śiva and Kālī. See Pechilis 2013; Wood 2004.

32. Mahalakshmi 2000: 24–48 offers an interpretation of Kāraikkāl Ammaiyār's appropriation through her thesis that Tamil *bhakti* marginalized local cults: "The specific focus here is on the deliberate attempts under the guise of *bhakti* to a single deity—Śiva—at marginalizing and even ignoring the other already existing local traditions in the Tamil region. The work of Kāraikkāl Ammaiyār, one of the earliest proponents of *bhakti*, will be examined in this connection. While it is well documented that the marginalization of local cults was never final . . . it is Kāraikkāl Ammaiyār's particular choice of a site known to be associated with an indigenous goddess that has led to this exploration" (Mahalakshmi 2000: 20). Much of her argument is repeated in Mahalakshmi 2011: 110–125. See also Shulman 1980: 194–223. I offer a different interpretation in what follows, which is more fully discussed in Pechilis 2011.

33. Kristeva 1982: 4.

34. The poet consistently uses the term *kāṭu* (wild, uncultivated, uninhabited land), a term that contrasts with *nāṭu* (cultivated land, city, political unit).

35. "meaning" (*porul*); "outsiders" (*pirar*); "ghoul" (*pēy*). "Fear-inducing" is implied.

36. "you" (*nī*); "cremation ground" (*īmap peruṅkāṭṭir*); "anklets ringing" (*kalalārppa*, literally, "noisy feet," which commentators interpret as the sound of anklets, indicating the strenuousness of the dance).

37. Cutler 1987: 122. In Tamil the term *pēy* often refers to the menacing spirit of a deceased person, which is also a meaning of the term *bhūta*. For contemporary ethnographies exploring this meaning of *pēy* in Tamil Nadu, see Kapadia 2000; Clark-Decès 2008.

38. I discuss this difference in locating Kāraikkāl Ammaiyār in the early Śaiva milieu in Pechilis 2016a.

39. Such as in the following excerpt from *Puṟanāṉūṟu* 359, "Kāviṭṭaṉār Sings Antuvaṉkīraṉ," translated in Hart and Heifetz 1999: 203:

> Even the rulers of countries go to the burning ground
> where the land is waste and desolate and filled with dry thorns,
> and owls are there with blazing mouths and undulating shrieks,
> and small foxes, their glistening teeth smeared with fat, chew at corpses;
> where demonesses [*peṇpēy*, "female *pēy*"], grasping and embracing the dead,
> dance swinging their legs on that salty land in terrifying movement
> by the light of the pyres, their bodies sending out the stench
> of hot meat because they have consumed the bloodless flesh.
> And that day will come when you must go there as well,
> but your bad reputation will remain, and your good reputation.

The connections between Tamil Śaiva *bhakti* and classical Caṅkam poetry have frequently been noted (see, for example, Cutler 1987; Mahalakshmi 2000). The connections among deities, *pēy*, and battle endured in Tamil literature. For example, Cayaṅkoṇṭār, a celebrated poet in the Chola court (late eleventh century to twelfth century CE), composed a poem celebrating one of the king's victories in which he homologizes the king and his army to the goddess Kālī and her host of *pēy* (Zvelebil 1975: 186–187; Thiagarajan and Muthuswamy 2006).

40. Heyes 2007: 22.

41. For the purposes of this essay, I will select relevant portions of Kāraikkāl Ammaiyār's story for discussion. For a translation and discussion of her complete story, see Pechilis 2006b and a revised and more elaborate discussion in Pechilis 2011. For a feminist interpretation of her story, see Pechilis 2008 and 2014.

42. *tirumaṭantai avatarittāḷ*, "an incarnation of the sacred lady," with *tiru* a reference to Lakṣmī.

43. "At that time, she became too beautiful to leave the house" (*vaṉappumīka kūra aru māṭciyiṉāl il ikavāp paruvattil*) (v. 6).

44. I explain my translation choices in Pechilis 2006b.

45. See my comparative discussion of these two saints in Pechilis 2005.

46. The story of the saint Tirumūlar represents him as changing bodies, but this is not a complete transformation of his own body.

47. See, for example, the cases of Ciṟuttoṇṭar, Caṇṭēcurar, Arivāṭṭāyar, Eṟipattaṉ, Kaṇampulla Nampi, and Ēyarkōṉ Kalikkāman.

48. See, for example, the wife of Kalikkampan̲, the daughter of Mān̲akkañcāran̲, and the wife of the king Kal̲aṟciṅkan̲.

49. Spivak 2001: 132. See Pechilis 2008 and 2014 for discussions of the affirmation and critique of social structures in Cēkkil̲ār's story of Kāraikkāl Ammaiyār.

50. As I suggested earlier, the poet's engagement with the frightening form and cremation-ground setting of Śiva is comprehensive in her Tiruvālaṅkāṭu hymns and prominent in her longest poem. However, it receives only brief representation in her shorter poem (certainly v. 15 and to some extent v. 17).

51. "May those who desire [you] with undying joyful love (*an̲pu*) not be reborn; if I am born again, may I never forget you; may I sit at your feet, happily singing while you, virtue itself, dance" (v. 60).

52. I translate and discuss Nampi's brief biography of Kāraikkāl Ammaiyār in Pechilis 1999: 112 and Pechilis 2006b: 175–176.

53. Monius 2004b: 183–185, 196.

54. Kāraikkāl Ammaiyār's *Tiruvālaṅkāṭṭut Tiruppatikam* (second decade) has *koṭṭa mul̲avaṅ kūḷi pāṭak kul̲akan̲ āṭumē* (v. 1), while Cēkkil̲ār's text has *koṭṭa mul̲avaṅ kul̲akan̲ āṭum en̲ap pāṭinār* (v. 64). The missing words from Cēkkil̲ār's text are *kūḷi pāṭak*, "goblins sing."

55. Monius 2004a: 139–152.

56. Ahmed 2012, esp. the chapter on "The Performativity of Disgust," 82–100. In Pechilis 1999: 69–76, I argued that the *proximity* of Jains underlay the critique of them in Tamil *bhakti* poetry by the three male saints' portrayal of them as disgusting; see Ahmed (2012: 97) on proximity.

57. For example, in the story of Mān̲akkañcāṟa, Śiva appears as a guest at his daughter's wedding ornamented with bones in his hair and across his chest. Śiva demands the daughter's hair so that he can use it as his sacred thread, and the father complies by chopping off her hair. The story does not represent her hair as being restored.

58. A contemporaneous poet-saint in the Vaiṣṇava tradition, Pēyāl̲vār, also seems to have explored the connection between being a *pēy* and the "othering" of consciousness. See Cutler 1987: 122, 128–130. Kāraikkāl Ammaiyār is also linked to another of the early Vaiṣṇava poet-saints, Pūtam, in a medieval commentary (Zvelebil 1975: 155 n. 164).

59. The later Tamil Śaiva philosophical tradition also noted this link. For example, Umāpati Civācāryār (fourteenth century CE) has the following passage in his text *Tiruvaruṭpayan̲* (The Fruit of Divine Grace): "Remain without performing any actions up until the nature of a *pēy* arises" (v. 8.7; translated and discussed in Prentiss 1999: 196). This sense of *pēy* was also used by Akappēyccittar (fifteenth century CE) (Zvelebil 1975: 242).

60. The Tamil term *aṟputam* is from the Sanskrit term *adbhuta,* which is one of the eight *rasas* enumerated in the *Nāṭya-Śāstra,* according to the *Tamil Lexicon* (vol. 1, 172). The term *adbhuta* is also used in the Bhagavad-Gītā in the eleventh chapter. There are differences in aesthetic theory between Sanskrit and Tamil traditions, however. Both Selby (2000: 31–33) and Cutler (1987: 65–70)

discuss the Tamil concept of *meyppāṭu* as a term corresponding to *rasa*, although there are significant differences between the two concepts. For example, Tamil poetics presumes a more direct experience of a performance than that ascribed to the connoisseur in Sanskrit aesthetics. In addition, the Tamil concept of *tiṇai*, or "context," is of central importance in Tamil poetry: "Just as *rasa* had become the primary focus of the Sanskrit rhetoricians and commentators, so had *tiṇai* become the chief concern of the Tamil critics" (Selby 2000: 33).

61. Another important recent study of wonder is Fuller 2006. While I appreciate Fuller's emphasis on wonder as a primary human emotion and as "the experience of contemplating how the various parts relate to a greater (if unobserved) whole" (8–9), I am less keen on his consistent prescriptive assertion, which forms a subtext of his book, that wonder constitutes a healthy way of living.

62. Fisher 1998: 8. It is the case that several of Fisher's examples relate to knowledge of the natural physical world, but he does have a chapter on aesthetic appreciation and wonder, so his study is not limited to nature.

63. According to Fisher (1998: 21), "Wonder and learning are tied by three things: by suddenness, by the moment of first seeing, and by the visual presence of the whole state or object." He contrasts the visual with the narrative in his discussion, ultimately concluding that the temporal unfolding of the latter diminishes the confrontational quality that is only possible with the sudden experience of a visual whole.

64. Fisher 1998: 33–56.

65. Cēkkiḻār can be said to have "miracle-ized" the life of Kāraikkāl Ammaiyār. In his discussion of Christian medieval female mystics and their male hagiographers, John Coakley notes a change in the construction of hagiography: "In the earlier medieval centuries, saints appeared to their admirers preeminently as the loci or media of a divine power that was expressed in miracles and great deeds of charity or asceticism. Newer saints still functioned in this way in hagiographical accounts, but they also appeared increasingly as people with a privileged subjective experience of the divine" (Coakley 2006: 9). (Regarding male hagiographers of female practitioners, see also Mooney 1999; Wilson 1996.) I submit that we can apply this characterization to the poet and her biographer, although in reverse chronological order from Coakley's examples. *She* was concerned with the exploration of her subjective experience of the divine, while *he* sought to foreground the miracle of her direct contact with Śiva, especially its culmination in what he represented as her bodily transformation.

References

Ahmed, Sara. 2012 [2004]. *The Cultural Politics of Emotion*. Abingdon and New York: Routledge.

Ali, Daud. 2000. "From *Nāyikā* to *Bhakta*: A Genealogy of Female Subjectivity in Early Medieval India." In *Invented Identities: The Interplay of Gender, Religion and Politics in India*, ed. Julia Leslie and Mary McGee, 157–180. New Delhi: Oxford University Press.

Cēkkiḻār. 2000 [1993]. *Cēkkiḻār Perumāṉ Aruḷiya Tiruttoṇṭar Purāṇam*, ed. A. Ca. Ñāṉacampantaṉ. Cennai: Cankai Puttaka Nilapam.

Clark-Decès, Isabelle. 2008. "From Wasteland to Bus Stand: The Relocation of Demons in Tamilnadu." In *Tamil Geographies: Cultural Constructions of Space and Place in South India*, ed. Martha Ann Selby and Indira Viswanathan Peterson, 173–197. Albany: State University of New York Press.

Coakley, John W. 2006. *Women, Men, and Spiritual Power*. New York: Columbia University Press.

Craddock, Elaine. 2007. "The Anatomy of Devotion: The Life and Poetry of Karaikkal Ammaiyar." In *Women's Lives, Women's Rituals in the Hindu Tradition*, ed. Tracy Pintchman, 131–147. New York: Oxford University Press.

Craddock, Elaine. 2010. *Śiva's Demon Devotee: Kāraikkāl Ammaiyār*. Albany: State University of New York Press.

Cutler, Norman J. 1987. *Songs of Experience: The Poetics of Tamil Devotion*. Bloomington: Indiana University Press.

Cutler, Norman J. 2003. "Tamil Hindu Literature." In *The Blackwell Companion to Hinduism*, ed. Gavin Flood, 145–158. Oxford: Blackwell.

DeNapoli, Antoinette Elizabeth. 2014. *Real Sadhus Sing to God: Gender, Asceticism, and Vernacular Religion in Rajasthan*. New York: Oxford University Press.

Doniger, Wendy. 1997. "Medical and Mythical Constructions of the Body in Hindu Texts." In *Religion and the Body*, ed. Sarah Coakley, 167–184. Cambridge: Cambridge University Press.

Fisher, Philip. 1998. *Wonder, the Rainbow, and the Aesthetics of Rare Experiences*. Cambridge: Harvard University Press.

Flood, Gavin. 2004. *The Ascetic Self: Subjectivity, Memory and Tradition*. Cambridge: Cambridge University Press.

Flood, Gavin. 2006. *The Tantric Body: The Secret Tradition of Hindu Religion*. London: I. B. Tauris.

Fuller, Robert C. 2006. *From Emotion to Spirituality*. Chapel Hill: University of North Carolina Press.

Gaston, Anne-Marie. 1982. *Śiva in Dance, Myth, and Iconography*. Delhi: Oxford University Press.

Gopala Iyer, T. V. 1996. "Iraṭṭai Maṇi Mālai." In *Encyclopaedia of Tamil Literature*, ed. Shu Hikosaka and G. John Samuel, vol. 3, 352–353. Madras: Institute of Asian Studies.

Hart, George L., and Hank Heifetz, trans. and ed. 1999. *The Four Hundred Songs of War and Wisdom: An Anthology of Poems from Classical Tamil, the Puṟanāṉūṟu*. New York: Columbia University Press.

Heyes, Cressida J. 2007. *Self-Transformations: Foucault, Ethics, and Normalized Bodies*. New York: Oxford University Press.

Holdrege, Barbara A. 2008. "Body." In *Studying Hinduism: Key Concepts and Methods*, ed. Sushil Mittal and Gene Thursby, 19–40. New York: Routledge.

Hopkins, Steven P. 2002. *Singing the Body of God: The Hymns of Vedāntadeśika in Their South Indian Tradition*. New York: Oxford University Press.

Hopkins, Steven P., trans. 2007. *An Ornament for Jewels: Love Poems for the Lord of Gods by Vedāntadeśika*. New York: Oxford University Press.

Jagadeesan, N. 1989. "The Life and Mission of Kāraikkāl Ammaiyār." In *Medieval Bhakti Movements in India: Śrī Caitanya Quincentenary Commemoration Volume*, ed. N. N. Bhattacharyya, 149–161. New Delhi: Munshiram Manoharlal.

Jorgensen, John. 2002. "Representing Wŏnch'ŭk: Meditations on Medieval East Asian Buddhist Biographies." In *Religion and Biography in China and Tibet*, ed. Benjamin Penny, 74–131. New York: Routledge.

Kaimal, Padma. 1999. "Shiva Nataraja: Shifting Meanings of an Icon." *The Art Bulletin* 81, no. 3: 390–419.

Kapadia, Karin. 2000. "Pierced by Love: Tamil Possession, Gender and Caste." In *Invented Identities: The Interplay of Gender, Religion and Politics in India*, ed. Julia Leslie and Mary McGee, 181–202. New Delhi: Oxford University Press.

Kāraikkāl Ammaiyār. 1982 [1956]. *Chants Dévotionnels Tamouls de Kāraikkālammaiyār*, ed. and trans. Karavelane. Pondichéry: Institut Français d'Indologie.

Kelting, M. Whitney. 2001. *Singing to the Jinas: Jain Laywomen, Maṇḍaḷ Singing, and the Negotiations of Jain Devotion*. New York: Oxford University Press.

Kristeva, Julia. 1982. *The Powers of Horror: An Essay on Abjection*. Translated by Leon S. Roudiez. New York: Columbia University Press.

Mahalakshmi, R. 2000. "Outside the Norm, within the Tradition: Kāraikkāl Ammaiyār and the Ideology of Tamil *Bhakti*." *Studies in History* 16, no. 1: 17–40.

Mahalakshmi, R. 2011. *The Making of the Goddess: Koṟṟavai-Durgā in the Tamil Traditions*. New Delhi: Penguin Books.

Monius, Anne E. 2004a. "Love, Violence, and the Aesthetics of Disgust: Śaivas and Jains in Medieval South India." *Journal of Indian Philosophy* 32, nos. 2–3: 113–172.

Monius, Anne E. 2004b. "Śiva as Heroic Father: Theology and Hagiography in Medieval South India." *Harvard Theological Review* 92, no. 2: 165–197.

Mooney, Catherine, ed. 1999. *Gendered Voices: Medieval Saints and Their Interpreters*. Philadelphia: University of Pennsylvania Press.

Novetzke, Christian Lee. 2008a. *Religion and Public Memory: A Cultural History of Saint Namdev in India*. New York: Columbia University Press.

Novetzke, Christian Lee. 2008b. "Memory." In *Studying Hinduism: Key Concepts and Methods*, ed. Sushil Mittal and Gene Thursby, 230–250. New York: Routledge.

Pāskar, Taraṇi. 2006. *Kāraikkāl Ammaiyār*. Poḷḷācci: Patippat tuṟai, Nallamuttuk Kavuṇṭar Mahaliṅkam Kallūri.

Patiṉoṉṟāṉ Tirumuṟai. 1995. Comm. Ñāṉacampantam Patippakam. Mayilāṭuturai: Tarumai Ātiṉam.

Pechilis, Karen. 2005. "The Story of Nantanar: Contesting the Order of Things." In *Untouchable Saints: An Indian Phenomenon,* ed. Eleanor Zelliot and Rohini Mokashi-Punekar, 95–107. New Delhi: Manohar.

Pechilis, Karen. 2006a. "Singing a Vow: Dedicating Oneself to Shiva through Song." In *Dealing with Deities: The Ritual Vow in South Asia,* ed. Selva J. Raj and William P. Harman, 147–163. Albany: State University of New York Press.

Pechilis, Karen. 2006b. "The Story of the Classical Woman Saint, Kāraikkāl Ammaiyār: A Translation of Her Story from Cēkkiḻār's *Periya Purāṇam.*" *International Journal of Hindu Studies* 10, no. 2: 171–184.

Pechilis, Karen. 2008. "Chosen Moments: Mediation and Direct Experience in the Life of the Classical Tamil Saint, Kāraikkāl Ammaiyār." *Journal of Feminist Studies in Religion* 24, no. 1: 11–31.

Pechilis, Karen. 2011. *Interpreting Devotion: The Poetry and Legacy of a Female Bhakti Saint of India.* New York: Routledge.

Pechilis, Karen. 2013. "Śiva as the Lord of Dance: What the Poetess Saw." *Journal of Hindu Studies* 6, no. 2: 131–153.

Pechilis, Karen. 2014. "Devotional Subjectivity and the Fiction of Femaleness: Feminist Hermeneutics and the Articulation of Difference." *Journal of Feminist Studies in Religion* 30, no. 2: 99–114.

Pechilis, Karen. 2016a. "Bhakti and Tantra Intertwined: The Explorations of the Tamil Poetess Kāraikkāl Ammaiyār." *International Journal of Dharma Studies* 4.2. doi: 10.1186/s40613-016-0024-x.

Pechilis, Karen. 2016b. "The Siva Nataraja Image: Poetic Origins." *Kalakshetra Journal* 4: 1–16.

Peterson, Indira Viswanathan. 1989. *Poems to Śiva: The Hymns of the Tamil Saints.* Princeton: Princeton University Press.

Prentiss, Karen Pechilis. 1999. *The Embodiment of Bhakti.* New York: Oxford University Press.

Prentiss, Karen Pechilis. 2001. "On the Making of a Canon: Historicity and Experience in the Tamil Śiva-*bhakti* Canon." *International Journal of Hindu Studies* 5, no. 1: 1–26.

Ramachandran, T. N., trans. 1993. *The Hymns of Kaaraikkaal Ammaiyaar.* Dharmapuram: Mayiladuthuri. Accessed June 4, 2011. http://www.shaivam.org/english/sen_thiru11_kkl_arputa_tiruvandadi.htm.

Ramaswamy, Vijaya. 1997. *Walking Naked: Women, Society, Spirituality in South India.* Shimla: Indian Institute of Advanced Study.

Sanford, A. Whitney. 2009. *Singing Krishna: Sound Becomes Sight in Paramānand's Poetry.* Albany: State University of New York Press.

Sasivalli, S. 1984. *Karaikkal Ammaiyar.* Chennai: International Institute of Tamil Studies.

Selby, Martha Ann. 2000. *Grow Long, Blessed Night: Love Poems from Classical India.* New York: Oxford University Press.

Shukla-Bhatt, Neelima. 2014. *Narasinha Mehta of Gujarat: A Legacy of Bhakti in Songs and Stories.* New York: Oxford University Press.

Shulman, David Dean. 1980. *Tamil Temple Myths: Sacrifice and Divine Marriage in the South Indian Śaiva Tradition*. Princeton: Princeton University Press.
Smith, David. 1996. *The Dance of Śiva: Religion, Art and Poetry in South India*. Cambridge: Cambridge University Press.
Spivak, Gayatri. 2001. "Moving Devi." *Cultural Critique* 47: 120–163.
Tamil Lexicon. 1924–1936. Madras: University of Madras. Accessed June 4, 2011. http://dsal.uchicago.edu/dictionaries/tamil-lex/.
Thiagarajan, P., and E. S. Muthuswamy, eds. 2006. *Kaliṅkattupparaṇi: English and Tamil, by Cayaṅkoṇṭār, 12th Century*. Chennai: Institute of Asian Studies.
Wilson, Liz. 1996. *Charming Cadavers: Horrific Figurations of the Feminine in Indian Buddhist Hagiographic Literature*. Chicago: University of Chicago Press.
Wood, Michael. 2004. "The Temple at Tiruvalangadu and the Myth of the Dance Competition." In *Chidambaram: Home of Nataraja*, ed. Vivek Nanda with George Michell, 106–117. Mumbai: Marg.
Younger, Paul. 1995. *The Home of Dancing Śivaṉ: The Traditions of the Hindu Temple in Citamparam*. New York: Oxford University Press.
Zubko, Katherine C. 2010. "Body." In *Brill's Encyclopedia of Hinduism*, ed. Knut A. Jacobsen, vol. 2, 720–724. Leiden: Brill.
Zvelebil, Kamil V. 1975. *Tamil Literature*. Leiden: E. J. Brill.

Chapter 8

Bodies of Desire, Bodies of Lament

Marking Emotion in a South Indian Vaiṣṇava Messenger Poem

Steven P. Hopkins

I will focus in this essay on a *sandeśa-kāvya*, or "messenger poem," the *Haṃsasandeśa* (Goose-Messenger), composed by the South Indian Śrīvaiṣṇava poet-saint, theologian, and philosopher Veṅkaṭanātha or Veṅkaṭeśa (ca. 1268–1369 CE), also known by his epithet Vedāntadeśika, "Preceptor of the Vedānta." The *sandeśa* is a genre of love poetry that has its roots as early as the fifth century CE in Sanskrit, flourishing in many different languages from the twelfth to the eighteenth centuries, yet also common right up to the present day. In most of the major messenger poems an exiled lover, human or divine, sends a message to a distant beloved via a messenger—a starling, a goose, a bee, a cuckoo, a parrot, a peacock, a language (Tamil), or, in the case of Kālidāsa's seminal sixth-century Sanskrit text the *Meghadūta*, a cloud. The *sandeśa* links the powerful emotions of love, separation, and the desire for reunion to beloved landscapes, literary visions of the natural world that echo the separated lovers' remembered past and anticipated future union. And not only the natural world of flora and fauna, idealized nature in its fecundities and its dangers, but also landscapes marked by culture, by religion, by the values—political and sectarian—of the poet who writes the poem. The *sandeśa-kāvya* is not only about love, the beauties of nature, and the transfigured time of eventual reunion; it is also about the individual poet's religio-geocultural *imaginaire*, reflecting regional identity and royal or sectarian patronage.

I have discussed elsewhere in some depth the geocultural landscapes of Veṅkaṭeśa's *sandeśa*—his southern refashioning of sacred space and his distinctive form of "southern" cosmopolitanism and decidedly "southern" Sanskrit.[1] This essay will not focus primarily on the *sandeśa*'s geocultural *imaginaire* and the vivid flowering of a regional Sanskrit but rather on the charged emotional landscapes of various particular *bodies* in the poem: there is indeed the affective body of a beloved territory—what is a fundamentally happy body of divine presences dripping with shrine-jewels—but there are also bodies of individualized lovers who desire and who lament in separation and bodies of animals that inspire and enflame the longings of lover and beloved. Veṅkaṭeśa's *Haṃsasandeśa* not only valorizes the excellence of particular South Indian landscapes, marking holy rivers, mountains, fields, and shrines, but it also eloquently marks emotional landscapes, the powers of erotic love and the turbulence of desire, onto the bodies of lover and beloved and also onto the body of the messenger, in this case a royal goose (*rāja-haṃsa*).[2] And there is the body of the text itself, a cultivated imaginal literary "body" that wills transformation in all it touches. This essay, and the larger project it reflects, is thus not about a presumed generic category of "the body" in Indian literatures but rather focuses on particularities, on beloved and loving *individual* bodies. I will explore the ways in which Veṅkaṭeśa refashions the story of Rāma and Sītā using motifs of vulnerable love and the virtues of violent emotion that inhere in his own South Indian *bhakti* (devotional) tradition: the agonies of separation, mourning, loss, and, through an act of visionary (presentational) literary imagination, the hoped-for time transfigured by love regained.

Rāma's Love-Madness and the Royal Goose

I will begin my analysis with a detailed portrayal of Rāma's love-madness, kindled by the sight of a royal goose.

The poem opens in autumn[3] with Rāma, the god and future king of the Sun Lineage, the Lord who honors humanity in his human birth, sleepless and vigilant (*jāgarūka*) in the forest of Kiṣkindha, suffering in love (*kāmin*), somehow lasting through a night that seems as long as a thousand ages (1.1).[4] He is pondering the message given to him by his monkey servant Hanumān: a vision of his beloved consort Sītā in agony, a captive in the demon king Rāvaṇa's palace in Laṅkā, alone in the *aśoka* grove, tormented by demonesses (*rākṣasīs*), and languishing in separation. He cannot wait until daybreak when he will muster his forces and head slowly toward Laṅkā to rescue his beloved. Veṅkaṭeśa thus combines in his *kāvya,* and indeed in the first two verses of the poem, two different *rasa*s, or conventional aesthetic moods according to Sanskrit literary theory: the poem oscillates between the poles of *vīra-rasa* and *śṛṅgāra-rasa,* the heroic and erotic moods, respectively. Although Rāma is a warrior, he also inevitably suffers in love.

The next day, as his troops ready for the march, still tormented in the depths of his heart (*dūyamānāntarātman*), he sees a royal gander (*rāja-haṃsa*) at play in a lotus tank, its white body shining like the full moon (1.2). Its gait is like Sītā's slow sensual walk, he thinks; its sweet voice, like the ring of her anklet;[5] its lovely body, like the bodies of geese woven into her fine *dukūla* (forest-bark) dress. Seeing the great gander, he falls into a swoon (*ceto vilaya*), overwhelmed by fierce emotion, struck dumb by the power of Kāma, the fish-bannered god of love:

His eye fixed unwavering on the slow sensual walk
 just like Sītā's, on the lovely white body like the bodies
  of geese
woven into her fine *dukūla* forest dress,
 on its sweet call like the low threshing ring of her anklet,

our hero lost for some time sense and self,
 his mind steeped in her alone:
as they say the call of the fish-bannered god of love
 can be cruel sometimes. (1.3)[6]

Somehow recovering, although still confused, he begins to speak to the gander as if it were human, offering it tender lotus petals, cajoling it, in a kind of a dark vehement madness (*gāḍhonmāda*) brought on by separation. It would be his messenger, he thinks, greater than aerial Hanumān, his servant; it would send his love back to her before he and his armies reach Rāvaṇa's gardens. Veṅkaṭeśa the poet then muses (1.4): like all lovers in the world who burn in separation, Rāma takes almost more solace in the messenger, in the tender message sent, than in the physical embrace of the beloved. And why not this goose? thinks the Rāma of the poem in verse 1.5. Have not lovers in the past, crazy with love, asked insensible things—clouds, mountains, trees—to bear their messages?

Honoring that royal gander in greater measure than he
  honored
 his old friend and servant Añjaneya [Hanumān],

in a dark vehement madness he worked hard to win the confidence
of a creature who could tell him nothing:

those shaken by love in separation are reduced to pleading
with clouds, begging mountains and trees,
insentient things—

how much more we expect
from an animal that knows feeling. (1.5)

These verses emphasize, in ways similar to the poetry of the ninth-century Tamil Vaiṣṇava poet-saint Nammāḻvār and the twelfth-century Tamil *Rāmāyaṇa* of Kampaṉ, *Irāmāvatāram*, the profoundly troublous, disruptive, mad world of love. Love's feelings are disruptive and turbulent, even for a god[7]—even for Rāma, who takes on his humanity only to "honor" the human. This leaky, unstable, vulnerable, turbulent world of love—haunted by the memories of the past, tormented by present loss, and fearful for the future—is linked in the history of *bhakti* literatures with patterns of Tamil poetry and with ideas of *pittu*, "lunacy," and *mayakkam*, "confusion," and Veṅkaṭeśa's Sanskrit text exudes their dark residue.[8] Rāma's mad romantic excess has its particular South Indian *bhakti* genealogy.[9]

Beginning with verse 6 of part 1 of the poem, we have Rāma's quite lengthy address to the royal goose, which goes on through verse 60 of part 1 and through verse 48 of part 2. He praises the goose, born in the great lineage of Viṣṇu, twin of the great goose that the creator god Brahmā rides through the heavens, which has the pale pure color of the goddess Sarasvatī's skin and a sweet voice that bears the sweetness, to the ear's touch, of the voice of Sarasvatī. In his hyperbolic praise Rāma emphasizes his own helplessness and earthbound humanity, and in verse 1.9 his rhetoric turns descriptive, anticipating the goose's journey south with an immediate reference to its sacred places (*divya-sthānas*). The southern region, birthplace of pearl fisheries, mother of fragrant sandalwood breezes blown down from the forests of the Malaya mountains, has only one blemish: it is also home to *rākṣasas*, pestilent southern demons. But no matter, says Rāma to the royal gander, this is a small thing compared to the blissful spectacles that await you (1.6–9).

An Ornament for Jewels: The Landscape's Beloved Body

Rāma then tells the goose in great detail where it is to go, across what beloved landscapes, to Laṅkā and to Sītā. He imagines in vivid detail stages of the southern route, an imaginal embodied geography that favors very specific southern regions that, although particular to this Śrīvaiṣṇava poet of northern Tamil Nadu, immediately bring to mind the literary Tamil landscapes described in Kampaṉ's *Irāmāvatāram*. We shift from the suffering and beautiful bodily surfaces, respectively, of Rāma and his goose messenger, to the emotionally marked bodies of beloved landscapes and the gods, spirits, and human folk who live in them, echoing their virtues. Veṅkaṭeśa praises the Toṇṭai, Cōḻa, and Pāṇṭiya regions, the exoticized charms of Āndhra and Karṇātic girls, the Kāverī and Tamrapāṇī rivers, the equally exoticized badlands of tribal forests, and a very few specific shrines—Tirupati temple, Kāḷahasti temple, Varadarāja and Ekāmranātha temples in Kāñcīpuram, the simple serpent shrine in the country in what will become Śrīraṅgam, and Vṛṣabha Hill and its anklet the Gaṅgā River—a landscape marked by particular beauties and the extravagant rhetoric of a lover's awe.[10]

With verse 1.11 begins a richly figured series of descriptions of a landscape redolent with the perfumes of night-flowering red lotus and *kuvalaya* blossoms that whirl about in the currents of the lakes and the honeyed exudations of elephants in rut, the air thick with the pollen of the *bandhu-jīva* flowers. Rich fare, and embodied lyric excess. A catalogue of flowers, animals, and regions at once real/concrete and symbolic. At one point (1.12) we hit upon an unusual detail: a lovely image of the god Śiva. The goose is compared to the crescent moon on Śiva's head, drowned in the waters of the Gaṅgā, reflecting the red-lac dye from the feet of his consort Pārvatī. The image is of the great god bowing down before his wife, doing homage to his *śakti*. This will not be the first vivid loving image of Lord Śiva. One might ask at this point, what is Śiva doing in this supposedly exclusively Vaiṣṇava poem? Some commentators emphasize that Śiva himself worships Viṣṇu at the famous shrines, although the poem does not allude to any such spiritual hierarchy. We will find that regional identity is most important in Veṅkaṭeśa's poem, not sectarian differences. At the southern shrines the gods are all friends, mingling their fragrances over the holy temple towns.[11]

This body of the southern territory is resplendent, "pressing out perfect bright pearls" and "heady perfumes" (1.9). To use an image from Veṅkaṭeśa's *stotras*, the shrines and places inscribed upon this magical land are like jewels adorning the beloved, and, in the extravagant rhetoric of lovers, the beloved's body itself, in its innate beauty, is an "ornament for the jewels."[12]

In Kālidāsa's *Meghadūta*, geese accompany the cloud on its journey. In Veṅkaṭeśa's poem, the autumn clouds serve as canopies for the goose in its journey southeast (1.13), and a wandering moon rushes overhead past the fine-eyed *śabara* hunter girls and their lovers in the thick bowers of the Sahya Hills (the Western Ghāṭas). Rāma tells his goose messenger (1.16–20) that with unblinking sleepless eyes it will cross a countryside marked by mountains, forests, and rivers, by young country girls who rush from their village houses to catch sight of it, and by girls who stand guard over paddy fields or lounge in the shade of sugarcane groves, prattling about their lovers and their wild lovemaking, singing bawdy sexual songs in mongrel tongues that mingle "Āndhra" with "Karṇāṭaka" (*karṇāṭāndhra-vyatikara-vaśāt*).[13] After this fascinating reference to songs in which two border vernaculars identified with their specific regions intermingle, we reach the first of the sacred places of the *sandeśa*: Añjanādri, or the Tirumalai Hills, Tirupati, home of Viṣṇu as Veṅkaṭeśvara/Śrīnivāsa (1.21).

The holy hills of Tirupati are studded with bright gems like serpents' hoods; no wonder, because they are thought to be the very incarnation of the serpent Ādiṣeśa. Dark thick autumn clouds tear off their peaks like skins slough off a serpent (1.22). This is a place for all to worship; Viṣṇu makes no distinction here between high and low. Therefore, Rāma says to his royal gander, worship to your heart's content that god who killed the demon Madhu (*madhu-vijayin*). Next, just before we reach the place that Veṅkaṭeśa favors over all other places, his Ujjayinī, he describes a river just south of the hill with subtle erotic touches, and once again we are graced with the awesome though invisible presence of Śiva:

> On the south slope of Añjana Hill you will see Kanakamukharā,
> a river that sings quietly in its golden beds,
> sandbanks now hidden, now naked, shining,
> as if drawing you down to stay:[14]
>
> it is she who gathers in her hands of bright long waves
> blossoms that fall from forest trees growing along her banks
> to honor the god who wears the crescent moon
> in his hair. (1.23)

This is Śiva as Śrīkāḷahastīśvara, Lord of the shrine of Kāḷahasti near the river Svarṇamukhī, one of the five most sacred places to Śaivas in South India—a form of Śiva praised by many later Telugu poets, including the great sixteenth-century poet-saint Dhūrjati.[15] He is here too, the local Śiva, in this Vaiṣṇava poem, being served by his river, which is called by its old name, the Kanakamukharā. Rāma imagines his goose will stop here, by these cool quiet sandbanks, although soon he will have to go:

Tasting her in secret, calling back to her in sweet low moans,
your feathers brushed so lightly by breezes
over sandbanks that breathe the heady scent of *vañjula* flowers,

with care but quickly, rise take your leave,
let no one follow,
may the fierce hunters who live near the river never catch
you. (1.24)

After these remarkable stanzas we encounter a group of eleven verses that give, in almost *stotra* (praise-poem) style, the longest extended description of a single place in the poem: the great city of Kāñcīpuram, in particular the temple and the temple icons of Varadarāja Perumāḷ, one of Veṅkaṭeśa's favorite shrines. This is where, according to the Sthala-Purāṇa, or "place legend," Brahmā himself earned a vision of Viṣṇu-Nārāyaṇa as Varadarāja, "Lord of the vows," in Satyavratakṣetra, the "land of true vows," the universal divine "person" particularized in a specific landscape. Before Varadarạja appeared in Brahmā's great sacrificial fire, his dark form burning, emerging along with the white shrine tower, the Lord himself had first come down in the form of a dam to stop Brahmā's jealous wife, Sarasvatī, who had become a torrential river, bent on flooding the sacrificial ground in anger. Today she is the swift-moving—but obedient—Vegavatī River:

Then catching sight of that famous Tuṇḍira country,
go to that place, the land of true vows that casts off sins,
where that god, the only dam for all beings to ford the
streams of births,
became a dam against the goddess of the tongue,
Sarasvatī, who took the shape of a river
out of anger at her husband. (1.25)[16]

There you will see the town of Kāñcī, an ornament for Earth,
whose splendors befit her shining wide hips,
whose walls endlessly echo sounds of songs and dances,
and whose virtues are magnified
by numberless precious jewels—

in that city will you not also see that great god who lives
on Elephant Hill,
whose passion is truth beyond the twin pairs of pain and
pleasure;
his searching passionate eye
never leaves this place. (1.26)

Drawing near to that city, do it honor with head bent low
in devotion,
for in the very first age of the world it was born
from the mere whim of Brahmā the creator.

In its streets the very dust kicked up by the swift horse
of the Lord of Elephant Hill
is worn on the foreheads with deep gratitude
by monarchs among the gods. (1.27)

Then the fragrant breeze, lover of dark lotus beds that hug
the banks
of the Kampā River,[17]
blown down from bowers of sacred mango groves that lightly
tremble at its passing,

will bear sweet dew from the crescent moon on the forehead
of Śiva,
Lord of the animals;
it will greet you like a dear friend just returned
from a far-off country. (1.28)

The allusion in the last stanza is to the temple of Ekāmranātha, "Lord of one mango," near the Kampā River in what is known now as "big Kāñcī." Varadarāja temple is in "little Kāñcī" on the other side of town. Once again we have a wonderful evocation of a kinship, even a kind of mutual honor, between the two gods Viṣṇu and Śiva, symbolized here by the breezes that pass through Śiva's mango grove, bearing his sweet dew as a sign of friendship.[18]

After this Rāma describes to the messenger the Vegavatī River, flowing clear and serene in the center of town, "queen of you birds and of poets" (1.29),[19] and he urges the goose to do homage and to bathe in the sacred waters. Then he describes the town's true center of gravity, the place that makes holy the entire southern country: the shrine of Varadarāja. Here Viṣṇu is a blue-black monsoon cloud that shrouds the hill of the shrine room, the site of Brahmā's old sacrificial altar, and his consort Lakṣmī is a streak of bright lightning (1.33). The central descriptive verses use lines from Veṅkaṭeśa's major Sanskrit *stotra* on Varadarāja, which allude to the Lord's union with his own consort, Viṣṇu as "mother of worlds":

> [I]nscrutable god goddess, mother of worlds, her shining
> dark body
> is made deeper dark by Lakṣmī's dark glances. . . . (1.32)[20]

From the central holy city and the region's divine *axis mundi*, we fly southwest over areca groves, rivers, and paddy fields of the Cōḻa country, over Tiruvaḷḷarai, doing special honor to the "daughter of Sahya," the holy river Kāverī, more eminent than the great Gaṅgā River of the north, which drives deep furrows into the countryside with her powerful streams, her banks clogged by pearls and sugarcane (1.36–42).[21] Then comes Candrapuṣkāriṇī Lake where goddesses bathe, and on its banks the serpent-couch (*śeṣa-pīṭhā*), future Śrīraṅgam, which awaits its ritual image of Lord Raṅganātha that Rāma is said to have later established in this place. (Veṅkaṭeśa is careful to avoid anachronism in this case.) From there Rāma imagines a flight to the Pāṇṭiya lands across the dangerous tribal forests "where thieves are thick and the crickets make harsh cries."

Vṛṣabha Hill is next, where Viṣṇu is known as Sundara or Aḻakar in Tamil (1.49). This is the hill-shrine of contemporary Tirumāliruñcōlai, and on the lap of the mountain shines a stream of the very Gaṅgā (*nūpura-gaṅgā*) that was "vomited" (*vānta*) out of the anklet of Viṣṇu as Trivikrama.[22] The Śiva stories say that the Gaṅgā fell into Śiva's red matted hair, but Veṅkaṭeśa writes here that the holy river remained "untouched by the matted hair of the Lord of animals" (*paśupati-jaṭā-sparśa-hīna*). Here is a bit of a sour sectarian note perhaps, but hardly extreme.

The remainder of the section is a praise of the Pāṇṭiya country, including allusions to the Pāṇṭiya kings who held the clouds captive, being royal storehouses of fertility and prosperity that bring dharmic rule to the land; to Agastya, who drank the ocean; and to the lucid Tamrapāṇī River, whose sandy banks are strewn with pearls like an earth-sky spread with stars. Next is the coast, the seashore with its palmyra groves, dark *tālī* and *tamāla* trees washed by the waves that throw up pearls and the pollen dust of *ketakī* flowers (1.50–53).[23] And from the shore the shape of a long-arched bow, loud with the ruckus of rivers descending into the sea, arrows let loose from the singing bowstring (1.54), the goose will fling itself into the sky, over coral reefs crimson like a jungle on fire, like the twilight sky and the yellow waist-cloth of Viṣṇu, and from there it will land at the great palace of Rāvaṇa on Laṅkā.

Sītā's Body of Desire and Lament

The second section (*āśvāsa*) begins with a long, conventional, image-rich description of the glories and terrors of Rāvaṇa's realm and his palace abode, so high "it darkens the sky's face," with its lamenting captive goddesses and floating "sky ships" (2.1–8).[24] But soon we are in the cloistered heart of the *aśoka* grove, and we see Sītā, dressed in her *dukūla* dress with its designs of geese, languishing in the fires of separation near her "solitary *śiṃśupa* tree" draped with her jewels. We return now to a suffering body in love, to a body marked by desire, separation, and lament, to Sītā in Rāma's eye. Rāma's description of Sītā's suffering body is vivid and detailed, finely rendered in Veṅkaṭeśa's *kāvya* style as a Mughal miniature, and represents within the *sandeśa* what might be termed *the bodily landscape of viraha*, "separation-iṇ-union" (2.10–24). Emotions here are not something exclusively mental and passion is not invisible feeling, something purely psychological, but rather emotions and passions are written into her body—into her breasts that themselves burn in fevers of separation (evoking Tamil notions of *aṇaṅku*, "heat," "power," "affliction"); into her hair, waist, eyebrows, and tears; and into her fine graceful arms and her skin—and are literally sewn into the clothes that she wears.[25] We have moved from the vivid body of a landscape, with its elegantly detailed contours, to the body of a woman suffering in love.

Rāma first visualizes Sītā as an extraordinary and otherworldly, divine, and precious gem (*kimapi divya-ratna*) that sits at the foot of the *śiṃśupa* tree. Then that gem slowly takes the shape of a woman:

That jewel with long shining eyes of *śaphara* fish
  and eyebrows arched like bows, fine dark hair, and
    slender body,
she leans forward just a little with the weight
  of her full high breasts, her skin shining like gold made
    pure in fire:

young with the slow sensual walk we so admire in you,
  her waist the slender altar of sacrifice;

lovely in every perfect limb, she hides in her body the
secret treasure
of love's essence itself;
equal to the goddess of luck and blessing,
she *is* my eye. (2.10)

Then follows Rāma's imagined map of Sītā's love-longing, emotions marked visually in a body of separation. Verbal forms in these verses make a subtle shift from the future sense of nominal verbal constructions to present participles and finite verbs, moving the listener into the heart of a future made vividly present before the eyes in the charmed time and space of the poem:

The moment you catch sight of her from the air she will be
mute,
dumb, confused with grief, or perhaps she will be talking
to birds,
begging they listen to her message
meant to reach me alone,

or, her eyes sealed shut with weeping, she will be fixing
her blind gaze
in our direction, the north,
for omens that speak of good news fast on the wing.
(2.11)

Or maybe out of her love-madness she prattles on,
talking to her own jewels that hang in the tree,
asking them whether or not they remember what it is like
to touch
the body of Rāma, Lord of the Raghus,

or, eyes shut tight in quiet meditation,
she lives again long hours so long past, the pleasures of
love-play
in their small single bed:
it can't be her, but only fate could have caused such pain.
(2.12)

Bright streams of purest moonlight in the hovel of an outcaste,
an eater of dogs,

a fresh branch of pure Pārijāta thrown into a wood
of poison trees,

the sweetest, most noble words of the finest of poets
sung in the ear of a criminal:
I think of the daughter of the king of Mithilā suffering
in the house of the Night-Prowler. (2.13)

Like clusters of lotus blossoms crushed by heavy rain,
like speech marred by contradiction,
like the tender lotus stalk choked by mud,
or the she-elephant separated from her husband,

like moon-rays muted by clouds,
like hope hemmed in by obstacles,
like the fawn approached by the tiger,
like the broken bowstring fallen on the battlefield. (2.14)

Remembering how once long ago she sought the shelter
of my close embrace,
in her fear of love's softest arrows
she now hugs the very ground, her Mother Earth,

with thin graceful arms fatigued even by the weight of her
bangles
and barely able to take the pressure
of fine unguents and herbs she has rubbed into her skin:
so weak she has become
she cannot even bear the weight
of memories. (2.15)

Taking my signet ring in her hands, slender as lotus blossoms,
over and over in waves of bliss
she feels the hairs of her body stand on end;
putting it on her head in her dark hair that once held the
precious crest-jewel
of a queen,
she is filled with deep delight;

then with care and reverence she presses it deep between
her two lovely breasts full as water pots

but sick with the love fever
that burns within them. (2.16)

The indelible heavenly unguent matching the grain of her
perfect body
that Anasuyā, another mother to her,
rubbed into her skin as a reward for her virtue

is yet washed clean away by her flow of heavy tears
hot with anguish;

they fall in torrents of some endless stream in a fierce rushing
along the sides of her breasts full as water pots. (2.17)

Her fine head of hair that I once bound
into hasty uneven braids because I could not hold it all
cleanly in my hands
now comes loose, spills down over her shoulders,
as if it desired to taste the perfume of her body,

her hair like a cluster of dark flowers from heavenly trees
thrown down to earth by Apsarases for the worship of
Ratī's husband,
the great god of love,
drawing in its fall a trail of fat
hungry bees. (2.18)

She is wearing a lovely dress the burning vermilion
of the young rising sun,
bearing a weave in gold thread on every border of your beloved
lady geese,

a twin to the blouse snatched with haste
by monkeys from the mountain:

so is she another crescent moon in a sky
dyed in red twilight. (2.19)

And then, after focusing on her left jeweled anklet that hangs from the tree in his visionary present, imagining Sītā remembering his touch on her feet as he fastened the anklets after their love-play

(2.20), and after envisioning her languishing and lamenting body like a drooping tender sprout, dimmed and withering, the "hot breath of her anguish" (2.21), he composes a tour de force of *yoga* "love metaphysics" in verse 2.22. There Sītā sits in formal yogic meditation, firmly fixing her thoughts (*dhī*) on Rāma as her inmost self. She achieves a level of *nirvikalpa samādhi*, pacification of the mind and the senses—literally, a "softening" (*mṛdunā*) of the mind's desire and a tranquilization of feeling (*śamāya*)—in union with the transcendental, formless, and non-changing goal far beyond the particular Rāma of her too-human desire. Here the power of love-*yoga* conquers individual, particular loss, but not for long.[26] Rather abruptly in verse 2.23 we return to a stark summary of Sītā's body in pain, the essential truth of separation, immediate and irreducibly particular:

> A vacant stare, unbounded sighing, too much of grief,
>   lotus face shut tight as a bud,
> yet tears flow from closed eyes in fierce rushing torrents
>   of rivers,
> lament without end;
>
>   by what inexorable law or fate has she,
> so deeply bound to me,
>   been drawn into such inconceivable misery—
> her slender sweet body—
>   O my heart now burns within me. (2.23)

This verse evokes indirectly, through Sītā's silent agonized pantomime imagined by Rāma, essential characteristics of female lament found in many cultures. It is an active witness to ruin, to irrevocable loss, written into the body—a refusal to resolve, domesticate, or ritually control and thereby "let go" of grief. Although it lacks the power of Sītā's direct speech, her great formal lament (*vilapana*) in Vālmīki's Sanskrit Rāmāyaṇa (after all, these are Rāma's words to his messenger, his verbal icon of suffering Sītā), this verse and the set piece that precedes it are a witness to familiar patterns of women's laments.[27] Like Constance in Shakespeare's *King John*, Sītā here holds "too heinous a respect of grief,"[28] although this does not mean that she is *merely* mad or *merely* an enfeebled passive victim of powerful emotions. Female lamenters hold on to particularity, a fidelity to individual loss that serves as an ethics of witness and a demand for justice (or revenge). To use a formulation of Jacques Derrida: the deep ambiguities of mourning and melancholy are expressed in an "unfaithful fidelity" in which "success" (to heal or even begin what Freud calls "the work of mourning") "fails," and "failure" (the continued witness to loss, what might be called "acute melancholia") paradoxically "succeeds."[29] In spite of the momentary solace offered by yogic *samādhi,* a metaphysical focus on a transcendent goal beyond immediate material suffering, it is Sītā's "systematic" witness to the present "misery"—a particular witness to particular loss—that holds Rāma's "eye" and drives the narrative forward, forcing Rāma to be the hero, to act against injustice done to him and to his realm. As Rāma himself says to the goose in the following verse (2.24), having seen Sītā in this miserable condition, "even you" will not be able to bear the intensity of your own grief that will have "welled up in you of its own accord." This material and performative bodily witness to grief will also inspire the messenger to action.

With Rāma's address to the goose, as at the beginning of this long recital of Sītā's imagined suffering, when Rāma says that Sītā *is* his eye, we have a direct immediate identification with another's suffering. Rāma, one might say, has pain in "his" Sītā.[30] Even more radically put: it is through their pain—through their separation—that Rāma and Sītā become real to one another; it is through their pain and the severing of connection, and not merely through yogic *samādhi,* that they are one.[31] And we readers/listeners are also meant to feel this in our bodies. Description here, for Rāma, for the goose, and also for us who look through the "eye" of the text—Rāma's eye (which is "Sītā")—is also participation. Rāma loves as we are meant to love, in full particularity, no matter the suffering.

The Body of the Text: Separation, Memory, and "Time Regained"

Finally, after this imaginary portrait of Sītā in separation, comes the poem's message: a series of love lyrics that express Rāma's deep pain of separation, emotional upheaval, and the weight of memory, an agony equal to that of his beloved (2.32–46). In lyrics that allude to and compare favorably with some of the finest Sanskrit love lyrics, we circle back, at the close of the poem, to the lover's confused sleepless madness that opened it.

Through his messenger the goose, who stands there in front of him, although he is imagined to have already arrived at his destination, Rāma addresses the absent Sītā as if she were present, "placing her in the path of his eyes" (*nayanoḥ vartmani sthāpayitvā*). Rāma muses to his Sītā in the third person (2.32): in the old days, he says, for Rāma even your ornaments, the very unguents on your skin, seemed to impede his close embraces, and now fate has carried you away to a distant island. Verse 2.33 is particularly evocative and alludes to a famous verse in Bhavabhūti's *Uttararāmacaritam* when Rāma describes his embraces of Sītā while the "night-watches passed unnoticed." Veṅkaṭeśa's verse is highly charged with erotic energy:

> In the old days, O lady of sweet body,
> consumed by a madness of passion that seemed to have no limit,
> we had barely begun to make love, our bodies pressed close together
> in tight embrace, when the night would vanish in an instant.
>
> But now broken into pieces by a thousand acts of love in my mind,
> this same night, made even deeper dark
> long with memories of you,
> never ends. (2.33)[32]

The fact of separation in a *sandeśa* is compounded by the fact that the so-called message that one hears or reads on the page has not yet been delivered but is simply being dictated *before the journey has even begun*. A double sense of separation. But this is not all. The *sandeśa* text itself, its very structure, is an act of creative imagination, an *anubhava* or *bhāvanā*, a kind of conjure. The *sandeśa* is binocular, drawing together in a stereoscopic vision two separate times and spaces as if they were simultaneous in experience. Actually more than two times are drawn together: in the *sandeśa* multiple time frames—past, present, and imagined future—coalesce, or to borrow a word from Proust, *miroiter*, flash back, one across the other; they "shimmer" together on the page. In this Proustian sense, the *sandeśa* is a kind of "magic lantern."[33]

The *sandeśa* is not only about the separation of lovers, but built into its imaginative structure is an experience of "time regained," the anticipation of a union that evokes auspiciousness, blessing, and well-being (*śreyas*). The austerities of love-in-separation in the *sandeśa* will ultimately bear fruit, generating good fortune and luck for the listener/reader. At the very end, Rāma tells Sītā that he and his armies will come and that autumn, when the four quarters are clear, is the time for war and the howling of a warrior's bow. Here the heroic (*vīra-rasa*) joins with the erotic (*śṛṅgāra-rasa*) in creating a most satisfying literary work, "polished on the whetstone of the intellect" (2.50), its goal to bestow, over and again, blessing and auspiciousness, an experience of full time.

Notes

1. See Hopkins 2004. For a discussion of Kālidāsa's *Meghadūta* and Veṅkaṭeśa's *Haṃsasandeśa* as examples of "southern Sanskrit" in what Sheldon Pollock has called "the vernacular millennium," see Bronner and Shulman 2006. I will not discuss in this essay the important elements of allegory applied by Śrīvaiṣṇava commentators to this poem and this literary genre. In the theological world of Śrīvaiṣṇava commentary (*anubhava-grantha*) and the tradition's secret teachings (*rahasya*), Rāma is the Lord, the goose is the Ācārya, and Sītā is the *saṃsārin*, the individual *jīva* suffering in this world of redeath in desperate need of consolation. Ajay Rao has studied this form of Śrīvaiṣṇava allegoresis quite extensively, and I refer to his indispensable work in my larger study on which this essay is based.

2. There is some lively controversy in Indological circles concerning exactly what the term *haṃsa* refers to in Indian poetry. Most translators of Indian literatures, from the seventeenth century to the present, have translated the word with some version of "swan" (*Cygnus*), influenced by European literary notions of that bird, with its many mythological associations. In his influential 1962 monograph *The Goose in Indian Literature and Art*, Vogel, using art historical and contemporary ornithological evidence, shed doubts on this easy identification of *haṃsa* with the swan, arguing that *haṃsa* or *rāja-haṃsa* mainly refers to the Indian "bar-headed" white goose (*anser indicus*) with its honking call, while *kala-haṃsa* is the graylag goose (*anser anser*). When the swan was eventually imported into India, the term *haṃsa* was used to refer to it as well. I follow recent post-Vogel Sanskrit scholarship in translating *haṃsa* as gander or goose, for reasons of precision and also to avoid inevitable poetic archaisms in English. The late Julia Leslie raised this issue again in a compelling way, challenging Vogel and arguing that the term denotes in Indian literatures a range of large aquatic birds, including swans, geese, and even flamingos and some ducks. I examine these issues in more detail in my larger study of the *Haṃsasandeśa* (Hopkins 2016).

3. "Autumn," *śarada*, the period after the rainy season when the geese fly south.

4. I have used three editions of the *Haṃsasandeśa* (1955, 1973a, 1973b) with commentaries in the preparation of this essay.

5. The phrase in the original Sanskrit contains a lovely fluid music: *tanmañjīrapratimaninade* (1.3).

6. All translations from Veṅkaṭeśa are my own, unless otherwise indicated. I have tried, in my English verse, to approximate the long, sometimes clipped,

sometimes loping rhythms of the original *mandākrānta*—"slowly approaching"—meter (four-line stanzas, each line containing seventeen syllables, with the following scheme: - - - - v v v v v - - v - - v - -). To best get a sense of this, I have chosen to compose English verse lines with phrases that flow one into the other, in single lines and in separate stanzas that visually mime the long original Sanskrit lines. For some general reflections on translation and for examples of very different English verse styles, see Hopkins 2002: 15–21, 2007a.

7. For a powerful set of verses that describe the confused, violent emotions of Rāma's love-in-separation from Sītā in Kampaṉ's Tamil *Rāmāyaṇa*, see *Irāmāvatāram*, Āraṇiyakāṇṭam 11, Ayōmuki Paṭalam, 1–34, which is translated beautifully in Hart and Heifetz 1988: 266–274 (citing the critical edition, where the passages occur in chapter 9, Ayōmuki Paṭalam).

8. For an account of this kind of emotionalism in Sītā in Kampaṉ's *Rāmāyaṇa*, see Shulman 1991: 89–113. This episode emphasizes Sītā's intense emotionalism and Rāma's stony silence. Suffering will also come eventually to Rāma himself. Shulman's descriptions of Sītā's experience in the fire-test episode (*agni-parīkṣā*) in Kampaṉ well describes Rāma in the opening of Veṅkaṭeśa's *sandeśa*: "Dynamic flux, instability, emotional excess and imbalance, the flooding of memory, the mingling of past and present, an inner experience of potential unity, the hesitations of language—this is the range of associations that Kampaṉ calls up at the outset of Sītā's ordeal" (1991: 99).

9. For an extended discussion of the extravagant emotions in Kampaṉ's aesthetics, with a focus on Rāma, Rāvaṇa, and Śūrpaṇakhā, see Hart and Heifetz 1988: 1–33. There are of course many analogues to such "love-madness" in Arabic and Persian literatures—notably in the famous Udhri poet Qays ibn al-Mulawwiḥ, who became known as Majnūn Layla, "Mad ['jinned'] for Layla." Majnūn would call out the name of his lost beloved Layla when looking at mountains, at wild animals, at other people; when asked his name and condition, he would say "Layla!" See the brief discussion in Sells 1996: 69–70. Pollock (2006: 29–31) notes, correctly I think, that Rāma's "love madness" in Vālmīki's Sanskrit Rāmāyaṇa is certainly about loss, the wounds of love, but it is even more about the terrible potential violence of a god enraged, the nascent destructive power of the king, and Rāma's identity as Rudra-Śiva. See also Pollock 1986.

10. For analogous descriptions that focus on particular details of a specifically Tamil landscape in Kampaṉ's *Rāmāyaṇa*, see Sugrīva's speech to Rāma describing the southern route the monkeys will take in their search for Sītā in *Irāmāvatāram*, Kiṭkintākāṇṭam 12, Nāṭaviṭṭa Paṭalam, 1–32. This passage in Kampaṉ continues with a structure very similar to a *sandeśa*: verses 32–66 provide a vivid "toenail to head" description of Sītā to Hanumān (what he will see), which is followed, in verses 67–74, by a "message" to be given to her. For another extended description of Tamil Toṇṭai, Cōḻa, and Pāṇṭiya landscapes on the monkeys' actual route, see *Irāmāvātaram*, Kiṭkintākāṇṭam 14, Āṟucel Paṭalam. For an analysis of Veṅkaṭeśa's distinctive Tamil geocultural *imaginaire*, see Hopkins 2004: 40–45.

11. See *Haṃsasandeśa* 1.28, translated later in this essay.

12. See Hopkins 2007a for a detailed treatment of this trope in Veṅkaṭeśa's devotional poetics. See also Hopkins 2007b.

13. Bronner and Shulman (2006: 18) refer to this as the poem's "genre ecology" (*gīti-bheda*).

14. There are vivid erotic undertones to this verse: the sandbanks evoke the image of a woman's thighs and allude to a famous verse in the Vālmīki Rāmāyaṇa (4.30.46) in which Rāma, mourning the loss of Sītā in autumn, sees and feels the presence of her body in the natural world around him (the same setting as Veṅkaṭeśa's *sandeśa*). In Merwin's translation (Merwin and Masson 1981: 68–69):

> Slowly slowly rivers in autumn show
> sand banks
> bashful in first love woman
> showing thighs.

15. For a fine short study and excellent anthology of translations from Dhūrjati's *Kāḷahastīśvara Śatakamu*, see Heifetz and Rao 1987.

16. For a detailed account of the Kāñcī Sthala-Purāṇa and the stories of Brahmā, Sarasvatī, and Brahmā's vision of Viṣṇu in Veṅkaṭeśa's Tamil *Attikiri Māhātmyam* and Sanskrit *stotra Varadarājapañcāśat*, see Hopkins 2002: 79–114, 169–198.

17. The phrase in the original is an exquisite example of the elegance of the *mandākrānta* meter (here broken by stress syllables): *kampāpāthaḥ—kamalavanikā—kāmuko gandhavāḥ.*

18. Sometimes, when visiting the Varadarāja temple in "little Kāñcī" in the evening, I would imagine catching just the very lightest scent in the air of Śiva, downwind from his temple's great mango tree.

19. *vaḥ kavinām svāmino* (1.29). Here *kavi* means both bird and poet.

20. For a translation of and commentary on this verse in Veṅkaṭeśa's *Varadarājapañcāśat*, see Hopkins 2002: 196–197.

21. See Peterson 1999.

22. There are important implications here for river imagery and goddesses, for in such narratives the Gaṅgā gets its purity from its source in the (male) body of Viṣṇu-Nārāyaṇa.

23. There are analogous descriptions of the same countryside in Kālidāsa's *Raghuvaṃśa*, Sarga 13. This itinerary, as I have already noted, follows closely the one described in Kampaṉ's *Irāmāvatāram*, Kiṭkintākāṇṭam 12, Nāṭaviṭṭa Paṭalam, 1–32.

24. The description evokes the virtues of the "old Tamil king," as Hart would have it. See his discussion of Rāvaṇa in Kampaṉ's Tamil *Rāmāyaṇa* in Hart and Heifetz 1988: 28–29.

25. For a vivid argument about the "materiality" of emotions, and particularly the passions, in Indian culture and literature, see Lynch 1990. For

a comparable set piece with Sītā's description in Kampaṉ, see *Irāmāvatāram*, Suntarakāṇṭam 3, Kāṭci Paṭalam, 3–29.

26. Bronner and Shulman (2006: 25) emphasize the ultimately positive nature of this imaginative fusion of Rāma and Sītā. I would stress a more paradoxical "unity" in the fact of their separation. Rāma and Sītā are made most real to one another through their pain in separation.

27. For Sītā's fine extended lament speech in the Vālmīki Rāmāyaṇa, an extraordinary performance that includes curses, threats, omens, jealousy, and fierce particularity, see Sundarakāṇḍa 23.10–27.19. Goldman and Sutherland Goldman (1996: 62) note, in their introduction to their translation of the Sundarakāṇḍa, that the Sundarakāṇḍa portrays a Sītā "softened and slightly complicated by deft touches of realism," evoking "the very humanity of Sītā" that "elevates her from the level of a static icon of unreasoning devotion to that of a woman of flesh and blood." I would argue that we see these "deft touches" of a realistic Sītā most powerfully in her long, formal lament in Sundarakāṇḍa 23.10–27.19. Sutherland Goldman (2001: 232) interprets this speech purely psychologically, speaking of its "narrative space" that allows for a "rhetoric of resistance." Sītā's final witness to irrevocable loss, her ultimate refusal to "give up" the particularity of her suffering, is her troublesome bodily withdrawal from Rāma's presence when she returns to her mother, the Earth, in the Uttarakāṇḍa, leaving Rāma and her two children alone for the rest of their days. A more detailed analysis of this Sītā is critical to a nuanced discussion of the literary figure of Sītā in the comparative study of women's lament traditions, although such an analysis is beyond the scope of the present essay.

28. See Shakespeare, *King John*, act 3, scene 3, for one of the most powerful female laments in English literature. Constance, "not mad," both cursing and calling on death and embracing grief as fondly as her dead child, her hair loose, unbound, eloquently "names, blames." And in the speeches beginning with "My name is Constance; I was Geoffrey's wife" and "Grief fills the room up of my absent child," she fixes her grief "in a landscape." See the Arden edition of *King John*, Shakespeare 1965: 80–84. I am currently working on a long-term project on women's laments cross-culturally, with a focus on the poetry of William Blake, although I also use comparative material from Gail Holst-Warhaft on Greek laments, Lila Abu-Lughod on Bedouin women, Veena Das on Sikh and Hindu mourning women, literary motifs in Sanskrit and Tamil literatures, and rabbinic narratives of Rachel the lamenter in Lamentations Rabbāh. See Hopkins 2009. Much more can be said about the performative power of Sītā's tears throughout the *sandeśa*. See the compelling comparative essays in Patton and Hawley 2005. Hawley (2005), in his essay "The Gopīs' Tears," discusses poetry to the Hindu god Kṛṣṇa and outlines patterns of religious weeping that resonate quite closely with my work on women's laments in Blake and that could also be extended to a discussion of Sītā. Hawley claims that "religious tears" are "enacted," never spontaneous; they open up communication rather than block it; they are gendered, "usually gendered female"; and they are frequently "about death." See also Hawley's (2004)

discussion of gender markings and *vyākulatā*, "desperate agitation," in the experience of love-in-separation (*viraha*) expressed by Ramakrishna and by male poets who adopt the poetic personae of the *gopīs*, Kṛṣṇa's cowmaiden lovers.

29. See Derrida 1986: 35. See also Zeiger 1997: 135–168. I am indebted to Amy Hollywood for these references. See Hollywood 2002: 335–356, 2006. See also Nussbaum's (2001: 248–294) insightful and moving discussion of "helplessness" and endless grief inscribed in the musical textures of Gustav Mahler's *Kindertotenlieder*. Mahler's deeply ambivalent musical writing and instrumental scoring belie the seeming consolation of a final peaceful "sleep" in the last lines of the song cycle: "For the [dead] children it is a sleep not of comfort but of nothingness. For the parent, it is the knowledge of the impossibility of any loving, any reparative effort. The oboe, the voice of active love, has fallen silent. The voice, immobilized by helplessness and a now irreparable guilt, falls silent. The world of the heart is dead" (Nussbaum 2001: 293). I think here too of Adorno's description of Mahler's "unconceptual language" in the Sixth Symphony as "unbounded weeping and unbounded love" and his summary remark about images of parting in "Der Abshied" from *Das Lied von der Erde*: "The subject cannot detach contemplative love from the irrecoverable." See Adorno 1992: 131–132, 166. Lament and an ethics of witness are at the heart of Mahler's music. See also Hopkins 2009 for citations in the context of Blake's poetry.

30. I am tempted to relate Rāma's vivid identification with Sītā's pain here to Wittgenstein's example in the *Blue and Brown Books* of the possibility of a person feeling *their own pain* in another's body: *my pain is inhabiting your body*. The experience of pain here, and the language of pain, is never merely interior but makes a claim on others, is shared, bodily, through radical bodily empathy. *My pain is in you*. According to Das (2007: 38), Wittgenstein's idea seems to suggest "that the experience of pain cries out for this response of the possibility that my pain could reside in your body and that the philosophical grammar of pain is an answer to that call." I also think here of Derrida's account (1993: 23, 119) of his sick mother's remarkable misprision in his Circumfession 4: "'I have pain *in* my mother,' as though she were speaking *for* me, both in my direction and in my place," and later on in Circumfession 23: "[B]ut like another, another wept over by another weeper, I weep *from* my mother over the child whose substitute I am. . . ." (italics mine). Using this example, Rāma has pain *in* his Sītā and weeps *from* his Sītā.

31. I am indebted to Katherine Ulrich for this insight regarding Rāma's and Sītā's "union" in pain and suffering.

32. See Bhavabhūti, *Uttararāmacaritam* 1.27 (translation mine):

When we talked at random—
  our cheeks pressed close
together, deep in love

softly, oh softly

of something unspeakable,
our arms busy in close embrace

only the darkness ended—

the night-watches passed
unnoticed.

See Hopkins 2002: 163 for a discussion of this verse in the context of another Veṅkaṭeśa poem and its commentary.

33. I borrow this image from Shattuck's work (2000: 99–136) on Proust and the experience of "time regained," memory, and recognition in *À la recherche du temps perdu*. The *sandeśa* in this sense operates as a kind of "magic lantern," an optical instrument where all time is projected, made present in shining ideal images. To use another image in Proust, Rāma's three different time frames—present separation, memory of the past, and the imaginative evocation of presence—*miroirtent*, or "mirror" each other, literally, "glisten, flash back and forth, shimmer." The *sandeśa* texts provide a multiple time space where past, present, and future "shimmer" together in the ear and on the page. See Shattuck 2000: 124. See also Proust 1993: 263–264, 1954: vol. 3, 872.

References

Adorno, Theodor W. 1992. *Mahler: A Musical Physiognomy*. Translated by Edmund Jephcott. Chicago: University of Chicago Press.

Bronner, Yigal, and David Shulman. 2006. "'A Cloud Turned Goose': Sanskrit in the Vernacular Millennium." *Indian Economic and Social History Review* 43, no. 1: 1–30.

Das, Veena. 2007. *Life and Words: Violence and the Descent into the Ordinary*. Berkeley: University of California Press.

Derrida, Jacques. 1986. *Mémoires: For Paul de Man*. Translated by Cecile Lindsay, Jonathan Culler, and Eduardo Cadava. New York: Columbia University Press.

Derrida, Jacques. 1993. "Circumfession." In Geoffrey Bennington and Jacques Derrida, *Jacques Derrida*, 3–315. Translated by Geoffrey Bennington. Chicago: University of Chicago Press.

Goldman, Robert P., and Sally J. Sutherland Goldman, trans. 1996. *The Rāmāyaṇa of Vālmīki: An Epic of Ancient India*. Vol. 5, *Sundarakāṇḍa*. Princeton: Princeton University Press.

Haṃsasandeśa of Veṅkaṭeśa. 1955. *Srimad Vedanta Desika's Hamsasandesa, Asvasas I and II*. Includes the commentary of Swetaranyam Narayana Sastry. Translated by S. Narayana Iyengar. Madras: V. Ramaswamy Sastrulu and Sons.

Haṃsasandeśa of Veṅkaṭeśa. 1973a. *Haṃsasandeśa*, ed. Uttamur T. Viraraghavacharya. Includes Sanskrit commentary. Madras: Ubhāya Vedānta Granthamālā.

Haṃsasandeśa of Veṅkaṭeśa. 1973b [1903]. *Haṃsasandeśa of Vedanta Desika*, ed. P. Anandacharlu. Includes the commentary of Mahāmahopadyāya Śrī Raṅga Chariar. Translated by N. V. Desika Chariar and Kasturi Ranga Ayengar. Madras: Vedanta Desika Research Society.

Hart, George L., and Hank Heifetz, trans. 1988. *The Forest Book of the Rāmāyaṇa of Kampaṉ*. Berkeley: University of California Press.

Hawley, John Stratton. 2004. "The Damage of Separation: Krishna's Loves and Kali's Child." *Journal of the American Academy of Religion* 72, no. 2: 369–393.

Hawley, John Stratton. 2005. "The Gopīs' Tears." In *Holy Tears: Weeping in the Religious Imagination*, ed. Kimberley Christine Patton and John Stratton Hawley, 94–111. Princeton: Princeton University Press.

Heifetz, Hank, and Velcheru Narayana Rao, trans. 1987. *For the Lord of Animals: Poems from the Telugu—The Kāḷahastīśvara Śatakamu of Dhūrjati*. Berkeley: University of California Press.

Hollywood, Amy. 2002. *Sensible Ecstasy: Mysticism, Sexual Difference, and the Demands of History*. Chicago: University of Chicago Press.

Hollywood, Amy. 2006. "Acute Melancholia." *Harvard Theological Review* 99, no. 4: 381–406.

Hopkins, Steven P. 2002. *Singing the Body of God: The Hymns of Vedāntadeśika in Their South Indian Tradition*. New York: Oxford University Press.

Hopkins, Steven P. 2004. "Lovers, Messengers, and Beloved Landscapes: *Sandeśakāvya* in Comparative Perspective." *International Journal of Hindu Studies* 8, nos. 1–3: 29–55.

Hopkins, Steven P., trans. 2007a. *An Ornament for Jewels: Love Poems for the Lord of Gods by Vedāntadeśika*. New York: Oxford University Press.

Hopkins, Steven P. 2007b. "Extravagant Beholding: Love, Ideal Bodies, and Particularity." *History of Religions* 47, no. 1: 1–50.

Hopkins, Steven P. 2009. "'I Walk Weeping in Pangs of a Mother's Torment for Her Children: Women's Laments in the Poetry and Prophecies of William Blake." *Journal of Religious Ethics* 37, no. 1: 39–81.

Hopkins, Steven P. 2016. *The Flight of Love: A Messenger Poem of Medieval South India by Veṅkaṭanātha*. New York: Oxford University Press.

Irāmāvatāram of Kampaṉ. 1984. *Kamparāmāyaṇam: Irāmāvatāram*. Chennai: Kampaṉ Kaḻakam.

Lynch, Owen. 1990. "The Social Construction of Emotion in India." In *Divine Passions: The Social Construction of Emotion in India*, ed. Owen M. Lynch, 3–34. Berkeley: University of California Press.

Meghadūta of Kālidāsa. 1979. *The Meghadūta*, ed. and trans. M. R. Kale. Includes the commentary of Mallinātha. Delhi: Motilal Banarsidass.

Merwin, W. S., and J. Moussaieff Masson. 1981. *The Peacock's Egg: Love Poems from Ancient India*. San Francisco: North Point Press.

Nussbaum, Martha. 2001. *Upheavals of Thought: The Intelligence of Emotions*. Cambridge: Cambridge University Press.

Patton, Kimberley Christine, and John Stratton Hawley, eds. 2005. *Holy Tears: Weeping in the Religious Imagination*. Princeton: Princeton University Press.

Peterson, Indira Viswanathan. 1999. "Kaveri in Legend and Literature." In *Eternal Kaveri: Historical Sites along South India's Greatest River*, ed. George Michell, 35–48. Mumbai: Marg Publications.

Pollock, Sheldon I., trans. 1986. *The Rāmāyaṇa of Vālmīki: An Epic of Ancient India*. Vol. 2, *Ayodhyākāṇḍa*. Princeton: Princeton University Press.

Pollock, Sheldon I., trans. 2006. *Rāmāyaṇa Book Three: The Forest, by Vālmīki*. New York: New York University Press and JJC Foundation.

Proust, Marcel. 1954. *À la recherche du temps perdu*. Edited by Pierre Clarac and André Ferré. 3 vols. Paris: Gallimard.

Proust, Marcel. 1993 [1981]. *In Search of Lost Time*. Vol. 6, *Time Regained. A Guide to Proust*. Translated by Andreas Mayor and Terence Kilmartin. Revised by D. J. Enright. New York: Modern Library.

Raghuvaṃśa of Kālidāsa. 1948. *The Raghuvaṃśa of Kālidāsa*, ed. Narayan Ram Acharya. Includes the commentary of Mallinātha and extracts from other commentaries. Bombay: Nirnaya Sagara Press.

Sells, Michael A., trans and ed. 1996. *Early Islamic Mysticism: Sufi, Qur'an, Mi'raj, Poetic and Theological Writings*. New York: Paulist Press.

Shakespeare, William. 1965. *King John*. Edited by E. A. J. Honigmann. London: Methuen; Cambridge: Harvard University Press.

Shattuck, Roger. 2000. *Proust's Way: A Field Guide to In Search of Lost Time*. New York: Norton.

Shulman, David. 1991. "Fire and Flood: The Testing of Sītā in Kampaṉ's *Irāmāvatāram*." In *Many Rāmāyaṇas: The Diversity of a Narrative Tradition in South Asia*, ed. Paula Richman, 89–113. Berkeley: University of California Press.

Sutherland Goldman, Sally. 2001. "The Voice of Sītā in Vālmīki's *Sundarakāṇḍa*." In *Questioning Rāmāyaṇas: A South Asian Tradition*, ed. Paula Richman, 223–238. Berkeley: University of California Press.

Uttararāmacaritam of Bhavabhūti. 1971 [1915]. *Uttara Rāmacharita of Bhavabhūti*, ed. and trans. P. V. Kane. Includes the commentary of Ghanaśyāma. Delhi: Motilal Banarsidass.

Vogel, Jean Philippe. 1962. *The Goose in Indian Literature and Art*. Leiden: E. J. Brill.

Zeiger, Melissa F. 1997. *Beyond Consolation: Death, Sexuality, and the Changing Shape of Elegy*. Ithaca: Cornell University Press.

Part 3

Gendered and Engendering Bodies

Chapter 9

Defining Women's Bodies in Indian Buddhist Monastic Literature

Carol S. Anderson

In the Pāli Buddhist canon of the Theravāda school, there is a list of what the redactors of the canon consider to be anomalous physical conditions that affect only women. This list appears twice in the Vinaya-Piṭaka, the first section of the Pāli Buddhist canon comprising monastic regulations for monks, *bhikkhus* (Sanskrit *bhikṣus*), and nuns, *bhikkhunīs* (Sanskrit *bhikṣuṇīs*): (1) in a passage that prohibits such women from becoming nuns, and (2) in a passage that abjures monks from using these terms as denigrating slurs for women. Using this list as a starting point to begin to untangle the regulation of women's bodies in Indian Buddhist traditions, the question I explore in this essay concerns how certain kinds of anomalous women's bodies are classified and defined in Indian Buddhist canonical and commentarial literature. The Pāli Buddhist tradition along with Hindu and Jain traditions recognize more than just two kinds of living beings—human and animal—and more than just two physical sexes—male and female. South Asian religions also recognize nonnormatively sexed bodies—termed *paṇḍakas*, *ṣaṇḍhas*, *ṣaṇḍhakas*, or *ṣaṇḍakas*—and intersex humans—termed *ubhatobyañjanakas* (Pāli) or *ubhaya-vyañjanas* (Sanskrit).[1] The distinction between male and female runs throughout this array of different types of bodies and beings. For example, the Vinaya-Piṭaka distinguishes between male and female humans, male and female animals and nonhumans, male *paṇḍakas*, and male and female *ubhatobyañjanakas*. The feature that differentiates male from female in the Vinaya-Piṭaka is how many "openings" (*magga*) a being has: males have a mouth and an anus (two openings), and females have a mouth, a vagina, and an anus (three openings).[2] We immediately see that the question of normative male and female bodies is embedded in a more complex array than a normative heterosexual model of a human and animal two-sex/two-gender system.[3]

The sophistication with which Indian Buddhist traditions explore the possible variations in women's bodies is strikingly similar to contemporary discussions about "disorders of sex development" (DSD) and "intersex," such as those found in Anne Fausto-Sterling's work and in medical journals.[4] However, Indian Buddhist literature analyzes such bodies in part to determine who can reliably undergo the discipline necessary for the successful pursuit of Buddhist knowledge. For example, the *Abhidharmakośa*, a Sanskrit compendium of Abhidharma (Pāli Abhidhamma) philosophy ascribed to Vasubandhu (ca. fourth or fifth century CE), explains that the three types of *paṇḍaka*s and *ubhaya-vyañjana*s—human, nonhuman, and animal—are incapable of maintaining the moral discipline needed to progress along the path.[5] When looking at the list of women's physical abnormalities in the Vinaya-Piṭaka, then, we need to first recognize that the Pāli Buddhist tradition is not the only tradition in the broader context of Indian religions that articulates connections between physically sexed bodies, gender, and an individual's capacity for religious attainment. Both Pāli and Sanskrit Indian Buddhist writings are quite clear on this point: one has to possess a whole and proper body in order to become a monastic follower of the Buddha.

What kind of bodies are considered to be normatively acceptable? We have the sources available to us to answer this question insofar as the requirements for admission into the *saṃgha*, monastic order, in the Vinaya-Piṭaka specify that monks and nuns have to have bodies that are free from disease, scars, or severed extremities and from such disabilities as a hunched back, dwarfism, or the inability to hear, speak, or see. The very ugly, very old, seriously ill, maimed, or crippled are also forbidden from joining the *saṃgha*. *Paṇḍaka*s, intersex individuals, and those guilty of killing their mother, father, or an *arhat* (one who has attained the highest level of enlightenment) are banned from ordination.[6] Pregnant women, mothers of nursing infants, and certain kinds of novices—those with insufficient training, those without permission of the order or one's family, or those who are rebellious—are not allowed to become nuns.[7] Having a normative body does not automatically ensure that one can join the monastic order, as there are other requirements that can affect eligibility, such as obligations to one's family, debt, service to a king, and so on. However, all candidates for ordination, both male and female, are required to have a particular kind of body: normatively sexed, free from disease, free from physical challenges, excessive old age, and so on. The cause of a disability appears not to matter. For example, if a candidate has been punished by having a finger or hand cut off, he or she is barred from the *saṃgha* on the same grounds as someone who has been missing a limb from birth. Normative bodies are those that are sexed according to a heterosexual two-sex system, and therefore *paṇḍaka*s and intersex individuals are barred from pursuing a monastic life along with physically abnormal women.

Judith Butler calls such bodies that fall outside of the heterosexual norm "abject" bodies. In *Bodies That Matter* Butler seeks to find a way to talk about actual physical bodies and the construction of gender in Western cultures that does not succumb to the extremes of either essentialism, in which physical bodies are considered the root of cultural definitions of gender, or "constructionism," in which physical bodies are rendered inaccessible beneath the layers of constructed meanings within cultures.[8] In her incisive essay arguing that Butler's discussion of abject bodies should be turned on its head when studying Buddhist bodies that matter, Susanne Mrozik accurately describes the points of intersection:

> As Butler argues, the constitutive constraints that produce the domain of "bodies that matter" also produce the domain of those that do not—that is, abject bodies. The threat of being reborn in abject material form encourages normative ethical behavior in Buddhist cultures. A striking feature of Buddhist literature is the sheer number and variety of bodies marked as abject, including—but hardly limited to—non-normatively sexed bodies. For instance, one medieval Indian monastic text warns that unrestrained sexual desire has the following karmic consequences: you will be reborn in hell or in a variety of demonic forms; if you are reborn as a human you will be one-eyed, lame, tongueless, deformed, blind from birth, deaf, or insensible; if you are reborn as an animal you will be a dog, swine, camel, donkey, monkey, elephant, horse, cow, tiger, moth, or fly. The same text warns that if the male head of a household prevents his son, daughter, or wife from being ordained as a monk or nun (and commits a few other crimes as well), he will be reborn blind from birth, retarded, tongueless, as an outcaste (*caṇḍāla*), permanent servant, woman, dog, swine, ass, camel, or venomous snake. He will also be reborn as a *ṣaṇḍaka* or a *paṇḍaka*.[9]

The text Mrozik refers to in this passage is the *Śikṣāsamuccaya*, which is a compendium of Mahāyāna Buddhist practice. Invoking Liz Wilson's *Charming Cadavers*, Mrozik suggests that women's bodies as a whole are "coded as abject" in Buddhist traditions.[10] Janet Gyatso suggests that the women in the Vinaya-Piṭaka's list of biologically nonnormative women represent a "female third sex" in a male monastic environment.[11] While women as a class are certainly *not* the norm in the androcentric texts of monastic Buddhism, as Wilson, Gyatso, Mrozik, and many others have pointed out, this list of women with nonnormative bodies indicates that not all women's bodies are considered to be abject in the same way. In other words, there is an awareness that certain kinds of women's bodies fall outside the normative range of women's bodies that matter to the redactors of the canonical and commentarial writings.

Women with Nonnormative Bodies

The list of nonnormative women's bodies in the Vinaya-Piṭaka of the Pāli canon is also found in the *Samantapāsādikā*, a commentary on the Vinaya-Piṭaka (which a later tradition has attributed to the compiler Buddhaghosa).[12] These works were composed between the first century BCE and the late fourth to early fifth centuries CE. The same list appears in a Chinese translation of a text closely related to the *Samantapāsādikā* by Saṃghabhadra in the fifth century CE. Within the Vinaya-Piṭaka, as mentioned earlier, the list appears (1) several times in a passage that prohibits women who have these nonnormative bodies from becoming nuns, and (2) in a passage that tells monks not to use the words in this list as derogatory terms when speaking to or about women.[13] Because this list of abject women's bodies appears in Indian and Chinese Buddhist Vinayas, we can conclude that the list was a minor but integral part of Indian Buddhist traditions.

The first passage is found in the Khandaka section of the Vinaya-Piṭaka. The Vinaya-Piṭaka is divided into three parts: (1) the Sutta-Vibhaṅga, which follows the structure of the rules as they are laid out in the Pāṭimokkha; (2) the Khandaka, which follows a different order for the rules, based on a historical narrative of the founding of the monastic order and the rules for different ceremonies and rituals; and (3) the Parivāra, which is a rather technical handbook of monastic law unique to the Pāli Vinaya-Piṭaka. In the Sutta-Vibhaṅga and the Khandaka, rules pertaining to nuns are found at the end of each part. In this first passage, which appears in the Khandaka, the list of nonnormative women's bodies is included in an enumeration of the "stumbling blocks" or obstacles to *dhamma* (*antarāyikā dhammā*) because women who have any of these varieties of physical bodies cannot become nuns. The list appears in the instructions from the Buddha to monks on what questions they should ask women seeking ordination as nuns; women must answer in the negative. The list of nonnormative women's bodies is repeated several times in this passage, embedded in a longer list of questions about disease, debt, royal service, and so on. The second occurrence of the list is found in the Sutta-Vibhaṅga, the rules according to the Pāṭimokkha, in the classification of rules for monks (Pāli Bhikkhu-Vibhaṅga). We find this list as part of the explanation of the third *saṃghādisesa*[14] for monks that prohibits monks from serving as "go-betweens" for a sexual liaison. In the course of the explanation, the Buddha tells monks not to use the terms in the list as slurs for women—which indicates that these terms may have been in circulation as derogatory terms for women.

The following list of eleven kinds of nonnormative women is found in both passages of the Vinaya-Piṭaka, and I have translated the terms based on the commentarial explanations found in the *Samantapāsādikā* and Saṃghabhadra's Chinese translation that is based on a text that is quite close to the *Samantapāsādikā* but not identical to it.[15]

(1) a woman without [female] genitalia (*animittā*)

(2) a woman with malformed genitalia (*nimitta-mattā*)

(3) a woman without [regular] menses (*alohitā*)

(4) a woman who is constantly bleeding (*dhuva-lohitā*)

(5) a woman who always wears a tampon (*dhuva-colā*)

(6) a woman who is dripping (*paggharantī*)

(7) a deformed woman (*sikhariṇī*)

(8) a woman *paṇḍaka* (*itthi-paṇḍakā*)

(9) a bearded woman (*vepurisikā*)

(10) a woman whose organs are mixed up (*sambhinnā*)

(11) an intersex woman (*ubhatobyañjanakā*)

The author of the *Samantapāsādikā* discusses these conditions in his commentary on the passage in the third *saṃghādisesa* of the Vinaya for monks. Saṃghabhadra, the Chinese translator of a text that drew from the *Samantapāsādikā*, provides different explanations than the *Samantapāsādikā* does for several of the conditions. This probably means that this list was not commonly known outside monastic communities, but the fact that we have a set of eleven conditions that define certain kinds of biologically sexed women as nonnormative indicates that there was an awareness of what counted as "normal" women. We do not find a comparable list of conditions for men who wish to become monks. Not all of these conditions are congenital, nor are they all considered to be disorders of sex development in contemporary diagnoses. Some conditions are behavioral, while others are unambiguously variations in sex development. All of these variations are unique to women, and each of the nonbehavioral cases can be explained with reference to conditions documented in contemporary medical literature, as we shall see in the following analyses of each term.[16] In the discussion of medical cases, I have not conducted a comprehensive study of all of the possible conditions that could fit the Pāli and Sanskrit terms; the examples are illustrative, not encyclopedic.

The first term, *animittā*, has two slightly different definitions according to the two commentators. The *Samantapāsādikā* explains that the term means simply that the woman is "without genitalia, not even as much as a crooked channel or an opening for water." Saṃghabhadra says that this kind of woman has "ill-formed sex organs." There are two contemporary medical conditions that can lead to a biologically sexed woman having incomplete or missing genitalia. The first is vaginal agenesis, which can result in the arrested development or lack of the uterus, vagina, and/or fallopian tubes.[17] This disorder occurs in an estimated 1 out of 5,000 female births, and diagnosis does not usually occur until a girl reaches puberty without developing a menstrual cycle. The second disorder is urorectal septum malformation sequence, which was identified in the mid-1980s. The anomalies of this condition include "ambiguous genitalia, lack of perineal openings, and müllerian and urinary tract anomalies."[18] The perineum is the area between the anus and the vulva in women, and there are cases in which infants have no vulva due to this condition. The müllerian ducts develop into the female genital tract—fallopian tubes, uterus, and upper portion of the vagina—during normal fetal development. Either one of these disorders could produce the conditions that the author of the *Samantapāsādikā* and Saṃghabhadra describe: a woman who appears to be missing any genitalia, including a missing urethra or vulva ("opening for water").

The second term, *nimitta-mattā*, is defined in a similar way according to both commentators. The *Samantapāsādikā* explains that the term means that the woman's "genitalia are incomplete, with barely a mark." Saṃghabhadra, on the other hand, explains in greater detail: this "means that the genitalia have an opening but no proper form, or it means that the genitalia have the proper form but no clear opening." The two conditions mentioned in my discussion of *animittā* could also be the cause of this condition insofar as either vaginal agenesis or urorectal septum malformation sequence can result in incomplete or malformed genital development. Epispadias is another condition that can produce the symptoms described as *nimitta-mattā*.[19] Far more common in men and boys, in women and girls it is a rare congenital malformation of the urogenital apparatus that consists of a defect of the urethra in which there is an opening from the urethra into the vagina. Labial adhesion is more common than any of these three conditions in children, and it often results from chronic inflammation of the vulva. Labial adhesion does not usually produce symptoms that seal the vulva but the possibility does exist, and there are cases in which labial adhesion can produce "an opening but no proper form, or . . . the proper form but no clear opening."[20] Finally, hydrocolpos and hydrometrocolpos are related disorders that can also result in missing or malformed genitalia.[21] These are conditions in which the uterus and vagina are distended due to an accumulation of watery fluid. This condition may appear as a mass or a bulge protruding from the vaginal introitus, or opening, thus satisfying the "no proper form" of Saṃghabhadra's definition.

The commentarial discussions by the *Samantapāsādikā* and Saṃghabhadra explaining the third, fourth, and fifth terms—in which a woman is "without [regular] menses" (*alohitā*), "constantly bleeding" (*dhuva-lohitā*), or "always wearing a tampon" (*dhuva-colā*)—are nearly the same for both commentators.[22] Regarding the third condition, *alohitā*, in which a woman does not have a regular menstrual period, the *Samantapāsādikā* says simply that her blood has dried up, while Saṃghabhadra explains that her vagina is dry, without any blood. Medically this condition is generally identified as amenorrhea, or the absence of menstruation. Primary amenorrhea is the absence of menarche at puberty that affects less than 1 percent of girls. Secondary amenorrhea is defined as the absence of a period for three to six months any time prior to menopause and has a wide variety of causes.

With respect to the fourth condition, *dhuva-lohitā*, in which a woman is constantly bleeding, this means that the "opening for water" is always wet, according to the *Samantapāsādikā*. Saṃghabhadra says that "the blood is constantly oozing by itself out of this woman's vagina." Metrorrhagia is a hormonal imbalance that results in nonmenstrual bleeding from the vagina, often from a tumor or other growth. The earliest articles in Western medical annals on metrorrhagia appear as early as 1879, so it is likely that the condition was well known historically.[23] In Āyurvedic medicine metrorrhagia, or dysfunctional uterine bleeding, is called *rakta pradara*.[24]

The fifth condition, *dhuva-colā*, in which a woman always wears a tampon, means that a small piece of cloth is always used as a "rag permanently inserted into the vagina," according to both commentators. However, Saṃghabhadra adds the explanation "so that blood is not allowed to come out." It seems a bit odd that such a condition would be included in this list, which suggests that such a practice was not unheard of—along the lines of wearing a tampon for too long, which leads to toxic shock syndrome, a potentially life-threatening infection in the vagina caused by the bacteria *Staphylococcus aureus*. The canonical list and commentarial explanations of the three conditions designated by the third, fourth, and fifth terms appear to reflect a relatively accurate understanding of women's menses and some of the more common associated abnormalities.

The sixth term, *paggharantī*, a woman who is constantly dripping, is defined in the *Samantapāsādikā* as one who is "flowing, [whose] urine is always flowing." Saṃghabhadra does not comment on this term. This condition is classified in contemporary medicine as a type of urinary incontinence. For example, it is not uncommon for adults to lose control of the external urethral sphincter that normally controls urination, particularly as they age.

The seventh term, *sikhariṇī*, the *Samantapāsādikā* explains, means a woman with a "small mass that protrudes outside." *Sikhara* literally means "the top or summit," as in a mountain or the point or edge of a sword. Saṃghabhadra's elaboration is a bit more vivid: "the sex-organ has long projections." Among the range of possible medical conditions that can produce such symptoms is hypertrophy of the clitoris, which can occur in cases of fetal exposure to androgens, resulting in a nontumorous bulge in the clitoris.[25] Different kinds of interlabial masses can also produce a "small mass that protrudes outside." This symptom is one of the more commonly recognized conditions that are currently discussed as kinds of intersex. Fausto-Sterling provides an excellent discussion of, for example, congenital adrenal hyperplasia: "When present in two doses (that is, when an individual is homozygous for the gene), it causes XX females to be born with masculinized external genitalia (although their internal reproductive organs are those of a potentially fertile woman)."[26]

The eighth term is *itthi-paṇḍakā*, which is a female *paṇḍaka*. This term appears to be an oxymoron because the term *paṇḍaka* in all other cases found throughout the Vinaya-Piṭaka refers to atypical males with either congenital or behavioral dispositions toward nonnormative sexual practices. Given the Vinaya definitions of biologically sexed males as those beings who have two openings (females have three), *paṇḍaka*s are defined as biologically male insofar as they have two openings. The lists generally enumerate five different kinds of *paṇḍaka*s who engage in a variety of sexual practices for biologically sexed men, several of which are no longer commonly recognized as congenitally determined.[27]

(1) Those who are not male (*napuṃsaka-paṇḍaka*s). This state is congenital, and it is defined as those who have "no nature" (*abhāvako*). It probably refers to people who look like men but do not have the full complement of male sexual organs.

(2) Those who, out of jealousy, watch others engage in sexual intercourse (*usūya-paṇḍaka*s; Sanskrit *īrṣya-paṇḍaka*s). This is accurately understood to refer to voyeurs.

(3) Those who are *paṇḍaka*s during the "dark" days of the month (full moon until the new moon), due to bad *karma* (*akusalavipākānubhāvena*), and whose passions are calm during the bright days of the month (*pakkha-paṇḍaka*s; Sanskrit *pakṣa-paṇḍaka*s). One commentary defines such people as those who are *paṇḍaka*s during the dark days of the month and women during the bright days. Another commentary says that such people are "mad" during the dark days.

(4) Those who take the penis of another into the mouth and are "sprinkled with impurity" (*āsitta-paṇḍaka*s; Sanskrit *āseka-paṇḍaka*s). These people are sprinkled with impurity as a result of their actions.

(5) Those whose seeds have been removed by means of some (medical) remedy (*opakkamika-paṇḍaka*; Sanskrit *āpat-paṇḍaka*). The subcommentaries explain this phenomenon in detail: "In one whose seeds are removed, the penis does not function with passion, male being disappears, [and] the beard and other features of maleness that have been present disappear."[28]

Vasubandhu explains that *paṇḍaka*s have other characteristics: "They are filled with defiling passions, their lust is not calm, and they lack masculinity (*napuṃsaka*). Overcome by the force of their lust, they desire friendship with anyone."[29] *Paṇḍaka*s are thus classified as biologically male (insofar as they have "two openings"), and the five types of *paṇḍaka*s previously enumerated reinforce the conclusion that *paṇḍaka*s are men with sexual inclinations that fall outside of the then-normative range of heterosexual practices. This combination of nonnormative sexual behaviors—voyeurism and fellatio—and medically anomalous conditions—lacking male sexual organs from birth, transformation, or castration—indicates that *paṇḍaka*s are defined according to both physical characteristics and behaviors and are considered to be male (with the exception of one case in which a commentator suggests that *pakkha-paṇḍaka*s are women during the bright half of the month).

The term *itthi-paṇḍakā*, female *paṇḍaka*, appears three times in the Vinaya-Piṭaka: twice in the Vinaya-Piṭaka's list of eleven kinds of biologically nonnormative women and once in the Sutta-Vibhaṅga in the third *saṃghādisesa*, at the end of a lengthy discussion concerning how a monk should not be a "go-between" for sexual liaisons. The term appears in the list of exceptions: a monk does not commit a formal offense if he seeks to examine a woman who turns out to be an *itthi-paṇḍakā*, in the same way that he is not guilty of a formal offense if the woman he inquires about is asleep, dead, has gone out, or is without female sex (*anitthī*).[30] In the commentarial discussions of *itthi-paṇḍakā*, the author of the *Samantapāsādikā* takes an abbreviated way out: he glosses *itthi-paṇḍakā* as simply *animittā*, without genitalia, as in the first term in this list. Saṃghabhadra offers a different explanation: *itthi-paṇḍakā*, he writes, means "the two sides have prominently bulged out—that is, out of the vagina has come a long fleshy projection that also has hair on it." The same conditions discussed earlier with reference to *sikhariṇī* could explain Saṃghabhadra's "long fleshy projection," although I have not been able to find a reference to hair on the sexual organ elsewhere in Buddhist sources.[31] Neither commentary addresses the fact that elsewhere in Buddhist canonical and commentarial literature *paṇḍaka*s are regarded as male. Furthermore, whereas male *paṇḍaka*s are considered to suffer from a combination of congenital variations and certain behavioral inclinations regarding sex, a female *paṇḍaka* is described only in terms of biological abnormalities, not in terms of anomalous sexual behaviors. Because they are included in this list, it is evident that *itthi-paṇḍakā*s are considered to be physically anomalous *women*—not men—probably with any of the several conditions that we would recognize today as intersex.

If we look at *sikhariṇīs* and *itthi-paṇḍakās* as a group—both of whom have a bulge or protrusion that appears outside the vagina—along with the last three kinds of women on our list—*vepurisikās*, bearded women; *sambhinnās*, women whose organs are mixed up; and *ubhatobyañjanakās*, intersex women—it appears that all five would be classified today as different kinds of intersex. In contemporary medical diagnoses, this group of nonnormative women would be diagnosed with different forms of disorders of sex development. The term "disorders of sex development" is not synonymous with the term "intersex."[32] The medical community tends to argue against the term intersex, but its popular use persists. In terms of diagnosing such variations in sex development, diagnostic trees—such as the one used by the National Institutes of Health and the International Statistical Classification of Diseases and Related Health Problems used by the World Health Organization—group diseases according to the system affected.[33] Thus disorders of sex development may be found under endocrine diseases, urogenital abnormalities, and so on. What all of these types of women have in common are documented medical conditions that violate the then-normative standards for women, according to our Buddhist sources.

The ninth term, *vepurisikā,* designates a woman who has "the form of a man with a beard or whiskers," according to both the *Samantapāsādikā* and Saṃghabhadra. In contemporary medical literature there are two different conditions that can give rise to this phenomenon. Hirsutism occurs in women or children and is caused by androgens from the ovaries, adrenal glands, or other sources. Hypertrichosis also causes male-pattern hair growth but is caused by genetic or acquired factors and is not related to the androgens that cause hirsutism.[34]

With regard to the tenth condition, *sambhinnā,* in which a woman's organs are mixed up, the *Samantapāsādikā* says that the "passages for urine and excrement are mixed up," and Saṃghabhadra remarks only that "the passages have met together." Such a condition is a biological possibility given that the development of the lower urinary tract, genital, and anorectal systems are closely correlated in females. There are documented malformations in contemporary medical literature in which the genital and urinary tracts are indeed mixed up. Depending on the timing of the arrested development, different kinds of anomalies may develop, including a persistent cloaca in which there is a single orifice behind the clitoris and no anus or vagina. A rare condition recently identified as cloacal dysgenesis sequence manifests in a "phallus-like structure, smooth perineum, and absence of urethral, vaginal, and anal openings as primary malformations."[35] Finally, mixed-up organs could also be explained with reference to a medical condition known as an obstetric fistula (a hole or passage between two organs that does not normally exist), which is a condition caused by complications in childbirth. This condition afflicts fifty thousand to one hundred thousand women annually today, and such a condition would not have been unusual among widows seeking to join the *saṃgha*.

The final term on the Vinaya-Piṭaka's list of eleven kinds of biologically nonnormative women is *ubhatobyañjanakā*, which designates an intersex woman. In the Vinaya classification of living beings with whom monks and nuns may not engage in sexual intercourse, *ubhatobyañjanaka*s are beings who are considered to be biologically female insofar as they are understood to have three openings, a mouth, anus, and vagina. However, *ubhatobyañjanaka*s are also explained as having only one faculty, or *indriya*, which is either male or female, but not both. The term *ubhatobyañjanaka* literally means "having both marks," with the term "mark" serving as a euphemism for the biological markers of sex, or the genitalia. The tradition understands *ubhatobyañjanaka*s as having both a functional penis *and* a functional vagina. Depending on their desire, intersex individuals can utilize their vagina or penis according to the sex of the person to whom they are attracted—based on a model of heterosexual desire. They are considered to be fully functional intersex humans insofar as male *ubhatobyañjanaka*s can impregnate others and female *ubhatobyañjanakā*s can become pregnant *and* impregnate others.[36] In its commentary on the term *ubhatobyañjanakā* in the Vinaya-Piṭaka's list, the *Samantapāsādikā* says that this kind of woman is endowed with characteristics of both female and male genitalia. Saṃghabhadra says much the same thing: such a person has "the mark of both sexes."

The word "hermaphrodite" is no longer used by medical practitioners; in Buddhist texts the word "eunuch" is used as a translation for this word. In current usage such conditions are commonly identified as disorders of sex development.[37] These conditions include female pseudohermaphroditism, male pseudohermaphroditism, true hermaphroditism (those individuals who have both well-developed ovarian and testicular tissues), and different forms of gonadal dysgenesis.[38] The frequency of such births is currently contested and ranges from Fausto-Sterling's estimate of 1.7 percent to one hundred times less than that, or .018 percent, depending on which conditions are included under the definition of intersex.[39] A survey of terms such as *paṇḍaka*, *ṣaṇḍha*, and *ubhatobyañjanaka* in Buddhist literature provides us with a similar range of physical conditions, but medical research today has not borne out the

Indian Buddhist tradition's claim that *ubhatobyañjanakas* can impregnate or become pregnant.

Taken together, the conditions identified in the Vinaya-Piṭaka's list of eleven kinds of women with nonnormative bodies are all exceptions to what Indian Buddhist traditions understand to be "normal women." They are all medically documented conditions, but this fact appears to be of little interest to the commentators. The author of the *Samantapāsādikā* is not at all interested in the medical implications. Rather, his commentary is intended to explain what these conditions are and to explain why monks should not call women by any of these terms. His point is proper monastic behavior. In a passage immediately following this list of eleven categories of women in the Sutta-Vibhaṅga, the *Samantapāsādikā* groups *sikharaṇī, sambhinnā,* and *ubhatobyañjanakā* together as more significant than the other terms in the list because they are related to sexual intercourse and thus may lead to violation of the prohibition against engaging in intercourse, which is the first of four rules, called the *pārājikas*, that, if violated, result in expulsion from the *saṃgha*.[40] Later subcommentaries follow the *Samantapāsādikā* in this tradition; it is common to find elaborations on these three terms in their explanations of the prohibition against calling women these names.[41] Even though the medical disorders themselves are of little interest to the commentators, the fact that these disorders correlate with medically recognized conditions suggests that the commentators may have possessed a greater degree of medical knowledge than scholars have previously recognized. The stability of these terms throughout the later commentarial traditions in the Pāli tradition is noteworthy but not unusual.

Nonnormative Women's Bodies in Indian Buddhist Traditions

These kinds of disorders of women's bodies are also found in other Buddhist Vinayas, which indicates that Indian Buddhist traditions were in fact familiar with such physical variations among women. Today there are extant Vinayas from six different Buddhist schools, many of which survive only in their Chinese translations. Up to this point I have discussed passages from the Pāli Vinaya-Piṭaka of the Theravāda school, along with two different sets of commentarial explanations, by the author of the *Samantapāsādikā,* who wrote in Pāli, and by the Chinese translator by the name of Saṃghabhadra. By tracing the list of nonnormative women's bodies in other Indian Buddhist Vinayas, we can get a sense of how widespread such conceptions of women's bodies were. Several of the conditions in the list do appear in the Vinayas of other Buddhist schools, but the full list of eleven conditions is found in its entirety only in the Pāli Vinaya-Piṭaka and in Saṃghabhadra's translation.

Throughout the extant Buddhist Vinayas, there is a relatively standard list of questions that women are to be asked before being admitted to the order of nuns. This list is comparable, but not identical, to the list of questions asked of men. These questions are called the "stumbling blocks" to *dhamma* (*antarāyikā dhammā*).[42] The list of stumbling blocks for men in the Khandaka section of the Pāli Vinaya-Piṭaka reads:

> And thus, monks, he should be asked: have you diseases like this: leprosy, boils, eczema, consumption, epilepsy? Are you a human being? Are you a man? Are you a freeman? Are you without debts? Are you not in the royal service? Have you your parents' consent? Are you full twenty years of age? Are you complete as to bowl and robes? What is your name? What is the name of your preceptor?[43]

In contrast, the list of stumbling blocks for women in the Khandaka section of the Pāli Vinaya-Piṭaka reads:

> *You are not without sexual characteristics? You are not defective in sex? You are not without a regular period? You are not constantly bleeding? You do not always wear a tampon? You are not always dripping? You are not deformed? You are not a female paṇḍaka? You are not a bearded woman? Your organs are not mixed up? You are not intersex?* Have you diseases like this: leprosy, boils, eczema, consumption, epilepsy? Are you a human? Are you a woman? Are you a free woman? Are you free of debt? You are not in royal service? Are you allowed by your mother and father, by your husband? Have you completed twenty years of age? Are you complete as to robe and bowl? What is your name? What is the name of your woman proposer?[44]

In other words, to the standard list of questions to be asked of a monk, the Pāli Vinaya adds questions referring to the eleven kinds of nonnormative women (italicized in the preceding passage).

There is significant variation in the lists of stumbling blocks for women found in other Buddhist schools, but they do contain references to some of the eleven conditions. The number of questions asked of women before ordination varies from twenty-three to thirty, according to the particular Buddhist school.[45] The questions posed by the Dharmaguptaka school are similar to the Pāli Vinaya questions, but only three terms (italicized in the following passage) corresponding to those on the Pāli list are included:

> What is your name? What is the name of your *upādhyāya*? Are you fully twenty years old? Do you have all the robes and the alms bowl? Do your parents give you the permission? Does your husband give you the permission? Do you have debts? Are you a slave? Are you a woman? Women have the following diseases: leprosy, ulcers, white leprosy, tuberculosis, and epilepsy; *they are hermaphrodite, the two tracts come together, they often lose control of their urine and excrement,* and they often discharge mucus and saliva. Do you have these diseases?[46]

The Mahāsaṃghika school poses a more extensive list of questions, which includes a number of questions (italicized in the following passage) that are parallel to those on the Pāli Vinaya list:

> (1) Do you or do you not have a mother and a father, a husband? If she says that she has, (the instructor *bhikṣuṇī*) ought to ask: Do you or do you not have permission from your mother and father, husband? (2) Have you already sought a preceptor *bhikṣuṇī*? (3) Have you been equipped with the five robes and the bowl? (4) Have you completed the two years' study in the precepts? (5) Have you already performed the *karma* of being taken as a disciple? (6) What is your name? (The person) shall answer name is so-and-so. (7) Have you or have you not killed your father and mother? (8) Have you or have you not killed an *arhat*? (9) Have you or have you not disrupted the Order? (10) Have you or have you not, with malicious mind, drawn blood from the body of the Buddha? (11) Have you or have you not broken the pure precepts of the *bhikṣus*? (12) Have you or have you not lived in the Order as a thief? (13) Have you or have you not lived a double religious life? (14) Have you or have you not received the *upasampadā* ordination by yourself? (15) Have you received the *upasampadā* ordination before? If she answers I have already received it, the instructor *bhikṣuṇī* ought to tell her: Depart, for you cannot receive the *upasampadā*

> ordination again. If she says I have not, the instructor *bhikṣuṇī* ought to ask (further). (16) Are you or are you not a female slave? (17) Are you or are you not an adopted daughter? (18) Do you or do you not bear debts to others? (19) Are you or are you not a female warrior? (20) Have you or have you not conspired against the family of the king? (21) Are you or are you not a woman? (22) *Are you or are you not a barren woman?* (23) *Have you or have you not suffered injury to your sexual organs?* (24) *Have you or have you not a joined anus and vagina?* (25) *Have you or have you not damaged your public* [*sic*] *regions?* (26) Have you or have you not lost your breasts? (27) Have you or have you not only one breast? (28) *Have you or have you not menstruation at all times?* (29) *Have you no menstruation at all?* (30) *Have you or have you not a monthly menstruation?* (31) *Are you or are you not impotent?* (32) Have you any of the following diseases? scabies, malaria, leprosy, carbuncles, hemorrhoids, uncontrollable bowel movements, yellow fever, fever and ague, coughing, tuberculosis, epilepsy, fever, swelling by gas, swelling by water, swelling in the stomach? Besides, have you any other diseases of the body?[47]

Finally, the Sarvāstivāda school has an equally long list of questions, with the following conditions included in the list: without genitalia, intersex woman, organs that are mixed up, blood always oozing out, without regular menses, and malformed genitalia.[48]

Variants of the list of nonnormative women's bodies found in the Pāli Vinaya-Piṭaka thus appear to be an integral part of the array of Indian Buddhist traditions, included in the broader list of questions asked of women seeking ordination. The fact that terms corresponding to those on the Pāli list of nonnormative women's bodies appear in the Vinayas of these different schools aids us in documenting the prevalence of the list.[49]

Demarcating Women's Bodies

What are we to make of this list of eleven kinds of women with nonnormative bodies? I suggest three concluding observations. The first requires us to locate this list of nonnormative women's bodies within a broader understanding of Buddhist conceptions of gender and of the faculties (*indriyas*), with implications for the relationship between biological sex and gender. The second observation concerns the medical knowledge displayed about women's bodies in these sources. The third observation highlights the boundary that distinguishes female bodies from male bodies in the category of *paṇḍakas*.

Regarding the first point, we have seen that Buddhist traditions define normative women as those who possess normally functioning reproductive organs and who appear in public as properly gendered women (for example, not as bearded women). In an earlier study Michael Sweet and Leonard Zwilling classify Indian Buddhist traditions as essentialist traditions in which the categories of biological sex accord closely with the socially constructed categories of a two-gendered system.[50] In their discussion, however, they give scant attention to the ways in which women are defined in the literature. We have found evidence concerning eleven kinds of nonnormative women's bodies that demonstrates a greater knowledge of women's bodies than Sweet's and Zwilling's study suggests. I would argue that Indian Buddhist traditions define women and men in sophisticated ways that recognize both biological sex and culturally constructed gender in a variety of normative and nonnormative men and women. It is important to emphasize in this context that Indian Buddhist traditions recognize more than a two-gendered system constructed upon an essentialist definition rooted in biology.

The broader argument about the relationship between biologically sexed bodies and early Buddhist conceptions of gender is a complex one, which I have laid out elsewhere as part of my refutation of Sweet's and Zwilling's conclusions. Briefly, their classification of Indian Buddhist traditions as essentialist and two-gendered is inaccurate, because they have overlooked the relationship between the *indriyas*, or faculties, and biological sex. According to Buddhist Abhidhamma thought, everything in the canonical and early commentarial traditions associated with what we understand as sex or gender is under the influence of the male or female *indriyas*. However, there is no *indriya* that refers to an overarching category of "sex" or "gender" in the Abhidhamma texts; when the topic of classically gendered behavior is discussed, *indriya* always refers to the male faculty *or* the female faculty. There are twenty-two *indriyas*, including the male and female faculties,[51] and these *indriyas* control physical bodies in Indian Buddhist traditions. Sweet and Zwilling's conclusion that Indian Buddhist teachings perpetuate a two-gendered system grounded in biological sex is thus problematic because the *indriyas* control biology, not the reverse.[52]

One more piece of evidence is key to this question of sex and gender, which I have also discussed elsewhere. Briefly, male and female *indriyas*—and genitalia—are changeable, according to both the Pāli Vinaya and Abhidhamma analyses. This phenomenon of sex change appears in the Pāli Vinaya-Piṭaka at two points: in the extensive discussion of the first *pārājika* for monks, and in the Parivāra. "Now, once the sexual characteristics of a woman (*itthi-liṅgaṃ*) appeared on a monk," and a few lines later, the reverse is laid out as a possibility: "the sexual characteristics of a man (*purisa-liṅgaṃ*) appeared on a nun."[53] The possibility of sex change is discussed at some length in the Pāli canon and commentaries, with the Abhidhamma analysis emphasizing the influence of the *indriyas* on both biologically sexed bodies and gender. Thus, although the list of nonnormative women's bodies might lead us at first glance to conclude that properly sexed bodies establish the basis for a two-gendered system, an examination of the role of the *indriyas* and of the phenomenon of sex change indicates that this characterization is inadequate to account for the complexity of Indian Buddhist perspectives. Even normatively sexed female bodies were not considered as fixed as we think of biologically sexed bodies today.

The second observation concerns the status of medical knowledge about women's bodies in Indian Buddhist sources. Several scholars have concluded that the author of the *Samantapāsādikā* was simply confused about biological sex and gender. Zwilling, for example, concludes that the *Samantapāsādikā*'s gloss of *itthi-paṇḍakā* as *animittā*, "without sexual organs," shows that there was a fundamental "confusion centering upon the signification of the traditional sexual category of *paṇḍaka* by the Indian classical authors."[54] Gyatso similarly suggests that there is a "recurring carelessness" with regard to the understanding of women's bodies in the Vinaya and commentaries, because the canon and the commentaries consistently use the term "path for water" (that is, the urethra) as a reference for the vagina. However, we have no way of knowing if this was a genuine misconception or a euphemism. Gyatso also remarks that these "gaffes are surprising" given Kenneth Zysk's arguments about the role of Buddhist monastics in the development of the Indian medical system of Āyurveda.[55] In his studies of the history of Indian medicine, Zysk emphasizes that early Buddhist traditions were the repository of a great deal of medical knowledge:

> In the beginning, medicine was part of an ascetically based religious movement, a portion of which became known as Buddhism. Medicine evolved along with the *saṅgha* and Buddhist monastery in India, became codified as part of the Buddhist scriptures, gave rise to the monk-healers and provided the

> basis for subsequent development of Buddhist monastic hospices and infirmaries, and finally became part of the standard curriculum in the Buddhist monastic "universities."[56]

Zysk provides us with a plausible framework for understanding why we find such graphic descriptions in Indian Buddhist sources of what can happen—medically—to women's bodies.

The details of precisely what the redactors of Indian Buddhist canonical and commentarial literature understood, however, may always elude us. Just because we have medically documented cases that fit the *Samantapāsādikā*'s and Saṃghabhadra's descriptions of these nonnormative women's bodies does not necessarily mean that the commentators themselves were aware of these conditions firsthand or even secondhand. The Buddhist canon and commentaries are compilations of lists, pericopes, and overlapping and intersecting teachings. In the case of the list of nonnormative women's bodies, I would suggest that we have a pericope, a fragment of tradition fixed in its number of disorders, that appears throughout the earliest layers of Buddhist canonical literature. Does this mean that the author of the *Samantapāsādikā* and Saṃghabhadra actually observed women's bodies with these afflictions? I doubt that this was the case; they were commenting upon a set list of conditions found in the root Vinaya texts. Did they receive these terms and a relatively consistent set of definitions, which were passed on with the Vinaya-Piṭaka from Sri Lanka to China in the fourth century CE? Here we need to answer in the affirmative. The *Samantapāsādikā* and Saṃghabhadra transmitted the received tradition regarding women's bodies that defined and classified variations in sex development—and those definitions indicate a fairly sophisticated knowledge of women's bodies. This list that describes variations in women's bodies is embedded firmly within Indian Buddhist monastic rules as a way of establishing the parameters for monastic behavior. Without a normative body, spiritual success as a monk or a nun is not possible.

Third, the fact that *itthi-paṇḍakā* appears in the list raises questions regarding our understanding of *paṇḍaka*s in Buddhist traditions as male. The five *paṇḍaka*s familiar to Buddhist traditions, which dovetail with those found in Jain and Hindu traditions, are all biologically sexed males: they have two openings, an anus and a mouth. How, then, can we have a female—*itthi*—*paṇḍaka*? The *Samantapāsādikā* defines *itthi-paṇḍakā* as a woman without sexual organs, but Saṃghabhadra defines this term as a woman whose labia bulge out and from which a "long fleshy projection that also has hair on it" protrudes. The intriguing thing about these diverging definitions is that in their comments on the other ten terms in the list the *Samantapāsādikā* and Saṃghabhadra agree, with variations only in the wording. When it comes to *itthi-paṇḍakā,* however, they provide two markedly different definitions. The *Samantapāsādikā* says that an *itthi-paṇḍakā* lacks sexual organs. Saṃghabhadra says that she has an anomalous penis-like protrusion (with hair on it). The element that both commentaries have in common is that they understand an *itthi-paṇḍakā* to have missing or anomalous female genitalia—which justifies their inclusion in the list of nonnormative women.[57]

Gyatso suggests that this list "amounts to a description of the class of female *paṇḍaka*s (even though at this point the term is but one member of the list)."[58] Although Gyatso's proposition may be accurate with respect to the Tibetan sources, I am not convinced that the Sanskrit sources recognize a class of female *paṇḍaka*s—and I am certain that the Pāli sources do not. I find it more likely that the commentator who wrote the *Samantapāsādikā* mapped his knowledge of the five kinds of male *paṇḍaka*s onto this list of eleven physical conditions that could afflict women and, in classic commentarial style, used the definition of the first kind of (male) *paṇḍaka* to clarify the nature of the *itthi-paṇḍakā*: both lacked genitalia. Saṃghabhadra's definition of a female *paṇḍaka,* in contrast, is the direct opposite of that found in the *Samantapāsādikā*: a woman who has a penis-like protrusion with hair on it. Given such different understandings of female *paṇḍaka*s, what seems evident is that the two commentators realized that female *paṇḍaka*s did not fit the proper classification for women, and each had a rather different way of explaining why. The noteworthy fact here for both commentaries is that *itthi-paṇḍakā*s appear in this list of abject women, *not* in the standardized list of male *paṇḍaka*s, suggesting that the overriding category is gender, not an emerging classification of a "third gender." In other words, female *paṇḍaka*s are still women, even though they are prohibited from becoming nuns in the same way that male *paṇḍaka*s are prohibited from becoming monks.

This list of eleven kinds of nonnormative women is quite explicit about what kind of bodies are considered to be abject in Indian Buddhist traditions. Proper women have female bodies with functioning reproductive systems and look like women. Any women who have medical conditions that we would refer to today as disorders of sex development or intersex are not considered proper women in these Buddhist traditions, even though, unlike male *paṇḍaka*s, they are not represented as possessing atypical sexual inclinations. It is worth pointing out that nonnormative women are barred from ordination as nuns based on physical aberrations, whereas most of the kinds of male *paṇḍaka*s are barred based on certain behaviors. The fact that the term *itthi-paṇḍakā* never appears in the lists of five (biologically male) *paṇḍaka*s underscores the clear boundary that demarcates male from female in Buddhist literature, even with regard to biologically atypical males and females.

Indian Buddhist traditions are thus far from straightforward when it comes to questions regarding biologically sexed bodies and gender. This has led to a variety of scholarly assertions concerning sex and gender in Buddhist literature. Sweet and Zwilling, as we have seen, assert that what we find in early Buddhist texts is an essentialist two-gendered system based on two sexes. Gyatso's starting point for her ethical reflections on the category of *paṇḍaka*s suggests that Buddhist traditions blurred the line that separates sex and gender:

> With the exception of one novel usage that does indeed seem to overlap with the function of the modern sense of gender, the traditional categories I explore in what follows seem to have been understood, perhaps unreflectively, as being based specifically upon sexual characteristics. Hence I have largely used the word "sex" to refer to those categories.[59]

Such scholarly assessments overlook the meticulous detail with which the Vinayas and their commentators examined bodies, and female bodies in particular. Because most scholars have assumed that male monks would not have much knowledge of women's bodies, this list of nonnormative women's bodies has been largely disregarded in current discussions of sex and gender in Buddhist traditions. However, we have found that the conditions described in this list are verifiable medical conditions. Moreover, we have seen that Indian Buddhist traditions present a sophisticated array of nuanced perspectives concerning sex and gender that define normative and nonnormative bodies with reference to the categories "male" and "female" while at the same time recognizing that these categories—as defined by the male and female *indriya*s and the genitalia—are themselves fluid and changeable. We must recall, however, that nonnormative bodies were prohibited from the monastic orders and were considered outside the range of acceptably sexed male and female bodies. The Vinaya-Piṭaka and commentaries detailed these nonnormative bodies in order to exclude them from proper Buddhist practice.

The principal concern of the Vinaya passages in which the list of nonnormative women occurs is proper behavior within the *saṃgha*. Preventing these kinds of women from joining the order of nuns and prohibiting monks from using these terms as derogatory names for women is about regulating proper behavior for monks and nuns. Furthermore, in the commentaries on the Vinaya-Piṭaka, the authors are particularly concerned that three kinds of women on our list not be the cause of violating the rule against sexual intercourse. The primary distinction between male and female is consistent throughout these sources, and, on the basis of this distinction, diseased male and female bodies are prohibited from joining the order. The fact that these kinds of disorders are enumerated in such detail for women may be attributed in part to the misogyny that underlies all of these texts. However, when we locate these kinds of nonnormative women's bodies within the broader framework of Abhidhamma analyses, we find a more complex conceptualization of sex and gender than has previously been recognized.

Notes

This essay is dedicated to Selva Raj (1953–2008), without whom this study would never have been included in this volume. I am indebted to him for his friendship, support, and insights and miss him greatly. I would also like to thank Barbara Holdrege, Ruth Vanita, Susanne Mrozik, Karen Pechilis, and Ann Heirman for their suggestions on this essay as well as the longer study of which this essay is one part.

1. For an overview of the literature, see Zwilling 1992; Sweet and Zwilling 1993, 1996; Gyatso 2003; Mrozik 2006. Regarding the terminology of "intersex" and "hermaphrodite," as I will discuss later, contemporary popular usage has shifted toward using the term intersex in lieu of hermaphrodite, due to the perceived derogatory connotations of the term hermaphrodite. In contemporary usage, intersex refers to a variety of congenital conditions, which means that those people who are born with such conditions do not fit the accepted definitions of male or female. Hermaphrodite has traditionally meant "between male and female." The medical community today prefers the term "disorders of sex development." However, some intersex individuals have argued that intersex communities should reclaim the term hermaphrodite as a positive form of self-identification, not unlike the way in which LGBT communities have reclaimed the term "queer."

2. Vinaya-Piṭaka, vol. 3, 23–24; trans. Horner 2000–2006: vol. 1, 40–42.

3. The terms used in this essay—*paṇḍaka*s, *ṣaṇḍha*s, *ṣaṇḍhaka*s, or *ṣaṇḍaka*s and *ubhatobyañjanaka*s (Pāli) or *ubhaya-vyañjana*s (Sanskrit)—are never precisely defined in the canon or commentaries. At best, as this essay will demonstrate, the terms are used to describe certain conditions. Furthermore, there is no accepted etymology for any of these terms among Pāli or Sanskrit scholars. Gyatso (2003: 94 n. 11) has discussed the problems with earlier translations of these terms. The

emerging practice among scholars of Buddhist traditions is to leave these terms untranslated, insofar as their use is becoming more widely known in scholarly literature (Bhikkhu Anālayo, personal communication).

4. Fausto-Sterling 2000; Koyama 2008; Consortium on the Management of Disorders of Sex Development 2006; Pasterski, Prentice, and Hughes 2010. The term "disorders of sex development" is not internationally accepted. The challenge to this classification is that nonnormative bodies are still regarded as diseased or "disordered." The terms "variations," "differences," and "divergence" have been suggested as alternatives to "disorders."

5. *Abhidharmakośabhāṣya* 4.96–97b–c; trans. Pruden 1988–1990: 679–681.

6. Vinaya-Piṭaka, vol. 1, 72–89; trans. Horner 2000–2006: vol. 4, 89–114.

7. Vinaya-Piṭaka, vol. 4, 317–334; trans. Horner 2000–2006: vol. 3, 364–395.

8. Butler 1993: 5–6.

9. Mrozik 2006: 22.

10. Mrozik (2006: 42 n. 40) cites Wilson 1996 as evidence that women's bodies as a whole are "coded as abject."

11. Gyatso 2003: 107, 112–114.

12. Many previous studies, including Zwilling 1992; Sweet and Zwilling 1993, 1996; and Gyatso 2003, erroneously follow the Pāli commentarial tradition that attributes authorship of the *Samantapāsādikā* to Buddhaghosa. Von Hinüber (2000: 104) suggests that the attribution of the *Samantapāsādikā* to Buddhaghosa was first made by Vajirabuddhi, a commentator who may be dated to 550–600 CE.

13. Vinaya-Piṭaka, vol. 2, 271–273; vol. 3, 129; trans. Horner 2000–2006: vol. 5, 375–377; vol. 1, 217.

14. *Saṃghādisesa* rules are those rules that, if violated, require a temporary separation from the order. A monk or nun may only be reinstated by a formal meeting of the *saṃgha*.

15. Vinaya-Piṭaka, vol. 2, 271–273; vol. 3, 129; trans. Horner 2000–2006: vol. 5, 375–377; vol. 1, 217. The commentary is found in *Samantapāsādikā* 548–549, where the author defines each term in the list as part of his comments on the third *saṃghādisesa* for monks. He does not discuss in his commentary the other occurrence of this list of terms in the Khandaka. Saṃghabhadra's Chinese translation of a text closely related to the *Samantapāsādikā*, the *Shan-chien-p'i-p'o-sha*, is translated into English in Bapat and Hirakawa 1970. My translations of the terms should be compared to those found in I. B. Horner's translation of the Vinaya-Piṭaka (2000–2006) and *The Pāli Text Society's Pāli-English Dictionary*. See also Gyatso's (2003: 112–113) translations and discussion of this list.

16. I am indebted to Janice Watch, who introduced me to the fact that these conditions are, in fact, medically documented conditions in an undergraduate paper she wrote in 2004. I am also grateful to Dr. David G. Addiss, a Fellow at the Arcus Center for Social Justice Leadership at Kalamazoo College, who read through these translations and introduced me to contemporary medical diagnostic trees, epidemiology, and the intricacies of the word "congenital."

17. Ulfelder and Robboy 1976; Marshall 1978.

18. Escobar et al. 1987.

19. Allen et al. 2004; Schey, Kandel, and Charles 1980. Allen et al. (2004) suggest that the incidence of female epispadias is as high as 1 in 160,000, instead of 1 in 500,000. In men and boys, epispadias and hypospadias are two of the conditions commonly defined as intersex today.

20. Girton, Kennedy, and Galask 2007.

21. Liu et al. 1999.

22. Von Hinüber (2005: 32–35) offers a very useful discussion concerning terms used for tampons and pads in the Vinaya-Piṭaka and commentaries.

23. Bennet 1879; Edis 1897.

24. Devi 2007.

25. Oyama et al. 2004.

26. Fausto-Sterling 2000: 53.

27. This list was not fully examined by Zwilling (1992: 204). Gyatso (2003: 96–98) revisits this list with material from Tibetan and other Vinayas. I have taken this list from *Samantapāsādikā* 1016–1017; *Abhidharmakośabhāṣya* 2.1c, 137, and I have also located similar definitions in medieval subcommentaries.

28. *bījesu pana apanītesu aṅgajātampi rāgena kammaniyaṃ na hoti, pumabhāvo vigacchati, massu-ādipurisaliṅgampi upasampadāpi vigacchati. Vimativinodanī-Ṭīkā* 2, para. 109, and *Vinayālaṃkāra-Ṭīkā* 1, para. 135.

29. *Samantapāsādikā* 991–992. The actual passage in Pāli reads: *paṇḍakā 'ti ussannakilesā avūpasantapariḷāhā napuṃsakā. pariḷāhavegābhibhūtā yena kenaci saddhiṃ mittabhāvaṃ patthenti.* Zwilling (1992: 205) offers this translation for these lines: "According to Buddhaghosa *paṇḍakas* are full of defiling passions (*ussanakilesa*); their lusts are unquenchable (*avūpasantapariḷāha*); and they are dominated by their libido (*pariḷāhavegābhibhūta*) and the desire for lovers just like prostitutes (*vesiyā*) and coarse young girls (*thulakumarikā*)." Zwilling seems to have conflated two different passages. *Samantapāsādikā* 991–992 does not mention *thullakumārikā*. However, Vinaya-Piṭaka, vol. 1, 70 (trans. Horner 2000–2006: vol. 4, 87) lists the five places that monks should not visit for alms, including prostitutes, *paṇḍakas*, and spinsters (not "coarse young girls"). The full list of women who are "off limits" to monks includes prostitutes (*vesiyāgocaro*), widows (*vidhavāgocaro*), spinsters (*thullakumārikagocaro*; see Horner 2000–2006: vol. 4, 87 n. 6; Collins 2007: 275), *paṇḍakas* (*paṇḍakagocaro*), and nuns (*bhikkhunīgocaro*).

30. Vinaya-Piṭaka, vol. 3, 143–144; trans. Horner 2000–2006: vol. 1, 244. In the canonical literature the term *anitthī*, "without female sex," is found only in this passage. However, the term does appear in later Pāli commentaries.

31. The only other references to "hairy sexual organs" of which I am aware, thanks to Steven Hopkins, are found in Ṛg-Veda 9.112.4 and 10.86.16–17; trans. Doniger 1981: 235, 260.

32. Dreger et al. 2005; Aaronson and Aaronson 2010.

33. Medical Subject Headings, The International Classification of Diseases.

34. Medical Subject Headings, s.v. "Hirsutism."

35. Bargaje et al. 2008.

36. *Atthasālinī* 1024; *Samantapāsādikā* 1024; trans. Bapat and Hirakawa 1970: 513.

37. Aaronson and Aaronson 2010.

38. Kim et al. 2002.

39. Sax 2002.

40. See Juo-Hsüeh's (2000: 128) discussion of the meaning of the term *pārājika*: "The canonical commentators do not gloss *pārājika* by its actual meaning but by its reference." The meaning of "expulsion" that is commonly associated with *pārājika* comes from the gloss *asaṃvāsa*, "no longer in communion" (Vinaya-Piṭaka, vol. 3, 28). Juo-Hsüeh (2000: 122–158, esp. 131) reviews contemporary scholarship on the problems with the etymologies attributed to *pārājika* and concludes that it is most useful to translate this term as "defeat," not on etymological grounds but because it evokes the meaning in the canonical commentaries that one who violates these rules is somehow fallen or defeated and should not be allowed to remain in the community. Heirman's (2002a: 119–124) discussion of the Chinese sources concerning the meaning of *pārājika* makes references to the same studies of the etymologies and definitions of the word.

41. See, for example, the *Vajirabuddhi-Ṭīkā*, written by Vajirabuddhi, who may be dated to 550–600 CE, and the *Khuddasikkhā*, composed by Dhammasiri, who was likely a younger contemporary of Vajirabuddhi. Two other commentaries that mention these terms date to the reign of Sri Lanka's King Parakkamabahu I (r. 1153–1186 CE): Bhadanta Sāriputta's commentary on the *Samantapāsādikā*, entitled *Sāratthadīpanī-Ṭīkā*, and the *Kaṅkhāvitaraṇī-Purāṇa-Ṭīkā*, written by Sāriputta's student Buddhanāga. A full examination of these commentaries (*ṭīkās*) lies beyond the scope of the present study. However, one can easily locate the terms *sikharaṇī*, *sambhinnā*, and *ubhatobyañjanakā* in the commentaries through a word search using the downloadable Chaṭṭa Saṅgayāna Tipiṭaka 4.0 Desktop Software published by the Vipassana Research Institute (www.tipitaka.org/cst4).

42. Horner (2000–2006: vol. 3, 21 n. 5) explains in some detail her translation of the term *antarāyikā* as "stumbling blocks," since the term is found elsewhere in the Pāli canon with different meanings.

43. Vinaya-Piṭaka, vol. 1, 93; trans. Horner 2000–2006: vol. 4, 120.

44. Vinaya-Piṭaka, vol. 2, 271; trans. Horner 2000–2006: vol. 5, 375. The translations here are my own, since Horner does not repeat the full list of eleven conditions.

45. Heng-Ching 2000: 514–515; Hirakawa 1982: 59 n. 25.

46. Heirman 2002a: 780–781.

47. Hirakawa 1982: 60–62.

48. Ridding and La Vallée Poussin 1920: 131. The Sanskrit terms are: *avyañjanā* (without genitalia), *ubhaya-vyañjanā* (intersex), *saṃbhinna-vyañjanā* (mixed-up organs), *sadā-prasrūta-lohinī* (blood always oozing out), *alohinī* (without regular menses), and *naimittikī* (malformed genitalia). Regarding the last term, Edgerton (2004: vol. 2, 312) defines this as "hermaphrodite," citing the Ridding

and La Vallée Poussin fragment as the source. Edgerton also cites the Tibetan rendering of this term, "of doubtful sexual characteristics." Linguistically, both the Sanskrit term *naimittikī* and the Pāli term *nimitta-mattā* derive from *nimitta*, "sign, sexual organ, mark."

49. A "school" should not be considered an entirely separate institution, but it does designate different Buddhist textual traditions. Without delving into the history of schisms and debates among different Buddhist schools, it will be helpful to briefly survey their origins and geographic locales in order to determine the extent of the geographic area across which these notions of nonnormative women's bodies were disseminated. The origin of the Mahāsaṃghika school is traced back to a dispute with the Sthaviravādas at the second Buddhist council over matters of discipline (*vinaya*) (Nakamura 1980: 102; Lamotte 1988: 523–528). The traditional home of the Mahāsaṃghika school was Magadha, with another center emerging in Mathurā in the first century BCE; there are also inscriptions at Kārli and at Nāgārjunikoṇḍa in Andhra Pradesh. The Sarvāstivāda and Dharmaguptaka schools developed out of the Sthaviravāda school. While the earliest geographic locations of the Sarvāstivāda school are unclear, the Sarvāstivādins were generally located in northwestern India and in Mathurā, with later influence in Central Asia. The Dharmaguptaka school also spread throughout Central Asia, with influence in Afghanistan and reaching as far as the border with Iran (Heirman 2002b: 396–399). The Theravāda school is traced back to the Sthaviravādas. This school originated in Avanti (now western Madhya Pradesh) and from there spread to Sri Lanka, where its center was established in Anuradhapura, at the Mahāvihāra (Great Monastery). Terms corresponding to those on the Pāli list of nonnormative women's bodies are found in the Vinayas of all of these schools, thus demonstrating a broad geographic range. I have not examined Tibetan sources, but Gyatso points out that terms corresponding to the Pāli terms appear in the *Mahāvyutpatti*, a Sanskrit and Tibetan encyclopedia of terms that dates to the eighth or ninth century CE (Gyatso 2003: 112 n. 71).

Looking more closely at Saṃghabhadra's Chinese translation of the *Samantapāsādikā* gives us greater appreciation of the range of these traditions. Heirman (2004) has suggested that we can glimpse the different Sri Lankan textual traditions by examining Saṃghabhadra himself. The Buddhist affiliation of this translator is unclear, although we know that he translated the Mahāvihāra-affiliated *Samantapāsādikā* in 488–489 CE. There is evidence that Saṃghabhadra had access to a different Sinhalese chronology than the usual one, but there is scant evidence from Saṃghabhadra's biographies to allow us to define his school affiliation with any certainty. Heirman suggests that Saṃghabhadra had access to the traditions of the Abhayagiri Vihāra, another important Sri Lankan Buddhist school, which he incorporated into his translation of the *Samantapāsādikā*. There is also evidence to suggest that Saṃghabhadra was familiar with the Dharmaguptaka Vinaya, although not enough evidence to identify him as Dharmaguptaka. Heirman argues that all of these influences suggest that Saṃghabhadra reflected the eclectic nature of Buddhist traditions in fifth-century China. By locating references to nonnormative women's bodies in the different Vinayas and in the commentaries of the author of the *Samantapāsādikā* and Saṃghabhadra, we thus obtain glimpses of the multiple and varied Buddhist traditions that gave rise to the different interpretations of these kinds of women's bodies.

50. Sweet and Zwilling 1993: 604.

51. The other *indriyas* include the five senses and the mind; vitality; pleasure, pain, happiness, unhappiness, and indifference; faith, energy, mindfulness, concentration, and wisdom; "I am knowing the known," knowing, and that of one who has fully known. Vibhaṅga 122.

52. See Anderson 2010: 53–56.

53. Vinaya-Piṭaka, vol. 3, 35. See Anderson 2010: 56, 2016a, 2016b.

54. Zwilling 1992: 208.

55. Gyatso 2003: 109; Zysk 1991.

56. Zysk 1991: 48–49.

57. Gyatso (2003: 113) points out that the Tibetan term *za ma* that is often used to translate the Sanskrit term *ṣaṇḍha* can also refer to a normal female.

58. Gyatso 2003: 112.

59. Gyatso 2003: 90.

References

Aaronson, Ian, and Alistair Aaronson. 2010. "How Should We Classify Intersex Disorders? [Letter to the Editor]." *Journal of Pediatric Urology* 6: 449.

Abhidharmakośabhāṣya. 1970–1972. *Abhidharmakośa and Bhāṣya of Ācārya Vasubandhu with Sphuṭārthā Commentary of Ācārya Yaśomitra*, ed. Swami Swarikadas Shastri. Varanasi: Bauddha Bharati.

Allen, L., A. Rodjani, A. Kelly, M. Inoue, and J. M. Huson. 2004. "Female Epispadias: Are We Missing the Diagnosis?" *BJU International* 94, no. 4: 613–615.

Anderson, Carol S. 2010. "The Agency of Buddhist Nuns." *Buddhist Studies Review* 27, no. 1: 41–60.

Anderson, Carol S. 2016a. "Changing Sex in Pāli Buddhist Monastic Literature." In *Queering Paradigms VI*. Oxford: Peter Lang.

Anderson, Carol S. 2016b. "Changing Sex or Changing Gender in Pāli Buddhist Literature." *Scholar & Feminist Online*.

Atthasālinī. 1979 [1897]. *Atthasālinī: Buddhaghosa's Commentary on the Dhammasaṅgaṇī*, ed. Edward Müller. Rev. ed. London: Pali Text Society.

Bapat, P. V., and Akira Hirakawa, trans. 1970. *Shan-chien-p'i-p'o-sha: A Chinese Version by Saṅghabhadra of Samantapāsādikā, Commentary on Pali Vinaya*. Poona: Bhandarkar Oriental Research Institute.

Bargaje, A., J. F. Yerger, A. Khouzami, and C. Jones. 2008. "Cloacal Dysgenesis Sequence." *Annals of Diagnostic Pathology* 12, no. 1: 62–66.

Bennet, Henry. 1879. "Metrorrhagia and Its Treatment by Plugging the Cervical Canal." *British Medical Journal* 2, no. 969: 122–123.

Butler, Judith. 1993. *Bodies That Matter: On the Discursive Limits of "Sex."* New York: Routledge.

Collins, Steven. 2007. "Remarks on the Third Precept." *Journal of the Pāli Text Society* 29: 263–284.

Consortium on the Management of Disorders of Sex Development. 2006. *Clinical Guidelines for the Management of Disorders of Sex Development in Children.* Rohnert Park: Intersex Society of North America. http://www.dsdguidelines.org.

Devi, K. Prameela. 2007. "Clinical Evaluation of Pushyanuga Choorna and Lodhrasava in Rakta Pradara (DUB)." *Indian Journal of Traditional Knowledge* 6, no. 3: 429–431.

Doniger, Wendy, trans. 1981. *The Rig Veda: An Anthology*. New York: Penguin.

Dreger, Alice D., Cheryl Chase, Aron Sousa, Phillip A. Gruppuoso, and Joel Frader. 2005. "Changing the Nomenclature/Taxonomy for Intersex: A Scientific and Clinical Rationale." *Journal of Pediatric Endocrinology and Metabolism* 18: 729–733.

Edgerton, Franklin. 2004 [1953]. *Buddhist Hybrid Sanskrit Grammar and Dictionary.* 2 vols. Delhi: Motilal Banarsidass.

Edis, Arthur W. 1897. "On the Diagnosis and Treatment of Metrorrhagia." *British Medical Journal* 1, no. 1536: 1298–1299.

Escobar, L. F., D. D. Weaver, D. Bixler, M. E. Hodes, and M. Mitchell. 1987. "Urorectal Septum Malformation Sequence: Report of Six Cases and Embryological Analysis." *American Journal of Diseases of Children* 141, no. 9: 1021–1024.

Fausto-Sterling, Anne. 2000. *Sexing the Body: Gender Politics and the Construction of Sexuality*. New York: Basic Books.

Girton, Stephanie, Colleen M. Kennedy, and Rudolph P. Galask. 2007. "Characteristics and Outcomes of 16 Patients with Symptomatic Labial Adhesion." *The Internet Journal of Gynecology and Obstetrics* 7, no. 1. http://www.ispub.com.

Gyatso, Janet. 2003. "One Plus One Makes Three: Buddhist Gender, Monasticism, and the Law of the Non-Excluded Middle." *History of Religions* 43, no. 2: 89–115.

Heirman, Ann, trans. 2002a. *Rules for Nuns according to the Dharmaguptakavinaya: The Discipline in Four Parts*. 3 vols. Delhi: Motilal Banarsidass.

Heirman, Ann. 2002b. "Can We Trace the Early Dharmaguptaka?" *T'oung Pao*, Second Series, 88, fasc. 4/5: 396–429.

Heirman, Ann. 2004. "The Chinese *Samantapāsādikā* and Its School Affiliation." *Zeitschrift der Deutschen Morgenländischen Gesellschaft* 154, no. 2: 371–396.

Heng-Ching Shih, Bhikkhunī. 2000. "Lineage and Transmission: Integrating the Chinese and Tibetan Orders of Buddhist Nuns." *Chung-Hwa Buddhist Journal* 13, no. 2: 503–548.

Hirakawa, Akira, trans. 1982. *Monastic Discipline for the Buddhist Nuns: An English Translation of the Chinese Text of the Mahāsāṃghika-Bhikṣuṇī-Vinaya*. Patna: Kashi Prasad Jayaswal Research Institute.

Horner, I. B., trans. 2000–2006 [1938–1952]. *The Book of the Discipline (Vinaya-Piṭaka)*. 6 vols. Oxford: Pali Text Society.

The International Classification of Diseases, 9th Revision, Clinical Modification (ICD-9-CM). 2008. 6th ed. National Center for Health Statistics. icd9cm.chrisendres.com.

Juo-Hsüeh Shih, Bhikkhunī. 2000. *Controversies over Buddhist Nuns*. Oxford: Pali Text Society.

Kim, Kyu-Rae, Youngmee Kwon, Jae Young Joung, Kun Suk Kim, Alberto G. Ayala, and Jae Y. Ro. 2002. "True Hermaphroditism and Mixed Gonadal Dysgenesis in Young Children: A Clinicopathologic Study of 10 Cases." *Modern Pathology* 15, no. 10: 1013–1019.

Koyama, Emi. 2008. "Intersex Initiative." http://www.ipdx.org.

Lamotte, Étienne. 1988. *History of Indian Buddhism: From the Origins to the Śaka Era*. Translated by Sara Webb-Boin. Louvain-la-Neuve: Institut Orientaliste.

Liu, William F., Orestes Borrego, Michael Weiss, and Craig R. Sweet. 1999. "Lethal Pulmonary Hypoplasia and Hydrocolpos with Transverse Vaginal Septum in a Newborn: A Case Report and Review of the Literature." *Journal of Perinatology* 19, no. 6: 454–459.

Marshall, F. F. 1978. "Vaginal Abnormalities." *Urologic Clinics of North America* 5, no. 1: 155–159.

Medical Subject Headings. Bethesda: U. S. National Library of Medicine, National Institutes of Health. http://www.nlm.nih.gov/mesh/MBrowser.html.

Mrozik, Susanne. 2006. "Materializations of Virtue: Buddhist Discourses on Bodies." In *Bodily Citations: Religion and Judith Butler*, ed. Ellen T. Armour and Susan M. St. Ville, 15–47. New York: Columbia University Press.

Nakamura, Hajime. 1980. *Indian Buddhism: A Survey with Bibliographical Notes*. Tokyo: Kansai University of Foreign Studies Publication.

Oyama, I. A., A. C. Steinberg, A. S. Holzberg, and J. L. Maccarone. 2004. "Reduction Clitoroplasty: A Technique for Debulking the Enlarged Clitoris." *Journal of Pediatric and Adolescent Gynecology* 17, no. 6: 393–395.

Pasterski, V., P. Prentice, and I. A. Hughes. 2010. "Impact of the Consensus Statement and the New DSD Classification System." *Best Practice and Research: Clinical Endocrinology and Metabolism* 24, no. 2: 187–195.

Pruden, Leo M., trans. 1988–1990. [1923–1931]. *Abhidharmakośabhāṣyam [Translated] by Louis de La Vallée Poussin*. 4 vols. Berkeley: Asian Humanities Press.

Ridding, C. M., and Louis de La Vallée Poussin. 1920. "A Fragment of the Sanskrit Vinaya Bhikṣunīkarmavacana." *Bulletin of the School of Oriental Studies* 1, no. 3: 123–143.

Samantapāsādikā. 1924. *Samantapāsādikā: Buddhaghosa's Commentary on the Vinaya-Piṭaka*, ed. Junijreo Takakusu and Nagai Makoto. 6 vols. London: Oxford University Press.

Sax, Leonard. 2002. "How Common Is Intersex? A Response to Anne Fausto-Sterling." *Journal of Sex Research* 39, no. 3: 174–178.

Schey, W. L., G. Kandel, and A. G. Charles. 1980. "Female Epispadias: Report of a Case and Review of the Literature." *Clinical Pediatrics (Philadelphia)* 19, no. 3: 212–215.

Sweet, Michael J., and Leonard Zwilling. 1993. "The First Medicalization: The Taxonomy and Etiology of Queerness in Classical Indian Medicine." *Journal of the History of Sexuality* 3, no. 4: 590–607.

Sweet, Michael J., and Leonard Zwilling. 1996. " 'Like a City Ablaze': The Third Sex and the Creation of Sexuality in Jain Religious Literature." *Journal of the History of Sexuality* 6, no. 3: 359–384.

Ulfelder, H., and S. J. Robboy. 1976. "The Embryologic Development of the Human Vagina." *American Journal of Obstetrics and Gynecology* 126, no. 7: 769–776.

Vibhaṅga. 1978 [1904]. *The Vibhaṅga, Being the Second Book of the Abhidhamma Piṭaka,* ed. Caroline A. F. Rhys Davids. London: Pali Text Society.

Vimativinodanī-Ṭīkā. Chaṭṭa Saṅgāyana Tipiṭaka, Vipassana Research Institute. http://www.tipitaka.org.

Vinayālaṅkāra-Ṭīkā. Chaṭṭa Saṅgāyana Tipiṭaka, Vipassana Research Institute. http://www.tipitaka.org.

Vinaya-Piṭaka. 1997 [1879]. *The Vinaya Piṭakaṃ,* ed. Hermann Oldenberg. 5 vols. Oxford: Pali Text Society.

von Hinüber, Oskar. 2000 [1996]. *A Handbook of Pāli Literature.* Berlin: Walter de Gruyter.

von Hinüber, Oskar. 2005 [1994]. "Remarks on the *Critical Pāli Dictionary* (I)." In his *Selected Papers on Pāli Studies,* 25–38. Oxford: Pali Text Society.

Wilson, Liz. 1996. *Charming Cadavers: Horrific Figurations of the Feminine in Indian Buddhist Hagiographic Literature.* Chicago: University of Chicago Press.

Zwilling, Leonard. 1992. "Homosexuality as Seen in Indian Buddhist Texts." In *Buddhism, Sexuality, and Gender,* ed. José Ignacio Cabezón, 203–214. Albany: State University of New York Press.

Zysk, Kenneth G. 1991. *Asceticism and Healing in Ancient India: Medicine in the Buddhist Monastery.* New York: Oxford University Press.

Chapter 10

Murderer, Saint, and Midwife

The Gendered Logic of Engendering in Buddhist Narratives of Aṅgulimāla's Conversion

LIZ WILSON

In this essay I analyze a set of narratives from the Pāli Buddhist canon about a murderer named Aṅgulimāla who became a patron saint of childbirth for Theravāda Buddhists.[1] The Pāli canon contains several recensions of Aṅgulimāla's story. The versions analyzed here are the Aṅgulimāla Sutta of the Majjhima Nikāya, along with Buddhaghosa's commentary on the narrative;[2] and a set of twenty-six verses in the Theragāthā that Aṅgulimāla is said to have uttered at the moment of his awakening, along with Dhammapāla's commentary on the verses.[3] That a murderer should become someone who ensures safe childbirth is quite a dramatic transformation. Is there something about a murderer—a person who takes life—that provides a foundation for him to become a saint who presides over the generation of new life in childbirth? In my analysis I will test the idea that the shedding of blood may provide the answer to this question. I focus on the death-dealing shedding of blood in murder and the life-giving shedding of blood in childbirth as a conceptual link between the criminal career of Aṅgulimāla and his saintly career empowering women to give birth successfully. In drawing a connection between the murderous act of shedding blood and the generative act of shedding blood in childbirth, I will invoke the work of Nancy Jay, a feminist sociologist of religion whose critique of sacrificial rhetoric highlights parallels between male and female forms of generativity. Using Jay's work as a lens allows me to reflect on the kinds of generativity that male and female bodies are endowed with in the literary imagination of Pāli-language Buddhist redactors and commentators. I will conclude the essay by suggesting that the Buddhist narratives analyzed here offer rich, complex possibilities for feminist readings.

Aṅgulimāla's Story

The saint who was once a mass murderer is well known to students and practitioners of South Asian religions. Aṅgulimāla's very name evokes the grisly details of his story: he is called "Garland (*mālā*) of Fingers (*aṅguli*)" in reference to his method for counting his victims by taking a finger from each as a tally. Among Buddhist practitioners, Aṅgulimāla stands as an icon of total transformation, a saintly exemplar who overcame his terrible *karma* to achieve the status of an *arhat*, an awakened being who is liberated from the cycle of birth and death. It is no wonder that Aṅgulimāla's name has been given to a British prison chaplaincy organization that provides Buddhist practice opportunities to prisoners in the United Kingdom.[4]

When Aṅgulimāla was born, his horoscope indicated a propensity for crime. And indeed, in a past life Aṅgulimāla had been a *yakkha*, or ghoul, who existed on a diet of human flesh. But as the child grew up, he proved to be well behaved and intelligent. He went off to a distant city as a young man, studied with a famous religious teacher, and excelled so much that his fellow students became jealous. They convinced the teacher that Aṅgulimāla had committed adultery with his wife. The furious teacher came up with a cunning ploy to get rid of Aṅgulimāla without having to harm the young man himself. He led Aṅgulimāla to believe that he must kill a thousand people, collect a finger from each, and give him the fingers as payment for the lessons taught by the teacher. Aṅgulimāla accepted the teacher's outrageous demand without much protest and went off to live on a high cliff in a forest where he could observe travelers on the road below and kill them. He strung the fingers of his victims on a necklace that he wore to keep an accurate tally. Word of the killer soon spread through the whole region. People came to call him Aṅgulimāla (Garland of Fingers). One day Aṅgulimāla had 999 fingers collected. His next victim would have been his own mother. She knew that the king's army was on its way to find and execute him, and she bravely set out alone to convince her son to change his ways and come home with her. On that fateful day, however, the Buddha intervened. The Buddha lured the murderer away from his mother and toward himself. When Aṅgulimāla saw the Buddha, he ran after him. He accelerated in hot pursuit but got no closer to the Buddha, who walked along at a normal pace. Aṅgulimāla demanded that the Buddha stop. The Buddha said, "I have stopped, Aṅgulimāla; now you too stop."[5] Aṅgulimāla heeded the Buddha's words and asked for ordination as a monk. And eventually this man became an *arhat*, an awakened or enlightened being.

Aṅgulimāla successfully turned his own life around and developed healing powers. He famously enabled a woman to deliver a healthy child after seven days of difficult labor by uttering a verbal formula safeguarding the life of the mother and her infant. In this way Aṅgulimāla facilitated the entry of new life into the world after being the agent of so much death in his past. This episode of healing turned his reputation around, from murderer to healer-saint or, if you will, midwife-saint. Aṅgulimāla continues to the present day to play this saintly role in popular Buddhist practices throughout the Theravāda Buddhist world, in places like Sri Lanka, Thailand, and Burma (Myanmar). For example, ceremonies for expediting childbirth are performed by monks who stand in the place of Aṅgulimāla and recite the Aṅgulimāla *paritta*—protective verses that are believed to be the saint's words.[6] Pregnant women drink water that carries the saint's blessings and touch objects that he is said to have handled while helping the woman give birth. For example, the *Saddharmaratnāvaliya*, a thirteenth-century Sinhala translation of a fifth-century Pāli commentary on the Dhammapada, claims that women in labor who drink water that was used to wash the seat where Aṅgulimāla spoke the protective verses "give birth painlessly."[7] Such practices are attested to in the early twentieth-century fieldwork of Charles Duroiselle in Burma, who was told that those who had witnessed Aṅgulimāla bring about the woman's safe delivery had established a bed, and a woman suffering a difficult childbirth could be immediately delivered of her child simply by touching the bed. If she could not travel to the bed, she could still deliver safely if she were to bathe in water that had been poured over the bed itself. There is an Aṅgulimāla image in the Shwezigon *stūpa* in Pagan, Burma, that is the focus of offerings by Burmese women seeking a safe delivery.[8] By such ritual procedures that extend the saint's power through time and space, safe childbirth is ensured. Such practices give us good reason to describe Aṅgulimāla's role in Theravāda Buddhism as that of a saintly male midwife for expectant mothers.

With this overview of Aṅgulimāla's story to provide context, I will proceed with my analysis in three sections. In the first section I will describe my sources, outline Jay's work, and consider the various forms of generativity that my sources suggest. Clearly we have a male saint helping to facilitate the generativity of laywomen—the woman whom Aṅgulimāla originally helped to deliver a baby and the many other Theravāda Buddhist women who have invoked the saint's powers through the centuries. But we also have men playing midwife to other men in the sense of facilitating a spiritual rebirth. For example, the Buddha's conversion of Aṅgulimāla can be seen as an act of regeneration that makes the Buddha a parent to the new man who Aṅgulimāla becomes. In the second section I will focus on this and other forms of male generativity seen in the narratives. In the third section I will ask whether my sources place greater value on male generativity than on female generativity. Both the Buddha's conversion of Aṅgulimāla and Aṅgulimāla's saintly midwifery could be adduced as evidence that those who redacted our texts viewed male spiritual fertility as more efficacious than ordinary women's fertility. I will consider this interpretation but will reject it based on evidence from the commentarial sources that highlights the agency of women in Aṅgulimāla's conversion, in his achievement of awakening, and in his attainment of the status of a celebrated saint.

Birth Done Better

Although there are narratives about Aṅgulimāla in Pāli, Sanskrit, Tibetan, and Chinese, I have limited my focus here to selected Pāli accounts, since these are the accounts known to the Theravāda ritual specialists who help women with childbirth rituals.[9] The earliest source is the Aṅgulimāla Sutta of the Majjhima Nikāya,[10] which gives the basic outline of Aṅgulimāla's conversion but offers little in the way of backstory. There are a number of Pāli-language commentaries that speak of Aṅgulimāla, three of which are especially useful in providing many details not given in the terse *sutta* account. Buddhaghosa's commentary on the Majjhima Nikāya, the *Papañcasūdanī,* is a key source.[11] The Theragāthā contains the twenty-six verses (verses 866–891) that are ascribed to Aṅgulimāla, which are commented upon in Dhammapāla's *Paramatthadīpanī.*[12] There are also two verses in the Dhammapada that are said to refer to Aṅgulimāla, and while the commentary on one verse is brief and contains little of the saint's story, the commentary on the second verse (verse 172) is extensive.[13]

In looking at all the Pāli accounts, it is clear that a lot of the narration is dedicated to the grislier parts of the story. Why is this? Is this a Buddhist version of a Freddy Krueger movie? Is the attention to gore a way to grab the interest of the audience so that the audience will stay for the moral lesson? Or is there something more to the emphasis on bloodshed in the texts? Is there something about a man who killed almost a thousand people that especially qualifies him to serve as a patron saint of childbirth? Plenty of Buddhist saints are said to have checkered pasts. That a figure who committed misdeeds in the past should become a saint is not unusual in Buddhist literature.[14] Our texts, however, dwell on the gory details of Aṅgulimāla's career as a killer in a way that brings the act of bloodshed into sharp focus.

Jay gives us one lens that can help to make sense of the textual focus on the shedding of blood. In her monograph *Throughout Your Generations Forever: Sacrifice, Religion, and Paternity,* Jay looks at the holy shedding of blood that goes on in rituals of animal sacrifice and the ways in which such rituals of killing may be akin to bringing new life into the world through childbirth.[15] The association of childbirth with bloodshed is of course directly observable. A successful childbirth entails the emission of blood from the birth canal. The emission of large amounts of blood can signal the possibility that both mother and child will lose their lives. Childbearing is often a violent process that poses danger for both mother and child. If we consider the blood imagery that is highlighted in our Buddhist sources, we can see parallels between the shedding of blood in killing and the shedding of blood in childbirth. We can see a logic that connects Aṅgulimāla as a killer to Aṅgulimāla as a healer who ensures safe childbirth.

In her monograph Jay focuses on a handful of different cultures that utilize sacrificial rites as a means of creating new patrilineal kinship groups that are thought to overcome the mortality of the individual. She finds in these examples common rhetorical strategies, ways of speaking about generativity.[16] Sacrifice is a kind of male childbirth procedure, to put it very crudely, whereby men claim to transcend natural birth and secure symbolic rebirth and immortality in male lineages. The work of men in sacrifice is "birth done better, under deliberate purposeful control, and on a more exalted level than ordinary mothers do it."[17] The termination of the lives of sacrificial victims in the controlled environment of sacrificial killing is understood to create enduring life and yield continuity, specifically intergenerational continuity. All who sacrifice together, or eat the flesh of sacrificed animals together, are thereby joined in enduring structures of affiliation around male ancestors. In these societies it is only through claiming affiliation through men, not women, that lasting intergenerational structures are thought be achieved.[18] Those who join such structures through sacrifice often claim to supplant the work of women in bringing children into the world. Sexual reproduction is associated with the unpredictable, chaotic work of nature, in contrast with the rule-bound predictability of culture. The activity of women as child-bearers is often denigrated in sacrificial rhetoric as merely a natural process, in contrast to the cultural work of men in social reproduction. Sacrifice as male reproduction is seen as grounded in the divine, the eternal, and the immortal. In contrast, biological reproduction is aligned with mortality and death.

Jay's monograph does not focus on Indian materials, but her work has relevance for Indian Buddhism. As Paul Mus has shown, the Vedic paradigm of sacrificial rebirth resonated with Buddhists as a model for framing and expressing religious transformation.[19] Although Jay does not include a chapter on Vedic sacrifice as practiced in ancient India in her selected set of case studies, it seems a logical candidate for inclusion. Vedic sacrifice can accurately be described by Jay's formulation as "birth done better."[20] It is a second birth, performed at the hands of male ritual specialists, that qualifies a male as a "twice-born" (*dvija*) man with the right to participate in the rituals that lead to postmortem felicity. Participation in the sacrificial cult gives a man the opportunity to go to the world of the male ancestors (Sanskrit *pitṛ-loka*, or "world of the fathers"). While Indian Buddhists rejected violent forms of Vedic sacrifice in which animals are killed, the Vedic paradigm of sacrificial rebirth continued to resonate with Buddhists as a model for describing religious achievement. In the Saṃyutta Nikāya, for example, the Buddha presents his path of self-discipline as an internalized kindling of the Vedic fire sacrifice: "I ignite an inward fire . . . the heart is the altar, self-discipline the flame."[21] Indian Buddhist texts describe entry into the monastic order as a second birth, a rebirth that makes one a son or daughter of the Buddha and establishes one in a line of descent from Buddhas of the past.[22] This line of descent is a patrilineal one, a lineage of male Buddhas who have realized the immortal condition of *nirvāṇa* and are no longer subject to death.

In the healing words of the Aṅgulimāla *paritta*—the words that he reportedly spoke to the woman suffering a difficult childbirth—Aṅgulimāla assumes rebirth in the lineage of the Buddhas. The story behind the words is this. After Aṅgulimāla's conversion and ordination as a monk, the Buddha and his monks were staying near the city of Sāvatthī. Aṅgulimāla went to beg for food in the city. He knew that the citizens were terrified of him and would not open their doors to him, but he went begging for alms as a matter of form, thus adhering to the rules of monastic discipline. As he was going from door to door on a certain street, he learned of a woman suffering a difficult and extended labor. He was moved by her pain, went back and told the Buddha about her, and was coached by the Buddha to return to her and say the words that are chanted today as a *paritta,* protective incantation. As soon as he uttered the words, she immediately gave birth to a healthy child.

Aṅgulimāla's words, rendered in English, are: "Sister, since being born in a noble birth, I have not deliberately taken the life of any living being. By this truth, may there be well-being for you and for your fetus."[23] He whose very name evokes methodical killing solemnly declared that he had intentionally taken no life since his birth. The words he spoke were technically true, because the birth about which Aṅgulimāla spoke was not his entry into this world through a birth canal but his second birth, his entry into a new order of being through ordination as a monk. He described himself as born in a noble birth (*ariyāya jātiyā*), and commentators identify the lineage of this new birth as the noble lineage of the Buddhas.[24] Aṅgulimāla's declaration is an example of a verbal formulation known in Pāli as a *saccā-kiriyā,* an act of truth, whereby a solemn utterance made by a person can have palpable consequences for that person and for others as well.[25]

Male Fertility

Jay's work helps us to identify textual claims to male forms of generativity. In addition to Aṅgulimāla, as a male saint, facilitating female generativity by helping a woman give birth, other male forms of generativity are operative in accounts of Aṅgulimāla's life. First I will examine how Aṅgulimāla came to exercise an asexual form of monastic fecundity as a saint after he helped the woman give birth. I will then analyze the Buddha's conversion of Aṅgulimāla, showing how it can be seen as an act of regeneration that makes the Buddha a progenitor of the new man who Aṅgulimāla becomes.

After performing the act of truth that ensured safe childbirth for the suffering woman that he encountered in Sāvatthī, Aṅgulimāla achieved the Theravādin goal of becoming an *arhat.* The woman of Sāvatthī was grateful. She and her family spread the word that the man who everyone thought was a cold-blooded killer was in fact a compassionate healer. At last Aṅgulimāla won the respect of the people of Sāvatthī. Instead of running from him and slamming their doors when he came begging food, they began providing him with food and robes. Aṅgulimāla came to be known as a field of merit—*puñña-kkhetta* in Pāli. In Theravāda

Buddhist traditions, this important status is reserved only for *arhats*. Donations given to an *arhat* who is a field of merit yield karmic benefits for those who give. Through planting seeds of merit in this way, the giver can achieve a better rebirth in future lives. In the agrarian metaphor of Theravāda Buddhist texts, the monk who is a fertile field of merit is the ritual equivalent of a field of earth that never fails to yield abundant crops. The donations planted in that field are like seeds guaranteed to sprout in the future, yielding fruit in the form of merit that has future karmic benefits for the donor. In Indian Buddhist literature the imagery of field and seed-planting evokes both agricultural fertility and sexual procreation. Buddhist texts show familiarity with pan–South Asian tropes of married women as fields to be plowed and seeded by their husbands. Thus once Aṅgulimāla became an *arhat* who had won the admiration and generosity of the citizens of Sāvatthī, he became a very fertile man. Although celibate, Aṅgulimāla achieved a form of fecundity, a womb-like function, with respect to the laity who supported him with their gifts.[26] The gifts that are offered to an *arhat* in this life are held to yield fruit after the death of the donor and enable the donor to achieve a better rebirth. Aṅgulimāla's fertility as a field of merit thus transcends death and is a form of generativity highly appropriate for those who have joined the Buddha's immortal lineage.

Another example of male fecundity in accounts of the life of Aṅgulimāla is found in the Buddha's conversion of Aṅgulimāla as an act of regeneration. We have already seen that Aṅgulimāla testified to something that was true when he declared himself to have done no intentional harm to any being since his noble birth. His ordination is so clearly marked as a second birth that the *sutta* account of the healing incident has the Buddha coach Aṅgulimāla in a way that draws attention to the difference between Aṅgulimāla's first and second births. The Buddha initially told Aṅgulimāla to say, "Sister, I have deliberately harmed no being since birth." Aṅgulimāla responded by asserting that he had indeed caused harm to living beings since his birth. The Buddha then modified the statement so that it referred to Aṅgulimāla's taking ordination and joining the Buddha lineage.[27] That second birth, a regeneration that made Aṅgulimāla the polar opposite of the man he had been, is the key one. By means of that rebirth, the killer who was Aṅgulimāla was terminated and a new being emerged. In having the Buddha coach Aṅgulimāla to modify his statement, the texts highlight the importance of ordination as rebirth and the Buddha's role as the agent of the killer's rebirth. In his role as someone who ushered Aṅgulimāla into a new life through a second birth, the Buddha functions as a male parent figure. The Buddha's conversion of Aṅgulimāla is represented as a form of male childbearing whereby the Buddha bloodlessly gave birth to a transformed man.

We are now in a position to ask if the Buddha's role as a giver of new life to Aṅgulimāla overshadows the role of Aṅgulimāla's biological mother in a way that diminishes the value of female generativity. Should we read the Buddha's conversion of Aṅgulimāla as an example of antinatal rhetoric? Is it "birth done better"? Does that make the Buddha the real parent to Aṅgulimāla? I take up such questions in the next section.

Will the Real Mother Please Stand Up?

In this section I will analyze the texts to see if one form of generativity—female or male—is treated as derivative of or dependent on the other. If female generativity depends on male intercession in the texts, this would be an indication that the redactors of our sources value men's generative powers over women's and consider male fertility to be a transcendent source of female fertility. In this case women's fertility would be derivative of male metafertility. In my view, the commentaries do not allow us to draw this conclusion. The commentaries suggest that it is the women in the story who are crucial catalysts enabling Aṅgulimāla to achieve the prerequisite conditions that make him a fertile man capable of bringing new life into the world. The commentaries showcase the agency of women in three aspects of Aṅgulimāla's life: in his conversion, in his achievement of awakening, and in his attainment of the status of a saintly field of merit.

Significantly, the killer's own mother, a woman named Mantāṇī, has an important role in the commentarial sources. Whereas the *sutta* account ascribes all agency for Aṅgulimāla's conversion to the Buddha, the commentaries decenter the Buddha. The commentaries have the Buddha intervene in response to the prior decision of Mantāṇī that she would herself undertake to save her son. Mantāṇī and her husband had not seen their son since he left home to be educated. Because of the horoscope and bad omens at the time of the child's birth, they knew that their son had a propensity to become an outlaw. When they heard that the king and his men were on their way to kill a murderer in the forest, they concluded that the outlaw was none other than their missing son. Mantāṇī discussed the matter with her husband, but her husband decided that they should not intervene. Mantāṇī's husband was the king's minister, and he felt that he could not compromise his reputation at court. It would be best just to let Aṅgulimāla be put to death by the king's men.[28] Mantāṇī, however, did not accept this opinion. She did not even try to change her husband's mind, but instead she immediately took action. She set off on a journey to Aṅgulimāla's forest hideaway, saying, "I'm going now to fetch my son."[29] It was in order to prevent Aṅgulimāla from encountering his mother and making her his next victim that the Buddha himself intervened. Buddhaghosa's commentary explains that the Buddha saw with his special powers of observation that the killer was ripe for conversion. Aṅgulimāla would in fact take ordination as a monk and attain a high level of realization if he could only hear one complete verse of the teaching spoken to him in the forest. But if Aṅgulimāla did not hear the teaching, he would go after his own mother as his final victim. If the killer took the life of the woman who gave him life, it would generate such negative *karma* that Aṅgulimāla would be beyond help.[30] That matricide is the ultimate sin here is indicative of the high value placed on the maternal role. This suggests a higher estimation of female generativity in the commentarial sources than Jay's interpretive model might lead us to expect.

Taking this commentarial framing of the story as our guide, Aṅgulimāla's mother Mantāṇī and the Buddha can be viewed as counterpart figures in their orientation to the killer. In fact, I am struck by how far we can go in reading the Buddha as a double of Mantāṇī, imitating her and confirming her in his actions. Mantāṇī is the first to set off in pursuit of Aṅgulimāla. She takes no weapon with her, intending to use words alone to stop her murderous son. In this, she sets an example that the Buddha follows. The fact that Mantāṇī sets out with the intention of stopping Aṅgulimāla and initiates the process that leads to conversion makes her a key player in her son's rebirth as a healer.

With respect to the more challenging case of the woman whom Aṅgulimāla saved after she had suffered seven days of fruitless labor pains, was her fertility dependent on Aṅgulimāla's male fertility? The newly minted monk Aṅgulimāla intervened to save the life of mother and child, but the woman herself played a decisive role as a catalyst in the saint's own awakening. The oldest of our sources, the Aṅgulimāla Sutta, makes it clear that Aṅgulimāla achieved awakening as an *arhat* only after seeing her and making his declaration of truth to her.[31] One wonders if Aṅgulimāla only came to empathize with his victims through identification with this woman's agony. Perhaps he only understood suffering after she instantiated it in a way that enabled him to identify with it and with her. Buddhaghosa's commentary on the Aṅgulimāla Sutta explains that it was not until Aṅgulimāla was able to assist the woman that he could set aside the guilt and remorse that had plagued him in his previous attempts at meditation. He could finally sit still in meditation without reliving horrible scenes from the past, full of people screaming and begging for their lives. Once he was able to engage in meditation with equanimity, Aṅgulimāla became an *arhat*.

Our texts suggest another more concrete sense in which Aṅgulimāla may be said to depend on the woman in labor for his fertility as a saint. Recall that this woman and her family helped Aṅgulimāla rehabilitate his reputation so that he became known as a field of merit. The criminal from whom people fled was transformed into a saint with a womb-like function with respect to the laity who supported him with their gifts. Given that this male form of religious fertility did not occur until Aṅgulimāla encountered a woman struggling to express her own fertility, we have another situation of interdependence, as in the pairing of the Buddha with Aṅgulimāla's mother. We are presented with a man becoming a fertile field of merit, fertile in his monastic discipline, in conjunction with a woman becoming fertile in childbirth.

Conclusion

Jay's theory allows us to discern a connection between ritualized acts of killing and childbirth that helps to explain why a man who took so many lives is well suited to perform the work of a patron saint of childbirth. Jay's work shows that fecundity or generativity can take male and female forms, and we have seen a number of ways in which the men in our sources exhibit forms of generativity appropriate to their situation as celibate monks. Having looked closely at the commentarial texts on Aṅgulimāla, however, my conclusion is that Jay's binary model with its devalued female and privileged male forms of generativity is too hierarchical to be used without modification. I agree with the critique that Kay Read raises in her review of Jay's book: some of the material that Jay covers has the potential for feminist readings that show female-led, if not female-dominated, social systems and ritual practices.[32]

I suggest that the Buddhist materials I have analyzed here reveal alternative readings that ascribe more agency to women than the strictly male-dominated systems that Jay emphasizes in her readings of sacrificial practices. If Jay were to analyze our Buddhist texts, she might suggest that Aṅgulimāla's mother merely gives physical birth to a son as an act of nature. Her childbearing work must be completed by the cultural work that the Buddha performs in converting her son. But it is the determination of Aṅgulimāla's mother to stop her son from continuing in his murderous ways that leads the Buddha to convert the killer, and the texts set up a parallel between the killer's mother and the Buddha that suggests that they are equally engaged in the "spiritual" work of regenerating Aṅgulimāla. The commentarial texts underscore the interdependence of men and women, monks and mothers. Binary oppositions of female versus male, natural versus cultural, are not helpful here. Aṅgulimāla's male fecundity depends on female fecundity operating on at least two distinct registers: first, his mother's determination to make her son into a new man; and, second, his encounter with the woman giving birth that led him to awaken as an *arhat* and become a fertile field of merit for others. If the conversion that Aṅgulimāla underwent from killer to saint is comparable to the birth of a new man, we can say that Aṅgulimāla had multiple mothers, male and female, who made the generation of the new man possible. Instead of the gendered hierarchy of male fecundity that trumps female fecundity that one would expect based on Jay's binary framework, the commentaries suggest interdependence: we see monks and mothers engaged together in the work of regeneration.

Notes

1. On Aṅgulimāla in Pāli literature, see Nyanaponika and Hecker 2003; Gombrich 2006; Loy 2000. For an overview of Aṅgulimāla narratives in Pāli, Sanskrit, Tibetan, and Chinese, see Furda 2005: 6–22. For iconographic references to Aṅgulimāla, see Parimoo 1995: esp. 133, 135; Lesbre 2001: esp. 314.

2. The Aṅgulimāla Sutta is found in the Majjhima Nikāya, which is the second of the five *nikāyas* (collections) in the Sutta-Piṭaka, the second section of the Pāli Buddhist canon. For the Aṅgulimāla Sutta, see *The Majjhima Nikāya*, ed. Trenckner and Chalmers, vol. 2, 97–105; Horner, trans., *The Collection of the Middle Length Sayings*, vol. 2, 284–292. For Buddhaghosa's commentary on the Aṅgulimāla Sutta, see *Papañcasūdanī*, ed. Woods, Kosambi, and Horner, vol. 3, 328–344.

3. The Theragāthā is the eighth book of the Khuddaka Nikāya, the last of the five *nikāyas* in the Sutta-Piṭaka, and consists of 264 poems that are attributed to the early monks of the Buddhist *saṃgha*, monastic order. For the twenty-six verses (verses 866–891) in the Theragāthā that are ascribed to Aṅgulimāla, see Norman, trans., *The Elders' Verses*, vol. 1, 82–84. For Dhammapāla's commentary on these verses, see *Paramatthadīpanī*, ed. Woodward, vol. 3, 54–64.

4. The website of Aṅgulimāla, The Buddhist Prison Chaplaincy is http://angulimala.org.uk.

5. Majjhima Nikāya, vol. 2, 99. All translations from Pāli and Sanskrit are my own unless otherwise specified.

6. On the uses of the Aṅgulimāla *paritta* in Sri Lanka, see de Silva 1981: 10; Gombrich 1971: 202, 224; Yalman 1964: esp. 140.

7. Dharmasēna 1991: 103–104.

8. Duroiselle 1922–1923.

9. For an overview of all versions of Aṅgulimāla's story, see Furda 2005: 6–22.

10. See n. 2.

11. See n. 2.

12. See n. 3.

13. The account that I draw on here is found in *Dhammapadaṭṭhakathā*, ed. Norman, vol. 3, 169–170; Burlingame, trans., *Buddhist Legends*, vol. 3, 6–14.

14. The Buddha, who is styled as a great physician, cured many sick minds. And the Buddha himself has a bit of a past. Theravāda Buddhists recognize that even the awakened Buddha had to endure hardships in his last life as a result of bad *karma* generated by his own hurtful actions in previous lives, including one instance of homicide. See Walters 1990.

15. Jay 1992.

16. For example, in chapter 4, "Creating Descent through Fathers and Sons," Jay (1992) compares selected agrarian and pastoral societies of European (specifically Mediterranean) antiquity and twentieth-century Africa. Jay limits her investigation to cultures concerned with the transmission of property and land from one generation to the next, surmising that we would not expect hunter-gatherers or members of industrial societies to construct elaborate kin groups that entitle people to bequeath land, herd, and other forms of productive property to their descendants. She shows that sacrificial cults in Mediterranean antiquity and twentieth-century Africa appeal to unbroken genealogical lines organized around men, despite the fact that the modes of social organization and religious life of the societies in question vary dramatically.

17. See Jay 1992: xxiv.

18. Jay (1992: 39–40) remarks, "It is through fathers and sons, not mothers and daughters, that 'eternal' social continuity is maintained. Daughters, who will marry out, are not members of the lineage in the same way as their brothers, nor do mothers have full membership in the husbands' and sons' lineage."

19. Mus 1935. See esp. the preface.

20. Jay 1992: xxiv.

21. Saṃyutta Nikāya, ed. Feer, vol. 1, 169. The Saṃyutta Nikāya is the third of the five *nikāya*s in the Sutta-Piṭaka.

22. Strong (1983: 82, 187–188, 217, 259) discusses the paternal lineage of Buddhist monks as "sons of Śākyamuni" (Śākyaputra) and "heirs of the Dharma" (*dharmadāyada*).

23. *Yato ahaṁ, bhagini, ariyāya jātiyā jāto nābhijānāmi sañcicca pāṇaṁ jīvitā voropetā; teṇa saccena sotthi te hotu sotthi gabbhassāti*. See Majjhima Nikāya, vol. 2, 103.

24. In the *paritta* verses the Pāli word for Aṅgulimāla's new identity is *jāti*. The same term, rendered as *jāt* in Hindi, is used by contemporary Hindi speakers

on the Indian subcontinent to refer to one's subcaste. In Buddhist literature *jāti* is glossed by commentators in Pāli as *gotta* and in Sanskrit as *gotra*, denoting a line of descent from a common ancestor—namely, the lineage of the Buddhas.

25. On the act of truth in Indian literature, see Burlingame 1917. On the Aṅgulimāla *paritta* as an act of truth, see Eckel and Thatamanil 2001: 67–68.

26. For a discussion of the epithet "worthy of gifts" (*dakkhiṇeyya*) and its Vedic antecedents, see Findly 1999: esp. 70ff.

27. Majjhima Nikāya, vol. 2, 103.

28. *Papañcasūdanī*, vol. 3, 331.

29. *Papañcasūdanī*, vol. 3, 331.

30. Buddhaghosa says the Buddha deduced the following: "There will be an auspicious outcome in my going to him. If he hears just one complete verse spoken in the forest, he will take ordination in my presence and attain the six super-knowledges. But if I do not go and he wrongs his mother, it will be irremediable." *Papañcasūdanī*, vol. 3, 331.

31. Majjhima Nikāya, vol. 2, 103–104.

32. Read 1994.

References

Angulimala, The Buddhist Prison Chaplaincy. Accessed May 4, 2014. http://angulimala.org.uk.

Burlingame, Eugene Watson. 1917. "The Act of Truth (*Saccakiriya*): A Hindu Spell and Its Employment as a Psychic Motif in Hindu Fiction." *Journal of the Royal Asiatic Society of Great Britain and Ireland* 49, no. 3: 429–467.

Burlingame, Eugene Watson, trans. 1921. *Buddhist Legends*. 3 vols. Cambridge: Harvard University Press.

de Silva, Lily. 1981. *Paritta: A Historical and Religious Study of the Buddhist Ceremony for Peace and Prosperity in Sri Lanka*. Colombo: National Museums.

Dhammapadaṭṭhakathā. 1992–1993 [1906–1915]. *Dhammapadaṭṭhakathā. The Commentary on the Dhammapada*, ed. H. C. Norman. 5 vols. Reprint. Oxford: Pali Text Society.

Dharmasēna, Thera. 1991. *Jewels of the Doctrine: Stories of the Saddharma Ratnāvaliya*. Translated by Ranjini Obeyesekere. Albany: State University of New York Press.

Duroiselle, Charles. 1922–1923. "Four Burmese Saints." *Annual Report of the Archaeological Survey of India, 1922–23*: 174–176.

Eckel, Malcolm David, with John J. Thatamanil. 2001. "'With Great Noise and Mighty Whirlpools the Ganges Flowed Backwards': Buddhist Approaches to Truth." In *Religious Truth*, ed. Robert Cummings Neville, 65–82. Albany: State University of New York Press.

Findly, Ellison Banks. 1999. "Women and the Arahant Issue in Early Pali Literature." *Journal of Feminist Studies in Religion* 15, no. 1: 57–76.

Furda, Danya. 2005. "Karma and Grace in the Legend of Aṅgulimāla." PhD diss., McMaster University.

Gombrich, Richard F. 1971. *Precept and Practice: Traditional Buddhism in the Rural Highlands of Ceylon*. Oxford: Clarendon Press.

Gombrich, Richard F. 2006 [1996]. "Who was Angulimala?" In his *How Buddhism Began: The Conditioned Genesis of the Early Teachings*, 135–164. 2nd ed. New York: Routledge.

Horner, I. B., trans. 1989–1993 [1954–1959]. *The Collection of the Middle Length Sayings*. 3 vols. Reprint. Oxford: Pali Text Society.

Jay, Nancy. 1992. *Throughout Your Generations Forever: Sacrifice, Religion, and Paternity*. Chicago: University of Chicago Press.

Lesbre, Emmanuelle. 2001. "An Attempt to Identify and Classify Scenes with a Central Buddha Depicted on Ceilings of the Kyzil Caves (Former Kingdom of Kutcha, Central Asia)." *Artibus Asiae* 61, no. 2: 305–352.

Loy, David. 2000. "How to Reform a Serial Killer: The Buddhist Approach to Restorative Justice." *Journal of Buddhist Ethics* 7: 145–168.

Majjhima Nikāya. 1977–1991 [1888–1902]. *The Majjhima-Nikāya*, ed. V. Trenckner and Robert Chalmers. 4 vols. Reprint. London: Pali Text Society.

Mus, Paul. 1935. *Barabudur: Esquisse d'une histoire du Bouddhisme fondée sur la critique archéologique des textes*. Hanoi: Impr. d'Extrême-Orient.

Norman, K. R., trans. 1990–1992 [1969–1970]. *The Elders' Verses*. 2 vols. Reprint. Oxford: Pali Text Society.

Nyanaponika, Thera, and Hellmuth Hecker. 2003. "Aṅgulimāla: A Murderer's Road to Sainthood." In their *Great Disciples of the Buddha: Their Lives, Their Works, Their Legacy*, 317–334. Reprint. Boston: Wisdom Publications.

Papañcasūdanī of Buddhaghosa. 1976–1979 [1922–1938]. *Papañcasūdanī*, ed. J. H. Woods, D. D. Kosambi, and I. B. Horner. 5 vols. Reprint. London: Pali Text Society.

Paramatthadīpanī of Dhammapāla. 1940–1959 [1926]. *Paramattha-dīpanī*, ed. F. L. Woodward. 3 vols. Reprint. London: Pali Text Society.

Parimoo, Ratan. 1995. "On Re-Identification of Āndhra Buddhist Jātaka Relief Sculptures." *Artibus Asiae* 55, no. 1/2: 125–154.

Read, Kay A. 1994. Review of *Throughout Your Generations Forever: Sacrifice, Religion, and Paternity*, by Nancy Jay. *Journal of Religion* 74, no. 3: 439–440.

Saṃyutta Nikāya. 1975–1998 [1884–1904]. *The Saṃyutta-Nikāya of the Sutta-Piṭaka*, ed. Léon Feer. 6 vols. Reprint. London: Pali Text Society.

Strong, John S. 1983. *The Legend of King Aśoka: A Study and Translation of the Aśokāvadāna*. Princeton: Princeton University Press.

Walters, Jonathan S. 1990. "The Buddha's Bad Karma: A Problem in the History of Theravāda Buddhism." *Numen* 37, no. 1: 70–95.

Yalman, Nur. 1964. "The Structure of Sinhalese Healing Rituals." *Journal of Asian Studies* 23, no. 1: 115–150.

Chapter 11

Fruitful Austerity

Paradigms of Embodiment in Hindu Women's *Vrat* Performances

TRACY PINTCHMAN

In contemporary India many Hindus perform votive rituals, called *vrat*s in Hindi, and they do so out of a variety of motivations and for a variety of ends. Although *vrat*s generally have their own particular structure, they are essentially devotional rites. There is a good measure of continuity between *vrat*s and other forms of *bhakti* observance, and the boundaries in this regard are rather fluid: a pilgrimage or daily *pūjā* (devotional ritual), for example, can be undertaken in the petitionary manner sometimes associated with *vrat*s, just as *vrat*s themselves can be undertaken without any desire whatsoever.[1] Although both men and women perform *vrat*s, several scholars have noted their special importance in the lives of women. Mary McGee and Anne Mackenzie Pearson, for example, have demonstrated that women in particular tend to understand the performance of these rites as continuous with their *strī-dharma*, their *dharma* as women, and especially their maternal and spousal roles as a *pativratā*, an auspiciously married woman with a living husband and children.[2]

In this essay I consider women's performance of one particular votive ritual, the Chaṭh *vrat*, focusing especially on ways in which both narratives and practices associated with this *vrat* address concerns about the body. I explore narratives I collected and performances of this *vrat* I observed in the city of Vārāṇasī, North India, where I conducted field research on women's devotional practices during three autumn seasons between 1995 and 1998.[3] The Chaṭh *vrat* is observed most fervently in the North Indian state of Bihar, but it is also quite popular throughout eastern Uttar Pradesh and has become increasingly important in Vārāṇasī as more and more Biharis have immigrated to the city. One *vrat* manual I purchased in Vārāṇasī emphasizes Chaṭh's importance by contending that Chaṭh is to eastern Uttar Pradesh and Bihar what Durgā Pūjā is to Bengal and Janmāṣṭamī is to western Uttar Pradesh.[4] It has spread throughout India wherever Biharis have settled.

There are two Chaṭh celebrations: one in the spring, and one in the autumn. The latter Chaṭh festival is the one most fervently celebrated and the one I will explore here. It takes place during the bright half of the Hindu month called Kārtik, which falls around October-November.[5] Chaṭh is observed over the course of four days, from the fourth to the seventh day of Kārtik's bright fortnight, but the main day of fasting (*upavāsa*) and ritual is the sixth, *chaṭh* or *ṣaṣṭhī*, after which the *vrat* is named. The *vrat* is also called Sūrya Chaṭh or Sūrya Ṣaṣṭhī, "Sun Sixth," but it is widely known in Vārāṇasī by the name Ḍāla Chaṭh, or "Basket Sixth," after the baskets used for holding and making offerings during the *vrat*'s main *pūjā*. Women who perform this *vrat* reported to me that, as with other *vrat*s, votaries may undertake it for a variety of reasons, including to ensure the general well-being of their families or to bring fulfillment of a variety of worldly desires. However, it is particularly associated—at least among the women with whom I spoke—with the conception, birth, and well-being of sons and, secondarily, the healing of serious illnesses.

Both narratives and practices pertaining to the Chaṭh *vrat* are centrally concerned with religious management of the human body in which four paradigms of embodiment pertaining to four pivotal Hindu values—auspiciousness, asceticism, purity, and devotion—are interwoven. In both narratives and practices auspiciousness emerges as the paramount value to be cultivated through performance of the Chaṭh *vrat*, with the other three values ascribed subsidiary roles in the service of promoting auspiciousness. Chaṭh *vrat* narratives valorize ascetic and devotional regulation of the votary's body as means of cultivating somatic auspiciousness, exemplified primarily in physical well-being and fecundity, not as biologically based bodily conditions but as states that must be deliberately and laboriously cultivated and maintained through religious performance. The ideals represented in the Chaṭh *vrat* narratives are actualized through the practices associated with contemporary Hindu women's observance of this *vrat*, which functions as a performative field in which the divergent models of the religiously managed body pertaining to asceticism, purity, and devotion converge with unique salience in concerns about somatic auspiciousness as it manifests in and through the female householder's body. The practices that women regularly perform in conjunction with the Chaṭh *vrat* are meant to create and perpetuate an auspicious female body through ritual manipulation, exemplifying preoccupation with bodily auspiciousness in unique ways while simultaneously participating in larger patterns that characterize women's *vrat* traditions more broadly.

Chaṭh *Vrat* Narratives

There are several different devotional narratives associated with this votive rite, but the ones I was able to collect are generally healing narratives centered on some kind of rupture to and subsequent restoration of bodily functioning. In these accounts Sūrya, the sun deity, who is also called Bhāskara, functions as the ultimate healing agent, and the *vrat* is performed as an expression of devotion directed to Sūrya. One *vrat* manual I purchased in Vārāṇasī, for example, associates Chaṭh with the story of an antireligious (*dharm virodh*) merchant named Mahīpāl, who one day says insulting words about Sūrya and defecates and urinates in front of his ritual image (*pratimā*). Sūrya becomes angry and blinds Mahīpāl in retaliation. Mahīpāl sinks into a deep depression over his blindness and eventually decides to commit suicide by drowning himself in the Gaṅgā, the Ganges River. He sets off toward the river but on the way meets Nārada, the celestial seer (*devarṣi*), who talks Mahīpāl out of killing himself and enjoins him to perform instead the Chaṭh *vrat*. Mahīpāl does so, and his sight is restored.

> Sūrya became angry and said, "Hey, you sinner! May your vision be destroyed." As soon as the Lord said this, the merchant became blind. He became terribly agonized by this, and he began to feel fed up with life. When he became too distressed, then one day he decided, "Why not end this miserable life by drowning in the Gaṅgā?" After a lot of deliberation, he decided to go ahead, and he set off for the riverbank. On the way, he met Nārada coming his way, singing the praises of Lord Hari (Viṣṇu) and playing his *vīṇā*. The divine seer said, "Hey, Lālā Mahīpāl! You are walking in great haste. What is the matter? Do you smell money?"[6] Mahīpāl said, "No, Lord! I was going to drown myself in the Gaṅgā, having

> become fed up with my blindness." Nārada said, "Do not do this second sin, Mahīpāl! Suicide is a heinous sin. You have already sinned by insulting Lord Bhāskara; you have become blind as a result of that." Mahīpāl asked humbly, "So, Lord! What can be done to get rid of the crime committed against Lord Sūrya?"
>
> Nārada said, "Great merchant! Soon the sixth (*chaṭh*) of Kārtik's bright half is coming. If you worship Lord Sūrya on that day, the sin of insulting the gods gets destroyed from its very root. So do the *vrat* with devotion and worship him on that day, and you will regain your eyesight." Having said this, Nārada left, and Mahīpāl fasted on Chaṭh and worshiped Lord Sūrya according to instruction. His blindness went away as a result. Hence one should feel inside, "Oh Lord Sūrya! Just as you gave vision to Mahīpāl, give the gift of vision to everyone."[7]

In this account Mahīpāl's transgression is an explicitly somatic one: he urinates and defecates where he should not, in front of a ritual image of Sūrya. His moral offense is also a corporeal one concerning the problematic release of polluting bodily effluvia in a place where such flowing should be blocked in the interest of ritual purity and devotional respect. In response, Sūrya, the sun deity, first compromises Mahīpāl's bodily integrity by destroying his vision, restoring it only when Mahīpāl relents and offers appropriate devotion, although the precise terms of that devotion are not made clear. Sin (*pāp*) manifests itself somatically as an immediate rupture to bodily functioning, blindness, underscoring Sūrya's dominion over illumination and vision. Blindness constitutes an obstruction of light to the eyes, a type of somatic blockage that here counterbalances the unrestrained and inappropriate flow of Mahīpāl's urine and feces. Mahīpāl's devotional penance "heals" the sin, resulting in the healing of his vision and marking the restoration of bodily integrity.

A second account that I collected in Vārāṇasī attributes to the Chaṭh *vrat* even greater healing powers. This more elaborate story is recounted in a short and inexpensive Chaṭh *vrat* manual that is sold all over Vārāṇasī.[8] In the Mahīpāl account narrated earlier, the votary is male, but in this more elaborate account only women perform the *vrat*. This more accurately reflects current practice, for several of my informants reported that Chaṭh is celebrated in North India exclusively by married women. Men act in the *vrat* only as "servants" (*sevak*) who perform supporting tasks, helping carry women's implements or wiping their foreheads. In Vārāṇasī I witnessed only women performing this *vrat*, and in fact some of my informants further insisted that only married women *with living sons* ought either to perform this *vrat* or, alternatively, to perform the basket *pūjā* from which the popular name of the *vrat* is derived.[9]

This more elaborate *vrat* narrative traces the performance of the *vrat* back to the events narrated in the Mahābhārata and recounts that Draupadī and her five husbands, the Pāṇḍavas, are wandering in exile when they are joined by eighty-eight thousand *ṛṣis* (seers). Yudhiṣṭhira immediately begins to worry about how he can possibly arrange to feed his guests, and Draupadī, seeing Yudhiṣṭhira's sadness, becomes despondent herself and asks her family priest, Dhaumya, to give her some *vrat* she may perform to restore happiness to the Pāṇḍavas, destroy their enemies, and provide milk for the *ṛṣi*-guests to drink. Dhaumya then advises her to perform the Chaṭh *vrat* and tells her the story behind the *vrat*.

Dhaumya recounts that once a powerful king, Śaryāti, had one thousand wives but only one child, a daughter Candramukhī, whom he adored. She was reportedly beautiful and hence was called Sukanyā, "lovely maiden." One day Sukanyā was out in the jungle with her girlfriends when they happened upon a *muni*, or ascetic, named Cyavana. Cyavana's entire body was leprous, infested with termites (*dīmak*), and buried in dirt, but his two eyes glowed from the middle of the mound, bright as fireflies. Sukanyā, astonished at the sight, poked Cyavana's eyes, from which a stream (*dhārā*) of blood (*rudhir*) then began to flow forth. She and her friends returned home, but because of Sukanyā's actions, the urine and feces of the king and his army became blocked, and they began to groan in pain.

After three days and nights, King Śaryāti asked his family priest what could be causing the distress. The priest explained that Sukanyā had poked Cyavana's eyes and caused blood to flow, angering the powerful *muni*, who was causing distress to the king and the king's army in retaliation. He suggested that Śaryāti give his daughter to Cyavana in marriage as an act of appeasement. Śaryāti therefore returned to Cyavana, taking Sukanyā with him. He poured water over the ascetic, revealing only bone, for Cyavana's eyes were now gone. He offered his beloved daughter to Cyavana to serve him, and Cyavana was appeased. Śaryāti returned to his palace, his difficulties gone, and Sukanyā remained with the now eyeless Cyavana.

One day, during the month of Kārtik, Sukanyā went to fetch water from a tank and saw there a lovely snake maiden (*nāg kanyā*), who was dressed in finery and jewels and was praying to Sūrya. Sukanyā asked the snake maiden what she was doing, and the snake maiden told her she was performing a *vrat* and its attendant *pūjā*. The snake maiden gave Sukanyā instructions concerning how to perform this *vrat*, the Chaṭh *vrat*, and reassured her that Sūrya removes all the miseries and fulfills all the desires of Chaṭh votaries. Sukanyā performed the *vrat*, and as a result the *muni* Cyavana's eyesight was restored, his body was healed and became free of all disease, and he and Sukanyā subsequently enjoyed a happy life together.

The story then returns to its frame of Dhaumya and Draupadī. Dhaumya assures Draupadī that if she, like Sukanyā, performs the Chaṭh *vrat*, she will restore prosperity to her husbands' kingdom. Draupadī does this, and as a consequence Yudhiṣṭhira is able to feed all the visiting *ṛṣis*. We are also told that the Pāṇḍavas were later able to recover their kingdom only because Draupadī kept this *vrat*.

Many elements of this narrative point to the general concern with auspiciousness that characterizes women's *vrat* traditions more broadly. Categories that exemplify auspiciousness, as Frederique Marglin has observed, include marriage, sexuality, and progeny; wetness, rains, abundance of food, and the well-being of crops; wealth; and health, medicines, and bodily well-being.[10] Kingship and lordly power also embody auspiciousness, for the strength of a king manifests itself in the production of rain and good crops. In the Sukanyā narrative water, snakes (*nāgas*), gold and jewels, the abundance of food to serve the eighty-eight thousand *ṛṣis*, the happiness of Sukanyā's alliance with Cyavana, and the restoration of the Pāṇḍavas' kingdom are all associated with auspiciousness. But the healing of bodily infirmity lies at the heart of both the Mahīpāl and Sukanyā narratives, with Sūrya functioning as the ultimate healing agent. While Mahīpāl performs the *vrat* on his own behalf, to restore his own vision after Sūrya has blinded him, Sukanyā performs the *vrat* in her capacity as a devoted wife, to heal not just the vision of Cyavana, whom she herself has accidentally blinded, but his entire infested body. Bodily flowing—the flowing of blood from Cyavana's eyes—as well as bodily blocking—the blocking of urine and feces in the bodies of the king and his army—both compromise somatic well-being, causing bodily disturbance, as they also do in the account of Mahīpāl's transgression against Sūrya. However, in the Sukanyā narrative the categories are reversed from the Mahīpāl account: the problematic flowing here involves the eyes, and the problematic blocking involves impeding feces and urine, rather than the other way around. In both cases, however, bodies are the problem; they either flow too much or they are blocked.

Interestingly, the problematic bodies in both narratives are male bodies; they are the ones that gush forth inappropriate substances or get stopped up and cease flowing in ways that are necessary for normal bodily function.[11] It is especially notable that in the Sukanyā narrative, the polluting gushing of blood from a bodily orifice, widely associated in Hindu traditions with menstruation, is displaced onto a male body, Cyavana's, as the seeming result of austerity, *tapas*, run amok. The fluid that counters the blood's polluting effect here is water, which again plays an important symbolic role. When Śaryāti first approaches Cyavana, he pours water (*jal choṛnā*) over him. Why? Is he washing away blood or dirt? Or is he cleansing the pollution caused by the gushing eyes? Or is he perhaps intent on healing Cyavana's eyes with life- and health-giving water? The connection of water to both auspiciousness and devotion is more clearly evident in Sukanyā's encounter with the snake maiden at the water tank. This encounter over water is what leads Sukanyā to perform the healing *vrat* that mends her husband's body, reinstating his eyesight.

The Chaṭh *vrat*'s association with healing and life-giving powers broadly construed is also exemplified in a third narrative that female informants in Vārāṇasī recounted to me in brief, attributing to the *vrat* the ability to restore life to dead bodies. Women's ability to revive the bodies of dead relatives, especially husbands, through ritual practice is of course a theme in other votive narratives and practices as well, as in the Sāvitrī and Karvā Cauth *vrat*s. Although I found no written version of this oral account, it seems nevertheless to be known to at least some Chaṭh votaries in Vārāṇasī and provides a prototype on which contemporary practice of the *vrat* is based.

One informant narrated the story in this way. One day a boy died. The boy's heartbroken mother took the dead child into her lap and went to stand in the river and pray to Sūrya to restore life to her son's body. She began praying and fasting in the evening before sunset and ended up remaining in the water all night long so that she could continue her prayers upon the Sun's rising. In the morning Sūrya saw the woman still standing in the river and, realizing that she had spent the entire night there, took pity on her and restored her son to life. In Bihar, the home state of the woman who recounted this narrative to me, some women observe the *vrat* in a similar fashion by remaining half-immersed in a river or pond for the entire night. A second informant who was originally from Bihar reported that in her village it was primarily women who were childless or were petitioning for relief from severe illness—either their own or that of someone in their family—who would remain standing all night in the river.

As in the story of Mahīpāl and the story of Sukanyā, here too the *vrat* is performed in response to a rupture in bodily well-being—in this case, the ultimate rupture, death. It is through the practice of bodily immersion in the river for a lengthy period of time, accompanied by fasting and prayer, that the rupture is redressed. Hence the mother's auspicious life-giving power—here manifested as the power to restore life to her son's body—is directly linked to her performance of bodily disciplines that are simultaneously devotional and ascetic. The flowing waters of the river are purifying, certainly, but they also function as the medium in which religious faith (*śraddhā*) and devotion (*bhakti*) are cultivated: the dead mother's child stands in the water to perform prayers to Sūrya, and she becomes so absorbed in her devotional practice that she loses awareness of her surroundings. The waters also function as an ascetic medium, for standing in the river's cool waters for hours on end is an exercise in bodily austerity. Finally, they function as a medium for cultivating fecundity and auspiciousness, for it is through immersing herself in these waters that this unnamed mother is able to bring her son back to life.[12]

The interweaving of devotion, asceticism, purity, and fecundity or auspiciousness that we see in these Chaṭh *vrat* narratives also characterizes the religious practices associated with women's observance of this *vrat* in Vārāṇasī.

Practice of the Chaṭh *Vrat*

Although some variations in how the Chaṭh *vrat* is performed were reported to me, almost everyone with whom I spoke about the *vrat* emphasized its physical arduousness. The performance of the Chaṭh *vrat* is spread out over four days, from the fourth day of Kārtik's bright fortnight to the morning of the seventh day when the final ritual observances take place. Preparations for the *vrat*, however, begin several days in advance. A votary's house must be thoroughly cleansed in preparation for the *vrat*, and the cleaning begins several days before the *vrat* begins. New bangles are also purchased and worn during Chaṭh, and new clothing is bought to be donned on the concluding day. Special ritual implements and foods must also be purchased. A new winnowing basket (*sūp*) must be bought for use on the sixth day of Kārtik's bright fortnight when the main rituals take place. Rice and wheat from the new harvest must be procured and thoroughly cleansed, for only such rice and wheat are supposed to be consumed during the course of the *vrat*.

The *vrat* proper begins on the evening of the fourth day of Kārtik's bright fortnight. In Vārāṇasī many women begin the observance of the Chaṭh *vrat* in the evening by consuming a simple vegetarian meal consisting of some kind of vegetable (often *laukī*, pumpkin or "bottle gourd"), lentils (*dāl*), and rice. *Parāṭhā*, a kind of fried unleavened wheat bread, may also be consumed, but all foods eaten on this day should be cooked without garlic or onion, both of which are considered polluting. One votary insisted that all foods consumed on this evening must be cooked only in *ghī*, clarified butter, not vegetable oil. As one of the five products of the cow (*pancagavya*), *ghī* is considered to be an especially pure substance and hence more suitable than oil for cooking ritual foods.

The following morning, the fifth day of Kārtik's bright fortnight, votaries fast for the entire day, consuming no food or liquid whatsoever. In either the morning or afternoon, they undertake a ritual bath in the Gaṅgā. Several votaries also reported that on this day they perform in the late afternoon a special *pūjā*, either at the bathing *ghāṭs* (after bathing in the river) or at home, to Chaṭh Mātā (also called Chath Maiyā), "Mother Chaṭh." Chaṭh Mātā is a goddess who is ascribed life-giving powers and is widely associated in Vārāṇasī with this *vrat*. In fact, some of the votaries with whom I spoke associated the *vrat* more strongly with Chaṭh Mātā than with Sūrya. Several of the songs associated with the *vrat* also invoke Mother Chaṭh as the object of devotion.[13] One informant identified Chaṭh Mātā with Pārvatī, but no one else could offer any further description of Chaṭh Mātā, and I found no textual references to her. Nevertheless, in Vārāṇasī she is widely perceived to play an important role in providing the auspicious boons associated with performance of this *vrat*.

To perform *pūjā* to Chaṭh Mātā on this day, some women reported to me that they make a kind of altar (*vedī*) out of mud, if they are at home, or clay from the banks of the Gaṅgā, if they are at the *ghāṭs*. One votary reported that on her altar, which she makes at the edge of the river, she places a small brass pot (*loṭā*), which she fills with water and smears with yellow rice paste. She then smears in six places on both the altar and the pot *sindūr*, vermillion powder that married women put in the part of their hair to signify their auspicious married state. After placing a garland of flowers around the pot and lighting six clay lamps, she places rice and *guṛ*, unrefined sugar made from boiled sugar cane juice, together in a bowl and puts the bowl on top of the brass pot. When she returns home, she cooks and consumes this mixture for her evening meal. In fact, all Chaṭh votaries are supposed to break the fast on this evening by consuming a meal that includes *pūrīs*, unleavened wheat bread deep fried in *ghī*, and *khīr*, a pudding of rice and milk made with *guṛ*. These foods—wheat, new rice, sugar—are those that represent the new fall harvest, and deliberately consuming them at this time expresses one's gratitude for the earth's abundance. One informant reported that this meal must be consumed in complete silence, while others reported that it must be consumed in solitude or only in the presence of other female votaries. Hence it is a religiously charged meal that is invested with the solemnity of the *vrat* itself.

On the sixth day of Kārtik's bright fortnight, votaries abstain from all food and drink for the entire day, which is spent in the kitchen cooking and preparing for the evening *pūjā*. On both the fifth and the sixth days, a new cooking fire or stove (*cūlhā*) is supposed to be installed and used to prepare the ritual foods, because one's regular stove, which is used daily to prepare ordinary meals, might be polluting. Some votaries told me that they banish children from the kitchen during the *vrat* for fear that the children will accidentally touch the stove, ritual implements, or ritual foods and thus pollute them.

In the late afternoon of the sixth day, crowds of women walk to the banks of the Gaṅgā, accompanied by family members. This is the central and most important practice of the Chaṭh *vrat*. The votaries take with them stalks of sugar cane and a decorated winnowing basket, in which they pile an offering of cloth along with abundant offerings of food, including coconuts and bananas, *pūrīs*, uncooked rice, and other fruits. Ideally, women who made altars by the edge of the river on the previous day return to those altars and begin the *pūjā* from that spot, but other votaries make their altars on the sixth day itself. A few of the votaries with whom I spoke complained that as the numbers of votaries and attendants has grown, the *ghāṭ*s have become impossibly crowded and chaotic, and they often return on the sixth to find the altar they had prepared the day before being used by another votary or, worse, smashed and trampled by the hordes of people at the river's edge. Votaries enter the water and root the sugar cane in the mud of the river bottom, with stalks rising above the water's surface. Standing in the water up to their chests, they pay homage to Sūrya with prayers, *bhajan*s (devotional songs), and libations (*argh*) of water or milk mixed with water, departing home only after sunset.

Votaries are enjoined to remain awake through the night, absorbed in the singing of *bhajan*s and the burning of *ghī* lamps. They continue their fast, abstaining from all food and drink until the following day. They return to the Gaṅgā starting around 3:00 or 4:00 a.m., parading through the streets of the city singing Chaṭh songs as they walk to the river's edge. They then reenter the water, spreading the *āṃcal*s, ends of their saris, out before them to greet Sūrya, and at sunrise they once again offer libations of water, milk, or a mixture of the two. The *āṃcal* of a sari is the portion that covers a woman's breasts and may be understood figuratively to stand for the breast. Hence a votary's spreading out of the *āṃcal* to catch Sūrya's blessings is a symbolic attempt to capture Sūrya's life-giving powers and invest one's own body with such power, embodied in a powerfully gendered form in the female (lactating) breast. After distributing *prasād* (ritually offered food) at the *ghāṭ*s, they return home by around 8:00 or 9:00 a.m., consume *prasād* themselves, and then eat a meal, marking the end of the *vrat*.

How might we begin to interpret women's engagement with their bodies in the performance of the Chaṭh *vrat*? Catherine Bell has stressed the role of the body in the analysis of ritual practices, noting that ritual entails performing specific actions with one's body, which in turn inscribe upon bodies values fundamental to the ritual situation. Bell is overwhelmingly concerned with the ways that ritual practices function to promote relations of power among human beings, and these are the values with which she is most concerned. In exploring the practice of kneeling during Christian prayer, for example, she emphasizes the way that kneeling produces relations of power in the very act of kneeling itself. Hence she remarks, "Kneeling does not merely communicate subordination to the kneeler. For all intents and purposes, kneeling produces a subordinated kneeler in and through the act itself."[14]

Bell is influenced in her analysis of bodies in ritual by the work of Michel Foucault, who chronicles the "technologies of power" through which bodies come to be disciplined and controlled. Foucault writes, for example, about the production of the "docile body"—which he understands to be a body that "may be subjected, used, transformed, and improved"—through the imposition of disciplines on the body that are rooted in European monastic disciplines.[15] Certainly applying a feminist hermeneutic of suspicion to women's engagement in the Chaṭh *vrat* could lead us toward viewing it as a practice that functions to produce docile female bodies ever more willing to engage in practices of bodily denial and bodily submission. With respect to social relations of power in bodily disciplines, gender plays a substantial role. Judith Butler has argued that gender is primarily performative and that gender identity is constituted through a stylized repetition of acts.[16] Butler is not speaking of ritual practices per se in this context, yet rituals are relevant to her analysis.

While it might be remiss *not* to acknowledge the role that social relations of power can indeed play in the deployment of the body in ritual, it would be equally remiss not to acknowledge the limitations of this model.[17] None of the women with whom I spoke described their own bodily engagement with the Chaṭh *vrat* in terms that could be interpreted as entailing docility, submission to covert mechanisms of social power, or ideological control over women's bodies. Instead, they spoke overwhelmingly of the physical difficulty of the *vrat* and the religious dedication it requires, as well as the boons gained by performing it. Analysis of the *vrat* and its performance solely in terms of human relations of power fails to account for the lived bodily experiences that Chaṭh votaries tended to report to me. Hence a hermeneutic of suspicion that accounts for gender ideology and women's subordination in North Indian culture may be appropriate to this context but not sufficient, as it does not take into account a wide range of cultural values that also come into play here.

Focusing on human relations of power in ritual practice also does not account in any meaningful way for religious models of the body and bodily discipline that come from within Hinduisms. Relevant in this regard is Gavin Flood's observation that cultural memory is somatic and is encoded in ritual and in the body. In his exploration of asceticism, Flood notes that ritual practice inscribes traditions on the body, and the performers of ritual "follow patterns established by others over very long periods of time."[18] Hence Hindu rituals can be read as the performance of context-specific, religious models of embodiment that are expressed in praxis. Barbara Holdrege, along these lines, has noted that Hindu traditions themselves provide "extensive, elaborate, and multiform discourses of the body" that can contribute in significant ways to scholarly explorations of the body in the study of religion.[19]

Focusing specifically on women's performance of the Chaṭh *vrat*, I would argue for the primacy of four paradigms of the religiously regulated female body that are rooted in broader Hindu conceptions of the body but are of special import in this ritual context: the auspicious body, the ascetic body, the purity body, and the devotional body. I borrow the latter three categories from Holdrege, who has contributed her own extensive analyses of models of embodiment in Hindu traditions.[20] But these models play out somewhat differently in women's Chaṭh performances than they do in the contexts that Holdrege explores at length in her work, for in this context the latter three bodily models—the ascetic body, the purity body, and the devotional body—largely function to support and promote the first—the auspicious body.

Auspicious Body

In Hindu votive practices fertility and human reproductive potential, as well as healing and general bodily well-being, may best be understood as encompassed by the larger value of auspiciousness, which is one of the main goals of women's participation in votive rituals. In this regard I have highlighted the special power that women ascribe to the performance of the Chaṭh *vrat* in promoting bodily fecundity, and more specifically in fulfilling their desire to produce and nurture sons—a theme that is prominent in women's *vrat* performances generally.

Symbolism of auspiciousness and bodily fertility comes to the fore especially in relationship to the *vrat*'s main *pūjā*, along with its practices of bodily immersion. The proffered winnowing basket, with its abundance of fruit and other foods, for example, acts as a model of the fertile womb. The votary's body, immersed so that the river's life-giving, fertile water bathes sexual organs and breasts, turns to seek the life-giving rays of the sun. Offerings of milk, the liquid of the fertile breast that embodies maternal love, and newly harvested sugar cane evoke the nourishing potential inherent in the fertile female body and the fertile land of the countryside. In contemporary Hindu votive practices more generally, the fertility of women's bodies, much more than that of men's bodies, is posited as in need of religious management. Among the women and men I encountered during field research in Vārāṇasī, human fertility and infertility tended generally to be viewed as primarily, if not exclusively, female concerns, not male ones, and in contemporary religious practice Hindu women's performances of *vrat*s are not infrequently for the purpose of promoting fertility.

Ascetic Body

In the Chaṭh *vrat*, as in some other *vrat*s, ascetic action functions as a paradigm through which bodily fertility comes to be regulated. Hence asceticism is conscripted in this context into serving domestic bodies and promoting auspiciousness within the domestic sphere.

Gavin Flood describes the term "asceticism" as referring to "a range of habits or bodily regimes designed to restrict or reverse the instinctual impulses of the body" as well as "an ideology that maintains that in so doing a greater good or happiness can be achieved."[21] In this regard the religiously appropriate bodily restraint entailed in the ascetic actions of the Chaṭh *vrat* function as a counterpoint to the inappropriate lack of restraint characterizing the gushing forth of feces, urine, and blood—all polluting substances—in the Chaṭh narratives detailed earlier. All this inappropriate flowing speaks to lack of discipline on the part of the narratives' actors, which is remedied by the ascetic bodily disciplines of ritual performance in which the votaries engage.

Flood notes as well that the goals of ascetic action "are not simply abstract ideologies or justifications for the power of institutions" but are also "the future orientations and narrative identities of people; their desire to achieve a goal, the goal of human perfection in this or in some other world."[22] In this regard *vrat*s function for many women as a form of domestic ascetic praxis, embracing bodily practices—fasting, subjecting the body to discomfort or pain, and so on—that are generally associated with a life of renunciation but incorporating them into the domestic realm to promote worldly goals associated with the *pativratā,* the perfectly devoted wife who brings auspicious boons to her family. In her work on women's *vrat*s, Pearson cites some of her *vrat*-performing female informants who, she argues, "have appropriated elements of the pervasive ideology of abstinence, self-control, and self-purification, articulated in the Yogasūtras, the Gītā and elsewhere."[23] She argues that women have seen "value and esteem placed by the Hindu tradition at large" on the self-disciplinary, or *niyama,* aspect of *vrat* performance, and so they also emphasize this aspect in their own performance of *vrat*s.[24] With respect to the deployment of human bodies in the practice of the Chaṭh *vrat,* it is important to note that the religious management of fertility presumes conceptualizing the body's fertility apart from sexuality (*kāma*) and reconstituting it within the domain of ascetic practice (*tapas*), to be managed through religious performance.

Water plays an important role in this context as well. In service of asceticism, water is withheld from votaries' bodies during the periods of fasting that take place throughout the days of the *vrat,* marking lack or paucity that is affiliated with self-denial. One does not drink; the body becomes dry. By way of contrast, the *vrat* culminates in an ascetic act marked by an overabundance of water, the water in which the body is submerged on the evening of the sixth day. Here we have the paradox of a body that is both too dry (inside) and too wet (outside), both ascetic (the dry body) and (one hopes) fecund (the wet body).

Purity Body

Concern with bodily purity is an important theme here as well. Purity is a concern in the first two Chaṭh *vrat* narratives recounted earlier, the Mahīpāl and Sukanyā narratives, where emission from human bodies of impure substances—urine, feces, blood—functions to instigate or communicate moral ruptures that require redress. The practice of the Chaṭh *vrat* maintains this concern with ritual purity. Foods permitted during *vrat*s are generally considered more conducive to purity than other foods and share certain features. Some, for example, are considered inherently pure or conveyers of purity; others are bland and hence unlikely to excite the senses or are covered by an outer husk or shell that prevents invasion of polluting substances.[25] In this regard there seems to be an especially robust concern in the Chaṭh *vrat* with the maintenance of ritual purity: a votary's home must be thoroughly cleansed before she undertakes the *vrat*, foods consumed or prepared for ritual use must be cooked on a new stove or fire to ensure that they are completely free of polluting substances, individuals who are not performing the *vrat* must be kept out of the kitchen where ritual foods are being made and consumed, and the votive body must be purified during the *vrat* through extreme fasting. Water is of course not just auspicious but also cleansing, and multiple ritual immersions of the votive body in the purifying waters of the Gaṅgā also work to ensure a state of ritual purity.

While purity is a central theme here, however, it seems not to function as an end in itself. Rather, a preoccupation with purity appears largely to function as support for the larger and seemingly more important goal of promoting auspiciousness. Scholarly discourse about auspiciousness has made much of the distinction between the values of auspiciousness and purity in Hindu culture, and such a distinction is unquestionably important and helpful in many contexts. However, while auspiciousness/inauspiciousness and purity/impurity represent different axes of value, they are not mutually exclusive.[26] Ritual activities that establish purity may also promote auspiciousness.[27] That clearly seems to be the case here.

Devotional Body

Asceticism and a preoccupation with purity in the Chaṭh *vrat* are also put to the service of *bhakti* to Sūrya, who functions as divine witness to the participating women's religious management of their bodies and ideally responds by participating in the process of transforming infertile bodies into fertile ones. The role of Chaṭh Mātā, who is clearly present in the performance of the *vrat* as a deity concerned with the flourishing and well-being of beloved family members, is less well defined. As the life-giving rays of the sun, however, Sūrya embodies the very possibility of life, especially when his (male) powers are united with the fecund powers of the (female) waters. Human male virility and procreative sex seem oddly peripheral to both the narratives and practices associated with the Chaṭh *vrat,* surfacing obliquely in this symbolic union between male and female powers brought together through the body of the religiously engaged votary as she spreads out her *āṃcal*—symbolically, her breast—to capture Sūrya's life-giving powers.

In her analysis of women's *vrat*s, Susan Wadley notes that bodily austerities normally associated with *vrat*s, such as fasting and sleeping on the floor, function as signals of one's faith and devotion, and the assumption is that "the deity will reward this faith and service with some kind of boon."[28] But in *vrat*s like the Chaṭh *vrat,* acts of austerity and purification might also be thought of as transformative practices that depend on the active bodily agency of the devotional participant, not just passive receptivity of a deity's favor. In the Chaṭh *vrat* women actively purify and inflict discomfort on their own bodies in order to make them more fertile at least in part by inducing Sūrya to act on their behalf. This is not mere passive receptivity but a form of engaged ritual coercion. In this context we might invoke Karen Pechilis Prentiss's suggestion that we reconceptualize *bhakti* as a theology of embodiment that necessitates active participation from human devotees and translate the term *bhakti* not as "devotion" but as "participation."[29] The devotional body is a relational one—that is, a body that participates in a relationship with a deity or deities—and action taken with one's body in the name of that relationship affects not only the body but also the bond between the devotee and the deity.

In many Hindu texts and traditions, the human body is postulated as permeable, transactional, and mutable; in other words, the body is not a closed system but is instead constituted by open boundaries that allow transactions and transformations to occur. Such a model of the human body helps account for the possibilities of somatic change associated with the narratives and performance of the Chaṭh *vrat*: blind eyes can again come to see, a body that is dead or reduced to bones can be restored to life, and an infertile womb can be rendered fertile through transactions with divine power. Outside influences certainly matter in effecting this kind of change, but so does individual effort. And active engagement of the body in religion helps make the spiritual tangible, as Meredith McGuire observes. She notes, "Performing religiously meaningful postures, gestures, and ritual acts, could also produce—physically as well as spiritually—a religious sense of awe and worshipfulness. Bodily sensations produce a confirmation that what one is experiencing is real, not just imaginary."[30] In the performance of the Chaṭh *vrat,* the votary becomes an active participant in any transformations that occur through and because of her bodily engagement.

Notes

1. See, for example, Pearson 1996: 204.

2. McGee 1987, 1991; Pearson 1996. Pearson (1996: 9) explicitly cautions against an overemphasis on domestic values when it comes to women's performance of *vrat*s, noting that, in her experience, "while women often spoke initially of *vrat*s as being for [maintaining] *suhāg* [Hindi for *saubhāgya*]—the auspicious married state—they also spoke directly or indirectly about the psychological, social, physical, and spiritual benefits for themselves," such as peace of mind or spiritual liberation. Nevertheless, both McGee and Pearson have detailed the strong connections that married women make between their performance of *vrat*s and the maintenance of their domestic status as wives and mothers.

3. During this period, I was researching religious dimensions of the month of Kārtik more generally. For a brief overview of the *Chaṭh vrat* as it is performed in Vārāṇasī, see Pintchman 2005: 71–72.

4. Vālā n.d.: 165.

5. Each Hindu month comprises two fortnights: the "dark" or "waning" fortnight (*kṛṣṇa pakṣa*), lasting from full moon to new moon, and the "bright" or "waxing" fortnight (*śukla pakṣa*), which lasts from new moon to full moon. Months may be calculated from new moon to new moon or from full moon to full moon. In Uttar Pradesh, the state in which Vārāṇasī is located, the latter system prevails.

6. "Lālā" is a vocative address for a merchant. Nārada is making a joke here about the merchant being greedy.

7. Gautam 1982: 182–184. All translations of Hindi passages are my own.

8. Singh n.d.

9. One *vrat* manual I purchased also notes that only married women with sons observe this *vrat* (Vālā n.d.: 165).

10. Marglin 1985: 175–181.

11. Many thanks to Jack Hawley for pointing this out in his response to our panel at the Annual Meeting of the American Academy of Religion in November 2007 in San Diego, where I presented a paper that included some of the material in this essay.

12. For an analysis of the association of rivers with fecundity, see Feldhaus 1995.

13. Chaṭh songs and video footage of women performing Chaṭh *pūjā* are now widely available on the Internet. Included among the items available are several songs to Chaṭh Mātā.

14. Bell 1992: 100.

15. Foucault 1995: 136.

16. Butler 1990: 171–180.

17. I am indebted to Marie Pagliarini (2006) for these remarks about the limitations of Foucault's model. In her work on the bodily and mental disciplines exercised by nuns living in the nineteenth-century Georgetown Visitation Convent, Pagliarini observes that analyzing the mechanics of power in the monastery is a necessary starting point but that any analysis must also move beyond this perspective.

18. Flood 2004: 214.

19. Holdrege 1998: 341. Holdrege herself articulates one such model, derived from her own close readings of classical Sanskrit sources, that accounts for five modalities of the human body: the ritual body, the ascetic body, the purity body, the devotional body, and the tantric body.

20. Holdrege 1998 and 2008.

21. Flood 2004: 4.

22. Flood 2004: 4.

23. Flood 2004: 214.

24. Flood 2004: 214.

25. McGee 1987: 97–99.

26. See, for example, Carman and Marglin 1985.

27. See Khare 1976: 109.

28. Wadley 1983: 149.

29. Prentiss 1999: 24.

30. McGuire 2003: 7.

References

Bell, Catherine. 1992. *Ritual Theory, Ritual Practice.* New York: Oxford University Press.

Butler, Judith. 1990. *Gender Trouble: Feminism and the Subversion of Identity.* New York: Routledge.

Carman, John B., and Frederique Marglin. 1985. *Purity and Auspiciousness in Indian Society.* Leiden: E. J. Brill.

Feldhaus, Anne. 1995. *Water and Womanhood: Religious Meanings of Rivers in Maharashtra.* New York: Oxford University Press.

Flood, Gavin. 2004. *The Ascetic Self.* Cambridge: Cambridge University Press.

Foucault, Michel. 1995 [1975]. *Discipline and Punish: The Birth of the Prison.* Translated by Alan Sheridan. New York: Random House, Vintage Books.

Gautam, Camanlāl. 1982. *Bārah māsoṅ ke sampūrṇ vrat evaṁ tyauhār.* Baroli: Saṃskṛti Saṃsthān.

Holdrege, Barbara A. 1998. "Body Connections: Hindu Discourses of the Body and the Study of Religion." In *The Study of Hinduism and the Study of Religion,* special issue, *International Journal of Hindu Studies* 2, no. 3: 341–386.

Holdrege, Barbara A. 2008. "Body." In *Studying Hinduism: Key Concepts and Methods*, ed. Sushil Mittal and Gene Thursby, 19–40. New York: Routledge.

Khare, R. S. 1976. *The Hindu Hearth and Home*. New Delhi: Vikas.

Marglin, Frederique. 1985. *Wives of the God King: The Rituals of the Devadasis of Puri*. Delhi: Oxford University Press.

McGee, Mary. 1987. "Feasting and Fasting: The Vrata Tradition and Its Significance for Hindu Women." ThD diss., Harvard University.

McGee, Mary. 1991."Desired Fruits: Motive and Intention in the Votive Rites of Hindu Women." In *Roles and Rituals for Hindu Women*, ed. Julia Leslie, 71–88. London: Pinter Publishers.

McGuire, Meredith. 2003. "Why Bodies Matter: A Sociological Reflection on Spirituality and Materiality." *Spiritus: A Journal of Christian Spirituality* 3, no. 1: 1–18.

Pagliarini, Marie. 2006. " 'Angels, Clothed in Mortal Flesh': The Practice of Sacred Comportment in Nineteenth-Century Visitation Monastic Life." Paper delivered at the Annual Meeting of the American Academy of Religion, Washington, DC.

Pearson, Anne Mackenzie. 1996. *"Because It Gives Me Peace of Mind": Ritual Fasts in the Religious Lives of Hindu Women*. Albany: State University of New York Press.

Pintchman, Tracy. 2005. *Guests at God's Wedding: Celebrating Kartik among the Women of Benares*. Albany: State University of New York Press.

Prentiss, Karen Pechilis. 1999. *The Embodiment of Bhakti*. New York: Oxford University Press.

Singh, Mahādev Prasād. N.d. *Śrī Chaṭh vrat kathā*. Varanasi: Ṭhākurprasād and Sons Booksellers.

Vālā, Rajanī, ed. N.d. *Hinduoṅ ke varṣbhar ke vrat aur tyauhār*. Delhi: Sumit Publication.

Wadley, Susan S. 1983. "*Vrats*: Transformers of Destiny." In *Karma: An Anthropological Inquiry*, ed. Charles F. Keyes and E. Valentine Daniel, 147–152. Berkeley: University of California Press.

Afterword

Bodies of Knowledge

Karen Pechilis

The essays in this volume are refigured versions of papers delivered at the Conference on the Study of Religions of India (CSRI) held at Albion College in Michigan in September 2007. This was the last CSRI program over which Selva J. Raj presided before his untimely death in March 2008. The theme of the conference was "Religion and the Body," and based on the strength of many of the conference papers, Selva believed that a volume of selected papers should be produced and asked Barbara and me to co-edit it. And so it is with fond tribute to Selva that we complete this volume now.

This collection of essays makes clear that any lingering popular idea that South Asian religions can be generally categorized as body-renouncing, transcendent, world-ignoring traditions is not accurate, especially when such a characterization is used as a foil in order to contrast South Asian traditions with a self-interested characterization of the West as an exemplar of the scientific mode that valorizes the study of physical processes. As the part titles in this volume suggest—"Material Bodies, Embodied Selves, and Perfected Embodiments," "Divine Bodies and Devotional Bodies," and "Gendered and Engendering Bodies"—South Asian traditions display a diversity of distinctive perspectives on the body. Readers of the essays will also have noted the significant overlap among perspectives within and across these categories in their representation of physical, subtle, and ultimate aspects of embodiment as dynamically engaged.

On a more theoretical level, these essays demonstrate that the terms used to consider, describe, and constitute the meaning of the body depend on the stance that a religious author or practitioner assumes with respect to the body. In this afterword I adopt a different schema that highlights three distinctive points of departure, each of which provides a discrete framework for its representations of the body: *materiality, self-awareness,* and *devotional participation*. In many ways devotional participation, which overtly thematizes both the material body and self-awareness, is a mediating term between the two other categories; however, as these essays demonstrate, negotiation of the relationship between materiality and the self is centrally implicated across the categories as they promote a transformative ideal. Such negotiation is also found across the various modes of inquiry and expression that constitute sources for these essays, including mythology, medical treatises, philosophy, performance, poetry, and ritual. These essays challenge us to see that South Asian traditions are intensely concerned with defining the body and assessing and promoting its capacity to instantiate an ideal, whether that ideal is defined as divinity, enlightenment, health, social validation, perfection, artistic mastery, devotion, love, or auspiciousness. From the details of these essays, patterns emerge according to whether the point of departure is materiality, self-awareness, or devotional participation. I will consider the essays that are representative of each category in order to identify these patterns, in a narrative that is not intended to supply a summary or abstract of each essay but rather theoretical reflections on them.

Traditions that take as their point of departure *materiality*, especially the materiality of the body, focus on the human body as providing a template and terms for imagining an ideal, including health (Cerulli), gender (Anderson), becoming alive (Wilson), and power (Busse). The complication is that, while the body can provide classifications of the ideal, it can also defy them. These essays provide us a provocative glimpse of bodily ideals, their contradictions, and ways in which that gap is addressed and, ideally, harmonized.

The essays by Carol Anderson and Anthony Cerulli both analyze classical texts that are centrally concerned with the physical body: Anderson discusses Indian Buddhist texts from the Vinaya-Piṭaka of the Pāli canon along with Buddhaghosa's commentary (ca. first century BCE to late fourth or early fifth century CE), and Cerulli considers classical Sanskrit medical sources, especially the *Caraka Saṃhitā* (ca. second century BCE to first century CE). The question that lies behind the materials that Anderson considers is, To what extent does a specific observable body measure up to the normative body ideals that are inscribed in the

Pāli Buddhist canon? The question that lies behind the materials that Cerulli considers is, What is the relationship of a healthy body to *dharma*? These questions, as raised and addressed by the texts, invest the material body with a significance that is wider than its own individuality while firmly grounding the instantiation of that significance in an individual observable body that must be dealt with insofar as its existence shapes the discourse.

In the case of Indian Buddhist monastic traditions, an unblemished body is viewed as a qualification for ordination, a first step toward the total perfection that can be realized through enlightenment or liberation. As Anderson discusses, women as a category are accepted as exemplars on the path insofar as they can become nuns: "all candidates for ordination, both male and female, are required to have a particular kind of body: normatively sexed, free from disease, free from physical challenges, excessive old age, and so on," and this includes a heterosexual orientation as a criterion as well. Anderson analyzes a classical list of eleven kinds of women who have disorders of sex development that disqualify them from ordination and thus from the attainment of Buddhist goals. Significantly, the list is included among the "'stumbling blocks' or obstacles to *dhamma* (*antarāyikā dhammā*)." This list is specific to women; there is no counterpart for men. Thus observations concerning the body operate on three levels if the person seeking ordination is a woman: it is observed that she is a woman; she is asked a set of questions about illness that is asked of any man or woman seeking ordination; and, on the basis of the observation that she is a woman, she is measured against a list of observable "obstacles" specific to women. That these "obstacles" are observable is highlighted by the fact that many of the conditions correlate with those described in today's medical literature. In these Buddhist texts the foundation of the enlightened path is observable physical normalcy.

In the case of Sanskrit medical texts, the material body must be maintained in a state of health because health is an instantiation of *dharma*. *Dharma* is a general ideal, a cosmic ordering principle that governs all beings. However, as Cerulli argues with his concept of the "body *dharma*" of Āyurveda, that ideal is both personalized and individualized in a physical body to the extent that the correct care of the body forms the foundation of all other forms of *dharma*, as a primary obligation that must be met before any other. The texts promote various strategies for enacting body *dharma*. Some of the strategies are physiological: the texts are well known for describing symptoms and suggesting therapies for their cure. The most famous is the physiological principle of the three bodily humors (*doṣas*): *vāta* (wind), *pitta* (bile), and *kapha* (phlegm), which are semi-fluid substances that circulate throughout the body and function as its primary pathogenic arbiters. The goal is to keep them in the balance appropriate to the individual body. But as Cerulli argues, these same texts also understand the body in a social context, and so they also articulate strategies for health such as keeping one's aspirations realistic, understanding fitness of the body to be a harmonized alignment of the physical body with the transcendent self, and acting morally. The healthy body is the observable body in its physical state of health, in its pursuit of appropriate livelihood, and in its moral actions. Thus the classical materials considered by Anderson and by Cerulli agree that the physical body is the foundation of the ideal of *dharma*: Anderson's essay provides us with negative examples of anomalous bodies that are obstacles to *dharma*, while Cerulli's essay provides us with positive examples of healthy bodies that uphold *dharma*.

Liz Wilson's essay explores seemingly disparate enactments of Buddhist ideals: a male murderer becomes an *arhat* (an awakened being liberated from the cycle of birth and death), and a woman gives birth to a healthy child after seven days of difficult labor. The two are connected in the popular Buddhist saint Aṅgulimāla, whose story is represented in classical Pāli sources, which are the focus of Wilson's essay, as well as in widely circulated Sinhala versions. Wilson's essay provides us with an analysis that demonstrates the interdependence of both birth and behavior in an individual's truly becoming alive in the world. Misled by a teacher who wants to get rid of him, Aṅgulimāla (whose name means "Garland of Fingers") believes that he must kill one thousand people and provide a finger from each to the teacher as payment for lessons. After the Buddha intervenes to stop his bloody campaign, Aṅgulimāla encounters a woman in labor and, moved by her suffering, declares an "act of truth" "whereby a solemn utterance made by a person can have palpable consequences for that person and for others as well," which enables her to immediately give birth to a healthy baby. It is this compassionate act that transforms Aṅgulimāla into an *arhat*. Aṅgulimāla's words continue to this day to function as protective verses (*paritta*) that are recited widely in Theravāda Buddhist communities to ensure that a woman gives birth painlessly. Through her analysis of images of birth, blood, awakening, and motherhood in tellings of this saint's story, Wilson challenges the dichotomy that male is transcendent/generative and female is physical/derivative, for Aṅgulimāla requires intervention by mothers to effect his transformation into an ideal Buddhist: "Aṅgulimāla's male fecundity depends on female fecundity operating on at least two distinct registers: first, his mother's determination to make her son into a new man; and, second, his encounter with the woman giving birth that led him to awaken as an *arhat* and become a fertile field of merit for others." Male generativity—becoming a fertile field of merit—and female generativity—giving birth—are thus interdependent, mutually and dynamically negotiating spiritual and physical realities.

The material body as a locus of power informs Kendall Busse's discussion of divine bodies as they are represented in the classical epic, the Mahābhārata (ca. second century BCE to second century CE). The epic period is a critical transition from Vedic to Hindu traditions, and, as Busse explains, one of the key issues is "the increasing importance of visual modes of apprehension in the epic period and the corresponding shifting understandings concerning the materiality of divine bodies," with the epic presenting alternative ways to imagine the bodies of gods: *vigraha* (human-like bodies that appear on earth), *mūrti* (multiple bodies with various shapes), and *yoga* (the power to manifest and become embodied in multiple forms). All of these forms are visible, although the degree to which they are material varies; *vigraha*s can be seen with the ordinary human eye, whereas *mūrti*s at times require an eye trained through *yoga*. The powers that gods enact through these graded forms of visual materiality also differ, with *vigraha*s providing a mode of direct intervention in human affairs and *mūrti*s the "power to structure reality." While as described in the epic, these divine bodies provide ways for human beings both to relate to divine beings and to be mystified by them, the larger point is that the variety of bodies can be harmonized to the divine order in distinctive ways.

Traditions that begin from the perspective of *self-awareness*, such as that exhibited by a transcendent self or some other psychic observer, focus on a truth or a cosmic order that has its source outside of the material body, and by which the material body must be controlled (Kamath), perfected (Skora), or even abandoned (Radich), in order to effect a transformed mode of being in the context of a performance or in the praxis of life itself.

Harshita Mruthinti Kamath offers a new theory of "performative selfhood" in her consideration of the role of the self in the performance of ritual possession in Tamil Nadu and in the performance of the classical South Indian dance forms of Kathakali and Kuchipudi. In contrast to the transformed modes of being discussed by Skora and Radich, Kamath considers moments of performance that are limited in duration. Nevertheless, the point of departure for her inquiry is the location of awareness. Her essay poses the key question, Where is the self in these intensely bodily practices? In response, she builds on and challenges past scholarship to develop her own tripartite classification of the self: the bodied self is "a visual selfhood expressed through the physical body of the performer"; the embodied self is "the constellation of psychoemotional faculties residing within the corporeal form of the bodied self"; and the reflective self is "the self-conscious faculty that exists independent of the performer's body but has the ability to observe, reflect upon, and control both bodied and embodied selves." The three examples Kamath discusses all configure these three modes in distinctive ways, creating a typology of their interactions, but all involve the intertwining of body and self. In possession, the reflective self cedes performative space to the bodied and embodied selves, but it watches—or "lingers," in Kamath's provocative language—and creates a memory of the uncontrolled bodily experience. In contrast, in Kathakali the reflective self maintains an active awareness of the rules of the dance, which keeps the performance of the bodied and embodied selves within the parameters of the dance's coded structure. Kuchipudi dance serves as a mediating example between the antistructure and structure of the two other examples. In this dance style mastery is defined as merging with the portrayed character's emotional state—a transformative experience in many ways akin to possession—and thus, according to Kamath's analysis, during the performance the reflective self exerts control only over the bodied self, not over the embodied self.

Kerry Skora explores the intertwining of Being and body in the *Tantrāloka*, the magnum opus of the Hindu tantric philosopher Abhinavagupta (ca. 975–1025 CE), and in a poetic text written by one of his disciples that describes the master at a religious gathering. The key term is *mudrā*, which generally means "bodily gesture," but which Abhinavagupta redescribes as an intertwining of external gesture and internal state of awareness, or, in Skora's terms, "bodily gesture that embodies awareness." Like Radich, Skora asks us to take seriously the revisioning of language that is involved: in his etymological discussions, Abhinavagupta is not providing "mere analytic representation in which words correspond in a conventional sense to the objects that they signify," but instead he seeks "to use language to empower each of his listeners in their flesh and bones to join him in the bodily experience of profound reality." Each bodily gesture reveals—or, in Abhinavagupta's foremost disciple Kṣemarāja's provocative language, "unseals"—Being itself. Again we see an emphasis on nonduality between internal and external: *mudrā* as gesture is "the bodying-forth of the perfected state of nondual consciousness" into the world of form. A poem by Abhinavagupta's disciple Madhurāja evokes his master's bodily presence through descriptions of his expressions and gestures, which are intended to catalyze the direct experience of the nondual consciousness of the master.

As Michael Radich discusses in his essay, it is difficult in the current Western scholarly and popular imagination to view a perfected body as real since the hegemonic scientific episteme takes "the biophysical, given human organism as the definitive point of reference." Widespread religiocultural images, such as that of the Fall, also play a role. Many of us have confronted this issue of perception with our students when we teach about perfected bodies in South Asian traditions, such as the bodies of realized *gurus*. Crucially, traditions that have awareness as their point of departure relate their teachings directly to the body, especially the body transformed. According to Radich, there is a large repertoire of transformed bodies imagined by cultures and religions that present alternatives to the materialist (ordinary bodies of flesh and blood) and descriptivist (which presuppose the materialist view of the body) inscriptions of the body in current Western theoretical discourse.

Many perspectives within Hindu and Buddhist traditions that thematize perfection promote a revolution in consciousness. The new mode of consciousness is distinctively and meticulously described in each tradition, but what these traditions tend to have in common is the claim that those who are perfected can holistically see things as they truly are, in contrast to the fragmented and partial half-truths viewed by ordinary persons. Simultaneously, the body is transformed by this radical knowledge: indeed, these changes render ordinary language and its dualistic conceptualizations—mind/body, spiritual/material—obsolete. Radich urges us to understand Buddhist texts that describe the transformations effected by radical knowledge not as metaphorical but instead as probably quite literal. He challenges us with a thought experiment concerning the Buddhist concept of *dharma-kāya,* the notion that "perfection, or Buddhahood, consists in the realization of an alternative embodiment in perfect gnostic identity with the highest metaphysical truth that inheres in all things." The Buddha taught that conceptualizing the body as the ordinary, given embodiment of material flesh and blood (*sat-kāya-dṛṣṭi*) and then identifying exclusively with that conception perpetuates a false view of our true existential makeup, which leads to suffering. In contrast, the being who radically, nondualistically, and completely identifies with the *dharma* is "embodied in the liberatory truth of all things" or, in contemporary terms, experiences "the complete 'upload,' in a manner of speaking, of embodiment into otherworldly, transcendent knowledge."

Traditions that begin from the perspective of *devotional participation* link embodied humanity to beings who are considered to be divine or perfected. Several essays demonstrate the depth of thought and emotion, especially in these cases love for and loyalty to the divine, that is a hallmark of Hindu *bhakti* traditions in India. *Bhakti* defines the devotee's mode of being as a response to the divine, and thus it is a path of participation. The body is valorized in *bhakti;* no type of body is disqualified, and thus devotional traditions came to include women, low-caste and below-caste men, people in various occupations, and those whose bodies lack wholeness. As a point of departure, devotional participation validates human imperfection through the forge of heartfelt commitment to the divine. Devotional participation enables the fusion of materiality and awareness toward enhanced embodiment in the world, which is actualized in a number of ways, including vivid descriptive imagination of the specific beauty of particularized bodies in a landscape (Hopkins), a devotional subjectivity developed through a transgressive exploratory impetus (Pechilis), a ritually cultivated auspiciousness (Pintchman), and transformation of the material body into a body of bliss (Holdrege).

Steven Hopkins takes up the issue of the particularized body in his discussion of the *Haṃsasandeśa,* the messenger poem of the Śrīvaiṣṇava poet-saint and theologian Veṅkaṭeśa (ca. 1268–1369 CE). His essay is "not about a presumed generic category of 'the body' in Indian literatures but rather focuses on particularities, on beloved and loving *individual* bodies," thus capturing a primary mode of *bhakti* that distinguishes its discourse from others that tend to evoke the body as a general category. For example, we witness the bodily markings of Lord Rāma's longing as he recalls the body of his beloved Sītā in the graceful walk of a goose. As he instructs his goose messenger to carry a message to his beloved, who is held captive in the demon Rāvaṇa's palace in Laṅkā, he describes in vivid detail the landscapes that the goose will cross. The elements of the landscapes come alive as embodied beings, such as a river "who gathers in her hands of bright long waves/ blossoms that fall from forest trees growing along her banks/ to honor the god who wears the crescent moon in his hair." As Rāma approaches in his imagination the land of Sītā's captivity, his feelings of loss and separation intensify, and he envisions Sītā's beautiful body, then tempers his vision by imagining her present suffering and recalling the distant memory of their union.

As discussed in my essay, both a female *bhakti* poet and her biographer centralize the repulsive body in their generative discussions of devotional subjectivity, and yet they are strikingly different in terms of the particular body on which they focus and the voice enabled by such a body. The poet Kāraikkāl Ammaiyār creates a devotional subjectivity that has exploration at its center by pondering the nature of Śiva's body and contextualizing his heroic valor with images of his fearsome aspect. Her poetry suggests that she bodily ventures to the cremation ground to witness his eternal dance and is transformed by the simultaneity of beauty and fear in that place. Her infrequent and generic mention of the human body touches only on universal human characteristics, and thus her poetic voice aspires to a universal. In contrast, her biographer places her gender and its limiting social location at the center of his construction of her devotional subjectivity, making for a dramatic narrative in which her body transforms from human to ghoul as a climactic moment but circumscribing the realism and accessibility of the *bhakti* path in the world as described by the poet herself.

Tracy Pintchman's essay explores the concrete devotional practices of contemporary Hindu women in Vārāṇasī through narratives and rituals associated with the Chaṭh *vrat*, a votive ritual directed to Sūrya, the sun deity, which is undertaken in the autumn. Both the narratives and the rituals are "centrally concerned with religious management of the human body." In particular, they promote bodies of physical well-being and fecundity and of auspiciousness "that must be deliberately and laboriously cultivated and maintained through religious performance." The holistic goals of the stories and practices call to mind the approach of the Āyurvedic texts discussed by Cerulli. Through their performance of the *vrat*, women cultivate bodies that possess the discipline of asceticism, the ritual purity of sacred waters, and the devotion of active participation in honoring Sūrya, which coalesce to transform a woman's body into one of overall female auspiciousness.

Barbara Holdrege presents the particularized bodies of both God and devotee in the discourse of embodiment developed by the Gauḍīya Vaiṣṇava tradition in the sixteenth century CE. This tradition envisions "multileveled models of embodiment and systems of bodily practices" in which divine bodies and human bodies are positioned as counterparts. Kṛṣṇa has limitless forms (*ananta-rūpa*) that can inhabit "transcosmic, macrocosmic, and microcosmic planes of existence," and he can also become embodied as a "concentrated presence" in concrete forms that can be accessed by devotees, which Holdrege calls "mesocosmic" modes of divine embodiment. The devotee engages the "material psychophysical complex" (*sādhaka-rūpa*) in external devotional practices enjoined by scripture in order to purify the material body, and at an advanced stage he or she engages in internal meditative practices in order to realize "a perfected devotional body that is an eternal, nonmaterial body of bliss" (*siddha-rūpa*). This developed philosophical tradition, which challenges both the nondualist philosophy of Advaita Vedānta and the dualist philosophy of Pātañjala Yoga, thus systematically describes both the transcendent and concrete aspects of divine embodiment as well as the nonmaterial and material aspects of human embodiment.

As these essays demonstrate, South Asian traditions of past and present offer rich resources on which to draw for imagining, deploying, critiquing, cultivating, and perfecting the body and notions of embodiment. As these distinctive yet interrelated discourses demonstrate, the question of the body is only very rarely settled, and such a resolution might be achieved only after much self-cultivation through knowledge and practice. For most of us, the body is a becoming, both subject and object of a history of decisions and a future of possibilities.

Contributors

Carol S. Anderson is Professor of Religion at Kalamazoo College. Her research interests as a scholar of South Asian religions focus on Buddhist traditions and feminist/queer approaches to the study of religions. She is the author of *Pain and Its Ending: The Four Noble Truths in Theravāda Buddhism* and co-editor of a festschrift in honor of Professor W. S. Karunatillake, *Embedded Languages: Studies in the Religion, Culture, and History of Sri Lanka*. Her most recent research project explores the range of sexualities found in the commentaries on the Pāli Buddhist canon.

Kendall Busse is a PhD candidate in Religious Studies at the University of California, Santa Barbara. Her research interests in South Asian religions and cultures focus on issues of embodiment, sacred space, and material culture. She completed a master's thesis on "*Mūrti*s and *Vigraha*s: Observations on the Bodies of the Gods in the Mahābhārata" and is currently completing a doctoral dissertation on deformity and disfigurement in South Asian traditions.

Anthony Cerulli is Associate Professor of Asian Languages and Cultures at the University of Wisconsin-Madison. His research interests include Sanskrit language and literature, the history of religions in South Asia, and the history of medicine in India. He is the author of *Somatic Lessons: Narrating Patienthood and Illness in Indian Medical Literature* and co-editor of *Medical Texts and Manuscripts in Indian Cultural History*. His research has been supported by fellowships from the American Council of Learned Societies, European Institutes for Advanced Study, and National Endowment for the Humanities. He was selected as a Fellow in South Asian Studies by the John Simon Guggenheim Memorial Foundation in 2015–2016.

Barbara A. Holdrege is Professor of Religious Studies and Chair of the South Asian Studies Committee at the University of California, Santa Barbara. Her research interests as a comparative historian of religions focus on historical and textual studies of Hindu and Jewish traditions and also engage broader theoretical issues arising out of critical interrogation of analytical categories such as the body, space, scripture, and ritual. Her current research is concerned with Hindu discourses of the body and constructions of sacred space in South Asia. Her publications include *Bhakti and Embodiment: Fashioning Divine Bodies and Devotional Bodies in Kṛṣṇa Bhakti*, *Veda and Torah: Transcending the Textuality of Scripture*, *Ritual and Power*, and a forthcoming monograph *The Body and the Self: Hindu Contributions to Theories of Embodiment*.

Steven P. Hopkins is Professor of Religion at Swarthmore College. His major field is South Indian Hindu traditions, with special attention to the work of the medieval South Indian poet-saint and philosopher Veṅkaṭeśa. He has also published in the area of comparative religious literatures on topics such as love, ideal bodies, and particularity; Sanskrit messenger poetry in South India; and women's laments in the poetry of William Blake. Hopkins received the 2010 A. K. Ramanujan Book Prize for Translation and is the author of *Singing the Body of God*, *An Ornament for Jewels: Love Poems for the Lord of Gods*, and *The Flight of Love: A Messenger Poem of Medieval South India by Veṅkaṭanātha*.

Harshita Mruthinti Kamath is Assistant Professor of Religious Studies at the University of North Carolina at Chapel Hill. Her research focuses on the textual and performance traditions of Telugu-speaking South India in conversation with theoretical discourses on gender and sexuality in South Asia. Her forthcoming book, *Constructing Artifice: An Ethnography of Impersonation in South India*, analyzes gender impersonation in the Telugu dance style of Kuchipudi. She has also co-translated the sixteenth-century classical Telugu text *Parijatapaharanamu* (Theft of the Parijata Tree) with Velcheru Narayana Rao, which will be published as part of the Murty Classical Library of India.

Karen Pechilis is NEH Distinguished Professor of Humanities in the Comparative Religion Department at Drew University. Her research interests include the study of *bhakti* (path of devotional participation), comparative analysis of female *gurus*, translation and critical discussion of Tamil devotional literature, reclaiming and restoring female voices from Indian traditions through gender and feminist analysis, and the historical development of the now global Naṭarāja image of Śiva. She is the author of *Interpreting Devotion: The Poetry and Legacy of a Female Bhakti Saint of India* and *The Embodiment of Bhakti*. She is also the editor of *The Graceful Guru: Hindu Female Gurus in India and the United States* and the co-editor with Selva J. Raj of *South Asian Religions: Tradition and Today*. Her work has been supported by the American Institute of Indian Studies, the Fulbright Program, and the Asian Cultural Council.

Tracy Pintchman is Professor of Theology and Director of the International Studies Program at Loyola University Chicago. Her research focuses on Hindu goddess traditions and Hindu women's ritual practices. She is the author, editor, or co-editor of seven books, including *The Rise of the Goddess in the Hindu Tradition*, *Guests at God's Wedding: Celebrating Kartik among the Women of Benares*, and *Hindu Ritual at the Margins: Innovations, Transformations, Reconsiderations*.

Michael Radich is Senior Lecturer in Religious Studies at Victoria University of Wellington, New Zealand. His research focuses on Chinese Buddhist traditions, early to middle Mahāyāna Buddhist traditions, problems of provenance and attribution in the Chinese Buddhist canon, and Buddha-body doctrine. He is the author of *How Ajātaśatru Was Reformed: The Domestication of "Ajase" and Stories in Buddhist History* and *The Mahāparinirvāṇa-mahāsūtra and the Emergence of Tathāgatagarbha Doctrine*. He is also the co-editor of *A Distant Mirror: Articulating Indic Ideas in Sixth and Seventh Century Chinese Buddhism*. He served as the Numata Visiting Professor of Buddhist Studies at the University of Hamburg in 2013–2014 and received an Alexander von Humboldt Foundation Fellowship for Experienced Researchers to support his work on the concept of *amalavijñāna* (taintless consciousness).

Kerry Martin Skora is Professor and Chair of Religious Studies at Hiram College. His research focuses on the religions of India, Tibet, and Bhutan. He is the author of several articles on Abhinavagupta, the renowned exponent of the nondual Trika Śaivism of Kashmir, in which he analyzes the category of the lived body from a phenomenological perspective. His articles have been published in a variety of venues, including the *International Journal of Hindu Studies* and *Numen: International Review for the History of Religions*. Having recently returned from Bhutan as a Fulbright Scholar, he explores in his current research the relationship between ecology, space, and consciousness in the thought of the Tibetan Buddhist visionary Longchenpa.

Liz Wilson is Professor of Comparative Religion at Miami University in Oxford, Ohio, where she is an affiliate in the Asian/Asian American Studies Program and in the Women's, Gender, and Sexuality Studies Program. Her training is in premodern South Asian religious history. Her research focuses on South Asian Buddhists in conversation with Hindus, Jains, and others on such topics as death and postmortem experience, sexuality, gender, family formations, and marriage. She is the author of *Charming Cadavers: Horrific Figurations of the Feminine in Indian Buddhist Hagiographic Literature* and the editor of *The Living and the Dead: Social Dimensions of Death in South Asian Religion* and *Family in Buddhism*.

Index